THE WORLD OF PARMENIDES

THE WORLD OF PARMENIDES

Essays on the Presocratic Enlightenment

Karl R. Popper

Edited by Arne F. Petersen,
with the assistance of Jørgen Mejer

London and New York

First published 1998
by Routledge
11 New Fetter Lane, London EC4P 4EE

Simultaneously published in the USA and Canada
by Routledge
29 West 35th Street, New York, NY 10001

Typeset in Garamond by J&L Composition Ltd, Filey, North Yorkshire.
Printed and bound in Great Britain by
Creative Print and Design (Wales), Ebbw Vale

British Library Cataloguing in Publication Data
A catalogue record for this book is available from the British
Library

Library of Congress Cataloging in Publication Data
Popper, Karl Raimund, Sir, 1902–1994
The world of Parmenides: Essays on the Presocratic Enlightenment
/ Karl Popper; edited by Arne F. Petersen, with the assistance of
Jørgen Mejer.
p.   cm.
Includes bibliographical references and index.
1. Pre-Socratic philosophers. 2. Parmenides. I. Petersen, Arne
Friemuth. II. Mejer, Jørgen. III. Title.
B187.5.P66 1998
182–dc21 97–17466

ISBN 0 415 17301 9

CONTENTS

CONTENTS

subjectivist interpretation of information theory –
29 Indeterminism in quantum physics as a breakdown
of Parmenideanism – 30 Other anti-Parmenidean
developments of modern physics – 31 Non-
Parmenidean explanations of the expanding universe –
32 Summary of the deviations from the Parmenidean
programme – 33 A lesson from non-Parmenidean
economics – 34 Beyond the search for invariants:
towards a logical theory of understanding – *Addendum*:
A note on opposites and existence in Presocratic
epistemology

PREFACE

The present book contains various attempts to understand early Greek philosophy, on which I have worked for many years. I hope that these essays may illustrate the thesis that all history is, or should be, the history of problem situations, and that in following this principle we may further our understanding of the Presocratics and other thinkers of the past. The essays also try to show the greatness of the early Greek philosophers, who gave Europe its philosophy, its science, and its humanism.

The essays have not been arranged in the order in which they were written. After one of the oldest essays, 'Back to the Presocratics', which presents some early attempts at understanding the main interests and achievements of the Presocratics, there follow a number of essays on the central problems that Xenophanes and Parmenides may have worked on. These later essays have been rewritten many times during recent years, and only one of them (Essay 3) has been published before. They supersede in some respects 'Back to the Presocratics', though that essay does deal with problems partly different from the more recent ones. This should also explain why there are recurrent themes and repeated attempts at rendering the ancient Greek texts: different translations have been retained in this collection since the main themes appear in different contexts and light from essay to essay — light reflected from the splendour of Presocratic philosophy.

The longest of the unpublished essays (Essay 7), originally entitled 'Rationality and the search for invariants', dates back to the 1960s. It tries to show that Heraclitus ('everything changes') and Parmenides ('nothing changes') have been reconciled and combined in modern science, which looks for Parmenidean invariance within Heraclitean flux. (As Emile Meyerson pointed out, this is done in physics by differential equations.) The final title of this essay indicates that 'the search for invariants' may advantageously be replaced by a theory of understanding founded on Xenophanes' early ideas.

When as a 16-year-old student I first read Parmenides' wonderful poem,

I learnt to look at Selene (the Moon) and Helios (the Sun) with new eyes — with eyes enlightened by his poetry. Parmenides opened my eyes to the poetic beauty of the Earth and the starry heavens, and he taught me to look at them with a new searching look: searching to determine, as does Selene herself, the position of Helios below the Earth's horizon, by following the direction of her 'eager look'. None of my friends whom I told about my rediscovery of Parmenides' discovery had looked for this before, and I hoped that some of them liked it as much as I did. It was, however, only some seventy years later that I realized the full significance of Parmenides' discovery, and this made me realize what it must have meant for him, the original discoverer. I have tried since to understand and explain the importance of this discovery for the world of Parmenides, for his Two Ways, and its great role in the history of science, and especially of epistemology and of theoretical physics.

As mentioned, these essays overlap in a number of respects, showing repeated attempts to solve the problem of understanding the ideas of the Presocratics. I apologize to my readers if the repetition is sometimes excessive. I am grateful, though, to my friends, in particular Arne F. Petersen, for their determination in putting together and editing the essays, in spite of their knowing that I am not an expert in this field, that I am a mere amateur, a lover of the Presocratics. I think that the essays reveal that I love three cosmologists above all the others: Xenophanes, Heraclitus, and Parmenides.

Karl R. Popper
Kenley, 27 February 1993

ABBREVIATIONS

C. & R.   Karl R. Popper, *Conjectures and Refutations*, London, 1963, 5th edn, 1989.

DK   H. Diels & W. Kranz, *Fragmente der Vorsokratiker*, 10th edn, Berlin, 1960.

L.d.F.   Karl R. Popper, *Logik der Forschung*, Vienna, 1934, 10th edn, 1994.

L.Sc.D.   Karl R. Popper, *The Logic of Scientific Discovery*, London, 1959.

O.K.   Karl R. Popper, *Objective Knowledge: An Evolutionary Approach*, Oxford, 1972, 2nd edn, 1979.

O.S.   Karl R. Popper, *The Open Society and Its Enemies*, 6th edn, vols I and II, London, 1969.

S.I.B.   Karl R. Popper, *The Self and Its Brain – An Argument for Interactionism*, Part I (Part II written by Sir John Eccles), Berlin–Heidelberg–New York, 1977, 3rd edn, 1990.

INTRODUCTION

Aristotle's invention of induction
and the eclipse of Presocratic cosmology

With the sole exception, perhaps, of Protagoras, who seems to argue against it, all serious thinkers before Aristotle made a sharp distinction between *knowledge*, real knowledge, certain truth (*saphes*, *alētheia*; later: *epistēmē*), which is divine and only accessible to the gods, and *opinion* (*doxa*), which mortals are able to possess, and is interpreted by Xenophanes as guesswork that could be improved.

It seems that the first who revolted against this view was Protagoras. There exists the beginning of a book by him, where he says: 'We don't know anything about the gods – neither whether they exist, nor whether they don't exist.' I suggest that his *homo mensura* proposition – 'Man is the measure of all things' – is derived from this, and that his argument was as follows: 'About the gods we don't know anything, so we don't know what they know. Thus human knowledge must be taken as our standard, as our *measure*.' In other words, the *homo mensura* proposition of Protagoras is a criticism of his predecessor's distinction between mere human opinion and divine knowledge. 'Therefore we must take human knowledge as our standard or measure.'

Other thinkers held similar views, but all of them can be placed historically after Protagoras: for example Democritus, whose native city, like Protagoras', was Abdera; although Democritus was, according to Diogenes Laertius, the teacher of Protagoras, more reliable historical sources place them in the inverse order. Protagoras was most probably an empiricist revolting against Parmenides' rationalism. This point is stressed several times in the present book.

Yet after Protagoras – but only until Aristotle – most thinkers of importance continued to hold the view of Parmenides and his predecessors that only the gods have knowledge. This is perfectly clear in Socrates. It is even clearer in the much more dogmatic Plato, because Plato's dogmatism pertains mainly to the laws of the state; although he does not want these laws to be written down, they should be rigid and quite immutable. Concerning the field that we now describe as natural science, Plato says explicitly (in the *Timaeus*, for example, but also in other places) that all he

1

can tell us is at best only 'truthlike' and *not* the truth: it is, at best, *like* the truth. This term is usually translated by 'probable', but we have to make the distinction between probability in the *mathematical sense* and in the totally different sense of *truthlikeness*. I therefore break with the tradition of mixing up these two notions; and since we cannot hope to change what mathematicians mean by 'probability', I use the term 'truthlikeness', or 'verisimilitude', especially for theories. The word that Plato uses is really '*similar*', and sometimes he says 'similar to truth'; the word is also connected with '*pictorial similarity or likeness*', and this seems, indeed, to be the root of the meaning.[1] According to Plato, humans can have only this kind of knowledge; he rarely calls it opinion, which is the usual term used, for example by his contemporary Isocrates, who says 'We have only opinion.'

The decisive break comes with Aristotle. Strangely enough, although Aristotle is a theist – he even has a kind of theology – he definitely breaks with the tradition of distinguishing between divine knowledge and human guesswork. *He believes that he knows*: that he himself has *epistēmē*, demonstrable scientific knowledge. This is the main reason why I do not like Aristotle: what to Plato is a scientific *hypothesis* becomes with Aristotle *epistēmē*, demonstrable knowledge. And for most epistemologists of the West, it has remained so ever since.

Thus Aristotle breaks with the reasonable tradition that says that we know very little. He thinks he knows a lot; and he tries to give a theory of *epistēmē*, of demonstrable knowledge; and being a clever man, and a good logician, he finds that his assumption that there is demonstrable knowledge involves him in an infinite regress, because this knowledge, if demonstrated, must be logically deduced from something else, which in turn must also be demonstrated knowledge, and therefore in its turn deduced from something else, and so on.

So he gets to the problem: how can this infinite regress be stopped? Or: what are the real original premises, and how do we make sure of their truth? He solves this fundamental problem of knowledge by the doctrine that the real original premises are statements of definitions. Here he invokes, at least sometimes, a kind of strange 'double thinking' or 'double talk'. Definitions, on the one hand, give to words a meaning by convention and are therefore certain (analytic, tautological). But if they are only conventional, and therefore certain, then all *epistēmē* is truth by convention and therefore certain. In other words, all *epistēmē* is tautological, deduced from our definitions. This conclusion Aristotle does not want, and he therefore proposes that there exist, on the other hand, also definitions that are not conventional and not certain. Yet he does not stress that they are not certain, only that they are the result of 'seeing the essence of a thing', and so synthetic; they are the result of induction.

This seems to have been the way in which induction entered into the theory of scientific method, of epistemology. According to Aristotle, induction is the procedure of leading the pupil (or the scholar in the sense of the learner) to a place, to an outlook, from which he can *see the essence* of the object of his interest. The description of this essence he then lays down by definition as one of his fundamental principles, the *archai*. In Aristotle these principles are definitions, and at the same time they become (I suggest by some kind of 'double talk') the certain truth that only conventional and tautological definitions can have.

Aristotle's method of induction is similar to the social initiation of a young man: it is the procedure of getting to an outlook from which you can actually see the essence of adult life. Inducing is a way of making definitions a rich source of knowledge. But definitions are in fact nothing like this: there cannot be such things as informative definitions.

Aristotle's theory of induction — the way we are led to see, to intuit, the essential property, the essence, the nature, of a thing — is double talk in another sense as well: it is achieved in part by regarding it critically from several sides (as in a Socratic discussion), and in part by considering many cases, many instances of it. The latter sense of induction leads to the construction of a kind of inductive syllogism. *Premises*: Socrates is mortal; Plato is mortal; Simmias is mortal; and so on. All these are men. *Conclusion* (which, Aristotle knows, is invalidly reached): All men are mortal. Or even the further conclusion, which goes to the essence of the problem: it is in the nature of every generated thing that it must decay and perish.

As just mentioned, Aristotle himself is perfectly clear that an inductive syllogism is invalid; but he does believe that we somehow arrive, by its help and by the intuition of the essences of things referred to, at statements that describe these essences, or some essential properties, and that these statements are, as definitions, true and certain and can serve as the ultimate premises of *epistēmē*, of demonstrated scientific knowledge.

I suspect that the logician Aristotle had a bad intellectual conscience when he introduced this theory. There are two arguments supporting this conjecture. One is that in spite of his generally very objectivist attitude, he becomes, in a strange way, a subjectivist in the theory of knowledge: he teaches that in knowing a thing, in intuiting it, the knower and his knowledge become one with the object known; a theory that may fairly be described as mysticism. [2] A theory that the knowing and the known are identical is, clearly, a form of subjectivism, and very different from the objectivism of demonstrable or syllogistic knowledge. But it helps somehow to get over the chasm across which induction offers a very insecure bridge.

The other indication that Aristotle had a bad conscience when he invented induction is that he projects his invention of induction on to Socrates, of all people. Yet Socrates would have been the last person to claim that he (or any man) possessed *epistēmē* that can be based upon such a procedure, simply because he always claims to have no *epistēmē*: *Socrates claims not to know*, as Aristotle himself puts it – though what he says, more literally translated, is that Socrates *professes* (or *pretends*) not to know.

It seems very strange to burden Socrates, of all men, with the responsibility for inventing induction. The motive may be the thought that if Socrates, of all men, saw the need for induction, *then it could not be as the result of a bad argument*, an uncritical argument. But Aristotle has to get over two difficulties. He has to deny that Socrates *seriously* claims not to know; and, indeed, he suggests that Socrates' profession of ignorance is just ironical. (This is 'Socratic irony'.) The other difficulty is to interpret (or convert) the Socratic method – the *elenchus*, critical refutation by counterexamples – into a positive method of proof.

What Socrates attempts, with his *elenchus*, is to prove ignorant those who believe that they know. At the start, they believe that they know all about a subject (virtue, for example); and then Socrates shows them *with the help of concrete, experiential instances* – of counterexamples – that they do not. This method Aristotle now interprets as a method of searching for the essence by way of concrete evidence. Although this interpretation has a certain plausibility the conversion of the *elenchus* into an *epagōgē* (inductive proof) creates for Aristotle a need to invoke Socratic irony.

It is now understandable why Aristotle chooses Socrates as the person to be burdened with the responsibility for an invention that he, Aristotle, himself had made and for which he, as it were, does not dare to bear the responsibility. That seems to have been the situation: Aristotle *knows* that he knows (and that he knows that he knows makes him a bit similar to Protagoras, who was also an empiricist). However, Aristotle does not admit what Protagoras might have perhaps admitted – namely, that human knowledge is not certain. Protagoras might have admitted indeed that, even though we are the measure of all things and cannot do much better than we actually do, we can perhaps improve our knowledge a little, but not a great deal, and therefore we have to take human knowledge as the measure of all knowledge. This does not say, however, that he believed in *epistēmē* in the way that Aristotle did.

Aristotle was described admiringly by Dante as 'The master of all who know'. In my opinion this is a correct description, but he should not be admired for it, since knowledge in the Aristotelian sense is really not accessible to man. Xenophanes and Socrates (and Plato too, to the extent that he dealt with problems of natural science) are right in saying '*We do not know, we only guess*.' Aristotle was undoubtedly a great scientist (though not as great as Democritus, whom Aristotle appreciates but Plato never mentions and – according to certain traditions – is supposed to have hated); but he was pre-eminently a scholar and a great logician, whom we can thank for the invention of logic, and a great biologist. There are many things that speak in his favour, although his theories are all studies

4

in dogmatism. Indeed Aristotle was the first real dogmatist – even Plato, though a political dogmatist, was not a dogmatist in epistemology.

We may say that the Aristotelian ideal of science is more or less an encyclopaedia full of concepts, the names of the essences. What is known about these essences defines the concepts, so that we can deduce everything about the concepts from their various definitions and their interconnections. This is the structure of a deductive encyclopaedia with all its concepts obtained by inductive procedures: the *archai* from which we can then derive everything else by means of logical deductions, the syllogisms.

Admittedly, Aristotle, by his theory of logical derivation, and by his theory of the four causes, or more precisely his third cause (the moving or proximate or efficient cause), achieved a considerable clarification of Plato's essentialism (which, for instance, made beauty the cause of the beautiful object).[3]

Nevertheless, I think that with Aristotle's theory, that science, *epistēmē*, is (demonstrable and therefore) *certain knowledge*, it may be said that the great enterprise of Greek critical rationalism came to an end. Aristotle killed the critical science to which he himself had made a leading contribution. The philosophy of nature, the theory of nature, the great original attempts in cosmology, broke down after Aristotle, owing mainly to the influence of his epistemology, which demanded *proof* (including inductive proof).

I think this is in brief the story of how epistemology as we know it came to be dominated by what Parmenides would have called a *wrong way*, the way of induction. This is also the main reason why these essays, which also contain a disproof of induction, have been collected under the title *The World of Parmenides: Essays on the Presocratic Enlightenment*. They are mostly about the three great Presocratics – Xenophanes, Heraclitus and Parmenides – but they also discuss Socrates and Plato, and what was later learnt and may still be learnt from the greatest and most inventive period in Greek philosophy; a period that came to an end with Aristotle's dogmatic epistemology, and from which even the most recent philosophy can be said hardly to have recovered.

Notes

1 See further Addenda 1 and 2 to Essay 1, below.
2 See *O.S.*, vol. I, p. 314.
3 For a detailed account of this improvement in the understanding and explanation of natural phenomena, see Svend Ranulf, *Der eleatische Satz vom Widerspruch*, Copenhagen, 1924. I am indebted to Dr Flemming Steen Nielsen for drawing my attention to this interesting work.

ESSAY 1

BACK TO THE PRESOCRATICS

I

'Back to Methuselah' was a progressive programme, compared with 'Back to Thales' or 'Back to Anaximander': what Shaw offered us was an improved expectation of life – something that was in the air, at any rate when he wrote it. I have nothing to offer you, I am afraid, that is in the air today; for what I want to return to is the simple straightforward *rationality* of the Presocratics. Wherein does this much-discussed 'rationality' of the Presocratics lie? The simplicity and boldness of their questions is part of it, but my thesis is that the decisive point is the critical attitude which, as I shall try to show, was first developed in the Ionian School.

The questions which the Presocratics tried to answer were primarily cosmological questions, but there were also questions of the theory of knowledge. It is my belief that philosophy must return to cosmology and to a simple theory of knowledge. There is at least one philosophical problem in which all thinking men are interested: the problem of understanding the world in which we live; and thus ourselves (who are part of that world) and our knowledge of it. All science is cosmology, I believe, and for me the interest of philosophy, no less than of science, lies solely in its bold attempt to add to our knowledge of the world, and to the theory of our knowledge of the world. I am interested in Wittgenstein, for example, not because of his linguistic philosophy, but because his *Tractatus* was a cosmological treatise (although a crude one), and because his theory of knowledge was closely linked with his cosmology.

For me, both philosophy and science lose all their attraction when they

The Presidential Address, delivered before the meeting of the Aristotelian Society on 13 October 1958; first published in the Proceedings of the Aristotelian Society, N.S. **59**, *1958–9. Footnotes were added to the reprint of the address in* C. & R., *1963. {In the present collection, the address is reprinted without the appendix but with two addenda on verisimilitude that first appeared in* C. & R., *1965 and 1969. Newly improved translations of Xenophanes' fragments (DK 21B23; 24; 25; 26; and DK B15; 16; 18; 34; and 35) have replaced the translations on p. 145 and on pp. 152–3 of the 5th edition of* C. & R., *1989. Ed.}*

give up that pursuit – when they become specialisms and cease to see, and to wonder at, the riddles of our world. Specialization may be a great temptation for the scientist. For the philosopher it is the mortal sin.

II

In this paper I speak as an amateur, as a lover of the beautiful story of the Presocratics. I am not a specialist or an expert: I am completely out of my depth when an expert begins to argue which words or phrases Heraclitus might, and which he could not possibly, have used. Yet when some expert replaces a beautiful story, based on the oldest texts we possess, by one which – to me at any rate – no longer makes any sense, then I feel that even an amateur may stand up and defend an old tradition. Thus I will at least look into the expert's arguments, and examine their consistency. This seems a harmless occupation to indulge in; and if an expert or anybody else should take the trouble to refute my criticism I shall be pleased and honoured.[1]

I shall be concerned with the cosmological theories of the Presocratics, but only to the extent to which they bear upon the development of *the problem of change*, as I call it, and only to the extent to which they are needed for understanding the approach of the Presocratic philosophers to the problem of knowledge – their practical as well as their theoretical approach. For it is of considerable interest to see how their practice as well as their theory of knowledge is connected with the cosmological and theological questions which they posed to themselves. Theirs was not a theory of knowledge that began with the question, 'How do I know that this is an orange?' or, 'How do I know that the object I am now perceiving is an orange?' Their theory of knowledge started from problems such as, 'How do we know that the world is made of water?' or, 'How do we know that the world is full of gods?' or, 'How can we know anything about the gods?'

There is a widespread belief, somewhat remotely due, I think, to the influence of Francis Bacon, that one should study the problems of the theory of knowledge in connection with our knowledge of an orange rather than our knowledge of the cosmos. I dissent from this belief, and it is one of the main purposes of my paper to convey to you some of my reasons for dissenting. At any rate it is good to remember from time to time that our Western science – and there seems to be no other – did not start with collecting observations of oranges, but with bold theories about the world.

III

Traditional empiricist epistemology and the traditional historiography of science are both deeply influenced by the Baconian myth that all science starts from observation and then slowly and cautiously proceeds to theories. That the facts are very different can be learnt from studying the early Presocratics. Here we find bold and fascinating ideas, some of which are strange and even staggering anticipations of modern results, while many others are wide of the mark, from our modern point of view; but most of them, and the best of them, have nothing to do with observation. Take, for example, some of the theories about the shape and position of the Earth. Thales said, we are told [A 15], 'that the Earth is supported by water on which it rides like a ship, and when we say that there is an earthquake, then the Earth is being shaken by the movement of the water'. No doubt Thales had observed earthquakes as well as the rolling of a ship before he arrived at his theory. But the point of his theory was to *explain* the support or suspension of the Earth, and also earthquakes, by the conjecture that the Earth floats on water; and for this conjecture (which so strangely anticipates the modern theory of continental drift) he could have no basis in his observations.

We must not forget that the function of the Baconian myth is to explain why scientific statements are *true*, by pointing out that observation is the *'true source'* of our scientific knowledge. Once we realize that all scientific statements are hypotheses, or guesses, or conjectures, and that the vast majority of these conjectures (including Bacon's own) have turned out to be false, the Baconian myth becomes irrelevant. For it is pointless to argue that the conjectures of science – those which have proved to be false as well as those which are still accepted – all start from observation.

However this may be, Thales' beautiful theory of the support or suspension of the Earth and of earthquakes, though in no sense based upon observation, is at least inspired by an empirical or observational analogy. But even this is no longer true of the theory proposed by Thales' great pupil, Anaximander. Anaximander's theory of the suspension of the Earth is still highly intuitive, but it no longer uses observational analogies. In fact it may be described as counter-observational. According to Anaximander's theory [A 11],

> The Earth . . . is held up by nothing, but remains stationary owing to the fact that it is equally distant from all other things. Its shape is . . . like that of a drum. . . . We walk on one of its flat surfaces, while the other is on the opposite side.

The drum, of course, is an observational analogy. But the idea of the Earth's free suspension in space, and the explanation of its stability, have no analogy whatever in the whole field of observable facts.

In my opinion this idea of Anaximander's is one of the boldest, most revolutionary, and most portentous ideas in the whole history of human thought. It made possible the theories of Aristarchus and Copernicus. But the step taken by Anaximander was even more difficult and audacious than the one taken by Aristarchus and Copernicus. To envisage the Earth as freely poised in mid-space, and to say 'that it remains motionless because of its equidistance or equilibrium' (as Aristotle paraphrases Anaximander), is to anticipate to some extent even Newton's idea of immaterial and invisible gravitational forces.[2]

IV

How did Anaximander arrive at this remarkable theory? Certainly not by observation but by reasoning. His theory is an attempt to solve one of the problems to which his teacher and kinsman Thales, the founder of the Milesian or Ionian School, had offered a solution before him. I therefore conjecture that Anaximander arrived at his theory by criticizing Thales' theory. This conjecture can be supported, I believe, by a consideration of the structure of Anaximander's theory.

Anaximander is likely to have argued against Thales' theory (according to which the Earth was floating on water) on the following lines. Thales' theory is a specimen of a type of theory which if consistently developed would lead to an infinite regress. If we explain the stable position of the Earth by the assumption that it is supported by water – that it is floating on the ocean (Okeanos) – should we not have to explain the stable position of the ocean by an analogous hypothesis? But this would mean looking for a support for the ocean, and then for a support for this support. This method of explanation is unsatisfactory: first, because we solve our problem by creating an exactly analogous one; and also for the less formal and more intuitive reason that in any such system of supports or props, failure to secure any one of the lower props must lead to the collapse of the whole edifice.

From this we see intuitively that the stability of the world cannot be secured by a system of supports or props. Instead Anaximander appeals to the internal or structural symmetry of the world, which ensures that there is no preferred direction in which a collapse can take place. He applies the principle that where there are no differences there can be no change. In this way he explains the stability of the Earth by the equality of its distances from all other things.

This, it seems, was Anaximander's argument. It is important to realize that it abolishes, even though not quite consciously, perhaps, and not quite consistently, the idea of an absolute direction – the absolute sense of 'upwards' and 'downwards'. This is not only contrary to all experience but notoriously difficult to grasp. Anaximenes ignored it, it seems, and even Anaximander himself did not grasp it completely. For the idea of an equal distance from all other things should have led him to the theory that the Earth has the shape of a globe. Instead he believed that it had the shape of a drum, with an upper and a lower flat surface. Yet it looks as if the remark, 'We walk on one of its flat surfaces, while the other is on the opposite side' [A 11], contained a hint that there was no absolute upper surface, but that on the contrary the surface on which we happened to walk was the one we might *call* the upper.

What prevented Anaximander from arriving at the theory that the Earth was a globe rather than a drum? There can be little doubt: it was *observational experience* which taught him that the surface of the Earth was, by and large, flat. Thus it was a speculative and critical argument, the abstract critical discussion of Thales' theory, which almost led him to the true theory of the shape of the Earth; and it was observational experience which led him astray.

V

There is an obvious objection to Anaximander's theory of symmetry, according to which the Earth is equally distant from all other things. The asymmetry of the universe can be easily seen from the existence of Sun and Moon, and especially from the fact that Sun and Moon are sometimes not far distant from each other, so that they are on the same side of the Earth, while there is nothing on the other side to balance them. It appears that Anaximander met this objection by another bold theory – his theory of the hidden nature of the Sun, the Moon, and the other heavenly bodies.

He envisages the rims of two huge chariot wheels rotating round the Earth, one 27 times the size of the Earth, the other 18 times its size. Each of these rims or circular pipes is filled with fire, and each has a breathing-hole through which the fire is visible. These holes we call the Sun and the Moon respectively. The rest of the wheel is invisible, presumably because it is dark (or misty) and far away. The fixed stars (and presumably the planets) are also holes on wheels which are nearer to the Earth than the wheels of the Sun and the Moon. The wheels of the fixed stars rotate on a common axis (which we now call the axis of the Earth) and together they form a sphere round the Earth, so the postulate of equal distance from the Earth is (roughly) satisfied. This makes Anaximander also a founder of the *theory of the spheres*. (For its relation to the wheels or circles see Aristotle *De Caelo* 289b10–290b10.)

VI

There can be no doubt whatever that Anaximander's theories are critical and speculative rather than empirical: and considered as approaches to truth, his critical and abstract speculations served him better than observational experience or analogy.

But, a follower of Bacon may reply, this is precisely why Anaximander was not a scientist. This is precisely why we speak of early Greek *philosophy* rather than of early Greek *science*. Philosophy is speculative: everybody knows this. And as everybody knows, science begins only when the speculative method is replaced by the observational method, and when deduction is replaced by induction.

This reply, of course, amounts to the thesis that, by definition, theories are (or are not) *scientific* according to their origin in observations, or in so-called 'inductive procedures'. Yet I believe that few, if any, physical theories would fall under this definition. And I do not see why the question of origin should be important in this connection. What is important about a theory is its explanatory power, and whether it stands up to criticism and to tests. The question of its origin, of how it is arrived at — whether by an 'inductive procedure', as some say, or by an act of intuition — may be extremely interesting, especially for the biographer of the man who invented the theory, but it has little to do with its scientific status or character.

VII

As to the Presocratics, I assert that there is the most perfect possible continuity of thought between their theories and the later developments in physics. Whether they are called philosophers, or pre-scientists, or scientists matters very little, I think. But I do assert that Anaximander's theory cleared the way for the theories of Aristarchus, Copernicus, Kepler, and Galileo. It is not that he merely 'influenced' these later thinkers; 'influence' is a very superficial category. I would rather put it like this: Anaximander's achievement is valuable in itself, like a work of art. Besides, his achievement made other achievements possible, among them those of the great scientists mentioned.

But are not Anaximander's theories false, and therefore non-scientific? They are false, I admit; but so are many theories, based upon countless experiments, which modern science accepted until recently, and whose scientific character nobody would dream of denying, even though they are now believed to be false. (An example is the theory that the typical chemical properties of hydrogen belong only to one kind of atom — the lightest of all atoms.) There were historians of science who tended to regard as unscientific (or even as superstitious) any view no longer accepted at the time they were writing; but this is an untenable attitude. A false theory may be as great an achievement as a true one. And many false theories have been more helpful in our search for truth than some less interesting theories which are still accepted. For false theories can be helpful in many ways; they may, for example, suggest some more or less radical modifications, and they may stimulate criticism. Thus Thales' theory that the Earth floats on water reappeared in a modified form in Anaximenes, and in more recent times in the form of Wegener's theory of continental drift. How Thales' theory stimulated Anaximander's criticism has been shown already.

Anaximander's theory, similarly, suggested a modified theory – the theory of an Earth globe, freely poised in the centre of the universe, and surrounded by spheres on which heavenly bodies were mounted. And by stimulating criticism it also led to the theory that the Moon shines by reflecting light; to the Pythagorean theory of a central fire; and ultimately to the heliocentric world-system of Aristarchus and Copernicus.

VIII

I believe that the Milesians, like their oriental predecessors who took the world for a tent, envisaged the world as a kind of house, the home of all creatures – our home. Thus there was no need to ask what it was for. But there was a real need to inquire into its architecture. The questions of its structure, its ground-plan, and its building material constitute the three main problems of Milesian cosmology. There is also a speculative interest in its origin, the question of cosmogony. It seems to me that the cosmological interest of the Milesians far exceeded their cosmogonical interest, especially if we consider the strong cosmogonical tradition, and the almost irresistible tendency to describe a thing by describing how it has been made, and thus to present a cosmological account in a cosmogonical form. The cosmological interest must be very strong, as compared with the cosmogonical one, if the presentation of a cosmological theory is even partially free from these cosmogonical trappings.

I believe that it was Thales who first discussed the architecture of the cosmos – its structure, ground-plan, and building material. In Anaximander we find answers to all three questions. I have briefly mentioned his answer to the question of structure. As to the question of the ground-plan of the world, he studied and expounded this too, as indicated by the tradition that he drew the first map of the world. And of course he had a theory about its building material – the 'endless' or 'boundless' or 'unbounded' or 'unformed' – the *apeiron*.

In Anaximander's world all kinds of *changes* were going on. There was a fire which needed air and breathing-holes, and these were at times blocked up ('obstructed'), so that the fire was smothered: [3] this was his theory of eclipses, and of the phases of the Moon. There were winds, which were responsible for the changing weather.[4] And there were the vapours, resulting from the drying up of water and air, which were the cause of the winds and of the 'turnings' of the Sun (the solstices) and of the Moon.

We have here the first hint of what was soon to come: of the *general problem of change*, which became the central problem of Greek cosmology, and which ultimately led, with Leucippus and Democritus, to *a general theory of change* that was accepted by modern science almost up to the

13

beginning of the twentieth century. (It was given up only with the breakdown of Maxwell's models of the ether, a historic event that was little noticed before 1905.)

This *general problem of change* is a philosophical problem; indeed in the hands of Parmenides and Zeno it almost turns into a logical one. *How is change possible* – logically possible, that is? How can a thing change, without losing its identity? If it remains the same, it does not change; yet if it loses its identity, then it is no longer that thing which has changed.

IX

The exciting story of the development of the problem of change appears to me in danger of being completely buried under the mounting heap of the minutiae of textual criticism. The story cannot, of course, be fully told in one short paper, and still less in one of its many sections. But in briefest outline, it is this.

For Anaximander, our own world, our own cosmic edifice, was only one of an infinity of worlds – an infinity without bounds in space and time. This system of worlds was eternal, and so was motion. There was thus no need to explain motion, no need to offer a *general* theory of change (in the sense in which we shall find a general problem and a general theory of change in Heraclitus; see below). But there was a need to explain the well-known changes occurring in our world. The most obvious changes – the change of day and night, of winds and of weather, of the seasons, from sowing to harvesting, and of the growth of plants and animals and men – all were connected with the contrast of temperatures, with the opposition between the hot and the cold, and with that between the dry and the wet. 'Living creatures came into being from moisture evaporated by the Sun', we are told [A 11]; and the hot and the cold also administer to the genesis of our own world edifice. The hot and the cold were also responsible for the vapours and winds, which in their turn were conceived as the agents of almost all other changes.

Anaximenes, a pupil of Anaximander and his successor, developed these ideas in much detail. Like Anaximander he was interested in the opposi-tions of the hot and the cold and of the moist and the dry, and he explained the transitions between these opposites by a theory of condensa-tion and rarefaction. Like Anaximander he believed in eternal motion and in the action of the winds; and it seems not unlikely that one of the two main points in which he deviated from Anaximander was reached by a criticism of the idea that what was completely boundless and formless (the *apeiron*) could yet be in motion. At any rate, he replaced the *Apeiron* by *Air* – something that was almost boundless and formless, and yet, according to Anaximander's old theory of vapours, not only capable of motion, but the main agent of motion and change. A similar unification of ideas was

14

achieved by Anaximenes' theory that 'the Sun consists of earth, and that it gets very hot owing to the rapidity of its motion' [A 6]. The replacement of the more abstract theory of the unbounded *Apeiron* by the less abstract and more common-sense theory of air is matched by the replacement of Anaximander's bold theory of the stability of the Earth by the more common-sense idea that the Earth's 'flatness is responsible for its stability; for it . . . covers like a lid the air beneath it' [A 20]. Thus the Earth rides on air as the lid of a pot may ride on steam, or as a ship may ride on water; Thales' question and Thales' answer are both reinstituted, and Anaximander's epoch-making argument is not understood. Anaximenes is an eclectic, a systematizer, an empiricist, a man of common sense. Of the three great Milesians he is least productive of revolutionary new ideas; he is the least philosophically minded.

The three Milesians all looked on our world as our home. There was movement, there was change in this home, there was hot and cold, fire and moisture. There was a fire in the hearth, and on it a kettle with water. The house was exposed to the winds, and a bit draughty, to be sure; but it was home, and it meant security and stability of a sort. But for Heraclitus the house was on fire.

There was no stability left in the world of Heraclitus. 'Everything is in flux, and nothing is at rest.' *Everything* is in flux, even the beams, the timber, the building material of which the world is made: earth and rocks, or the bronze of a cauldron – they are all in flux. The beams are rotting, the earth is washed away and blown away, the very rocks split and wither, the bronze cauldron turns into green patina, or into verdigris: 'All things are in motion all the time, even though . . . this escapes our senses', as Aristotle expressed it. Those who do not know and do not think believe that only the fuel is burned, while the bowl in which it burns (cp. DK A1) remains unchanged; for we do not see the bowl burning. And yet it burns; it is eaten up by the fire it holds. We do not *see* our children grow up, and change, and grow old, but they do.

Thus there are no solid bodies. Things are not really things, they are processes, they are in flux. They are like fire, like a flame which, though it may have a definite shape, is a process, a stream of matter, a river. All things are flames: *Fire* is the very building material of our world; and the apparent stability of things is merely due to the laws, the measures, which the processes in our world are subject to.

This, I believe, is Heraclitus' story; it is his 'message', the 'true word' (the *logos*), to which we ought to listen: 'Listening not to me but to the true account, it is wise to admit that all things are one': they are 'an everlasting fire, flaring up in measures, and dying down in measures'.

I know very well that the traditional interpretation of Heraclitus' philosophy here restated is not generally accepted at present. But the critics have put nothing in its place – nothing, that is, of philosophical

15

interest. I shall briefly discuss their new interpretation in the next section. Here I wish only to stress that Heraclitus' philosophy, by appealing to thought, to the word, to argument, to reason, and by pointing out that we are living in a world of things whose changes escape our senses, though we *know* that they do change, created two new problems: *the problem of change* and *the problem of knowledge*. These problems were the more urgent as his own account of change was difficult to understand. But this, I believe, is due to the fact that he saw more clearly than his predecessors the difficulties that were involved in the very idea of change.

For all change is the change of something: change presupposes something that changes. And it presupposes that, while changing, this something must remain the same. We may say that a green leaf changes when it turns brown; but we do not say that the green leaf changes when we substitute for it a brown leaf. It is essential to the idea of change that the thing which changes retains its identity while changing. And yet it must become something else: it was green, and it becomes brown; it was moist, and it becomes dry; it was hot, and it becomes cold.

Thus every change is the transition of a thing into something with, in a way, opposite qualities (as Anaximander and Anaximenes had seen). And yet, while changing, the changing thing must remain identical with itself.

This is the problem of change. It led Heraclitus to a theory which (partly anticipating Parmenides) distinguishes between reality and appearance. 'The real nature of things loves to hide itself. An unapparent harmony is stronger than the apparent one' [B 123]. Things are *in appearance* (and for us) opposites, but in truth (and for God) they are the same.

> Life and death, being awake and being asleep, youth and old age, all these are the same . . . for the one turned round is the other and the other turned round is the first. . . . The path that leads up and the path that leads down are the same path. . . . Good and bad are identical. . . . For God all things are beautiful and good and just, but men assume some things to be unjust, and others to be just. . . . It is not in the nature or character of man to possess true knowledge, though it is in the divine nature [B 88, 60, 58, 102, 78].

Thus in truth (and for God) the opposites are identical; it is only to man that they appear as non-identical. And all things are one — they are all part of the process of the world, the everlasting *Fire*.

This theory of change appeals to the 'true word', to the *logos*, to reason; nothing is more real for Heraclitus than change. Yet his doctrine of the oneness of the world, of the identity of opposites, and of appearance and reality threatens his doctrine of the reality of change.

For change is the transition from one opposite to the other. Thus if in truth the opposites are identical, though they appear different, then change itself might be only apparent. If in truth, and for God, all things are one, there might, in truth, be no change.

This consequence was drawn by Parmenides, the pupil (*pace* Burnet and others) of the monotheist Xenophanes, who said of the one God (DK B23; 26; 25; and 24):

> One God, alone among gods and alone among men is the greatest.
> Neither in body nor in mind does he resemble the mortals.
> Always in one place he remains, without ever moving,
> Nor is it fitting for him to wander now hereto now thereto.
> Effortless he swings the All, by mere thought and intention.
> All of him is sight; all is knowledge; and all is hearing.

Xenophanes' pupil Parmenides taught that the real world was one, and that it always remained in the same place, never moving. It was not *fitting* that it should go to different places at different times. It was in no way similar to what it appeared to be to mortal men. The world was one, an undivided whole, without parts, homogeneous and motionless: motion was impossible in such a world. In truth there was no change. The world of change was an illusion.

Parmenides based this theory of an unchanging reality on something like a logical proof; a proof which can be presented as proceeding from the single premise, 'What is not is not'. From this we can derive that the nothing – that which is not – does not exist; a result which Parmenides interprets to mean that the void does not exist. Thus the world is full: it consists of one undivided block, since any division into parts could only be due to separation of the parts by the void. (This is 'the well-rounded truth' which the goddess revealed to Parmenides, B1: 29.) In this full world there is no room for motion.

Only the delusive belief in the reality of opposites – the belief that not only *what is* exists but also *what is not* – leads to the illusion of a world of change.

Parmenides' theory may be described as the first hypothetico-deductive theory of the world. The atomists took it as such; and they asserted that it was refuted by experience, since motion does exist. Accepting the formal validity of Parmenides' argument, they inferred from the falsity of his conclusion the falsity of his premise. But this meant that the nothing – the void, or empty space – existed. Consequently there was now no need to assume that 'what is' – the full, that which fills some space – had no parts; for its parts could now be separated by the void. Thus there are many parts, each of which is 'full': there are full particles in the world, separated by empty space, and able to move in empty space, each of them being 'full', undivided, indivisible, and unchanging. Thus what exists is *atoms and the void*. In this way the atomists arrived at a *theory of change* – a theory that dominated scientific thought until 1900. It is the theory that *all change, and especially all qualitative change, has to be explained by the spatial movement of unchanging bits of matter – by atoms moving in the void.*

The next great step in our cosmology and the theory of change was made when Maxwell, developing certain ideas of Faraday's, replaced this theory by a theory of changing intensities of fields.

X

I have sketched the story, as I see it, of the Presocratic theory of change. I am, of course, well aware of the fact that my story (which is based on Plato, Aristotle, and the doxographic tradition) clashes at many points with the views of some experts, English as well as German, and especially with the views expressed by G. S. Kirk and J. E. Raven in their book *The Presocratic Philosophers*, Cambridge, 1957. I cannot, of course, examine their arguments in detail here, and especially not their minute exegeses of various passages, some of which are relevant to the differences between their interpretation and mine. (See, for example, Kirk and Raven's discussion of the question whether there is a reference to Heraclitus in Parmenides; cp. their note 1 on pp. 193f., and note 1 on p. 272.) But I wish to say that I have examined their arguments and that I have found them unconvincing and often quite unacceptable.

I will mention here only some points regarding Heraclitus (although there are other points of equal importance, such as their comments on Parmenides).

The traditional view, according to which Heraclitus' central doctrine was that all things are in flux, was attacked forty years ago by Burnet. His main argument (discussed by me at length in note 2 of ch. 2 of my *Open Society*) was that the theory of change was not new, and that only a new message could explain the urgency with which Heraclitus speaks. This argument is repeated by Kirk and Raven when they write (pp. 186f.): 'But all Presocratic thinkers were struck by the predominance of change in the world of our experience.' About this attitude I said in my *Open Society*: 'Those who suggest . . . that the doctrine of universal flux was not new . . . are, I feel, unconscious witnesses to Heraclitus' originality, for they fail now, after 2,400 years, to grasp his main point.' In brief, they do not see the difference between the Milesian message, 'There is a fire in the house', and Heraclitus' somewhat more urgent message, 'The house is on fire.' An implicit reply to this criticism can be found on p. 197 of the book by Kirk and Raven, where they write: 'Can Heraclitus really have thought that a rock or a bronze cauldron, for example, was invariably undergoing invisible changes of material? Perhaps so; but nothing in the extant fragments suggests that he did.' But is this so? Heraclitus' extant fragments about the *Fire* (Kirk and Raven, fragm. 220–2) are interpreted by

Kirk and Raven themselves as follows (p. 200): 'Fire is the archetypal form of matter.' Now, I am not at all sure what 'archetypal' means here (especially in view of the fact that we read a few lines later, 'Cosmogony . . . is not to be found in Heraclitus'). But whatever 'archetypal' may mean, it is clear that once it is admitted that Heraclitus says in the extant fragments that all matter is somehow (whether archetypally or otherwise) fire, he also says that all matter, like fire, is a process; which is precisely the theory denied to Heraclitus by Kirk and Raven.

Immediately after saying that 'nothing in the extant fragments suggests' that Heraclitus believed in continuous invisible changes, Kirk and Raven make the following methodological remark: 'It cannot be too strongly emphasized that [in texts] before Parmenides and his apparent proof that the senses were completely fallacious . . . gross departures from common sense must only be accepted when the evidence for them is extremely strong.' This is intended to mean that the doctrine that bodies (of any substance) constantly undergo invisible changes represents a gross departure from common sense, a departure which one ought not to expect in Heraclitus.

But to quote Heraclitus: 'He who does not expect the unexpected will not detect it: for him it will remain undetectable, and unapproachable' (DK B18). In fact Kirk and Raven's last argument is invalid on many grounds. Long before Parmenides we find ideas far removed from common sense in Anaximander, Pythagoras, Xenophanes, and especially in Heraclitus. Indeed the suggestion that we should test the historicity of the ideas ascribed to Heraclitus – as we might indeed test the historicity of those ascribed to Anaximenes – by standards of 'common sense' is a little surprising (whatever 'common sense' may mean here). For this suggestion runs counter not only to Heraclitus' notorious obscurity and oracular style, confirmed by Kirk and Raven, but also to his burning interest in antinomy and paradox. And it runs counter, last but not least, to the (in my view quite absurd) doctrine which Kirk and Raven finally attribute to Heraclitus (the italics are mine): 'that natural changes of all kinds [and thus presumably also earthquakes and great fires] are regular *and balanced*, and *that the cause of this balance is fire, the common constituent of things that was also termed their Logos*'. But why, I ask, should fire be 'the cause' of any balance – either 'this balance' or any other? And where does Heraclitus say such things? Indeed, had this been Heraclitus' philosophy, then I could see no reason to take any interest in it; at any rate, it would be much further removed from common sense (as I see it) than the inspired philosophy which tradition ascribes to Heraclitus and which, in the name of common sense, is rejected by Kirk and Raven.

But the decisive point is, of course, that this inspired philosophy is *true*, for all we know.[5] With his uncanny intuition Heraclitus saw that things are processes, that our bodies are flames, that 'a rock or a bronze cauldron

19

. . . was invariably undergoing invisible changes'. Kirk and Raven say (p. 197, note 1; the argument reads like an answer to Melissus): 'Every time the finger rubs, it rubs off an invisible portion of iron; yet when it does not rub, what reason is there to think that the iron is still changing?' The reason is that the wind rubs, and that there is always wind; or that iron turns invisibly into rust – by oxidation, and this means by slow burning; or that old iron looks different from new iron, just as an old man looks different from a child (cp. DK B88). This was Heraclitus' teaching, as the extant fragments show.

I suggest that Kirk and Raven's methodological principle 'that gross departures from common sense must only be accepted when the evidence for them is extremely strong' might well be replaced by the clearer and more important principle that *gross departures from the historical tradition must only be accepted when the evidence for them is extremely strong*. This, in fact, is a universal principle of historiography. Without it history would be impossible. Yet it is constantly violated by Kirk and Raven: when, for example, they try to make Plato's and Aristotle's evidence suspect, with arguments which are partly circular and partly (like the one from common sense) in contradiction to their own story. And when they say that 'little serious attempt seems to have been made by Plato and Aristotle to penetrate his [i.e. Heraclitus'] real meaning', then I can only say that the philosophy outlined by Plato and Aristotle seems to me a philosophy that has real meaning and real depth. It is a philosophy worthy of a great philosopher. Who, if not Heraclitus, was the great thinker who first realized that men are flames and that things are processes? Are we really to believe that this great philosophy was a 'post-Heraclitean exaggeration' (p. 197), and that it may have been suggested to Plato, 'in particular, perhaps, by Cratylus'? Who, I ask, was this unknown philosopher – perhaps the greatest and the boldest thinker among the Presocratics? Who was he, if not Heraclitus?

XI

The early history of Greek philosophy, especially the history from Thales to Plato, is a splendid story. It is almost too good to be true. In every generation we find at least one new philosophy, one new cosmology of staggering originality and depth. How was this possible? Of course one cannot explain originality and genius. But one can try to throw some light on them. What was the secret of the ancients? I suggest that it was a *tradition – the tradition of critical discussion*.

I will try to put the problem more sharply. In all or almost all civilizations we find something like religious and cosmological teaching, and in many societies we find schools. Now schools, especially primitive schools, all have, it appears, a characteristic structure and function. Far from being places of critical discussion they make it their task to impart a definite doctrine, and to preserve it, pure and unchanged. It is the task of a school to hand on the tradition, the doctrine of its founder, its first master, to the next generation, and to this end the most important thing is to keep the doctrine inviolate. A school of this kind never admits a new idea. New ideas are heresies, and lead to schisms; should a member of the school try to change the doctrine, then he is expelled as a heretic. But the heretic claims, as a rule, that his is the true doctrine of the founder. Thus not even the inventor admits that he has introduced an invention; he believes, rather, that he is returning to the true orthodoxy which has somehow been perverted.

In this way all changes of doctrine – if any – are surreptitious changes. They are all presented as restatements of the true sayings of the master, of his own words, his own meaning, his own intentions.

It is clear that in a school of this kind we cannot expect to find a history of ideas, or even the material for such a history. For new ideas are not admitted to be new. Everything is ascribed to the master. All we might reconstruct is a history of schisms, and perhaps a history of the defence of certain doctrines against the heretics.

There cannot, of course, be any rational discussion in a school of this kind. There may be arguments against dissenters and heretics, or against some competing schools. But in the main it is with assertion and dogma and condemnation rather than argument that the doctrine is defended.

The great example of a school of this kind among the Greek philosophical schools is the Italian School founded by Pythagoras. Compared with the Ionian School, or with that of Elea, it had the character of a religious order, with a characteristic way of life and a secret doctrine. The story that a member, Hippasus of Metapontum, was drowned at sea because he revealed the secret of the irrationality of certain square roots is characteristic of the atmosphere surrounding the Pythagorean School, whether or not there is any truth in this story.

But among Greek philosophical schools the early Pythagoreans were an exception. Leaving them aside, we could say that the character of Greek philosophy, and of the philosophical schools, is strikingly different from the dogmatic type of school here described. I have shown this by an example: *the story of the problem of change which I have told is the story of a critical debate, of a rational discussion.* New ideas are propounded as such, and arise as the result of open criticism. There are few, if any, surreptitious changes. Instead of anonymity we find a history of ideas and of their originators.

Here is a unique phenomenon, and it is closely connected with the astonishing freedom and creativeness of Greek philosophy. How can we explain this phenomenon? *What we have to explain is the rise of a tradition.* It is a tradition that allows or encourages critical discussions between various schools and, more surprisingly still, within one and the same school. For nowhere outside the Pythagorean School do we find a school devoted to the preservation of a doctrine. Instead we find changes, new ideas, modifications, and outright criticism of the master.

(In Parmenides we even find, at an early date, a most remarkable phenomenon – that of a philosopher who propounds *two* doctrines, one which he says is true, and one which he himself describes as false. Yet he makes the false doctrine not simply an object of condemnation or of criticism; rather he presents it as the best possible account of the delusive opinion of mortal men, and of the world of mere appearance – the best account which a mortal man can give.)

How and where was this critical tradition founded? This is a problem deserving serious thought. This much is certain: Xenophanes, who brought the Ionian tradition to Elea, was fully conscious of the fact that his own teaching was purely conjectural, and that others might come who would know better. I shall come back to this point again in my next and last section.

If we look for the first signs of this new critical attitude, this new freedom of thought, we are led back to Anaximander's criticism of Thales. Here is a most striking fact: Anaximander criticizes his master and kinsman, one of the Seven Sages, the founder of the Ionian School. He was, according to tradition, only about fourteen years younger than Thales, and he must have developed his criticism and his new ideas while his master was alive. (They seem to have died within a few years of each other.) But there is no trace in the sources of a story of dissent, of any quarrel, or of any schism.

This suggests, I think, that it was Thales who founded the new tradition of freedom – based upon a new relation between master and pupil – and who thus created a new type of school, utterly different from the Pythagorean School. He seems to have been able to tolerate criticism. And what is more, he seems to have created the tradition that one ought to tolerate criticism.

Yet I like to think that he did even more than this. I can hardly imagine a relationship between master and pupil in which the master merely tolerates criticism without actively encouraging it. It does not seem to me possible that a pupil who is being trained in the dogmatic attitude would ever dare to criticize the dogma (least of all that of a famous sage) and to voice his criticism. And it seems to me an easier and simpler explanation to assume that the master encouraged a critical attitude; possibly not from the outset, but only after he was struck by the pertinence of some questions, asked by the pupil perhaps without any critical intention.

However this may be, the conjecture that Thales actively encouraged criticism in his pupils would explain the fact that the critical attitude towards the master's doctrine became part of the Ionian School tradition. I like to think that Thales was the first teacher who said to his pupils: 'This is how I see things – how I believe that things are. Try to improve upon my teaching.' (Those who believe that it is 'unhistorical' to attribute this undogmatic attitude to Thales may again be reminded of the fact that only two generations later we find a similar attitude consciously and clearly formulated in the fragments of Xenophanes.) At any rate, there is the historical fact that the Ionian School was the first in which pupils criticized their masters, in one generation after the other. There can be little doubt that the Greek tradition of philosophical criticism had its main source in Ionia.

It was a momentous innovation. It meant a break with the dogmatic tradition which permits only *one* school doctrine, and the introduction in its place of a tradition that admits a *plurality* of doctrines which all try to approach the truth by means of critical discussion.

It thus leads, almost by necessity, to the realization that our attempts to see and to find the truth are not final, but open to improvement; that our knowledge, our doctrine, is conjectural; that it consists of guesses, of hypotheses, rather than of final and certain truths; and that criticism and critical discussion are our only means of getting nearer to the truth. It thus leads to the tradition of bold conjectures and of free criticism, the tradition which created the rational or scientific attitude, and with it our Western civilization, the only civilization which is based upon science (though, of course, not upon science alone).

In this rationalist tradition bold changes of doctrine are not forbidden. On the contrary, innovation is encouraged, and is regarded as success, as improvement, if it is based on the result of a critical discussion of its predecessors. The very boldness of an innovation is admired; for it can be controlled by the severity of its critical examination. This is why changes of doctrine, far from being made surreptitiously, are traditionally handed down together with the older doctrines and the names of the innovators. And the material for a history of ideas becomes part of the school tradition.

To my knowledge the critical or rationalist tradition was invented only once. It was lost after two or three centuries, perhaps owing to the rise of the Aristotelian doctrine of *epistēmē*, of certain and demonstrable knowledge (a development of the Eleatic and Heraclitean distinction between certain truth and mere guesswork). It was rediscovered and consciously revived in the Renaissance, especially by Galileo Galilei.

XII

I now come to my last and most central contention. It is this. The rationalist tradition, the tradition of critical discussion, represents the only practicable way of expanding our knowledge – conjectural or hypothetical knowledge, of course. There is no other way. More especially,

23

there is no way that starts from observation or experiment. In the development of science, observations and experiments play only the role of critical arguments. And they play this role alongside other, non-observational arguments. It is an important role; but the significance of observations and experiments depends *entirely* upon the question whether or not they may be used to *criticize theories*.

According to the theory of knowledge here outlined there are in the main only two ways in which theories may be superior to others: they may explain more; and they may be better tested – that is, they may be more fully and more critically discussed, in the light of all we know, of all the objections we can think of, and especially also in the light of observational or experimental tests which were designed with the aim of criticizing the theory.

There is only one element of rationality in our attempts to know the world: it is the critical examination of our theories. These theories themselves are guesswork. We do not know, we only guess. If you ask me, 'How do you know?' my reply would be, 'I don't; I only propose a guess. If you are interested in my problem, I shall be most happy if you criticize my guess, and if you offer counter-proposals, I in turn will try to criticize them.'

This, I believe, is the true theory of knowledge (which I wish to submit for your criticism): the true description of a practice which arose in Ionia and which is incorporated in modern science (though there are many scientists who still believe in the Baconian myth of induction): the theory that knowledge proceeds by way of *conjectures and refutations*.

Two of the greatest men who clearly saw that there was no such thing as an inductive procedure, and who clearly understood what I regard as the true theory of knowledge, were Galileo and Einstein. Yet the ancients also knew it. Incredible as it sounds, we find a clear recognition and formulation of this theory of rational knowledge almost immediately after the practice of critical discussion had begun. Our oldest extant fragments in this field are those of Xenophanes. I will present here five of them in an order that suggests that it was the boldness of his attack and the gravity of his problems which made him conscious of the fact that all our knowledge was guesswork, yet that we may nevertheless, by searching for that knowledge 'which is the better', find it in the course of time. Here are the five fragments (DK B16 and 15; 18; 35; and 34) from Xenophanes' writings.

The Ethiops say that their gods are flat-nosed and black
While the Thracians say that theirs have blue eyes and red hair.
Yet if cattle or horses or lions had hands and could draw
And could sculpture like men, then the horses would draw their gods
Like horses, and cattle like cattle, and each would then shape
Bodies of gods in the likeness, each kind, of its own.

The gods did not reveal, from the beginning,
All things to us; but in the course of time,
Through seeking we may learn, and know things better . . .

This, as we well may conjecture, resembles the truth.

But as for certain truth, no man has known it,
Nor will he know it; neither of the gods
Nor yet of all the things of which I speak.
And even if perchance he were to utter
The perfect truth, he would himself not know it;
For all is but a woven web of guesses.

To show that Xenophanes was not alone I may also repeat here two of Heraclitus' sayings (DK B78 and 18) which I have quoted before in a different context. Both express the conjectural character of human knowledge, and the second refers to its daring, to the need to anticipate boldly what we do not know.

It is not in the nature or character of man to possess true knowledge, though it is in the divine nature. . . . He who does not expect the unexpected will not detect it: for him it will remain undetectable, and unapproachable.

My last quotation is a very famous one from Democritus (DK B117):

But in fact, nothing do we know from having seen it; for the truth is hidden in the deep.

This is how the critical attitude of the Presocratics foreshadowed, and prepared for, the ethical rationalism of Socrates: his belief that the search for truth through critical discussion was a way of life – the best he knew.

Notes

1 I am glad to be able to report that Mr G. S. Kirk has indeed replied to my address; see below, notes 4 and 5, and the Appendix to this paper, *C. & R.*, pp. 153–65.
2 Aristotle himself understood Anaximander in this way; for he caricatures Anaximander's 'ingenious but untrue' theory by comparing the situation of its Earth to that of a man who, being equally hungry and thirsty yet equidistant from food and drink, is unable to move (*De Caelo* 295b32. The idea has become known by the name of 'Buridan's ass'). Clearly Aristotle conceives this man as being held in equilibrium by immaterial and invisible attractive forces similar to Newtonian forces; and it is interesting that this 'animistic' or 'occult'

character of his forces was deeply (though mistakenly) felt by Newton himself, and by his opponents, such as Berkeley, to be a blot on his theory (see Addendum 2, below).

3 I do not suggest that the smothering is due to blocking breathing-in holes: according to the phlogiston theory, for example, fire is smothered by obstructing breathing-out holes. But I do not wish to ascribe to Anaximander either a phlogiston theory of combustion, or an anticipation of Lavoisier.

4 In my address, as it was originally published, I continued here 'and indeed for all other changes within the cosmic edifice', relying on Zeller, who wrote (appealing to the testimony of Aristotle's *Meteor.* 353b6): 'Anaximander, it seems, explained the motion of the heavenly bodies by the currents of the air which are responsible for the turning of the stellar spheres' (E. Zeller, *Die Philosophie der Griechen*, 5th edn, vol. I, Leipzig, 1892, p. 223; see also p. 220, note 2; T. Heath, *Aristarchus of Samos*, Oxford, 1913, p. 33; and H. D. P. Lee's edition of the *Meteorologica*, London, 1952, p. 125). But I should perhaps not have interpreted Zeller's 'currents of air' as 'winds', especially as Zeller should have said 'vapours' (they are evaporations resulting from a process of drying up). I have twice inserted 'vapours and' before 'winds', and 'almost' before 'all' in the second paragraph of Section IX; and I have replaced, in the third paragraph of Section IX, 'winds' by 'vapours'. I have made these changes in the hope of meeting Mr G. S. Kirk's criticism on p. 332 of his article (discussed in the appendix to this paper, *C. & R.*, pp. 153ff.).

5 This should establish that it makes sense, at any rate. I hope it is clear from the text that I appeal to truth here in order (a) to make clear that my interpretation at least makes sense, and (b) to refute the arguments of Kirk and Raven (discussed later in this paragraph) that the theory is absurd. An answer to G. S. Kirk which was too long to be appended here (although it refers to the present passage and to the present paragraph) will be found in the aforementioned appendix to this paper.

ADDENDUM 1
A HISTORICAL NOTE ON VERISIMILITUDE
(1964)

Some further remarks on the early history of the confusion between verisimilitude and probability (in addition to those in the Introduction) will be given here.

1. In brief, my thesis is this. The earliest sayings at our disposal unambiguously use the idea of truthlikeness or verisimilitude. In time, 'like the truth' becomes ambiguous: it acquires additional meanings such as 'likely' or 'likely to be true' or 'probable' or 'possible', so that in some cases it is not clear which meaning is intended.

This ambiguity becomes significant in Plato because of his crucially important theory of imitation or *mimēsis*: just as the empirical world *imitates* the (true) world of ideas, so the accounts or theories or myths of the empirical world (of seeming) 'imitate' the truth, and thus are merely *'like the truth'*; or, translating the same expressions in their other meanings, these theories are not provable, or necessary, or true, but merely probable, or possible, or (more or less) seemingly true.

In this way Plato's theory of *mimēsis* furnishes something like a philosophical basis for the (then already current) mistaken and misleading equation of '*truthlike*' and '*probable*'.

With Aristotle an additional meaning becomes fairly prominent: 'probable' = 'frequently occurring'.

2. To give a few details, we have first a passage in the *Odyssey* 19.203: wily Odysseus tells Penelope (who does not recognize him) a story which is false, but which contains quite a few elements of truth; or as Homer puts it, 'he made the many lies similar to the truth' (*etumoisin homoia*). The phrase is repeated in the *Theogony*, 27f.: the Muses of Olympus, daughters of Zeus, say to Hesiod: 'we know how to speak many lies similar to the truth; but we also know, if we want to, how to speak the truth (*alētheia*)'.

The passage is interesting also because in it *etymos* and *alēthēs* occur as synonyms for 'true'.

A third passage in which the phrase *etumoisin homoia* occurs is Theognis 713, where cunning is extolled (as in the *Odyssey*) and the power of making lies sound like truth is described as divine (perhaps an allusion to the Muses in the *Theogony*): 'you would make lies similar to the truth with the good tongue of godlike Nestor'.

Now, one thing about these passages is that they are all related to what we call today 'literary criticism'. For the issue is the *telling of stories* which are (and which sound) *like the truth*.

A very similar passage is to be found in Xenophanes, himself a poet and perhaps the first literary critic. He introduces (DK B35) the term *eoikota* in place of *homoia*. Referring perhaps to his own theological theories, he says: 'these things, we may conjecture, are similar to the truth' (*eoikota tois etumoisi*; see also above, p. 25, and Plato's *Phaedrus* 272 d/e, 273b and d).

Here we have again a phrase which expresses unambiguously the idea of *verisimilitude* (*not* probability) in conjunction with a term (I have translated it by 'we . . . may conjecture') which is derived from the term *doxa* ('opinion'), which plays so important a role in and after Parmenides. (The same term occurs also in the last line of Xenophanes B34, quoted on p. 25 above, and is there used in contrast to *saphes*, that is, *certain truth*.)

The next step is important. Parmenides B8: 60 uses *eoikota* ('similar' or 'like') without explicitly mentioning 'truth'. I suggest that it means nevertheless, as in Xenophanes, 'like the truth', and I have translated the passage accordingly ('wholly like truth'; see Essay 9, Section 4). My main argument is the similarity between the passage and Xenophanes B35. Both passages speak of the conjectures (*doxa*) of mortal men, and both say something relatively favourable about them; and both clearly imply that a relatively 'good' conjecture is not really a true story. In spite of these similarities, the phrase of Parmenides has often been translated by 'probable and plausible' (see *C. & R.*, p. 236, note 19).

This passage is interesting also because an important passage in Plato's *Timaeus* (27e–30c) is closely related to it. In this passage, Plato starts (27e–28a) from the Parmenidean distinction between 'That which always Is and has no Becoming', on the one hand, and 'That which is always Becoming and never Is' on the other; and he says with Parmenides that the first of these can be known by reason, while the second 'is an object of opinion and unreasoning sensation' (compare also *C. & R.*, p. 165).

From this he proceeds to explain that the changing and becoming world (*ouranos* or *kosmos*: 28b) was made by the Creator as a copy or likeness (*eikon*) whose original or paradigm is the eternally unchanging Being that Is.

The transition from the paradigm to the copy (*eikon*) corresponds to the transition, in Parmenides, from the Way of Truth to the Way of Seeming. I have quoted the latter transition below (in Essay 9, Section IV), and it contains the term *eoikota*, which is related to Plato's *eikon*, i.e. the *likeness of Truth*, or *of What Is*; from which we may perhaps conclude that Plato read *eoikota* as 'like (the truth)' rather than 'probable' or 'likely'.

However, Plato also says that the copy, in being like the truth, cannot be known with certainty, but that we can only have *opinions* of it which are *uncertain* or '*likely*', or '*probable*'. For he says that accounts of the paradigm will be 'abiding, unshakable, irrefutable, and invincible' (29b–c) while 'accounts of that which is (merely) a copy's likeness of the paradigm will . . . possess (mere) likelihood; for as Being is to Becoming, so is Truth to (mere) Belief'. (See also *Phaedrus* 259e–260e, 266e–267a.)

This is the passage which introduces likelihood or probability (*eikota*) in the sense of imperfectly certain belief or partial belief, at the same time relating it to verisimilitude.

The passage concludes with yet another echo from the transition to the Way of Seeming: just as the goddess promised Parmenides an account so 'wholly like truth' that no better could be given (Essay 9, Section 4), so we read in the *Timaeus* (29d): 'we should be content if we can give an account which is inferior to none in likelihood (*eikota*), remembering that [we] . . . are human creatures and that it becomes us to accept a likely story (*eikota muthon*) . . .' (To this, 'Socrates' replies: 'Excellent, Timaeus!')

It is very interesting to note that this introduction of a systematic ambiguity of 'truthlikeness' and 'likelihood' (i.e. 'probability') does not prevent Plato from using the term *eikota* later, in the *Critias* (107d/e), in the sense of 'truthlike account'. For considering what precedes it, that passage should be read: 'in respect to matters celestial and divine, we should be satisfied with an account which has a small degree of truthlikeness, while we should check carefully the accuracy of accounts that pertain to mortal men'.

3. Apart from this systematic and no doubt conscious ambiguity in

Plato's use of *eikota* (and kindred terms), and apart from a wide range of differing usages in which its meaning is definite, there is also a wide range of usages in which its meaning is simply vague. Examples of different usages in Plato (and Aristotle) are: its use in opposition to 'demonstrable' and to 'necessary'; its use to express 'the next best to certainty'. It is also often used as a synonym for 'to be sure' or 'certainly', or 'this seems all right to me', especially by way of interjections in the dialogues. It is used in the sense of 'perhaps'; and it is even used in the sense of 'occurring frequently'; for example, in Aristotle's *Rhetoric* 1402b22: 'the probable (*eikos*) is that which occurs not invariably but only in most cases'.

4. I should like to end with another passage of literary criticism, one that occurs twice in Aristotle's *Poetics* (1456a22–5, and 1461b12–15) and which on its first occurrence he attributes to the poet Agathon. 'It is likely that the unlikely should happen.' Or less elegantly, but also less vaguely: '*It is like the truth that improbable things should happen.*'

ADDENDUM 2
SOME FURTHER HINTS ON VERISIMILITUDE
(1968)

1. Since my interest in the distinction between verisimilitude on the one hand, and probability (in its many meanings) on the other, seems to be open to misinterpretation, I will first stress that I am not at all interested in words and their meanings, but only in *problems*. Least of all am I interested in making the meanings of words 'precise', or in 'defining' or 'explicating' them.

There is an analogy between words or concepts and the question of their meaning on the one hand, and statements or theories and the question of their truth on the other, as I demonstrated in a 'Table of ideas', *C. & R.*, p. 19. *Yet I regard only statements or theories and the question of their truth or falsity as important.*

The mistaken ('essentialist') doctrine that we can 'define' (or 'explicate') a word or term or concept, that we can make its meaning 'definite' or 'precise', is in every way analogous to the mistaken doctrine that we can prove or establish or justify the truth of a theory; in fact, it is part of the latter ('justificationist') doctrine.

While words and their precise meanings are never important, the clearing up of confusions may be important for solving problems; problems concerning theories, of course. *We cannot define, but we must often distinguish.* For confusions, or merely the lack of distinctions, may prevent us from solving our problems.

2. In connection with verisimilitude, the main problem at stake is *the*

realist's problem of truth – the correspondence of a theory with the facts, or with reality.

The dangerous confusion or muddle which has to be cleared up is that between truth in the realist's sense – the 'objective' or 'absolute' truth – and truth in the subjectivist sense as that in which I (or we) 'believe'.

This distinction is of fundamental importance, especially for the theory of knowledge. The only important problem of knowledge concerns the problem of truth in the objective sense. My thesis is, simply, that the theory of subjective belief is utterly irrelevant to the philosophical theory of knowledge. Indeed, it is destructive of the latter if the two are mixed up (as they still are, in accordance with tradition).

3. Now it is decisively important that the need to distinguish sharply between objective truth and subjective belief remains as urgent as ever if we bring *approximation to truth* (or truthlikeness or verisimilitude) into the picture: verisimilitude as an objective idea must be sharply distinguished from all such subjective ideas as degrees of belief, or conviction, or persuasion; or of apparent or seeming truth, or plausibility, or of probability in any one of its subjective meanings. (Incidentally, it so happens that even if we take probability in some of its objective meanings, such as propensity, or perhaps frequency, it should still be distinguished from verisimilitude; and the degree of objective verisimilitude should be also sharply distinguished from the degree of corroboration, even though this is an objective notion; for the degree of verisimilitude of a theory, like the idea of truth itself, is timeless, even though it differs from the idea of truth in being a relative concept; while the degree of corroboration of a theory is essentially time-dependent – as pointed out in Section 84 of my *L. Sc. D.* – and thus essentially a historical concept.)

The confusion between verisimilitude and subjective notions like degrees of belief, or of plausibility, or of the appearance of truth, or of subjective probability, is traditional.

The history of this tradition ought to be written. It will turn out to be more or less identical with the history of the theory of knowledge.

In the preceding addendum I sketched, very superficially, this history so far as it was connected with the early philosophical use of the words 'the truth' (words connected with the Greek root *eikō*, such as *eikōn*, a likeness, a picture, *eoika*, to be like, to seem like, etc.). That is to say, with words which have at least at times (at any rate in Xenophanes or in Parmenides) been used in connection with a *realist* or *objectivist* idea of truth (whether as 'approximation to truth', as in Xenophanes, B35, or in the sense of a deceptive likeness to truth as in Parmenides, B8: 60).

4. In the present addendum I will just add a few brief remarks on the use of certain words which had from the start a *subjective* meaning. I will refer to two main Greek roots. One is *dokeō* (*dokē*, etc.), to think, to expect, to believe, to have in mind, to hold an opinion, with *doxa*, opinion.

(Related are also *dekomai*, to accept, to expect, with *dokimos*, accepted, approved, and *dokeuō*, to expect, to watch closely, to lie in wait.) The second is *peithō*, to persuade (also the power, or the goddess, Persuasion), with the meaning to win over, to make things appear plausible or probable – *subjectively* probable, of course; and with the forms *pithanoō*, to make probable; *pithanos*, persuasive, plausible, probable, even specious; *pistis*, faith, belief (with *kata pistin*, according to belief, according to probability); *pistos*, faithful, believed, deserving belief, probable; *pisteuō*, to trust, to believe; *pistoō*, to make trustworthy, to confirm, to make probable, etc.

There is never a doubt about the fundamentally subjective meaning of these words. They play an important role in philosophy from the earliest times. *Dokos*, for example, occurs in Xenophanes, DK B34, in the beautiful fragment quoted on p. 25 above, where I translated the term *dokos* by 'guess' ('guesses'), since it clearly means *'mere* opinion' or *'mere* conjecture'. (Cp. Xenophanes B35; and B14, where *dokeousi* means 'believe wrongly' or 'imagine wrongly'.) One might say that this disparaging usage of *dokein* is the birth of scepticism. It may be perhaps contrasted with the more neutral usage in Heraclitus B5 ('one would think that') or B27: 'When men die, there waits for them what they do not expect or *imagine (dokou-sin)*.' But Heraclitus seems to use the term also in the sense of 'mere opinion', as in B17, or in B28: '[For] it is mere opinion what even the most trustworthy [of men] defend [or preserve, or cling to] as knowledge.'

In Parmenides, *doxa*, opinion, is used in direct opposition to truth (*alētheia*); and it is, more than once (B1: 30; B8: 51), associated with a disparaging reference to 'the mortals'. (Cp. Xenophanes B14, and Heraclitus B27).

At any rate, *dokei moi* means 'it seems to me', 'it appears to me', and thus comes very near to 'it seems to me plausible, or acceptable' (*dokimōs einai*, 'acceptable as real'; cp. Parmenides B1: 32; Essay 9, Section 4).

5. The term 'probable' itself (*probabilis*) seems to have been invented by Cicero as a translation of the Stoic and Sceptic terms *pithanos*, *pithanē*, *pistin*, etc. (*kata pistin kai apistian* – 'as to probability and improbability', Sextus, *Outline of Pyrrhonism* i.10, and i.232). Two hundred and fifty years after Cicero, Sextus, *Against the Logicians* i.174, distinguishes three 'Academic' senses of the term 'probability' (*to pithanon*, 'the probable'): (1) 'What appears true and is in fact true'; (2) 'What appears true and is in fact false', (3) 'What is both true and false'.

Under (3), appearance is not specially mentioned: it seems that approximation to truth or verisimilitude in our sense is intended. Elsewhere, appearance is sharply distinguished from objective truth; yet appearance is all we can attain. 'Probable' is, in Sextus' use, that which induces belief. Incidentally, Sextus says (*Pyrrhonism* i.231), with a reference to Carneades and Cleitomachus, that 'the men who . . . use *probability as the guide of life'* are dogmatists: by contrast, 'we [the new Sceptics] live in an undogmatic way by following laws, customs, and our natural affections'. At times, Sextus uses 'probability' (or 'apparent probabilities', which seems almost a pleonasm; cp. *Pyrrhonism* ii.229) in the sense of 'specious'. Cicero's usage is different.

6. 'Such', says Cicero, 'are those things which I felt I should call probable (*probabilia*) or similar to the truth (*veri similia*). I do not mind if you prefer another name' (*Academica*, fragm. 11).

Elsewhere he writes of the Sceptics: 'For them something is probable (*probabile*) or resembling the truth (*veri simile*), and this [characteristic] provides them with a rule in the conduct of life, and in philosophical investigations' (*Academica* ii.32; in 33 Cicero refers to Carneades, as does Sextus in the same context; cp. *Academica* ii.104: 'guided by probability'). In *De Natura Deorum*, probabilities enter *because* falsity may be deceptively similar to truth; yet in *Tusc.* i.17, and ii.5, the two terms are synonyms.

7. There is thus no doubt that the terms 'probability' and 'verisimilitude' were introduced by Cicero as synonyms, and in a subjectivist sense. There is also no doubt that Sextus, who uses a subjectivist sense of 'probable', thought of truth and falsity in an objectivist sense, and did clearly distinguish between the subjective appearance of truth – seeming truth – and something like partial truth or approximation to truth.

My proposal is to use, *pace* Cicero, his originally subjectivist term 'verisimilitude' in the objectivist sense of 'like the truth'.

8. As to the terms 'probable', and 'probability', the situation has changed radically since the invention of the *calculus of probability*.

It now seems essential to realize that *there are many interpretations of the calculus of probability* (as I stressed in 1934 in Section 48 of my *L.d.F.*), and among them *subjective and objective interpretations* (later called by Carnap 'probability$_1$' and 'probability$_2$').

Some of the objective interpretations, especially the *propensity interpretation*, have been briefly mentioned in *C. & R.*, pp. 59 and 119, in my *L.Sc.D*, and further developed in my *Postscript to The Logic of Scientific Discovery*, 3 vols, Totowa, NJ, 1982–3.

ESSAY 2

THE UNKNOWN XENOPHANES

An attempt to establish his greatness

> Xenophanes . . . has become a figure in the history of Greek
> philosophy by mistake.
>
> (Harold F. Cherniss)

Xenophanes was a poet and rhapsode, and he was a historian, perhaps the
real father of history. As a highly creative thinker, unusually critical, and
unique in his self-criticism, he became the founder of the Greek Enlightenment. He developed Anaximander's cosmology in defending it against
Anaximenes. His very original rationalist theology was closely connected
with the cosmology that, late in life, he may have arrived at under the
influence of the astronomical discoveries of Parmenides. He was a literary
critic, perhaps the first, and a moralist. He was the founder of what today
are called geology and meteorology. He was an acute critic, again the first,
of society and of social institutions. And of decisive importance to Western
science and philosophy, he was the founder of epistemology, the theory of
knowledge. [Yet most, if not all, of these great contributions to our
civilization have been either attributed to somebody else, ignored, partly
forgotten, or simply misunderstood. In this essay I propose a more just and
historically plausible picture of Xenophanes and his achievements than I
think has been drawn before.]

1   Founder of the Greek Enlightenment

The crisp lines that I have chosen as a motto[1] stem from the pen of Harold
F. Cherniss, an outstanding[2] historian of Greek philosophy (but one, I am
afraid, who may never 'become a figure in the history of . . . philosophy'
even 'by mistake'). The lines I have quoted conform to a pattern, to a
tradition that allows anyone to abuse Xenophanes with impunity.

   The roots of this pattern may be discerned in a masterly sneer, due to
the great Heraclitus, a younger contemporary of Xenophanes (DK B40):

[*Section 1 of this essay was completed by Popper himself. The other sections and the preamble have been
compiled from the Author's* Nachlass *according to a plan described in the editorial note following the
addenda to this essay. Ed.*]

33

> To know everything does not help to know anything. For it helped
> neither Hesiod to know, nor Pythagoras, neither Xenophanes nor
> Hecataeus.

Although this was no doubt intended as a sneer, unintentionally it paid
homage to Xenophanes by making him a member of an exalted company.
Moreover, Heraclitus credits him here with knowing much – rather too
much, yet not the right thing. The right thing was, presumably, to know
that day and night (and so all the opposites) were *one*;[3] because day cannot
exist without night, and *vice versa*.

But Heraclitus' sneer may tell us even more: it seems to me that it
might be used as an argument – admittedly a weak one – that Heraclitus
did not look upon Pythagoras as a mere soothsayer, as a shaman, since he
put him together with Xenophanes. For of all the philosophers of the
period who believed in the existence of gods, Xenophanes was, according
to Cicero, 'the only one who strongly repudiated the practice of divining
the future'.[4] This, no doubt, makes Xenophanes also a strong opponent of
shamanism.

I think it was Xenophanes' leadership of the early Enlightenment which
explains the pattern mentioned before: the old tradition of dismissing him.
We know all too well the platitude that you cannot be a real philosopher
unless you despise the Enlightenment for its total lack of depth in contrast
to the Essence of all real Philosophy. For if you are a philosopher, you
must be deep. You must try to attain that lofty depth (*'die erhabene Tiefe'*)
that Hegel credits to himself. (This, of course, is an unmixed metaphor
that works out to flatness, as Schopenhauer was quick to see. But what
Hegel really meant was that he was elevated beyond everybody else
because of the bottomless depth of his thought.) It is this 'knowledge of
themselves' that makes some philosophers more fashionable than others.
And since followers of the Enlightenment cannot attain this knowledge,
they can get into the history of philosophy only 'by mistake'.

I think that Xenophanes came most close to anticipating the ideas of
the European Enlightenment. But these ideas were never respected among
intellectuals, who practised the misuse of ideas for the sake of enlarging
their own power – especially priestly power or (later) political power.[5]
This misuse of ideas was always connected with the attempt to impress
people by the depth of one's ideas – by their transcendentally (that is,
non-empirically) inspired – even divine – source, by their prophetic
significance.

Some of this, but very little, we can find even among the great Presocratics. When Heraclitus was called 'the obscure', it was presumably
because his brilliant formulations had a prophetic flavour. But in fact,
there was not much of it in them, and he may well be said to have himself
belonged to the Enlightenment (compare, for example, DK B43, 44, 55,

but also B47–54), although it was, no doubt, his 'obscurity' that saved him from the central accusation: he is never accused of superficiality, which is the standard accusation against Xenophanes.

It is an accusation greatly feared by the many who are superficial; and it is therefore widely used by them because they hope to distance themselves from their own superficiality – by directing the accusation towards others – and, of course, also by the use of an ununderstandable and impressive language. 'I did not understand a word; but *I know: this is philosophy*' was the deep conviction of a highly gifted young physicist after he had heard Heidegger speak. (I admit: if this is philosophy, then Xenophanes entered the history of philosophy by mistake.)

Note that I do not suggest that all those who belittle Xenophanes are enemies of the Enlightenment. All the great founders of the Milesian School belonged in their different ways to a phase of the Enlightenment, including Heraclitus. And the misunderstanding of Xenophanes' cosmology discussed below in Section 3, and the attacks on him provoked by these misunderstandings, have hardly anything to do with anti-Enlightenment tendencies; they were simply due to the fact that he seemed to his critics to be completely muddleheaded. But from Galen's defence of Xenophanes it emerges that some of these critics did indeed belong to the anti-Xenophanes and anti-Enlightenment tradition.

I suggest that it was one of Xenophanes' greatest achievements that he anticipated and strongly represented all the main ideas of the European Enlightenment. Among these were the ideas of fighting for truth and against obscurity; of talking and writing lucidly and modestly; of practising irony and especially self-irony; of avoiding the pose of a deep thinker; of looking critically at society; and of looking upon the world with wonder, and with an infectious curiosity.

2 Xenophanes' early years and his encounter with the Milesian School

Xenophanes of Colophon in Asia Minor, about three or four days' brisk walking north of Miletus, was born in 570 BC. Colophon was a wealthy Ionian city with a long literary tradition, once 'the capital of Ionia with respect to the poetry of the earliest period'.[6] It was an inland city. Not very far to the north was the great harbour of Phocaea, and to the south, less distant than Miletus, was the great city of Ephesus. Phocaea and Miletus both played an important part in the life of Xenophanes.

In his youth Xenophanes became a pupil of Anaximander, born in 610 BC at Miletus, the greatest of the Milesian natural philosophers. Anaximander's teaching amounted to a cosmogony and a cosmology: he attempted to describe how the world originated and, in so doing, what its present structure was. His principle of explanation was clear and radical: replace the gods, the mythology of Hesiod, by something we can come to understand by studying nature. Anaximander had himself been a pupil of Thales, the founder of the Ionian School, and was one of his relatives. In sharp contrast to all other known schools, which typically would have as one of their main preoccupations the upholding of the founder's teaching unchanged,[7] it was part of the Ionian School tradition to be critical, and to try to improve not only the founder's teaching, but also that of the later members. Perhaps for this reason, each generation produced at least one important change, and the name of the innovator is openly transmitted. This must have been due to the fact that not only were the doctrines, the theories, and the innovations traditionally transmitted, but so was a kind of second-order methodological advice: 'Try to improve upon the theories! Try to make them better, for they are not perfect!' I suggest that this self-critical methodology must have come from the founder, Thales, and that it was transmitted by Anaximander to his followers, especially to Anaximenes and Xenophanes.

One of the central problems Anaximander discussed with his students was the Earth and its stability. Thales had taught that it was floating on water (thus explaining earthquakes),[8] *Water* being the 'principle' and origin of all things, incapable of further explanation and not requiring any explanation itself. Anaximander changed all this. His Earth (of drumlike shape, a short circular column; DK 12A10, 11) was not supported by anything: it was freely suspended in the centre of things and kept there by a symmetrical attraction exerted by all things, in empty or almost empty, infinite space – somewhat like our ether or 'empty' space – which he called the *Apeiron* (*apeiron* = 'infinite').[9] And he replaced *Water* as the principle and origin of all things by this *Apeiron* (= the Unbounded), an infinite fine substance that fills the entire infinite space (with which it is, indeed, identical), that *Apeiron* which is eternal and out of which all other substances emerge.[10] In contradistinction to water, the *apeiron* is an invented hypothetical substance, and the term '*Apeiron*' as used by Anaximander is the first *technical term* of which we have any knowledge. Although it does not, as does Thales' *Water*, *support* the Earth from below, it does undoubtedly help a little to keep the Earth *suspended* and balanced.

This theory of a freely suspended Earth, held in place by forces acting at a distance and apparently emanating from all heavenly bodies, is one of the boldest and most ingenious theories in the history of science. The boldness of this rather abstract theory was too revolutionary for Anaximander's more pedestrian pupil Anaximenes: he wanted to replace the *Apeiron* by something more familiar, namely *Air* – including mist and heavy clouds. The emergence of clouds from air seems to demonstrate the possible emergence of even more solid matter floating in air, such as the Sun, the Moon, and the stars – and, indeed, airborne animals such as insects and birds.

Anaximenes explained the stability of the Earth by the assumption that it is supported by air, as the solid lid of a kettle is supported by steam.

I suggest that it was in this debate between Anaximander and Anaximenes over the two competing principles, *Apeiron* and *Air*, that the young Xenophanes intervened on the side of Anaximander; an intervention that led to a crucial misinterpretation (due to Empedocles and, through him, to Aristotle, as described below in Section 3). As a consequence of this misinterpretation, we are left with two sharply conflicting and indeed contradictory sets of traditional reports that constitute our historical evidence about Xenophanes' theory of the Earth, and about his cosmology.

Fortunately, we have Xenophanes' own brisk wording of his intervention in the *Apeiron–Air* debate (DK 21B28):

γαίης μὲν τόδε πεῖρας ἄνω παρὰ ποσσὶν ὁρᾶται
ἠέρι προσπλάζον, τὸ κάτω δ' ἐς ἄπειρον ἱκνεῖται.

At our feet we can see how the Earth with her uppermost limit
Borders on air; with her lowest, she reaches down to *Apeiron*.

It seems to me almost obvious that with these two verses, written by a member of the Milesian School, Xenophanes was defending Anaximander's theory against Anaximenes, that is, against the theory that the Earth floats on *Air*. No, say these two verses: the air is, as we can see, above the upper side (or the upper surface) of the Earth; but below the lower side there is just the *Apeiron* – and thus *no* supporting body (neither *Water* nor *Air*).

Indeed (Xenophanes may have continued), the theory that the Earth is stable because it is supported by some body or bodies such as Thales' *Water* or Anaximenes' *Air* is absurd. For did not Anaximander indicate that any such theory would merely raise the question 'and what supports the water? Or, what supports the air?' We should arrive at an infinite regress. Had Anaximander (Xenophanes seems to ask) invented in vain his beautiful theory of the Earth being in a state of equilibrium, owing to its being equidistant from everything?

We may [thus] assume that B 28 can be supported by a drawing like the following:

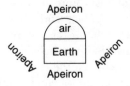

Here the Earth is Anaximander's; and air does not support it (as it would a flat leaf) as reported of Anaximenes' theories.[11] Writing on Xenophanes'

fragment B 28, Charles H. Kahn in his splendid book on Anaximander says: 'The conception of *apeiron* . . . surrounding the world is a permanent feature of Ionian cosmology.'[12] He also stresses that we have to translate as 'reaching . . . below [or down] to *apeiron*'. Kahn continues: 'Presumably [Xenophanes] had the theory of Anaximander in mind, but exactly what he meant is as obscure to us as it was to Simplicius (Xenoph. A47)'. Yet Xenophanes' fragment B28 is [as I have suggested above] an attempt to support Anaximander's theory of the postition of the Earth against Anaximenes.

I have tried to describe the (conjectured) problem situation in which Xenophanes intervened, and to extract the implied content of the brisk two verses of his intervention, as I have translated them. (If I am right, then B28 supports independently the reports that assert that Xenophanes was a pupil of Anaximander.) However, I must admit that, so far as I know and remember the literature on Presocratic philosophy, I am alone in my interpretation – although I know of three authors who, like myself, connect the two lines of Xenophanes (DK B28) with the Milesian problem of the stability and support of the Earth. They are C. H. Kahn, F. M. Cornford and J. Mansfeld.

I now turn to discuss and defend my translation and interpretation. With the exception of the two excellent scholars, Charles H. Kahn and Felix M. Cleve,[13] all translations known to me have ended Xenophanes' second line somewhat as follows:

on the lower side, it [= the Earth] reaches down to infinity.

This translation – universally accepted, so far as I know, with only the exception of Kahn and Cleve – says that *the Earth goes down infinitely, or indefinitely*, or down into the inmeasurable,[14] in contrast to Cleve's and my interpretation, which attributes to the Earth a *lower side* or *end*. This, in its turn, borders on the 'infinite'; which Kahn and I (but not Cleve) propose to identify with Anaximander's 'principle' – his *Apeiron*.

Cleve mentions in his chapter on Xenophanes neither Anaximander nor Anaximenes. Both are mentioned by Cornford, in his *Principium Sapientiae*,[15] and by Mansfeld, in his commentaries on the two lines of Xenophanes and on the term *'apeiron'*; and they associate them with the discussions of the Milesian School. Yet Mansfeld translates them twice in the usual way (with 'ins Unermessliche' or, op. cit., p. 208, 'hin ins Unbegrenzte'); and he comments on the term *'apeiron'* that 'in this case . . . this Milesian concept is here in an original manner reinterpreted: not the . . . Air of Anaximenes is carrying the Earth, but the Earth itself is unlimited, in one direction' (that is, downward). So my interpretation[16] is, in part, supported by Kahn and Cleve and, in another part, by Cornford and Mansfeld, but also contradicted by Mansfeld. In combination, the four seem to me to support strongly the interpretation.

My translation is, from a linguistic point of view, almost the same as Kahn's and Cleve's. Where we differ from others is clearly over the translation of a few words of the second line: '*to katō d'es apeiron ikneitai*', which Kahn, Cleve and I would read, word for word, 'the lower [limit or end] to the *Apeiron* reaches'. The decisive point is that we construe this phrase as a parallel to 'the upper(most)[17] limit . . . borders on Air'. Thus we get:

> The upper limit of the Earth borders on *Air*,
> The lower limit of the Earth reaches down to the Unlimited, [i.e. the *Apeiron*].

To Kahn, Cleve and me this seems to be the most natural rendering of the Greek. And it is greatly strengthened by what I take to have been the problem situation of this important cosmological discussion in Miletus at the time. Most translators assume silently (with DK) that 'the lower' refers to 'limit', as the Greek text suggests. In this way, however, they do not only overlook the glaring contradiction that 'the lower limit' simply *does not exist* if the Earth goes down to the unlimited, but they also take *es Apeiron* to mean 'to infinity' or 'infinitely', whereas '*Apeiron*' is really the name of Anaximander's principle (*archē*). Thus Xenophanes' argument, typically compressed into a few brilliant and lucid verses, was misunderstood. Many infinities were wrongly attributed to Xenophanes in antiquity forming the Xenophanes legend which was encouraged by the passage from Aristotle, discussed in the next section. Only after their rejection can one begin to see that Xenophanes was a great and original philosopher of science. He gives a new version of the theory of the Sun and the stars: he proposes to see them as burning masses of gas. Such things can be seen on Earth — igniting gases over swamps, or emerging from volcanoes.[18] It seems that Xenophanes used the term *nephos* for formulating his excellent conjecture that *the Sun and the stars are {balls of} burning gas*. This seems to me an improvement on Anaximander's theory. Moreover, it is an almost necessary intermediate step between Anaximander's and Heraclitus' theories and the famous theory of Anaxagoras that the Sun is a glowing stone. (It is reported in DK A32.)

Anaximander died in 546BC (DK 12 A1), and we may assume that Xenophanes left Miletus at about this time, going north. Returning to Colophon, he did not much like any longer the social and intellectual atmosphere he found there (DK 21B3).

The next year, 545, was a year of catastrophe for the Ionian Greeks. A huge Persian army, commanded by Harpagus, a Median general, invaded Ionia and destroyed its freedom. Xenophanes left Colophon and emigrated.

We have no detailed reports about the circumstances of his emigration. But Theodor Gomperz's suggestion that Xenophanes joined the citizens of Phocaea and shared their wildly adventurous emigration does not seem to me too far-fetched. (See Section 7 below.)

3   The misunderstood cosmology of Xenophanes

I now come to what may be called the central misunderstanding of Xenophanes as a cosmologist; a misunderstanding that is responsible for attributing to him silly and even contradictory doctrines. The story is, indeed, very exciting.[19]

This misunderstanding is due to the authority of Aristotle, who wrote in *De Caelo* (294a21) that Xenophanes is one of those who hold that the Earth extends downward infinitely; and that these people adhere to this view 'in order to save themselves the trouble of looking for a reason' (that is, a reason for the apparent stability of the Earth). That Aristotle did not know the two crucial verses of Xenophanes (that is, DK B28) is obvious; for he cites instead, lacking better evidence, three contemptuous verses by Empedocles, who derides those who hold that 'the depth of the Earth and the ample ether are infinite'. From the fact that Aristotle cites the lines of Empedocles in order to endorse them as a criticism of Xenophanes, we must conclude (or so it seems) that, somewhere in the same context, Empedocles named Xenophanes as one of the culprits responsible for this silly theory of the infinite 'roots' of the Earth.

This passage of Aristotle (*De Caelo* 294a21 = DK 31B39), in which, somewhat rashly, he quotes, accepts, and endorses Empedocles' derisive and arrogant attack on Xenophanes, is the sole source of the almost universal misinterpretation of Xenophanes' B28, and indeed of a whole lot of other misinterpretations which are all the consequences of this first and basic misinterpretation. But we must not accept Aristotle's authority here. Indeed, Aristotle himself said things about Xenophanes which sharply contradict certain consequences of this Aristotelian misinterpretation.

There are, if we over-simplify things a little, *two sets of reports about Xenophanes' cosmology*.[20] The *first set* consists of reports that attribute implicitly to Xenophanes the doctrine that his one god and the universe are both finite and spherical, and a unity. Clearly, these reports, which began with Plato and Aristotle, make Xenophanes a forerunner of Parmenides, and tend to assimilate him to the latter. I think that certain linguistic reasons speak for a (loose) connection between the two, but the attempt to assimilate them seems to me suspicious. However, we just don't know. The *second set* of reports attributes to Xenophanes the teaching that the Earth (and therefore also the universe) is infinite in depth (and also, perhaps, even infinite in width); a view that makes the setting of the Sun impossible, thus leading on to a perverse attribution to Xenophanes:

to the doctrine that the Sun moves in an infinite straight line over the infinite Earth and does not set but disappears because it becomes infinitely distant. (Tell this to a man who has sailed the oceans, as Xenophanes did more than once!) So the Sun has to be daily renewed or, rather, recreated as a new body in the East. [For further comments on this, see Popper Fragment 11, below. Ed.]

This is only one of the impossible theories attributed to Xenophanes. Just as important, perhaps, is the attribution to him of a 'principle' like those of Thales (*Water*), Anaximenes (*Air*) and Heraclitus (*Fire*),[21] and that his 'principle' – the fourth – was *Earth*. So, like the other 'principles', the *Earth* was infinite and so needed no further support. And in some of the reports belonging to the *second set*, several doctrines of the *first set* are included.

Now, the teaching attributed to Xenophanes by the *second set* of reports is nowhere supported in the fragments B27 and 29 written by Xenophanes himself – provided that B28 is translated as Kahn, Cleve and I (and the text) suggest. So the interpretation of B28 becomes indeed crucial: if this fragment is translated as almost everybody else translates it, then the stories in the *second set* of reports become at least in part plausible. If it is translated as Kahn, Cleve and I translate it, these stories not only can be rejected, but their mistakes can be explained as ultimately due to a misinterpretation encouraged by Aristotle's authority.

But Plato's and Aristotle's own reports belong mainly to the *first set* (with the exception of that fatal passage in *De Caelo*). Both see in Xenophanes a precursor of Parmenides of Elea, whose teachings about *The One* – that is, a spherical indivisible universe – they emphasize. Aristotle complains in his *Metaphysics* (986b21 = DK A30) of Xenophanes that what he said was not very clear, illustrating his complaint by the story that Xenophanes said (referring to the universe) that *The One* was God ('*to hen einei . . . ton theon*'). This, indeed, is a vague saying, and it does not give us much information about Xenophanes, beyond perhaps illustrating that Aristotle, like Plato, took him to be a forerunner of Parmenides. But in other and later reports belonging to the *first set*, Xenophanes' antici-pation of Parmenides is elaborated. Xenophanes' one God – who 'does neither in body nor in mind resemble the mortals' (DK B23) – is said to have a body of spherical shape: indeed, not resembling the human shape! And elsewhere this body is identified with the physical universe, an identification that is a little difficult to accept (in view of B25: 'Effortless over the All he reigns by mere thought and intention'). Of course, this would make the physical universe of Xenophanes also finite, like that of Parmenides, since only a finite body can have a (spherical) shape.

All this indicates that there is a tradition that clashes with the infinitist interpretation of our two verses, B28, and with the *second set* of reports.

If, therefore, Kahn's and Cleve's and my finitist interpretation of B28 is accepted, the *first set* of reports *may* be accepted, but the *second set must* be rejected as based on a misinterpretation. But whether or not the *first set* should be accepted is a more difficult question; for it could be, perhaps, just the result of Plato's ascription to Xenophanes (in the *Sophist* 242d5) of founding the Eleatic School, whose outstanding member was Parmenides.

This is a problem on which it is difficult to have an opinion. The elaborate arguments of my late friend W. K. C. Guthrie, in volume I of his great *History of Greek Philosophy*, seem the best I know, and they seem strengthened by my translation and interpretation of B28 (which Guthrie translated with the majority). However, we should take seriously a possibility first mentioned by the ingenious Karl Reinhardt (whom I greatly admire, but with whom I very frequently disagree – especially with what he says about Xenophanes in his book *Parmenides*). Reinhardt says that Xenophanes (whom he dislikes) may have been, late in life, influenced by the younger Parmenides, who is said to have been, at some stage, a disciple of Xenophanes. This – or a mutual influence between the two – is certainly a serious possibility. It would make it probable that Xenophanes was led to drop Anaximander's drum model of the Earth in favour of Parmenides' spherical Earth – while adhering, perhaps, to B28, or else correcting it to an Earth surrounded, first, by an envelope of Air, which in turn was surrounded by the *Apeiron*. And it would make Plato's and Aristotle's remarks and all the reports of the *first set* much easier to understand.

I cannot close without mentioning that two very great ancient scholars were dissatisfied with the then current reports about Xenophanes. Simplicius in his commentary on *De Caelo* (522.7 = DK A47) complained that he felt doubtful whether Aristotle was correct in his ascription to Xenophanes of an infinitely deep Earth; and whether we might not perhaps even misunderstand Aristotle. He says that he could not find Xenophanes' own words – our B28? – and could therefore not feel sure. At another place, in his commentary on Aristotle's *Physics* (22. 22 = DK A31), Simplicius seems to be confused about Xenophanes, obviously owing to the conflicting reports of the *first* and the *second* set.

The other great scholar of antiquity I have in mind is Galen. He is most explicit. He writes (DK A36): 'In a malicious and slanderous way some commentators on Xenophanes have lied about him.' He mentions Sabinus (who apparently reported that Xenophanes' 'principle' was *Earth*), and continues: 'For nowhere can Xenophanes be found to have said anything like that.' This remark makes it probable that Galen still had access to Xenophanes' lost writings *On Nature*, and that they did not contain any of the preposterous remarks attributed to him by what I have here called the *second set* of reports.

4 Xenophanes as a philosophical theologian and the influence of Parmenides

The one short fragment (B1) we possess from Anaximander tells us that the world process is not merely a natural process but a moral process; and although few may agree with it today, everyone will feel that this is a poetico-philosophical idea that deserves to be called a deep thought – especially as it originates from a highly creative natural scientist. Heraclitus also achieves a poetic effect. Although his aphorisms, many of which are strikingly impressive, do not belong to poetry in the contemporary sense of metrical composition, they might be said to belong to the form of poetry now sometimes called 'free verse'. Parmenides, of course, also writes poetry, and he too writes, like Anaximander and Heraclitus, as a kind of prophet: he too has an all-important message, and he also wishes to impress us with it.

Xenophanes who, of these four, seems to have the greatest interest in religious problems, is the only who does not think of himself as a prophet. He argues with us rationally, as does Parmenides; but his message has no divine authority, as has Parmenides': he is very conscious of his fallibility. He is also a moralist, but he does not preach. All this gives his language a touch of ease, and of modesty.[22] Xenophanes' language is the least impressive of the four mentioned. He is not speaking to us as a man conscious of his superior wisdom. (This, I conjecture, is one main reason why German scholars – and perhaps also some Greek philosophers – are not impressed by him. A second, and very different, reason is to be found in the above-mentioned misunderstandings of his teachings in the Greek doxographic tradition.)

Xenophanes even carries *argument* into theology. As a rhapsode reciting the poems of Homer and Hesiod professionally, he turned, under the influence of the Milesians, into a severe critic of both of them: he criticized them from a moral and educational point of view. He objected to their stories, which made the gods steal, lie, and commit adultery. So he was moved to reconsider their theologies from a highly critical point of view. One of his main achievements was to discover and attack a way of thinking that today we call 'anthropomorphism': he discovered that the stories of Homer and of Hesiod must not be taken seriously, simply because they describe the gods as if they were men.[23] I quote Xenophanes' arguments in verse form (from my almost literal translation; B16, B15):

> Αἰθίοπές τε {θεοὺς σφετέρους} σιμοὺς μέλανάς τε
> Θρῆικές τε γλαυκοὺς καὶ πυρρούς {φασι πέλεσθαι}.
> ἀλλ' εἰ χεῖρας ἔχον βόες {ἵπποι τ'} ἠὲ λέοντες
> ἢ γράψαι χείρεσσι καὶ ἔργα τελεῖν ἅπερ ἄνδρες,
> ἵπποι μέν θ' ἵπποισι βόες δέ τε βουσὶν ὁμοίας

καί {κε} θεῶν ἰδέας ἔγραφον καὶ σώματ' ἐποίουν
τοιαῦθ' οἷόν περ καὐτοὶ δέμας εἶχον {ἕκαστοι}.

The Ethiops say that their gods are flat-nosed and black,
While the Thracians say that theirs have blue eyes and red hair.
Yet if cattle or horses or lions had hands and could draw
And could sculpture like men, then the horses would draw their gods
Like horses, and cattle like cattle, and each would then shape
Bodies of gods in the likeness, each kind, of its own.

What all this teaches us is that we must never relax our critical – a highly critical – search for truth, always trying to learn from those who hold a different view. But in order to avoid relativism we have to say more than this. What we should say is: 'I may be wrong and you may be right; and by talking things over rationally we may be able to correct some of our mistakes; and we may perhaps both of us get nearer to the truth.'

Thus Xenophanes arrived at his problem: how should we think of our gods, *after* taking account of this criticism of anthropomorphism? There are four fragments that contain part of his answer. The answer is monotheistic (even though Xenophanes, like Luther in his translation of the First Commandment, uses the plural 'gods' in the formulation of his monotheism; B23, B26, B25, B24):

εἷς θεός, ἔν τε θεοῖσι καὶ ἀνθρώποισι μέγιστος
οὔτι δέμας θνητοῖσιν ὁμοίιος οὐδὲ νόημα.
αἰεὶ δ' ἐν ταὐτῶι μίμνει κινούμενος οὐδέν
οὐδὲ μετέρχεσθαί μιν ἐπιπρέπει ἄλλοτε ἄλληι.
ἀλλ' ἀπάνευθε πόνοιο νόου φρενὶ πάντα κραδαίνει.
οὖλος ὁρᾶι, οὖλος δὲ νοεῖ, οὖλος δέ τ' ἀκούει.

One God alone among gods and alone among men is the greatest.
Neither in mind nor in body does he resemble the mortals.
Always in one place he remains, without ever moving.
Nor is it fitting for him to wander now hereto now thereto.
Effortless over the All he reigns by mere thought and intention.
All of him is sight; all is knowledge; and all is hearing.

These are the fragments that give an account of Xenophanes' speculative theology. (As to my translation 'he reigns' in DK B25, see Addendum 1 to this essay.) They report on the results of his analysis of the *logic of supreme power* that first led him to a rejection of anthropomorphism, then to the discovery of monotheism, and finally to the insight that God is, in body and mind, unlike man.

It is clear that this completely new theory was the solution of a difficult problem for Xenophanes. In fact, it came to him as a solution of the greatest of all problems, the problem of the universe. Nobody who knows anything about the psychology of knowledge can doubt that this new insight must have appeared like a revelation to Xenophanes.

Yet he stated clearly and honestly that his theory was no more than a conjecture. That was a self-critical victory without equal, a victory of his intellectual honesty and of his modesty. Xenophanes generalized this self-criticism in a manner that was completely characteristic of him: it was clear to him that what he had discovered about his own theory – that in spite of its intuitive power of persuasion it was nothing more than a conjecture – must be true of all human theories: everything is only conjecture. But it also seems to me to reveal that, psychologically, it was not easy for him to view his own theory as conjecture.

Later scholars of Greek philosophy such as Cicero (A34), Sextus Empiricus (A35), Simplicius (A31), and Aristotle, who in his *Metaphysics* (quoted above) adds that Xenophanes *identified his One God with the universe*, have ascribed to Xenophanes the doctrine that *the shape of his One God is spherical*. I consider both assertions mistaken, the latter probably due to an exaggeration of the Platonic-Aristotelian thesis of an Eleatic Unitary School. As mentioned in Section 3, it may be that Xenophanes encountered Parmenides late in life, as Karl Reinhardt suggests, but what he learnt from the much younger Parmenides is most probably different from what this group of scholars believe. I think that the most he *may* have learnt in his old age is that *the Earth is a sphere*. This would have appealed to him, and it could be related to an early astronomical result of Parmenides. And this may have led to Xenophanes' name being attached to the untenable view that the shape of God is spherical.

5 Xenophanes' theory of knowledge

I now turn to Xenophanes' epistemology. We have seen before that he was a highly critical thinker: straightforward yet subtle, lucid with well thought-out and highly polished arguments presented in briefest formulations of almost deceptive simplicity and robustness. I am thinking, of course, of his two-line rectification of Anaximenes; his theological criticism – his presentation of anthropomorphism in a manner that shows its absurdity without even a word of criticism (although he can be openly critical and hit hard, again with astonishingly few words).

Let us consider the two verses of DK 21B38:

εἰ μὴ χλωρὸν ἔφυσε θεὸς μέλι, πολλὸν ἔφασκον
γλύσσονα σῦκα πέλεσθαι.

If God never had chosen to make the light-yellow honey,
Many a man would think of figs as being much sweeter.

Admittedly, reading this, one has to add in one's mind 'sweeter than figs appear to him now, because the comparison with honey reduces the impact of the sweetness of figs'. Yet if you make this addition, you have been induced to be mentally active – one of the aims of any teacher who wants to enlighten his students. So these lines are perhaps only a little difficult; but the simplicity of the picture ensures that they are nevertheless very lucid, and cannot be misunderstood by anybody unless he is not prepared to make an effort – a very modest effort indeed.

Regarding the content of this parable, some people have said that Xenophanes was here preaching – or teaching – an epistemological relativism. This is a misunderstanding. It is, on the contrary, merely a psychological relativism: in trying to judge reality (objective reality) don't forget, he repeatedly reminds us, that your immediate reaction is often tainted by comparison: 100 drachmae are a lot when you expected 20, but they are disappointing when you expected 200. But objectively they are the same in each case.

So if you wish to obtain knowledge of the objective world, Xenophanes teaches, know thyself and mistrust your own impressions! Obviously an early version of *critical empiricism*, explained with easy examples.

Yet there is more in these verses: they probably represent the first step towards a distinction between primary and secondary qualities. Or rather, they contain a better distinction between what were much later called 'secondary qualities', on the one hand, and 'primary qualities' on the other – qualities due to a certain priming of the senses.

Xenophanes most probably arrived at his critical theory of knowledge in connection with his revelation-like solution to the problem of the universe, described in Section 3. He states his theory in four beautiful verses (I need six verses to translate them in verse form).[24] To me there is nothing in the whole literature of philosophy that is so critical, so self-critical, so correct, and so true as B34:

> καί τὸ μὲν οὖν σαφὲς οὔτις ἀνὴρ ἴδεν οὐδέ τις ἔσται
> εἰδὼς ἀμφὶ θεῶν τε καὶ ἄσσα λέγω περὶ πάντων·
> εἰ γὰρ καὶ τὰ μάλιστα τύχοι τετελεσμένον εἰπών,
> αὐτὸς ὅμως οὐκ οἶδε· δόκος δ' ἐπὶ πᾶσι τέτυκται.

> But as for certain truth, no man has known it,
> Nor will he know it; neither of the gods
> Nor yet of all the things of which I speak.
> And even if by chance he were to utter
> The perfect truth, he would himself not know it;
> For all is but a woven web of guesses.

In what follows I shall first defend this translation, and afterwards I shall give my interpretation of it.

(a) It would perhaps be slightly closer to the text to translate τὸ σαφές by 'certainty' rather than by 'certain truth'. But I find that 'certain truth' not only sounds a little better in English, it is also more explicit and therefore closer to Xenophanes' intention as an enlightened teacher.

I have also inserted the word 'truth' in line 5 of my translation. Here again I find it implied by the text (τετελεσμένον εἰπών = 'speaking the most perfect reality'). I may even call for support from Kirk, Raven, and Schofield, who likewise have 'truth' twice in their translation of the fragments (*The Presocratic Philosophers*, 2nd edn, Cambridge, 1983, p. 179). They translate B34 as follows:

No man knows, or ever will know, the truth about
the gods and about everything I speak of; for even if one
chanced to say the complete truth, yet oneself knows it
not; but seeming is wrought over all things.

I find their translation very good (although I prefer my own), and it seems to me that the intended meaning is the same as in my translation: 'for even if one chanced to say' may indeed be slightly closer to the text than my 'And even if by chance he were to utter', but the difference is negligible. On the other hand, 'but seeming is wrought over all things' seems to me less good English than, say, 'For all is guesswork' or 'guesses interwoven with everything', which with a slight degree of poetic licence led me to my version: 'For all is but a woven web of guesses'.

For τεύχω meaning 'weave', see, for example, the famous passage in the *Odyssey* 7.235 and 8.276–81.

In the same line I prefer to translate δόκος by 'conjectures' rather than by 'seeming' (which hardly exists as a noun); and 'guesses' I regard here as poetic for 'conjectures'.

This ends the detailed verbal defence of my translation.

(b) I now proceed to give my interpretation of the fragment, which is at the same time a defence of the significance of B34 against the onslaught due to Hermann Fränkel.[25] To my limited knowledge this onslaught is the most elaborate attempt to destroy the significance of these most important and indeed masterly four verses of Xenophanes.

The verses contain more than a theory of the conjectural character of human knowledge. They contain *a theory of objective knowledge*. For here Xenophanes teaches that, whilst something I say may be true, neither I nor anybody else will *know* that it is true. This means, however, that truth is objective: truth is *the correspondence with the facts* of what I say, whether *I know or do not know* that the correspondence holds. But this means that the

47

correspondence holds independently of my knowing it: truth is *objective*; the truth or falsity of what I have said depends only upon the facts.

In addition these lines contain another very important theory. They contain a clue to the difference between objective *truth* and subjective *certainty*. For Xenophanes says that, even when I utter the most perfect truth, I cannot know this with certainty: I can only conjecture it. Thus we may know the truth in a hypothetical sense of 'know', but we cannot know that we have reached it. There is no infallible criterion of truth. We can never, or hardly ever, be really sure that we are not mistaken: our reasons are never fully sufficient.

However, Xenophanes was not an epistemological pessimist. He was a searcher; and during the course of his long life he was able, by way of critical re-examination, to improve some of his own conjectures, especially his scientific theories. In B18 Xenophanes formulates what may be called his *licence to search*:

οὔτοι ἀπ' ἀρχῆς πάντα θεοὶ θνητοῖσ' ὑπέδειξαν,
ἀλλὰ χρόνωι ζητοῦντες ἐφευρίσκουσιν ἄμεινον.

The gods did not reveal, from the beginning,
All things to the mortals; but in the course of time,
Through seeking they may get to know things better.

Xenophanes also explains what he means by 'to know things better': he means the approximation to objective truth: closeness to truth, affinity with truth. For (in B35) he says:

Let us conjecture that these things are like the truth.

It is possible that when he uses the word *doxazein* (which I here translate by 'conjecture') in this fragment, Xenophanes alludes to his own mono-theistic theory of deity.

We can say that Xenophanes' theory of human knowledge contains the following points:

1 Our knowledge consists of statements.
2 Statements are either true or false.
3 Truth is objective. It is the correspondence of the content of a state-ment with the facts.
4 Even when we express the most perfect truth, we cannot know this — that is, we cannot know it with certainty. We can never have sufficient reasons.
5 Since 'knowledge' in the usual sense of the word is 'certain knowl-

edge', there can be no knowledge. There can only be *conjectural knowledge*: 'For all is but a woven web of guesses'.

6 But in our conjectural knowledge there can be progress to something better.

7 Better knowledge is a better approximation to the truth.

8 But it always remains conjectural knowledge – a web of guesses.

For a full understanding of Xenophanes' theory of truth, it is especially important to appreciate his clear distinction between objective *truth* and subjective *certainty*. Objective truth is the correspondence of a statement with the facts, whether we know this – know it for certain – or not. Thus, *truth must not be confused with certainty or with certain knowledge*. Admittedly, he who knows something for certain must know the truth. But it often happens that someone conjectures something without knowing it for certain; and that his conjecture is actually true, without his knowledge. Xenophanes implies that there are many truths – and important truths – that nobody knows for certain; yes, that nobody can know, even though they may be conjectured by some. He further implies that there are truths that nobody can even conjecture. And, of course, he is correct in all that.

Even today there are many philosophers who think that truth can be of significance for us only if we actually possess it; that is, know it with certainty. Yet the very knowledge of the existence of conjectural knowledge – and so, of unpossessed truth – is of great importance. There are truths that we can approach only by luck; others, only by laborious searching. Our path, nearly always, winds its way through error; and without truth there can be no error (and without error there is no fallibility).

Some of the views that I have just described were already more or less clear to me before I read Xenophanes' fragments. I would otherwise, perhaps, not have understood his words. It had become clear to me through Einstein's achievement that even our best knowledge is a woven web of guesses, that it is uncertain.

Much later I found that Kepler had a similar view of science, as may be seen from the following case [which also shows that mistakes may be hidden in our best-corroborated theories as Xenophanes taught. The story is briefly this]. Kepler had been worried about a deviation from circularity of Tycho's measurements of the orbit of the planet Mars. The deviation was a very small one, as he explains in a letter to Christen Longomontanus, Tycho's former collaborator: 'Yes, my Christen, had I wished to leave [a difference] of 8 minutes in doubt, I could have saved myself the enormous effort of the whole last year 1604.'[26]

Why did he not assume that the 8 minutes' difference was due to the unavoidable inaccuracy of every measurement? It would seem an obvious way out, in view of the fact that the Earth, from where Tycho's measurements were made, was a moving platform whose movements had not yet been fully determined. The answer is: Tycho's measurements, taken over several Mars-years, made the distance of Mars from the Sun exceed the expected distance (calculated on the circle hypothesis) always at the same place: the inaccuracy would have been a *systematic* inaccuracy.

This, Kepler felt, was unacceptable. So he tried other trajectories than circular ones: non-circular orbits that resemble a circle as a fat pear resembles an apple! This was, quite literally, what he did. He felt the deviation from the circle to be a deviation of the empirical world from mathematical purity, and so he did not think of an ellipse – a well-known mathematical entity – but rather of vegetable shapes. Thus he tried several vegetable models before he remembered that an ellipse might fit after all. It did.

So Kepler did not derive his ellipse hypothesis from Tycho's measurements: he operated by trial and the elimination of error: by the method of conjecture and refutation. [As mentioned above, this case also illustrates the importance of the fourth principle of Addendum 2 to this essay – that searching for mistakes in our best-corroborated theories may lead to discoveries of the greatest importance.]

I do not believe that the conjectural character of all our knowledge would ever have become clear to me without the work of Newton and Einstein; and so I asked myself how it could have become clear to Xenophanes 2,500 years ago. A possible answer is this. Originally Xenophanes believed in Homer's picture of the world and the gods. This picture was shattered for him, just as my Newtonian picture was shattered for me. For him it was shattered by his own criticism of Homer: by his discovery that the Homeric gods were anthropomorphic; for me Newton's theory was shattered by Einstein's discovery of an alternative theory that explains the facts at least as well as Newton's, and even better than Newton's. Xenophanes, like Einstein, replaced the criticized picture of the universe by another; and each of them was aware that his new picture was conjectural.

The realization that Xenophanes had anticipated by 2,500 years my theory of knowledge taught me to be modest.[27] But the importance of intellectual modesty too had been anticipated as long ago, by both Xenophanes and Socrates.

Socrates was the second, and much more influential, founder of the sceptical tradition. He taught: only he is wise who knows that he is not. Although many people are aware that this is Socrates' teaching, few realize that his 'Know thyself!' means 'Know how little you know!', and that his demand that the statesman should be wise, or at least a 'lover of wisdom' (a 'philosopher'), is intended to demand of the politician, who bears such immense responsibilities, that he should be constantly aware of his ignorance. Few have seen how this demand (which we know of through Plato's *Apology*) clashes with Plato's interpretation of it (in the *Republic*) that philosophers ought to be kings, and kings fully trained philosophers.

Socrates and, at about the same time, Democritus, independently of each other, made the same ethical discovery. Both said, in very similar words: 'It is better to suffer injustice than to inflict it' (Democritus, DK 68B45). It was this insight – combined with the knowledge of how little we know – that led to toleration, as Voltaire taught later.

6 On Xenophanes' moralism: the defence of civilization against the gods[28]

[I shall now discuss the significance of Xenophanes' self-critical philosophy or his ethical attitude. But in order to do so,] I shall first consider the following important objection. It is correct, somebody might say, that Xenophanes, Democritus, and Socrates did not know anything; and it was indeed wisdom that they recognized their own lack of knowledge, and perhaps even wiser of them to adopt the attitude of searchers for truth. Today, we – or more correctly contemporary scientists – are still searchers for the truth, but today's scientists are not only searchers, but also finders. For they know a great deal; so much that the very volume of our scientific knowledge has become a grave problem. So it hardly can be right that we should still build our philosophy of knowledge on the basis of the Socratic thesis of lack of knowledge.

The objection is correct, but only with four very important qualifications.

Firstly: The suggestion that present-day science knows a great deal is of course correct, but the idea of 'knowledge' employed here, apparently unconsciously, is completely different from that of Xenophanes and Socrates, and from the meaning given to it when used, with emphasis, in everyday usage. For when we speak of knowledge in a non-casual way, by 'knowledge' we always mean *'certain* knowledge'. If someone should say 'I *know* that today is Tuesday, yet I am *not sure* that today is Tuesday', then he would be contradicting himself, for he is retracting in the second half of his statement what he is saying in the first half.

But scientific knowledge simply is *not* certain knowledge. It is always open to revision. It consists of testable *conjectures* – at best, of conjectures that have been subjected to the most stringent tests; yet still, of *conjectures only*. It is hypothetical knowledge, conjectural knowledge. This is my first comment, and by itself a full defence of the application to modern science of the insights of Xenophanes and of Socrates.

My *second* comment on the remark that we know so much nowadays is this: with almost every new scientific achievement – with every hypothetical solution of a scientific problem – both the number of unsolved problems and the degree of their difficulty increase; they increase much faster than do the solutions. And it would be correct to say that *whilst our conjectural knowledge is finite, our ignorance is infinite*. But not only that. For the genuine scientist with a feeling for unsolved problems, the world is becoming more and more difficult to understand.

My *third* comment is this: when we say that we know *more* today than did Xenophanes or Socrates, then it is probably incorrect as long as we interpret 'know' in a subjective sense. Presumably none of us *knows more*; rather we have heard that more is known, and also we know a greater variety of things. We have replaced particular theories, particular hypotheses, particular conjectures by others; admittedly in most cases by better ones: better in the sense of being better approximations to the truth.

The *content* of these theories, hypotheses, conjectures may be called *knowledge in the objective sense*, as opposed to subjective or personal knowledge. For example, the contents of an encyclopaedia of physics is impersonal or objective knowledge – though still, of course, conjectural knowledge. But it far exceeds what the most learned physicist can possibly 'know' (in any sense of the word). What a physicist knows – or, more exactly, conjectures – may be called his personal or subjective knowledge. Both impersonal, or objective, and personal, or subjective, knowledge are, on the whole, hypothetical and capable of improvement. But these days not only does impersonal knowledge exceed by far that which any human can know for himself, but the advances in impersonal, objective knowledge are so rapid that personal knowledge can keep up only in small areas and for short periods of time; it is being superseded all the time.

Here we have a *fourth* reason for saying that Xenophanes and Socrates are right, even today. For this outdated personal knowledge consists of theories that have been found to be false.[29] Outdated knowledge is, therefore, definitely not knowledge, at least not in the ordinary sense of the word.

We have thus four considerations that show that even today the Socratic insight, 'I know that I do not know, and hardly that', is highly topical – I think even more so than in Socrates' time. And we have reason, in the defence of toleration, to derive from this Socratic insight those ethical consequences that were derived by Erasmus, Montaigne, Voltaire, and Lessing. We may even derive further consequences.

Every rational discussion, that is, every discussion devoted to the search for truth, is based on principles, which in actual fact are *ethical principles*. I should like to state three of them.

1   *The principle of fallibility.* Perhaps I am wrong and perhaps you are right; but, of course, we may both be wrong.
2   *The principle of rational discussion.* We need to test critically and, of course, as impersonally as possible the various (criticizable) theories that are in dispute.
3   *The principle of approximation to truth.* We can nearly always come closer

to the truth with the help of such critical discussions; and we can nearly always improve our understanding, even in cases where we do not reach agreement.

It is remarkable that these three principles are epistemological and, at the same time, also ethical principles. For they imply, among other things, toleration: if I can learn from you, and if I want to learn, then in the interest of truth I have not only to tolerate you but also to recognize you as a potential equal; the potential unity of man and the potential equality of all humans are prerequisites of our willingness to discuss matters rationally. Of further importance is the principle that we can learn from a discussion, even when it does not lead to agreement. For a rational discussion can help to shed light upon some of our errors.

All this shows that ethical principles form the basis of science. The most important of all such ethical principles is the principle that objective truth is the fundamental regulative idea of all rational discussion. Further ethical principles embody our commitment to the search for truth and the idea of approximation to truth; and the importance of intellectual integrity and of fallibility, which lead us to a self-critical attitude and to toleration. It is also very important that we can *learn* in the field of ethics.

[In Addendum 2 to this essay I have demonstrated this by proposing twelve principles constituting what I have called a new professional ethics, principles closely connected with the demand for toleration and intellectual honesty which Xenophanes formulated and practised 2,500 years ago.]

As shown above, Xenophanes' 'licence to search' for truth is rooted in both epistemological and ethical demands or principles, which have criticism and self-criticism as their main impetus. How could this dynamism between a search for truth and a critical methodology have come about? Most probably as a result of Xenophanes' experience as a rhapsode, who recited the classic works of Hesiod and Homer but also, no doubt, performed contemporary poetry, including his own poetry, in parts of the Mediterranean region where a great many cultures were meeting with all their different expectations and conceptions of such performances.

In Xenophanes' time culture-clash could be felt also in the world of art, and in his profession it was not necessary to search long to find fundamental differences between, say, oriental and Greek drama. For example, while oriental dramatists would by necessity include a prostrating gesture of reverence before their gods as part of their divine service, this kind of submission is not part of Greek dramatic tradition. On the contrary, Greek dramatists argue with the gods, even accusing them of senseless cruelty. The gods are told to be more rational and responsible: 'You are despots and ought to be ashamed of yourselves. You play with us, but we humans shall show up your play!'

I suggest that this defence of civilization against the family of gods and their whims led Xenophanes to the view that the existence of the world and the world of humanity depends on equity or righteousness, and that the *ethics of the supreme power* presupposes that God, the almighty, must be right; and that this view ought to be a guiding principle for our human search for peace and our fight against war. I further suggest that Xenophanes carried over this view to the domains of epistemology and science, to our search for truth.

It seems to me that Xenophanes' monotheism is here as good as, or better than, the Christian or Jewish monotheism (the Old Testament God being a jealous and avenging god). Xenophanes' moralism much better characterizes the present-day situation in science and politics, and is certainly to be preferred to the idiocy expressed by modern slogans such as 'Anything goes!', the password of some influential but irresponsible intellectuals.

7   Did Xenophanes inaugurate historical writing?

[As announced in Section 2, I shall end by trying to answer the question of this section by a new interpretation of a passage in Herodotus, who is traditionally considered to have given the first historical account of a period of Western civilization.]

We know from two fragments of Xenophanes (B8 and B22), written when he was 92 years old, that he left Miletus at about the time when Anaximander died (546BC) and that the following year, when 25 years old, he was forced into exile for the rest of his life. These moving fragments[30] also give us the year in which Xenophanes emigrated (545) and the year of his birth (570):

> Sixty-seven years it is now that the burden of life
> I am dragging to and fro through the regions of Greece.
> Counting the years from the day of my birth, I was then twenty-five
> – If I still correctly remember.

> This is the stuff one best talks about by the fire in winter,
> Comfortably inclined, sipping sweet wine and nibbling some nuts:
> 'Tell me, who are you, my friend, and where do you come from?
> How old are you, my dear, and what was your age
> At the time of the Median invasion?'

The last question posed in the second fragment relates to the catastrophe which hit the Ionian Greeks as a consequence of the sudden war of conquest launched by the Persian king Cyrus against the Medians and Lydians, and forced the Greeks, who were taken by surprise long before they had even learnt to distinguish between Persians and Medians, to leave their settlements in Asia Minor. We know that these events were described by Xenophanes in a long epic poem in which there also was an account of the founding of Elea (Hyele). This epos is lost, as is another one that described the founding of Colophon.[31]

What is known about this terrible but also very human story is a detailed account in Herodotus' *History* (I.163–7). It is a story in which the love of freedom clashes with the love of one's country, in which determination to resist enslavement ends in ultimate defeat. The story is briefly this. When the Persian army, commanded by Harpagus, a Median general, invaded Ionia and besieged Phocaea (Xenophanes speaks of him as 'the Mede'), all citizens of Phocaea decided unanimously to leave rather than to be enslaved. They left apparently with a great number of ships (perhaps more than 60, each of 50 oars) and tried to buy from the Chians some small inhabited islands. Being unsuccessful, they returned to Phocaea, where they killed the garrisons that Harpagus had left. Then there arose a deep division among them: although they had sworn a great oath that they would all continue together, more than half the citizens broke their oath. One part of them, longing for their home city, preferred to stay in Phocaea (Herodotus says nothing about their fate), while the others left for Corsica (Kyrnos) – as we are told later, because of a misunderstood oracle that had spoken of the hero Kyrnos, not of the island. In Corsica they joined some of their countrymen 'who had come first'. There they settled down, and built houses and temples. Later some of them, Xenophanes among them, departed after some of their fellow-citizens had done injustice to their neighbours, the Tyrrhenians and the Carchedonians, and left for southern Italy. Here, south of Naples, they founded the city of Elea, where presumably Xenophanes wrote the two fragments rendered above, which together with his earlier critique of the Colophonian life style seem to be the only autobiographical passages we possess.

But if Theodor Gomperz is right,[32] then the story in Herodotus is, possibly, an outline of Xenophanes' autobiographical report of a most tragic and indeed devastating period in his life. There seem to me to be three kinds of evidence that could support this interesting hypothesis:

(i) Herodotus does *not* say, as he sometimes does, that he knows this story from hearsay (see, for example I.170, the first sentence).

(ii) For Herodotus, the main interest is in this context the story of Ionia, of Cyrus and Harpagus; I.162–4 fits this 'plan'.

With I.165, a major deviation begins: here the interest turns to the tragic story of the Phocaean refugees. From here on – though the story is exciting and tragic – it is sketchy and written as if Herodotus were explaining certain points only because later passages demanded their insertion. Thus especially in I.165, the first sentence becomes *very* long because the beginning of the story of the relations of the Phocaeans to Corsica and the founding of Alalia is squeezed in at the end, before the full stop. Then there is another squeezed-in, short sentence that explains why the Phocaeans did not get any help from Arganthonius. All this suggests that a long poem is being cut and exploited, and not too well: corrections have to be made later to insert omissions somehow and somewhere because otherwise the later passages at the beginning of I.166 (τῶν πρότερον ἀπικομένων) would be incoherent, or would be necessarily misunderstood: one would not know who had arrived first! The passage (I.166) that tells about those 'who had come first' also suggests that the story told is in fact a personal report by one who sailed not with those Phocaeans who arrived first, but with a later wave of immigrants.

(iii) If Herodotus had a source, could this have been Xenophanes' epos? Herodotus, who wrote his *History* about 100 years after the events, would undoubtedly have tried to get some written source,[33] and it is most unlikely that another written source existed: an author writing history 100 years before the 'Father of History' was not easily come by; and as we know that Xenophanes was such an author, it is likely that he was indeed the source of what we can now read in Herodotus.

There are several implicit or explicit evaluations in the text. In the first sentence of I.165, the egotistic attitude of the Chians is just touched upon. Later, when the oath is broken by more than half the Phocaeans, the breach is clearly condemned, but the condemnation is very tolerant towards the weakness of those who broke the oath. The brief description reads like an outline from a report of one who was present and who had some sympathy with those he had to condemn on principle. This reminds one of Xenophanes' humane moralism.

Herodotus seems touched by the tragic events of this story, and there-fore he tells it very succinctly; perhaps he also wishes to get back to his main topic. But I for one – the other and earlier one was Gomperz (who, however, does not even refer to Herodotus' story) – get the feeling that the source was the epos by Xenophanes, who witnessed and participated in this terrible adventure from which survived fewer than one-sixth of the citizens of Phocaea who had taken the oath of comradeship against the Persian threat.

[I think this interpretation of Herodotus fits well into the account of how Western science and philosophy originated in the Greek colonies in Asia Minor and the Ionian islands and how it was transported to the mainland of Greece and Graecia Magna by highly learned and educated refugees. Among the most important of these emigrants we may count Pythagoras of Samos, Xenophanes of Colophon, Anaxagoras of Klazomenai, and Her-odotus of Halicarnassus. I need hardly say that I consider it a most fortunate unintended consequence of the tragic events, about which Xen-ophanes sang for his fellow-citizens, that the unique cultural development of these great scientists and scholars was brought to bear upon our Western civilization.]

Notes

1 See H. F. Cherniss, 'The Characteristics and Effects of Presocratic Philosophy', *Journal of the History of Ideas*, vol. 12, 1951, pp. 319–45; reprinted in D. J. Furley and R. E. Allen, *Studies in Presocratic Philosophy*, vol. 1, London & New York, 1970, pp. 1–28 (the quotation is on p. 18).

2 Although Cherniss is, in my opinion, truly outstanding, he is not always reliable in his analyses. For example, he says (op. cit., p. 21): 'The whole argument of Parmenides proceeds by applying the law of excluded middle to prove that the identity of what-*is* precludes the possibility of any characteristic except just *being*.' This is doubly mistaken. (1) Parmenides' *Being* has many 'characteristics', such as 'taking up space' or 'filling space'; 'impenetrable'; 'capable of stopping anything that touches it'; therefore it is unmovable in bulk, unchanging, uncoloured, limited, spherical, hard, and dense. So Cherniss is mistaken when he says that, for Parmenides, 'the identity of what-*is* precludes the possibility of any [other] characteristics'. (2) It is not the law of the excluded middle to which Parmenides appeals, but his battle axe, his often-used fighting argument, is the *polydērin elenchon*, as he calls it (DK 28B7: 5), a *reductio ad absurdum*, a refutation that appeals to the law of non-contradiction, rather than to that of the excluded middle: if you were to admit that non-being exists, then you would have to admit

$$non\text{-}being = being,$$

which obviously is absurd: it is a contradiction. *This* is 'the whole argument in Parmenides', repeated any number of times – but not often enough to escape being wholly misrepresented by an outstanding historian of Greek philosophy.

3 See Heraclitus, DK B57, where Hesiod again is attacked for knowing much but not the right thing.

4 *De Divinatione* 1.3.5 = DK 21A52; also in Aetius. This report of Cicero is very interesting. For 'the practice of divining the future' – the practice of prophecy – has remained the most widespread form of superstition down to our own days. Even today, an intellectual is evaluated by his prophetic powers. I myself am still asked by every newspaper correspondent what the future will bring, although I have spent my long life in preaching (apparently in vain) against the fraudulent practice and still more fraudulent theory of historical prediction. (To the latter ideology I have given the somewhat unfortunate name of 'historicism'.)

5 For a very clear description of the authoritarian misuse of the intellect, see Julien Benda, *La trahison des clercs*, Paris, 1928.

6 U. von Wilamowitz-Möllendorff, *Sappho und Simonides*, Berlin, 1913, p. 279.

7 An example of a school in this sense is the school founded by Pythagoras. Here changes in the teachings tend to be secret and credited to the founder of the school in order to obtain legitimation. Since changes were here illicit, we can hardly expect ever to have any history of early Pythagoreanism.

8 Seneca reports, DK 11A15, the following on Thales' theory: 'Thaletis . . . sententia est . . . terrarum orbem aqua sustineri et vehi more navigii mobilitateque eius fluctuare tunc cum dicitur tremere.' ('Thales' . . . theory is . . . that the Earth was supported by water, and that she was swimming on it like a

vessel; and it is owing to the movability of the water that she fluctuates when she is said to quake.')

9 DK 12A11: 3: τὴν δὲ γῆν εἶναι μετέωρον ὑπὸ μηδενὸς κρατουμένην, μένουσαν δὲ διὰ τὴν ὁμοίαν πάντων ἀπόστασιν. Or in English translation: '[Anaximander says] that the Earth is freely suspended [in space = in the *apeiron*] and at rest owing to the equality of her distances from all [heavenly bodies].'

10 The *Apeiron* is an as yet indeterminate and unlimited first 'principle', almost insubstantial, unstructured, and incorporeal, and almost the same as what we now call 'space' (compare 'spaceship'). From the *Apeiron* all substances and bodies derive by an evolutionary process of assuming some structure or other which they impose, for a limited time, upon the *Apeiron*.

11 My figure is a revision of a figure due to Felix M. Cleve, *The Giants of Pre-Sophistic Greek Philosophy*, The Hague, 1965, 2nd edn. 1969, vol. I, p. 11.

12 C. H. Kahn, *Anaximander and the Origins of Greek Cosmology*, New York, 1960, p. 234.

13 See C. H. Kahn, op. cit., pp. 234f., and F. M. Cleve, op. cit., pp. 11f. Cleve translates:

> This upper end of the earth is seen contacting the air
> At [our] feet. But the lower [end] comes to the infinite.

And on the same page he puts it: 'borders on the infinite'.

14 As Mansfeld translates ('*ins Unermessliche*') in his *Die Vorsokratiker I*, Stuttgart, 1983, p. 221.

15 F. M. Cornford, *Principium Sapientiae*, Cambridge, 1952, p. 147, note 1.

16 My interpretation stems from the late 1970s. It was first published very briefly as part of an endnote, which the present text replaces, in the first German edition of my book *Auf der Suche nach einer besseren Welt*, Munich, 1984, p. 229. In this endnote I referred to Cleve's book, a copy of which he had kindly sent me shortly before.

17 In colloquial English, comparatives like 'the upper' and 'the lower' are often replaced, equivalently, by superlatives; thus Jane Austen writes normally 'the eldest' and 'the youngest' when speaking of *two* sisters.

18 There was no Greek word for 'gas' only for 'cloud', for 'vapour', or for 'mist'. The term '*nephos*' is later found in the Latin '*nubis*', '*nubes*' (cloud), '*nebula*'; in German '*Nebel*' (fog), and in English 'nebulous'. The same idea seems to underlie the report that Xenophanes believed that burning gas consists of little burning (or ignited) particles. It is fairly clear that fog or mist consists of little droplets or particles; and so does smoke, which sometimes ignites.

19 It has been told by Cleve, op. cit., pp. 11f. I arrived independently at a slightly different version of the story much later.

20 In the *first* set of reports we have Plato and Aristotle, and in the *second* set of reports Empedocles and again Aristotle. [In another manuscript dealing with the misunderstandings of Xenophanes' cosmology, Popper talks about *three* sets of traditional reports, and on a separate sheet he has enlarged the two mentioned sets as follows: (1) Plato, Aristotle, Cicero (A34), Sextus Empiricus (A35), Simplicius (A31), Hippolytus (A33), Theodoretus (A36), MXG (A28: 7); (2) Empedocles (DK 31 B39), Aristotle (A47), Aetius (A41, 41a), and he counts as the *third* set (3) Simplicius (A47) and Galen (A36); finally a *fourth* set is mentioned as a 'neutral group', including (4) Ps. Plutarch *Stromateis* (A32), Theodoretus (A36), Stobaeus (A36), and Hippolytus (A33). Ed.]

21 That the *Air* of Anaximenes corresponds to the *Water* of Thales may be

acceptable, but the *Fire* of Heraclitus seems to me far from analogous to these two; and obviously the four elements are due to Empedocles, who only later assigned them to some of his predecessors.

22 The only known case where he deviates slightly from this modesty is in fragment B2, where he measures thought against (what we now call) sport. And no doubt rightly: he would be surprised that after 2,500 years we know of him and study his thought – even though nobody remembers the Olympiad winners [of his time] in spite of Pindar (who is remembered).

23 There were atheists in Xenophanes' time. Thales' famous remark about magnets is atheistic in the sense of denying the omniscience of *personal* gods. For atheists, Xenophanes' criticism of anthropomorphism might be comparatively easy, but for deeply religious people, who want a personal god, his criticism might be an unforgivable offence.

24 However, I managed an adequate four-line German translation:

Sichere Wahrheit erkennte kein Mensch und wird keiner erkennen
Über die Götter und alle die Dinge von denen ich spreche.
Selbst wenn es einem auch glückt die vollkommene Wahrheit zu künden,
Wissen kann er es nicht: es ist alles durchwebt von Vermutung.

25 H. Fränkel, 'Xenophanesstudien I und II', *Hermes*, vol. 60, 1925, pp. 174–92; partly reprinted in Fränkel, *Wege und Formen frühgriechischen Denkens*, Munich, 1955, pp. 335–49. [English translation in A. P. D. Mourelatos (ed.), *The Pre-Socratics: A Collection of Critical Essays*, Garden City, 1974, pp. 118–31. Describing Xenophanes as a narrow-minded pragmatist and a stubborn moralist, Fränkel characterizes fragment B34 as relativistic and altogether untenable, and he considers Xenophanes' method as that of a 'rough empiricism' and Xenophanes' haphazard view of knowledge as a doubtful support for his joyful idea of progress expressed in fragment B18. Ed.]

26 M. Caspar and W. von Dyck, *Johannes Kepler in seinen Briefen*, Munich, 1930; quoted from E. Oeser, *Die Entstehung der neuzeitlichen Wissenschaft*, Göttingen, 1971, p. 53.

27 Xenophanes' teaching that we *may* hit upon the truth (by good luck) but could not *know* that we have attained it does *perhaps* assume that the gods (but not we) would know that we have found the truth. But *here* the gods can be omitted, and it appears that Xenophanes knew that: his theory anticipates mine.

28 [Here reference is made to E. R. Dodds, *The Greeks and the Irrational*, Berkeley and Los Angeles, 1951. Regarding the importance of rationalism and moralism for the defence of civilization against the gods, there is some similarity in the point of view when Dodds, who has adopted Popper's idea of the open society, writes the following (op. cit., p. 252) about the decline of rationalism in the first century BC: 'I have already suggested that behind the acceptance of astral determinism there lay, among other things, the fear of freedom – the unconscious flight from the heavy burden of individual choice which an open society lays upon its members.' Ed.]

29 Michael Polanyi's book *Personal Knowledge* (London, 1965), belonged to this outdated personal knowledge from the day it appeared; if for no other reason than for its absurdly mistaken interpretation of Tarski's theory of truth and its attempt to replace it with an authoritarian theory of truth.

30 [Translated into English by Sir Ernst Gombrich based on a German translation of the same fragments that Popper worked on shortly before his death. Popper's translation reads like this:

Siebenundsechzig Jahre sind verflossen seit ich
Auf und ab durch Hellas meiner Seele Sorgen trage.
Damals war ich fünfundzwanzig Jahre alt –
Wenn ich das alles richtig noch berichten kann.

Beim Feuer ziemt sich solch Gespräch im Winter,
Wenn man gesättigt ruht und süssen Wein trinkt,
Und dazu Nüsse kunspert: 'Von wo kommst du her?
Wer war dein Vater? Wie alt bist du Freund?
Und wie alt warst du als der Meder kam?']

31 We do not have a line of either of them, which is not very surprising, since a
longish epos is not copied very easily, and since in those days books were not
published. (No market for books existed: the oldest report of a book market – in
Athens – stems from about 450; cp. my *In Search of a Better World*, London 1992,
pp. 99–116.) However, this does not exclude that Herodotus can have known
Xenophanes' epos and used it as a source for writing about the Ionian tragedy.

32 [Theodor Gomperz, *Griechische Denker: Eine Geschichte der antiken Philosophie*,
Berlin–Leipzig, 1922, Bd 1, pp. 129f., speaks of 'thousands of verses' that
describe the foundations of Colophon and Elea, and on p. 217 Herodotus is
mentioned as 'a pupil of Anaximander and Xenophanes', but mainly regarding geology. Indications like these may have inspired Popper to his hypothesis
about Herodotus' sources. Nowhere does Gomperz suggest, however, that
Xenophanes' epos on the history of his hometown and its inhabitants and
their fate could have been a source for Herodotus. Ed.]

33 The story told by Herodotus was too old to be told with such detail without a
source, and too recent to have been just invented. The correctness of the story
was never questioned, and a reason for this could be that those of Herodotus'
contemporaries who might have questioned its authenticity knew about
Xenophanes' epic poem.

ADDENDUM 1
A NOTE TO THE QUOTATION FROM
XENOPHANES (DK 21B25) IN SECTION 4 ABOVE

I suggest that Xenophanes B25 ($\kappa\rho\alpha\delta\alpha\acute{\iota}\nu\epsilon\iota$) be translated as follows:

(1) Effortless over the All he reigns by mere thought and intention.

The word 'reigns' in this translation deviates from most previous translations known to me, including my own earlier translation, which was:

(2) Effortless he swings the All, by mere thought and intention.

The word 'swing' may be interpreted as an allusion to something like a
pre-Aristotelian 'first mover' who sets in motion the starry heavens by
swinging them like a lance; thus instead of 'swing' we may put 'move'.
Translation (2) follows a suggestion of Hermann Diels, who was severely

criticized by Karl Reinhardt in his famous book *Parmenides* (1916, pp. 112f.); Reinhardt proposed another interpretation that was accepted by most scholars and might be turned into English verse perhaps as follows:

(3) Effortless he shakes the All by mere thought and intention.

With a reference to Reinhardt, this translation was accepted by Walter Kranz and used in the 5th edition of *Die Fragmente der Vorsokratiker* (DK, 1934–7), and it has thereby acquired almost universal approval and authority.

Obviously, the Greek text must be scrutinized with care in order to decide between these three somewhat different translations. But before doing this I wish to say that translation (1) seems to me straightforward and best fitting the context, both the context of B25 and the (perhaps problematic) wider context of B23, 26, 25, and 24 – always provided that it can be linguistically defended.

But is translation (1) really acceptable with a view to the Greek wording? Not at first appearance. The dictionaries do *not* give for κραδαίνω a meaning like 'to rule'. I shall try to show that either the dictionaries are incomplete, or alternatively, an emendation should be adopted.

The dictionary of Liddel and Scott (revised by Jones) tells us that *kradainō* is another form of *kradaō*, giving as translations: 'to swing, wave, brandish' [especially a lance or a spear], 'to quiver' [of a lance after it has fixed itself in the ground], and also 'to make tremble'; even to cause an earthquake or a cosmic upheaval, as described by Aeschylus in *Prometheus Bound*, line 1047, the best passage in support of Reinhardt's interpretation (referred to him, op. cit., p. 112, footnote 2).

Clearly, Reinhardt's interpretation is perfectly possible from a linguistic point of view. Yet to me it does not seem to fit. Xenophanes' God is most powerful, and so he could perhaps cause not only the Earth but even the universe to quake. But Xenophanes was a great critic of anthropomorphism and bitterly opposed to Homer's and Hesiod's attribution to their gods of all kinds of human vices, misdeeds, and outbursts of temper. So we may take it that his God is not given to outbursts of temper, as Zeus is: he is not, like Zeus, human in his ways of thinking and in his emotions. He would not display his power in order to prove that he is powerful. Zeus' treatment of Prometheus in *Prometheus Bound* would not fit at all Xenophanes' idea of Godhead, which is (or so it seems to me) far removed from that scene of brutal cruelty, revenge, and destruction. And it is equally far removed from another famous scene to which Reinhardt also refers (*Iliad* 1.530) a scene in which Zeus makes Olympus tremble by nodding his heavy head and thereby affirming his promise. But Xenophanes' God does not move! Incidentally, the word we are discussing – *kradainō* – does *not* occur in this Homeric passage, so that this reference is hardly relevant. Also for good measure, Homer's scene does not fit because Zeus clearly shakes Olympus unintentionally – it just happens. For this reason, neither an effort nor the lack of an effort fits the situation, and an allusion to this scene could hardly occur to Xenophanes. Besides, the scene is again anthropomorphic; and Reinhardt's suggestion (that Xenophanes wants his god to outdo Zeus by making the All tremble rather than merely Olympus) seems to me to clash with the main tendencies of Xenophanes. To sum up, Reinhardt's interpretation (3) seems to me technically possible, but not to fit the context.

Diels's interpretation (2), which I once accepted and supported, also seems to me possible. *Kradainō* certainly can mean 'swing' in the sense of swinging a lance – there are comparatively many occurrences of this meaning in Homer, although 'brandish a lance' or 'threaten with a lance' is perhaps more often what is meant. At any rate, if a hero can swing, and set in motion, 'an awful lance' (*Iliad* 7.213; *Odyssey* 19.438), then a god can swing, and set in motion, the starry heavens. And yet, I now think that this idea is, again, too anthropomorphic for what Xenophanes intends. Xenophanes' God is the ruler of the All. Why, then, does Xenophanes not say so, in a straightforward way?

With this I come to the defence of my own interpretation (1): to the hypothesis that Xenophanes did indeed say, in a direct and straightforward way, that his God rules or reigns over the universe.

This hypothesis seems to me linguistically defensible in view of a strange (and, it seems, so far unnoticed) similarity between two Greek dictionary words: *kradainō* (or *kradaō*) is the first of these words and *kraainō* (also occurring in the forms *kraiainō* and *krainō*) is the other. The first word, *kradainō*, has as one of its basic meanings 'to brandish a lance' (that is, a sharpened stick). The second word, *kraainō* or *krainō*, has as one of its basic meanings 'to brandish the staff of rule' (the stick that has become a symbol of power, the *skeptron* or sceptre; see Sophocles, *Oedipus Coloneus* 449), and it therefore also means 'to exercise sway' or 'to reign' (*ibid.* 296, 926; *Odyssey* 8.391). This similarity in meaning of two apparently unrelated yet very similar words (though *kradainō* has a short first syllable while *kraiainō* has a long first syllable) can hardly be an accident. The two words must be somehow related, either by origin or possibly by some kind of muddle. At any rate, translation (1) seems to me linguistically justified, with or without emendation.

ADDENDUM 2
SOME PRINCIPLES FOR
A NEW PROFESSIONAL ETHICS
BASED ON XENOPHANES' THEORY OF TRUTH

I should like to put forward some principles for a new professional ethics, which for a long time I have felt is badly needed, principles based on

Xenophanes' theory of truth and connected with his moralism and intellectual honesty.

For this purpose I shall first characterize the old professional ethics, and perhaps caricature it a little, in order to compare and contrast it later with the new professional ethics that I propose. Should this new ethics turn out to be a better guide for human conduct than the traditional ethics of the intellectual professions – the ethics of scientists, physicians, lawyers, engineers, architects, and also civil servants, and most importantly, the ethics of politicians – then I may be allowed to claim that new things can be learnt even in the field of ethics.

Both the *old* and the *new* professional ethics are based, admittedly, upon the ideas of truth, of rationality, and of intellectual responsibility. But the old ethics was based upon the ideas of personal knowledge and of the possibility of reaching certainty; and therefore upon the idea of *authority*. The new ethics, by contrast, is based upon the ideas of objective knowledge and of uncertain knowledge. This means a fundamental change in thinking, and with it a change in the *role* played by the ideas of truth, of rationality, and of intellectual honesty and responsibility.

The old ideal was to *possess* both truth and certainty and, whenever possible, to *guarantee* truth by means of a proof. This ideal, which to this day is widely accepted, corresponds to the personal ideal of the sage – not, of course, to the Socratic ideal of wisdom, but rather to the Platonic ideal of the initiated seer: of the Platonic philosopher who is, at the same time, a royal ruler, an authority.

The old imperative for the intellectual was: 'Be an authority! Know everything (at least in your chosen field of expertise)!' Once you are recognized as an authority, your authority will be protected by your colleagues; and you must, of course, reciprocate by protecting their authority.

The old ethics here described leaves no room for mistakes. Mistakes are not allowed; and therefore the confession of mistakes is not allowed. I do not need to stress that this old professional ethics is intolerant. Moreover, it has always been intellectually dishonest: it leads especially in medicine and politics to the covering up of mistakes for the sake of authority ('closing ranks').

I suggest, therefore, that a *new* professional ethics, fit not only for scientists, be based upon the following twelve principles.

1   Our objective conjectural knowledge continues to exceed more and more what *one* person can master. *Therefore there are no authorities.* This holds true even within the various medical specialities.

2   *It is impossible to avoid all mistakes,* or even all those mistakes that are, in themselves, avoidable. Mistakes are continually being made by *all* scientists. The old idea that mistakes can be avoided and that one is

63

therefore in duty bound to avoid them must be revised: it is itself a mistake.

3 *It still remains our duty to do everything we can to avoid mistakes.* But it is precisely in order to avoid them that we must be aware of the difficulty in avoiding them, and of the fact that nobody succeeds in avoiding them all; not even the most creative scientists who are guided by intuition succeed. Although we can do nothing without it, intuition is more often wrong than right.

4 *Mistakes may be hidden in our best-corroborated theories*, and it is the specific task of the scientist to search for such mistakes. Finding that a well-corroborated theory or a much-used practical technique is mistaken may be a discovery of the greatest importance.

5 *We must therefore change our attitude to our mistakes.* It is *here* that our practical ethical reform must begin. For the attitude of the old professional ethics leads us to cover up our mistakes, keep them secret, and to forget all about them as soon as possible.

6 The new basic principle is that in order to avoid making more mistakes than we need make *we must learn from the mistakes we do make*. To cover up mistakes, therefore, is the greatest intellectual sin.

7 *We must, therefore, be constantly on the lookout for mistakes*, especially our own mistakes. When we find them we must remember them; and we must scrutinize them from all aspects, in order to understand better what went wrong.

8 A *self-critical attitude*, frankness, and openness towards oneself become, therefore, part of everyone's duty.

9 Since we must learn from our mistakes, *we must also learn to accept*, indeed accept with thanks, *their being pointed out to us by others*. When we draw other people's attention to their mistakes, we should always remember that we ourselves have made similar mistakes. And we should remember that the greatest scientists have made great mistakes. This is certainly not meant to imply that our mistakes are, generally, forgivable: we must never let our attention slacken. But it is humanly impossible to avoid making mistakes, and when we draw the attention of others to their mistakes, we might help them by pointing this out too.

10 We must be clear in our minds that *we need other people to discover and correct some of our mistakes (as they need us)*; especially people who have grown up with different ideas, in a different cultural atmosphere. This too leads to toleration.

11 We must learn that self-criticism is the best criticism; but that *criticism by others is a necessity*. It is nearly as good as self-criticism.

12 *Rational (or objective) criticism must always be specific*: it must give specific reasons why specific statements, specific hypotheses appear to be false, or specific arguments invalid. It must be guided by the idea of getting

nearer to objective truth. In this sense it must be impersonal, but also sympathetic.

I ask the reader to consider what I am proposing here as suggestions. They are meant to point out that, in the field of ethics too, one can put forward suggestions which may be discussed and improved by critical discussion, as Xenophanes and his successors, it seems, were among the first to discover.

The more or less universal acceptance of the conjectural character of science has meant a fundamental change in the attitude of scientists towards refutations of mistaken theories, even of their own. A similar change in attitude to human fallibility has not yet taken place in politics and within our different institutions. If I dream of a democratic utopia, it will be one in which a parliamentary candidate can hope to attract votes by the boast that he discovered during the last year 31 serious mistakes made by himself and managed to correct thirteen of them; while his rival discovered only 27, even though he admitted correcting thirteen of his own mistakes. I need not say that this will be a Utopia *of toleration*.

Editorial note

Owing to its fairytale origin, which will not be related here, no part of this volume got into 'the Popper Archive', so from that point of view *The World of Parmenides* may be considered Sir Karl Popper's last philosophical publication on which he worked to the end of his life. Essay 2 on Xenophanes, which is the only essay among those printed here that Sir Karl left unfinished, has been completed from numerous handwritten drafts and other documents, kindly made available by Mr and Mrs Raymond Mew, Sir Karl's literary executors, according to two main lists of contents found among the papers of Sir Karl's *Nachlass*: (X_1) three structurally similar lists with various keywords added over a period of time, and (X_2) one list entirely different from the others.

The X_1-lists comprise seven sections and carry a number of keywords (here written in brackets): (I) 'Xenophanes as a Co-founder of the Greek Enlightenment' (a teacher who wanted to teach so as to become unnecessary!); (II) 'Notes on the Life of Xenophanes' (Colophon, Miletus, Anaximander; refugee); (III) 'The Misunderstood Cosmology' (fields of force in which disturbances cause vibrations that spread like waves); (IV) 'Relation to Parmenides' (*demas* versus *melea* or *melos* – *melea* hardly occurs in Xenophanes? Cartesian Rationalism, sphere); (V) 'Enlightened Theology' (the Logic of Supreme Power, the Ethics of Supreme Power; the Critique of Anthropomorphism is fundamental, see Mansfeld I, p. 16, Back to Anaximander! das Zitat); (VI) 'Moralism: the Defence of Civilization Against the Gods' (the dramatists; Die Existenz der Welt und der Menschenwelt beruht auf Gerechtigkeit: Gott, der Mächtige, muss gerecht sein); (VII) 'Logic and Epistemology'. (Between Sections VI and VII a reference to E. R. Dodds, *The Greeks and the Irrational*, 1951, is noted.)

The X_2-list of contents also sketches out seven sections, but with different titles, and it gives other keywords and carries the heading 'On the Greatness of Xenophanes': (1) 'Anti-Anthropomorphism, Theology'; (2) 'The Summary of Theology, B34, Truth versus Certainty' (Monotheism – as good, or better, than the Christian or Jewish one. The Old Testament God is an envious god: you must not have other gods besides me!); (3) 'Two Popular Senses of Scepticism' (both deriving from 'no criterium of truth'); (4) 'Two Kinds of Objects of Knowledge: Laws and Stable Environment – the *Momentary* Dangers and Gain-Situations'; (5) 'Xenophanes the First and Best of Greek Epistemologists' (he said 'no criterion of truth, but, if we go on searching, then our conjectural knowledge may become better'. This is the only sound epistemology); (6) 'B27 and Empedocles' Misinterpretation, confirmed by Aristotle'. (All B27 is correct: the Sun is a big gas ball); (7) '"The Spherical God"' (Three possibilities: (i) The god is spherical according to Aristotle: the unmoved mover; (ii) Xenophanes got it from Parmenides; (iii) Xenophanes' god is not spherical. We cannot know, but I would opt for the third (1), the first (2), the second (3)).

Destiny allowed Sir Karl to cover only a part of the topics indicated in these lists of contents and, for some of them, only in a very first approximation. This has invariably affected both the order of presentation and the contents of the present sections of the Xenophanes essay. No doubt, had this essay been completed by Sir Karl himself the shape of it would have been different; however, the main topics and arguments have been saved and reproduced according to his views on Xenophanes – although with an emphasis and detail less characteristic than he would have given it had he been allowed to write out as a whole his original reconstruction of Xenophanes' contribution to science and philosophy.

In the present version of Essay 2, *Section 1*, which originally introduced the essay, describes Xenophanes as a founder of the Greek Enlightenment. The Preamble that now precedes Section 1 comes from a separate, handwritten note. The first part of *Section 2* on Xenophanes' early life has been carried over from a larger manuscript beginning with the words 'Xenophanes had a hard life', while the second part of this section stems from a typescript entitled 'Three Notes on Xenophanes'; the model of Xenophanes' Earth and the text to notes 11 and 12 as well as the text to note 18 have been copied from an inscription made by Sir Karl in June 1984 on the flyleaf and p.[I] of his master copy of *Die beiden Grundprobleme der Erkenntnistheorie*, Tübingen, 1979. The main text of *Section 3* on Xenophanes' misunderstood cosmology also comes from 'Three Notes on Xenophanes'. *Section 4* about Xenophanes' theology has been compiled from one manuscript joined with several shorter manuscripts and comments noted in separate handwritten documents. The same holds for *Section 5* on Xenophanes' theory of knowledge, where the first part (including the paragraphs to which notes 24 and 25 refer) has been adapted from two manuscripts, while the last part draws on some pages of a paper entitled 'Toleration and Intellectual Responsibility', published in K. R. Popper, *In Search of a Better World*, London, 1992, where Xenophanes' theory of truth is outlined; the four paragraphs on Kepler come from a footnote which Sir Karl prepared in 1990 for a revised version of the latter paper when he still wanted it included as an essay in the present collection. The main text of *Section 6* on Xenophanes' moralism comes from the paper on toleration, while the last four paragraphs of this section have been pieced together from scattered remarks, some of which were noted directly on the lists of contents. The main text of *Section 7* comes from shorter manuscripts in German and English; the hypothesis about Xenophanes as a precursor of Herodotus has been carried over from the manuscript starting 'Xenophanes had a hard life'. *Addendum 1* comes from 'Three Notes on Xenophanes' and *Addendum 2* has been adapted from the paper on toleration. (Wording in square brackets has been inserted to connect manuscript fragments not originally combined by Sir Karl himself. Notes indicated or planned by the author have been tentatively written out by the editor and similarly bracketed. The titles of Sections 2–7, not in brackets, have been adapted from the preliminary lists of contents to announce the main themes of the appropriate sections. Ed.)

Among the restored notes to Essay 2 a few words on note 20 should be added. The distinction between four sets of traditional reports on Xenophanes' cosmology with which Popper operates in his analysis are not unequivocal. With some emendation the following version of the note may be preferable: 'In the *first* set of reports we have Plato and Aristotle, and in the *second* set of reports Empedocles and again Aristotle. [In another manuscript dealing with the misunderstandings of Xenophanes' cosmology, Popper talks about *three* sets of traditional reports, and on a separate sheet he has enlarged the two mentioned sets (corresponding to respectively (1) and (2) + (3) as follows: (1) Plato (A29), Aristotle (A30), Cicero (A34), Sextus (A35), Theodoretus (A33), *MXG* (A28, 7); (2) Empedocles (DK 31B39), Aristotle (A47), Aetius (B27, A41, 41a, 47), Hippolytus (A33); and he counts as a *third* set (3) Ps. Plutarch *Stromateis* (A32) and Stobaeus (A36); finally, a *fourth* set is mentioned as a "neutral" group, including (4) Galen (A36) and Simplicius (A31, 47).' JM]

ESSAY 3

HOW THE MOON MIGHT SHED SOME OF HER LIGHT UPON THE TWO WAYS OF PARMENIDES (I)

I first met Parmenides – together with Anaximander, Xenophanes, Heraclitus, and the other great Presocratics – in a German translation by Wilhelm Nestle, famous as the editor of the later editions of Zeller's *magnun opus*. I was 15 or 16 years old, and I was overwhelmed by the meeting. Here were the first of the steps that led to Newton. The verses that I liked best were Parmenides' story of Selene's love for radiant Helios (DK 28 B14–15). But I did not like it that the translation made the Moon male and the Sun female (according to the genders of their German names), and it occurred to me to give the couplet in German a title like 'Moongoddess and Sungod', or perhaps 'Selene and Helios', in order to rectify the genders. So I began fiddling about with the translations. The volume, which I still possess, shows many traces of this.

In those days I was an enthusiastic Newtonian (I still am) and, of course, aware of the theory of the Moon. But before reading Parmenides' story it had not occurred to me to watch how Selene always looks at Helios' rays.

νυκτιφαὲς περὶ γαῖαν ἀλώμενον ἀλλότριον φῶς,
αἰεὶ παπταίνουσα πρὸς αὐγὰς ἠελίοιο.

Bright in the night with the gift of his light,
Round the Earth she is erring,
Evermore letting her gaze
Turn towards Helios' rays.

Since the day when I first read these lines (in Nestle's translation[1]), 74 or 75 years ago, I have never looked at Selene without working out how her gaze does indeed turn towards Helios' rays (though he is often below the horizon). And I have always remembered Parmenides with gratitude.

This essay is an improved and expanded version of a paper published in The Classical Quarterly, N.S. *42, 1992, pp. 12–19. All translations are the author's, except where otherwise attributed. [Sketches for a second paper, 'Parmenides II', are printed as Popper Fragments 0–5, below. Ed.]*

1   The structure of Parmenides' epos

Parmenides' epos consists of a proem, followed by two main parts: the Way of Truth and the Way of Human Conjectures (if I may give the second main part that name); or the Way of True Knowledge and the Way of Conjectural Knowledge.

In the proem, Parmenides describes his own journey to the goddess[2] – an experience of enrapture – and her kind welcome. It ends with a brief but invaluable abstract (in five lines) of her impending revelation. We possess the proem complete. Then comes the first part – Part 1 – of her revelation, the Way of Truth. This we possess almost complete, and its two main messages are perfectly clear, though very startling. They are a theory of knowledge and a theory of the real world, as known to the gods. Both are delivered by the goddess with divine authority, but not in the spirit of dogmatism. The listener, Parmenides, is treated as a critical thinker. The appeal is to his intellect, and perhaps to his intellectual pride.

Part 2, the Way of Human Conjectures, is a shambles. What remains are a dozen brief fragments, highly interesting and poetic. They belong to cosmogony, astronomy, and human biology. One of them (DK B10) is a programme of what the poem is to tell us, and this is supported by a very interesting report due to Plutarch.[3] These two passages allow us to estimate how much must be missing from this part. Incidentally, Plutarch makes it clear that he regards this part of Parmenides' work as extended, and as highly original.

2   The revelation of the goddess

But it is Part 1, the Way of Truth – of demonstrable Truth as revealed by the goddess – that created a sensation. Here the goddess reveals to Parmenides two things that are so monstrous that they cannot be accepted unless they are given a logical proof.

The first is that we must not trust our senses, but only reason and logical proof (or disproof).[4]

The second is that the real world is full: it is a spherical block of continuous matter. (Parmenides is a materialist who believes in the power of pure thought.) And this has the consequence that, in this world, there can be no movement. Nothing ever happens.

To any normal person this teaching must have appeared not merely false but outrageous. What is shocking in Parmenides' poem (and constitutes a complete break with the old tradition that distinguishes between divine knowledge and human fallible conjecture) is not that the goddess declares our human world of experience to be false and illusory, but that she reveals, and claims to be true – and even proves! – a theory of reality that must seem impossible and even insane to every sane person. (We get an echo of this about a century later in Plato's *Parmenides* 128d, and in Aristotle, *De Gen. et Corr.* 325a13; and again in *Adv. Col.*, as reported by Plutarch, *Moralia* 1113f., almost 500 years later.)

3   The problem

And yet, Parmenides tries to describe a real revelation of the goddess, and what the goddess said to him, he believed to be true. There has been a real revelation – a great flash of light. This is what he wishes to tell us, especially in the proem. It must have come to him as a great enlightenment; it must have solved for him a great problem. What is this problem?

To discover Parmenides' problem and to understand his enraptured feeling of enlightenment: this is my problem here.

4   A proposed solution of my problem

Parmenides was a philosopher of nature (in the sense of Newton's *philosophia naturalis*). A whole series of highly important astronomical discoveries is credited to him: that the Morning Star and the Evening Star are one and the same; that the Earth has the shape of a sphere (rather than of a drum of a column, as Anaximander thought). About equally important is his discovery that the phases of the Moon are due to the changing way in which the illuminated half-sphere of the Moon is seen from the Earth.[5]

Before this, the most ingenious theory of the phases of the Moon was due to Heraclitus.[6] He explained the phases of the Moon and the eclipses of Moon and Sun by the assumption that these were fires held in (metal?) bowls which circled round the Earth: they could turn their black sides partly, or fully, towards us. According to this theory, the Moon was no longer waxing and waning, but its phases were still the result of a real movement in the Moon. But according to Parmenides' new discovery, the phases of the Moon were nothing of the kind. They involved no real change or movement in the Moon. They were, rather, an illusion – the deceptive result of a play of light and shadow.

So our senses are misleading us. We must not trust them. They deceive us: we believe that the Moon moves whilst, in truth, she does not; instead, light plays on her dark and unchanging body.

But what is light? No thing, no matter. Light does not resist – it has no body, just as heat and cold (though they can be sensed, say, by our face) have no body. It is mere appearance, only affecting our senses, our eyes. It has no reality, no real existence. We should never have given light a name: only real, existing things deserve names.

Our senses are to be rejected. They lead us to impossible conjectures. We see movement very clearly where there is none. And we can even prove

70

that there is none: we can disprove, refute, the movement which we once saw in the phases of the Moon (B7):

> Never shall it prevail that things that are not are existing.
> Keep back your thought from this way of inquiry; don't let experience,
> Much-tried habit, constrain you. And do not let wander your blinded
> Eye, or your deafened ear, or even your tongue along this way!
> But by reason alone decide on the often-contested
> Argument that I have here expounded to you as disproof.

This is the intellectualism or rationalism of the goddess, and her disproof of empiricism and, especially, of the acceptability of the senses as sources of knowledge.

But a great discoverer is bound to try to generalize his discovery. Selene does not truly possess those movements that she exhibits to us. Perhaps we can generalize this?

And then came the great intellectual illumination, the revelation: in one flash Parmenides saw not only that reality was a dark sphere of dense matter (like the Moon), but that he could prove it! And that movement was, indeed, impossible.

The proof was (more or less simplifed):

(1) Only being is (only what is, is).
(2) The nothing, the non-being, cannot be.
(3) The non-being would be the absence of being: it would be the void.
(4) There can be no void.
(5) The world is full: a block.
(6) Movement is impossible.

Or to quote Parmenides B2 for his basic rational assumptions (1) and (2), formulated together in the first four lines of his Way of Truth, which contain what he calls his *First Path*:

> Listen! And carry away my message when you have grasped it!
> Note the only two ways of inquiry that can be thought of:
> One is the way that *it is*; and that *non-being* cannot be *being*.
> That is the path of Persuasion, Truth's handmaid; now to the other!
> This path is that *it is not*; and that *it* may *not* be *being*.
> That path – take it from me! – is a path that just cannot be thought of.
> For you can't know what is *not*: it can't be done; nor can you say it. [7]

The rejection of the *Second Path*, on the grounds of both deduction and intuitive logical thought, destroys movement (except perhaps local rotation), and with it common sense.

71

It must be admitted that, in his first formulations of the Way of Truth, which I have here quoted, Parmenides omits the subject '*it*'. But later he speaks more naturally. It seems that he was afraid that by naming his subject he would do something like begging the question: the question of existence, of being. But this omission is a question that does not in any way affect the main argument, with its astounding combination of offering an outrageous theory and a splendidly simple and intuitively convincing proof for it.

5 Traces? Or evidence?

My proposed solution makes use of the well-established fact that a great discovery has often blinded its author like a powerful flash of light, making him believe that it explains far more than it actually does – perhaps everything.[8]

Parmenides' crucial discovery of the true explanation of the phases of the Moon was a great one. It soon led to the explanation of the eclipses, and to Aristarchus' anticipation of Copernicus. But, of course, my proposed solution cannot be proved. It is a historical hypothesis about the thoughts of a person. The only thing one can do for it is to show that it has some explanatory power: there are certain traces in our fragments which otherwise are not explicable, but in the light of my theory they might be fairly well understood. These could serve as something like evidence in its favour, weak evidence, admittedly.

My theory explains the relation between Part 1 and Part 2 of the speech of the goddess. And it explains especially the fascinating story, told by the goddess, of the epistemological fall of man (*der Sündenfall der Erkenntnis*, as Karl Reinhardt calls it[9]) that links the two parts. According to Parmenides, as here interpreted, the fall consists in the giving of names to two things – light and night – instead of only one – night, the dark Moon, the dark heavy matter. The forbidden move was to name 'light' – a no-thing. This is where 'they' – the mortals, the intellectual sinners – 'went astray'. It led them to believe in no-things, in the void, in empty space, and so in (the possibility of) motion. My hypothesis, therefore, singles out 'light' as the forbidden name, whilst the name 'night' would be permitted: the thing in itself, with no light playing on it, is dark, as is the Moon in itself. In giving a name to a no-thing, to a non-being, we are deceiving ourselves, and upsetting our world-picture, our conjectures, our 'opinions'. So the goddess promises at the end of the proem (B1: 31–2), referring to the story of the fall (B8: 53–61):

> But you also shall learn how it came that illusive conjecture,
> Bound to be taken for real, was forcing its way through all things.

When she then really comes to the end of the Way of Truth, and to the story of our intellectual fall, she says (B8: 50–2):

Here I am ending my discourse, so far as it can be relied on,
And my clear thoughts about truth. Now learn of human conjectures,
When you will listen to my so beguilingly ordered verses.

But before she begins with these beguiling verses that treat of human conjectures about our cosmos, she tells the story of our intellectual fall; and this story seems to me most important. It is certainly easier to understand in the light of my historical hypothesis than it was before (when the influence of Hesiod was often appealed to for an explanation).

I shall quote the story; remember that 'they' are the intellectual culprits, responsible for the fall (B8: 53–4):

Two forms they made up their minds that they would give names to;
But of these two, one was not permitted to have a name given.
This is where they have gone astray . . .

The two named 'forms' are, as mentioned, light and night. They provide me with something that may almost be claimed to be a test of my hypothesis.

For most scholars so far (all those whom I have checked) have assumed on intuitive grounds that it was *light* which could be 'named', because it was existing, being, and that *night* was unreal, and the one that should not have been named; whilst my hypothesis suggests the opposite. Who is right?

Only years after I had formulated my hypothesis (including the hypothesis that light should not have been named) did it occur to me to develop a method of solving this problem. The method is easy enough. Make a list of opposites! This leads, I think unambiguously, to the result that *light* is on the side of non-being, the void, unreality, change, movement, warmth, youth, love, illusion, desire (for example for Helios' rays, B15); whilst *night* is on the side of darkness, heaviness, body (B8: 59, πυκινὸν δέμας – the most crucial place), cold, old age, death, non-movement, matter; the one real being: the permanent, unchanging, timeless truth.

Everybody can check this.[10] It fuses the Way of Truth and the Way of Conjectures into one well-articulated – but pessimistic – whole work. Parmenides sees life in all its warmth and movement and beauty and poetry. But the icy truth is death.

6 A few scattered comments

I am at the end of my story. I only wish to add a few more comments on what I regard as shocking mistranslations. (I think the mistranslations have become worse since Diels' Parmenides book of 1897.)

The worst of these translations are those of B16. I have discussed some of its shockingly bad translations in my book *Conjectures and Refutations*

(5th edn, 1989, first published 1963, whose criticism is partly complementary to my present criticism), but my old criticism was ignored, it
seems: I have seen new and very bad translations years later. Famous
scholars have simply not understood the (admittedly difficult) text. The
best translation was, I believe, that of Hermann Diels. A sample translation, unfortunately representative of the texts transmitted by Aristotle,
Metaphysics 1009b22–5 – Theophrastus' text is better – was that of Sir
David Ross (I am quoting from the 2nd edn, 1928, of his translation of
the *Metaphysics*), which reads like this:

> For as at each time the much-bent limbs are composed,
> So is the mind of men; for in each and all men
> 'Tis one thing thinks – the substance of their limbs:
> For that of which there is more is thought.

I find that this is not English. The words are all English, of course, but
they are woven into an impenetrable fog – almost as if on purpose. The
same holds for all the other translations known to me (except perhaps that
by Diels; yet Diels–Kranz has one of the worst). But in the light of one of
the two main truths revealed by the goddess – Parmenides' aggressive
anti-empiricism or anti-sensualism – B16 becomes perfectly clear and
immensely interesting: when properly translated, it is a scathing and
highly ironical attack on sensualistic empiricism – in fact, on the teaching
that is best known in the famous (but somewhat weak) formulation *Nihil
est in intellectu quod non antea fuerat in sensu*. (So far the earliest known
doctrine of this kind was that of Protagoras; but it must have existed half a
century earlier. Of course, it is mentioned and mildly criticized, but not
dated, in Aristotle's *Metaphysics* 1009b13; see below.)

We must start from the sources of B16, Aristotle's *Metaphysics* 1009b21,
and Theophrastus, *De Sensu* (DK A46). The context in which both Aristotle and Theophrastus report and discuss their versions of Parmenides DK
B16 is sense perception.

Aristotle begins the paragraph in which the quotation occurs with an
important reference to philosophers who 'suppose that thought is sense
perception and that sense perception is physical change'; a crisp formulation of precisely that sensualist (and mechanist) theory of thinking
which, as we shall see, Parmenides attacks in B16 with scathing irony.
Theophrastus, who transmits the better text, puts it into the middle of a
passage that also discusses sense perception, yet mainly with a problem
that has nothing to do with our B16, and that goes back to Empedocles
(for example DK 31B90): whether or not we perceive cold with cold and
sweet with sweet, or possibly with the opposite – cold with hot and sweet
with bitter. (Theophrastus links this problem with still another one that
also has nothing to do with our B16.)

At any rate, Aristotle and Theophrastus agree in reporting B16 in a context concerning sense perception. But nothing in the usual translations shows this. They translate μελέων (genitive plural of μέλος) by 'limbs'. But you can find the following in Aristotle's *De Partibus Animalium* 645b36–646a1: 'Examples of parts are Nose, Eye, Face; each of these is named μέλος.' This the Loeb edition translates 'a "limb" or "member"'. But this is not English! Who would call the nose or the eye or the face in English a 'limb' or a 'member'? We would, of course, call the nose or the eye a sense organ; and the face also, if we used it for perceiving, say, a cold wind. However, the dictionary says 'limb' or 'member', but not 'sense organ'; and that is it, even though it is not proper English (just as *Glied* is in this context simply not correct German; as Hermann Diels realized, in using the right term).

I now turn to translating the passage, remembering Aristotle's context (but *not* Theophrastus') and Parmenides' rationalism and his hatred and contempt of sensualism and, no doubt, of the doctrine he hates: that rational thought (intellect) is sense perception linked with physical change. And I assume that both Aristotle and Theophrastus knew well that μέλος meant: a nose for smelling or an eye for seeing, or an ear for hearing. As a result, the translation now looks like this:

What is, at any one time, in their much-erring sense organs' mixture,
That's what men use as standby for thought. For they treat, as if equal,
Reasoning powers of man, and his sense organs' nature or compound.
What in this mixture prevails becomes thought, for each man and all.

This is obviously a violently sarcastic presentation of precisely the theory that Aristotle thought that Parmenides was defending. (Aristotle misremembered the crucial, and for Parmenides very characteristic, word 'much-erring', replacing it by 'much-humbled', so that he might have thought that Parmenides wanted to defend the senses against being undervalued.)

Karl Reinhardt was well aware of Parmenides' scorn and contempt, but he nevertheless believed that B16 was one of the false yet serious human conjectures to be found in Part 2 of the speech of the goddess.[11] I admit that this is possible: it could have been a serious conjecture of the working of the minds of blockheads (or doubleheads).[12] But I cannot quite imagine the context. To me it is easier to think that B16 was a straightforward ironical attack like B6, and probably belonging with it.[13]

My reason is that the goddess was, after all, making propaganda through Parmenides (B2: 1) for rational, logical thought and against sensualism. This could not be combined with propagating amongst the best conjectures the view that humans cannot, in general, think, but can only perceive, and can only mistake their sense impressions for thought.

However, I wish to stress that we just do not know in which context B16 occurred. But if forced, I should vote for a place in the Way of Truth, near to B6.

A sign, apart from B7, that Parmenides also analysed his own way of logical thinking is, I believe, B5:

> . . . It's all the same to me where I begin:
> Just to that very place I shall come back again.

I think B5 shows that he saw that most of his intuitive logical steps were logical equivalences rather than one-sided entailments. (This does not hold, however, for the last step, (6).)

7   A brief assessment

I think that Parmenides was the first great theoretician, the first creator of a deductive theory: one of the very greatest thinkers ever. He built not only the first deductive system, but the most ambitious, the boldest and most staggering ever; and one whose logical validity was intuitively immaculate.[14]

It took far more than 2,000 years before logicians learnt that there was no natural or intuitively fully satisfactory way of avoiding logically catastrophic conclusions, and that up to a point we had to choose our own logical conventions for avoiding them: an almost Parmenidean lesson (and one never learnt by most of the philosophers who made 'ontology' their business and got nowhere).

The next step, made possible only by Parmenides, was the recognition by Leucippus and Democritus that a deductive theory of the world, a theory of such power as that created by Parmenides, could only be *hypothetico*-deductive. So they accepted the existence of motion as an empirical refutation of Parmenides' hypothetical system and concluded from it that both the full *and* the empty existed: atoms *and* the void.

In this way, the greatest physical theory ever was born from a critically inspired discussion of Parmenides' thought that led to the refutation of his theory.

But the war still continues, the war of observation and experiment against theory, of believers in sense perception against thinkers; both within science and within scholarship.

Notes

1 Wilhelm Nestle, *Die Vorsokratiker, in Auswahl übersetzt*, Jena, 1908. I have since translated B14–15 (*Mondgöttin und Sonnengott*): 'Leuchtend bei Nacht mit dem

Licht, das er schenkt, / so umirrt sie die Erde. // Immerzu blickt sie gebannt / hin auf den strahlenden Gott.'

2　I do not see why the goddess should be regarded as anonymous. It must be Dikē (Justice), although Parmenides could have made this clearer. But why should Dikē, if she is merely a turn-key for a higher goddess, have so much fuss made about her by the Heliads, and be described by a fear-inspiring epithet? I cannot believe that it was Parmenides' intention to inform us that he passed her without exchanging a word with her, the divine turn-key, in order to be taken by the hand at once in a friendly fashion by a higher goddess, and welcomed. Is it not more probable that he was not an experienced writer and did not anticipate that we might want an explicit identification (although there was not a syllable in his text to make us suspect that there could be more than one goddess on his stage)? I believe the idea that there may be a second goddess involved is the unconscious result of translating 'high road' instead of, say, 'wide road' (i.e. wide enough for a wagon). Incidentally, it seeems to me highly appropriate that a youth, turned speechless by a goddess's kind reception, thinks of her now as the 'goddess', and so addresses her in his mind, rather than by her name Dikē, which (he must feel) would be an impermissible familiarity. So the change in the text from 'Dikē' to the 'goddess' is determined by the situation. And the choice of Dikē, the guardian of truth (in courts of law), as the speaker is of course also highly appropriate. (See DK, vol. I, pp. 32, lines 20f.; and especially Heraclitus B28.)

3　DK B10 contains an extract, perhaps too brief, from Plutarch's *Moralia* 1114b.

4　The old pre-Aristotelian formal proof was, it seems, mainly the indirect proof, the ἔλεγχος, *elenchos* (*reductio ad absurdum*). Parmenides mentions it by name in B7: 5. It is good that there can be no doubt about its meaning, as it derives from ἐλέγχω ('to disgrace', 'scorn', 'dishonour'; in this case, to dishonour an assertion).

5　Parmenides speaks therefore of the round-eyed (κύκλωπος) Selene, B10: 4. He clearly knew that she was always half lit up.

6　See DK 22A1, p. 142, 2–6. Diogenes Laertius 9.10: eclipses of the Sun and of the Moon occur when the bowls (that contain the burning fuel) are turned upwards; the phases of the Moon occur when the bowl rotates, little by little, in its place.

7　I have tried in my translation to be as close to the text as is compatible with the use of clear English. The deviations of Parmenides from ordinary Greek have been sufficiently discussed elsewhere, by many scholars, and I do not believe that his meaning is in any doubt. Concerning the proof in six steps (preceding the quotation which refers to only the initial statements of the premise(s)), these steps extend, very repetitively, over the whole Way of Truth – apart from the fact that Parmenides does not consider the possibility that his total cosmic sphere might rotate (a possibility which would not have impressed him since his sphere was 'immovable and unchangeable in the bounds of mighty chains': B8: 26–7). At any rate, his intuitive proof seems to me (not valid but) intuitively in order: within his logic, which seems intuitively to work, there is no obviously invalid step; and the premise 'what exists, exists', or 'what is, is ', seems to be a tautology; which would turn the valid derivation into a valid proof.

8　One of the rare exceptions is Xenophanes; cp. his modest comment (B34) on his revolutionary theology.

9　Karl Reinhardt, *Parmenides und die Geschichte der griechischen Philosophie*, Frankfurt-am-Main, 1st edn 1916; 2nd edn, 1959, p. 26; see Essay 9, Section 4, below.

10 See, for example, the scholium to Simplicius, *Physics* 31.3 (= DK, vol. I, p. 240, lines 12ff.: 'On the side of the [fire] is the slender, the warm, the shiny, the soft, and the light [in contrast to the heavy]; opposed is the dense, the cold and the hard and the heavy.'

11 Reinhardt, op. cit., especially pp. 77f.

12 The 'doubleheads' (or the 'two-headed' ones) in B6 create a problem. The expression is certainly used in anger, like 'blockhead'. But has it a special meaning, at least one like blockhead? And perhaps even a meaning that links it with the argument? Or are they just ordinary mortals looking Janus-faced towards being *and* towards not-being?

13 Gadamer has raised a very serious objection in a letter addressed to me in August 1992: the reference to κρᾶσις = mixture in B16: 1 is certainly a reason to place B16 into the same part as B12: 1 and B12: 4. (We should consider also A43.) [See further Popper Fragment 1(d), below. Ed.]

14 See above, note 7. The problem of paradoxes – simple inferences which, it seems, cannot be intuitively shown to contain a mistake, but lead to impossible conclusions — was known in antiquity and has not left us. The most famous one is the Epimenides (a form of the Liar).

This essay is dedicated in gratitude to Jaap Mansfeld for his book *Die Offenbarung des Parmenides und die menschliche Welt*, Assen, 1964. Mansfeld has also encouraged me to add this note on Parmenides' conventionalist attitude towards language, although the note is unconnected with my argument.

A child born blind may know very little about its being disabled (especially in a society in which no fuss is made about it). But it may exhibit an unusual attitude towards language similar to that of Parmenides. For it will by example and convention learn to adopt, and to use, words that mean little or nothing to it (like 'blind', 'see'; 'green', 'red'; 'dark', 'light'; . . .). Parmenides was clearly not blind: he was an astronomer! But he may have been brought up by (or with) someone who was. Or he may have been colour-blind, which may lead to a similar attitude (as Dr Noel Bradley, a psychotherapist, informs me).

My favourite hypothesis (or shall I say 'dream'?) to explain the language of Parmenides is that he was brought up with and by a beloved blind sister, older by three years, who at 11 took full charge of him. Something like this may explain her great influence.

Apart from numerous places where names and naming occur (e.g. B8: 38, 53; B9: 1; B19: 3), the hypothesis would explain the many places where 'way' and 'sign' (or 'signpost') occur, and 'erring (ways)' etc. (remember also πολυπλάγκτων = polyplanktōn). Moreover, B4 ('Attempt to see, with your thinking eye, the absent as it if were present!') becomes quite clear: the admonition is far from trivial for a blind speaker. [See further Popper Fragment 3, below. Ed.]

ESSAY 4

HOW THE MOON MIGHT THROW SOME OF HER LIGHT UPON THE TWO WAYS OF PARMENIDES (1989)

In this essay I shall not speak about the times and the personality of Parmenides of Elea, who lived about 515–445 BC, or of his influence: historical notes may be found in the Addendum to Essay 6, and elsewhere in this volume.

I shall, rather, try to solve what I believe to be the two central problems to which the extant fragments of Parmenides' great epos give rise. It has the form of an epic poem, written in hexameters, clearly influenced by Homer. But it is a philosophical work, and probably it bore the title 'On Nature', thereby alluding to its predecessors, the works of the Ionian philosophers of nature, especially Anaximander and Heraclitus.

I

The poem consisted of two parts and an introduction (the proem). In the introduction, the young Parmenides travels by superhuman means to be received by 'the goddess' (probably identical with Dikē[1]). 'The goddess' announces that she will reveal to him (1) the so far unrevealed and therefore secret truth about nature or reality, but also (2) the mistaken opinions of mortal men. Then she proceeds with her speech, which is clearly divided into these two parts, usually distinguished as (1) the Way of Truth and (2) the Way of Opinion.

The contents of Part 1, the Way of Truth, are completely surprising, especially in the context of the philosophy of nature of Parmenides' predecessors (a context into which Part 2 clearly fits): the goddess (a) first establishes a radically rationalist and anti-sensualist epistemology and (b) then proceeds to a kind of (purely logical) proof culminating in the thesis that movement is impossible, and that the world consists, in reality, of one

This essay, written in March 1989, is an enlarged version of Essay 5 and a preliminary study for Essay 3. {Notes 12 (last three sentences), 13 and 15 were written in 1991. Ed.}

huge, unmoving, homogeneous, solid block of spherical shape in which nothing can ever happen; there is no past or future.

This world of reality of Part 1, the Way of Truth, is sharply contrasted with the world of appearance of Part 2, the Way of Opinion. This is the world as experienced by ordinary mortals, the rich and variegated world of movement, change, development, the colourful world of contrasts, of 'light and night'.

The extant fragments of Part 1 seem capable of being fitted together so as to be very nearly complete; those of Part 2 are obviously quite incomplete, as are the fragments of all other philosophical works preceding Parmenides. Presumably the unusual near-completeness of Part 1 is due to the fact that it created a sensation and was therefore more often quoted and copied than any work of Parmenides' predecessors. The incompleteness of Part 2 is obvious in the light of Plutarch's testimony.[2]

II

So much for a very brief description of the facts surrounding Parmenides' great poem. It is often described by Greek scholars as written in a tedious, unpoetic, quasi-logical style. To me this judgement seems mistaken: I think that his writing is more lively and often more beautiful than his subject matter leads one to expect; but I cannot claim to be a competent judge.

Having mentioned all this, I can now state my two central problems.

We have reliable reports that Parmenides made at least five empirical (astronomical) discoveries of the first order: (i) The Moon (Selene) is a sphere;[3] (ii) The Moon receives her light from the Sun;[4] (iii) The waxing and waning of the Moon are unreal: they are shadow play (and can be modelled with the help of a little globe exposed to light from the Sun or a lamp);[5] (iv) The Evening Star (Hesperus) and the Morning Star (Phosphorus) are one and the same;[6] (v) The shape of the Earth is spherical.[7]

With these results in mind I can now formulate my *first problem*:

(I) *How is it possible that a successful astronomer and empiricist can turn radically against observation and the senses, as Parmenides did in his Way of Truth?*

I shall call this problem *Parmenides' recoil from sensualism*.

That Part 2 of Parmenides' poem was rich in ideas and comments fitting in with the scientific and cosmological tradition of his time, and carrying it further, is shown by the well-known comment on it made by Plutarch (see note 2 below), which shows that Plutarch knew well the content of Part 2 of Parmenides' poem and regarded it as an excellent and very full treatment of cosmology and of natural history, and as a work that was highly original (i.e. containing genuine discoveries); this was in contrast to many – or most – works by other authors, who were merely snapping at their colleagues in order to put themselves forward.

In order to formulate my second problem, I have first to make clear the unprecedented abyss between Parmenides' two worlds, the world of reality and the world of appearance.

Admittedly, the discrepancy between the Way of Truth, the world of reality as revealed by the goddess, and the Way of Opinion, the world of appearance of mortal men, is in the tradition of Parmenides' forerunners in so far as it carries on their distinction between Truth which is certain, and which is attainable only for gods (and those to whom the gods revealed it), and mere opinion and guesswork, which is all that can be obtained by mortal human beings. Moreover, Parmenides' forerunners invented, one might say, a world (a world of gods and demons) behind the ordinary world as it appears to us in order to explain the unusual (such as thunder and lightning; or unusually high waves in the sea; or strange human behaviour; or the power of love; or the strange motions of the planets).

But all this is completely eclipsed by the Parmenidean opposition between his two worlds, the world of reality and the world of appearance. For (i) while the world of reality is (of course) the true world, the world of appearance is *totally* false: it is nothing, no-thing, at best a shadow play. (ii) Nothing belonging to the world of reality (that is, Part 1 (b)) explains anything that might need explanation in the world of appearance; nor would such an explanation solve any problem of the world of appearance, since this world is totally false, totally illusory. (The only explanation of any interest would be one that explains how such illusions can arise; and this, indeed, is explained in Part 1 (a): it arises from our trusting sense experience instead of wholly relying on reason: sense experience, according to Parmenides, leads to self-contradictions.)

Each of these two points, (i) and (ii), opens an unbridgeable abyss between the two 'worlds'; and I know of no other philosophy that contains anything similar – except, possibly, the philosophy of Kant: Kant also has a world of reality, the completely unknowable world of the things in themselves, and a world of appearance, the world of things as they appear to us, to our senses *and* to our reason. Kant's world of the things in themselves resembles the Parmenidean in so far as his world of reality does not function in any way as an explanation of any unexplained events in the world of appearance. Yet the difference between Kant's and Parmenides' systems is very great. For Kant, the world of appearance also has reality: it is what natural science tries to describe by descriptions which are true, and to explain by theories which are true; while the world of reality – of the things in themselves – is for ever unknowable, hidden from us, and therefore – for us – only something like a shadow world.

All other (Western) philosophies known to me that are two-world systems, and especially those that came after Parmenides and were influenced by him, tried to bridge the gap that was unbridgeable in Parmenides' system:

they all fell back upon systems in which the world of reality had the function of explaining our human world of appearance. (I shall call this methodology *'the traditional style'*.) This holds very clearly of the atomists, and it holds even for Plato's world of ideas; ideas that are real, and *true and unchanging* like Parmenides' real world, the world described in Part 1. In these 'traditional systems' ideas help to explain the less real and less true world of appearances in which we live and die.

Now I can formulate my *second problem*: Parmenides' two-world system is not only unprecedented, but looks like a historical impossibility, like a glaring 'anachronism', to use Burnet's expression.[8] *This apparent anachronism – almost a historical paradox – has to be explained.*

Burnet tried to explain this paradox away by saying, if I understand him correctly, that what I have called the *world of opinion* or of *illusion* simply does not exist for Parmenides.[9] Parmenides' system contains only *one* world. The other is for him nothing whatever – a false view which others (the Pythagoreans?) may hold and which he himself may have held once. In other words, all Parmenides really wishes to tell us is that reality is as the goddess says, in Part 1. And Part 2 functions only as a warning not to persist in our false belief in a plurality of moving things: such a world (in which Parmenides himself obviously believed before he received the revelation) does not exist. This is the content of the revelation, and nothing else. The revelation simply destroyed all that Parmenides believed before he received it; and it destroyed all that is, or was, believed by every other mortal man.

Obviously, Burnet thought that in this way the anachronism and the historical paradox disappear, since the apparent similarity with the Kantian dualism of a world of things in themselves and a world of appearances disappears.

Now, it may be granted that Burnet's suggestion greatly reduces the similarity between Parmenides and Kant. But does it solve my problem? I do not think so. My reason is simple: all contemporaries of Parmenides felt that his system was a scandalous paradox, which is the strongest proof there can be of its anachronism. Not only is his great pupil and friend Zeno a witness to this reception of the work of Parmenides, but all he could do to counter the outcry was to show that the idea of a real motion is at least as paradoxical as Parmenides' doctrine that motion does not exist. And all Western philosophers of all later ages starting with Aristotle also found that Parmenides' and Zeno's system was (and still is) paradoxical. The only exception is, perhaps, Plato.

Burnet's remark (*Early Greek Philosophy*, 1908 edn, p. 209, note 3) may be taken as a hint that after Kant, Parmenides' system would have been felt less paradoxical, and that it would therefore have been no anachronism had it appeared after Kant. Indeed, after Berkeley and even more after Kant, it might have been felt as a philosopher's clever inversion of a

Berkeleian or a Kantian idealism – perhaps as an attempt to show the absurdity of these systems. But since it came out 2,300 years before Kant, and was, in fact, both an anachronism and a paradox, my *second problem* might be reformulated this way:

(II) *How can we explain, or make it understandable, that a passionate seeker for truth, at the time of Parmenides and in his intellectual situation, could produce such a paradoxical view of the world, of a strange yet material Reality, and believe it to be true?*

I shall call this problem that of *the apparent anachronism of Parmenides.*

There is a third problem – that of the explanatory relation between Part 1 and Part 2 of the revelation of the goddess. This problem will be formulated and solved in Section VII below.

III

These are my two problems. Before going on with an attempt to solve them I shall briefly add a few comments on them.

As to my first problem, Parmenides' recoil from sense experience is, it seems to me, once formulated, very obvious. But I do not think that it has been seen, or even vaguely felt, by any of the many commentators on Parmenides. Some of them have, admittedly, tried to find some solution to the Parmenidean riddle in Part 2 (as one must, I suggest, if my first problem is to be solved in harmony with the textual evidence). But I do not think that they approached my problem (I) any nearer than this.

My other problem has, I think, been felt, and even seen, by everybody, and more clearly and more strongly by Burnet than by anybody else. But Burnet was strangely mistaken when he thought that it was solved by putting Part 2 – the Way of the Opinion of the Mortals – in its proper place. He is right that Parmenides both describes the illusory world of appearance and teaches its absolute non-existence. But this does not help. It does not make his poem less anachronistic. For it is timelessly paradoxical and remained anachronistic *at least* until Berkeley, owing to the fact that the denial of the existence of the world in which we all live, Parmenides (and Zeno) included, is anachronistic and paradoxical (even if we forget the anachronistic and paradoxical character of Parmenides' Part 1 in isolation from Part 2).

IV

Before turning to introduce a solution – of course a hypothetical solution – of my two problems I wish to say that it is based only on textually well-founded facts – with *one* exception: one psychological assumption is made. I assume that it quite often occurs that a discoverer is so impressed by one of his discoveries, and so excited by it, that he feels that he has now discovered the philosopher's stone, the solution of all riddles: that his discovery illuminates everything (and indeed, it sometimes does). Examples from older times are: Pythagoras' idea that number is the essence of *all* things; Protagoras' *homo mensura* principle: man is the measure of *all* things. Or from very recent times: Bohr's extension of his 'principle of complementarity', first derived from the quantum theoretical 'dualism of particle and waves', to problems of biology such as the difficulty of saying what is the secret of life, or to psychological and philosophical problems such as the problem of free will; or Heisenberg's early belief that his principle of indeterminacy means that physics is (almost? or already?) at an end, since it has demonstrably arrived at a place where finer measurements are impossible, so that one might say: it is impossible to penetrate to a more profound level.

To these examples of what may be called 'the tendency to universalize and to dogmatize a discovery', I may propose an apparently rare counter-example: Xenophanes, who, after discovering a (monotheistic) solution to his problem that the Homeric gods are crudely anthropomorphic and that the divine power that moves and rules the world must be totally different, writes (B34, my translation):

> But as for certain truth, no man has known it,
> Nor will he know it; neither of the gods,
> Nor yet of all the things of which I speak.
> And even if by chance he were to utter
> The perfect truth, he would himself not know it.
> For all is but a woven web of guesses.

Xenophanes is a rare thinker: instead of trying to make of his discovery a universal dogma, he recognizes his own discovery as a conjecture; as a hypothesis. Like all merely human knowledge it is not more than 'a woven web of guesses'. It cannot be more since man is fallible.

As this counterexample shows, the 'tendency to universalize and dog-matize a discovery' must not, in its turn, be universalized and dogmatized. But it exists; and I shall assume, in my solution, that Parmenides had this tendency. (This seems to me to emerge from his poem; but I am aware that my impression is no more than guesswork.)

V

Now I come to my proposal for a solution of my first problem, *the problem of Parmenides' recoil from sensualism.*

Parmenides discovered that the observation (which everybody can make with marvellous clarity) that the Moon – Selene – waxes and wanes during the course of time is false. Selene does nothing of the kind. She does not change in any way. Her apparent changes are an illusion. Although they seem to repeat themselves so regularly that the observation can be done by everybody, the changes are, in truth, non-existent. So clear observations, especially those of change or motion, are utterly untrustworthy; and observed movement may not exist. In fact Selene is a globe that is always of the same size and shape.

But we may say more: the discovery that the Moon neither waxes nor wanes was in its turn made with the help of observation. It could not have been made without observing that Selene always seems to look at the Sun (DK 28B15); which means (reason tells us) that she receives her light from the Sun. So observation may imply the falsity of observation – a clear case of a disproof (*elenchus*, or more specifically, a *reductio ad absurdum*, an indirect proof of falsity). The apparent bodily change of the Moon turn out to be a mere play of shadows, as anybody can see who holds a sphere into the Sun and observes the play of light and shadow on it while he moves round the sphere (or moves the sphere round himself).

However, none of this could have been found without (logical) reasoning. And reasoning is reliable: it is, indeed, the way of truth; the one and only way.

This is my proposed solution of the first central problem. It seems to me clear that Parmenides may easily have come to his strict rationalism by arguing like this. And he may easily have experienced it as a blinding eye opener – as opening his mental eye to the poverty of his sensual eye. To him it was like a divine revelation. This was the truth, and this was the way to truth. This way of truth must be first established, even before the world of observations is denounced.

Now I turn to my second problem, that of *the apparent anachronism of Parmenides*. Here my assumption concerning Parmenides' tendency to universalize and dogmatize comes into play.

The great discovery that the Moon is an unchanging spherical body is generalized by Parmenides to the view that perhaps the whole world is unchanging and immovable. Perhaps *all* change, all motion is an illusory play of lights and shadows, a play of light and night? [10] Perhaps one can rationally *prove* that all motion is impossible? Indeed, Parmenides proves it. His proof is the positive cosmological result of his Part 1, the Way of Truth.

The Way of Truth has two main functions in his poem: it asserts the finding that sensualism always refutes itself, and that rationalism is the only way to truth; and it proves that motion in the real world, the material world, is impossible.

The proof is most ingenious. It is completely *a priori*, free of all empirical assumptions. It may be put as follows:

(1) Only what is, is;
(2) The nothing cannot be.
(3) There is no empty space.
(4) The world is full.
(5) Since the world is full there is no room for motion – and thus for change (which is a kind of motion).
(6) Motion and change are impossible.

This is the proof of the goddess: as a proof it is infallible and thus divine. There is no clever trick in Parmenides' argument; on the contrary, there is simplicity, great care, and some clumsiness: all signs of a great pioneer.

It is an *a priori* deduction of Parmenides' great empirical discovery of the unchanging Moon, and it generalizes it. So this discovery is explained, and with it the cosmos! Even for us, 2,500 years later, it is almost as difficult to find a flaw in Parmenides' proof as it is to find a flaw in Zeno's famous proofs that show that the assumption of movement leads to paradox.

Note that Parmenides *had* to give a proof, a compelling logical proof. Without it, his doctrine that reason rather than the senses gives us truth would lead nowhere; and his doctrine of the impossibility of change would be a stillborn paradox. No doubt, he needed it for himself, to convince himself: he had himself been one of the mortals who believed in the reality of the changing world, changing in the light and even in the night.

But note that Parmenides' proof is a *refutation*. It is an *elenchus*, an obviously much-contested refutation (DK 28B7: 5, πολύδηριν ἔλεγχον) of the doctrine of empiricism and of the doctrine of the existence of change. So are Zeno's and Gorgias' proofs. And this is the case of most (or all?) of the early mathematical proofs, for they are indirect: the *elenchus* rules supreme in the field of the logic of demonstration, of proof. It still rules supreme with Socrates and, I think, with Plato. And indeed the *reductio ad absurdum* is a method of almost absolute proof, in contrast to the axiomatic method (say, of Euclid), which works with unproved assumptions. And it is in contrast to Aristotle's use of syllogisms (that is, derivations) as proofs, an attempt which drove him to invent induction (as we saw on p. 2 above) and which, in despair, he fathered on Socrates, because Socrates had used examples, instances – though only in his disproofs – in the Socratic *elenchus*. In their use of disproof, or refutation, lies at least part of the superiority of the Presocratics over Aristotle, though he was a great physicist and an even greater biologist.

But let us now return to Parmenides and to my two central problems. I have shown that the proposed solution of my first problem is a very fertile theory: it has a great explanatory power. It explains why Part 1 denounces the method (= the Way) of observation as self-contradictory and why (owing to a tendency to universalize) it sets itself the task of proving logically the impossibility of movement, by the same method of refutation that, according to my proposed solution, destroyed observational empiricism for Parmenides. So my solution of the first problem explains even more than this problem requires. And it leads, immediately, to a solution of the second problem of Parmenides' alleged anachronism.

The second problem is solved, simply, by pointing out that everything, including the strange Way of Truth, depends on his great astronomical discovery and its cosmological generalization. The solution is clear: Parmenides, as we have seen, thinks and acts fully in the historical tradition of the 'physicists' of his century; his great discovery, his new theory of the Moon is entirely in this tradition, and so is his universalizing method – compare Thales' theory *'everything* is (a form of) water' and Heraclitus' theory *'everything* is (a form of) fire' and *'everything* changes' (*'everything* is in flux'). So even Parmenides' doctrine *'everything* is at rest since the world is packed full' is entirely within this tradition. Only the radical rejection of observational empiricism and the astonishingly successful adoption of the method of rational proof (the *elenchus*) clearly transcend the tradition of his forerunners; but this departure is fully explained by our proposed solution to the first problem. Parmenides' view is therefore far from anachronistic, but entirely in the tradition of the great Ionian cosmologists.

But the explanatory power of my proposed solution is even greater. It solves a most vexing problem of the interpretation of Part 2. Parmenides, or rather his goddess, says in the very beginning of Part 2 something that is very difficult to understand. She says that the illusion of the world of appearance arises from this, that mortal men, by convention, agree to adopt and to name two entities (or forms), *light* and *night*, instead of only adopting one of these, which presumably is *night*: 'a compact and heavy body'; obviously the material block universe, the one and only reality (B8: 59, νύκτ' ἀδαῆ: the absence of *light*, that is, of the illusion of reality). This convention, this verbal invention of a second reality, 'light', is where the mortals have gone astray, and have become the victims of illusion.

The explanation of this strange passage is not one of my main problems, and my solution of the first central problem (which happens to solve the second also) was not intended to explain, or even to throw light upon, this passage which, on the face of it, seems to be merely a problem of the linguistic clarification and interpretation of the text. And yet, the solution of the first problem seems to me to solve this apparently linguistic problem also.

To see this, let us return to the Moon. What is the explanation of the illusion that it waxes and wanes? Obviously the changing *light* (which comes from the Sun): the waxing and waning of the Moon is nothing real, but, quite literally, a *shadow play* – the playing of light and night on a spherical body! (This can be shown also on a small scale by the model mentioned at the beginning of Section 2 above.) But light is *no-thing*: it is not a *thing*; and only a thing can be: the nothing does not exist! And only a thing can rightly bear a name: the nothing should never have been given a name, and taken for real. Only the Moon as such, the dark material Moon, independently of its illumination is a thing (indeed, a compact and heavy body): the thing itself rather than the thing lit up; however, as we all know, mortal men not only have given a name to this unreal no-thing, *light*, but even prefer it to the real, perhaps because it appeals to one of their senses, and flatters the sense of sight: they cannot see without light. But beware of your senses, Parmenides warns, trust only your reason! It is reason that tells you of the invisible black Moon and of the invisible reality!

So the illusion of movement is the illusion of sight, because of the no-thing called *light*, which should never have been named. This is the explanation of how men have become victims of The Great Illusion. This is why the non-existing world of illusive appearance, the non-existing world of change and motion, is believed in by mortals who trust their senses.

This is the solution of the apparently only verbal problem of the transition from Part 1 to Part 2, and the interpretation of this difficult passage (DK 28B8: 53–9). Here at least, it seems to me, no textual problem is left.

VI

I will now sum up the solution of the first two problems. What is real is the well-rounded, heavy and dense unchanging block universe, which is a generalization of the well-rounded, heavy and unchanging Moon. The illusion of a changing universe is, like that of a waxing and waning Moon, the result of *light* (a no-thing) which produces unreal shadow plays. All this can be established, but only by reason and the method of (dis)proof. This must first be established. Once it is established, we can even without danger describe the non-existing illusory world in which mortal men believe because they are stupid enough to trust their senses – especially sight – and even mistake illusion-creating sensation for thought (DK 28B16) – while only reasoning is real thought, that is, thinking about reality.

The last remarks allow us to solve another apparently merely textual problem: the problem of Parmenides' fragment B16, which has been (in my opinion) always mistranslated; in fact even one of the latest translations seem to me quite senseless. For example Kirk, Raven, and Schofield (1983) translate as follows:[11]

> As is at any moment the mixture of the wandering limbs,
>   so mind is present to men; for that which thinks is the same thing,

namely the substance of their limbs, in each and all men;
for what preponderates is thought.

I am afraid that this is incomprehensible for anybody who is not a classical scholar. My verse translation (in pseudo-hexameters) is now, slightly touched up since 1963, as follows: [12]

What is, at any one time, in the much-erring sense organs' mixture,
That seems genuine knowledge to men. For they take as the same thing
Man's intellectual mind, and his sense organs' varying nature.
'Thought' they call what in this muddle prevails, in each man and all.

This is a typical Parmenidean attack on mortal men, their sense-generated illusions and their underrating of rational thought. It is, admittedly, like the Greek original in being not quite easy to understand (though not more difficult than that); but if one reads it twice it makes good sense, I think, and it fits perfectly with the goddess's message: it is, one can say, a scathing parody of the empiricist principle 'Nothing is in our intellect that was not previously in our senses.'

I think that this fragment 16 belongs to Part 1, where Parmenides formulates his own theory of knowledge in opposition to the theory which he ridicules in this fragment. (The present place of fragment 16 in Part 2 is due, I think, to its misinterpretation as a serious pro-empiricist passage which one could put, of course, only into the false Part 2.) Understood as I suggest, fragment 16 should be placed somewhere near fragment 6 – perhaps between B6 and B7, where Parmenides warns:

Never shall it prevail that things that are not are existing.
Keep back your thought from this way of inquiry; don't let experience,
Much-tried highways, constrain you; and do not let wander your blinded
Eye, or your deafened ear, or even your tongue, along this way!
But by reason alone decide on the often-contested
Argument that I have here expounded to you as disproof.

VII

My *third problem*, less central than the others, may be formulated as follows. In a way, all the cosmologists construct a world behind the world of appearances, in an attempt to *explain* the latter. (Indeed, this is the method of non-positivist science, or what I have called above the 'traditional style'.) But in this, Parmenides breaks with the tradition, even though the tradition culminates in his own great discoveries: his real world, the world of the Way of Truth, is not to be regarded as an explanation of his world of illusion (which is just a mistake). So we arrive at the question:

(III) *What is now the explanation of the interrelation between the real world (of Part 1) and the illusionary world (of Part 2)?*

Answer: The relation is a kind of *inversion* of the 'traditional style'. The whole world of illusion is, indeed, needed in order to explain that *its total abolition* – the discovery of its illusionary character – is a discovery and a highly important step. It is *The Great Revelation* which forces us to construct the true world: the screen upon which *light* and *night* project their illusion.

This answer, which explains the mistaken world of illusion, also links up the two parts of the poem. To understand Parmenides' view of the world it does not suffice to consider only Part 1: the world of illusion, in Part 2, is necessary for the understanding of Part 1. The view that only Part 1 is Parmenides' theory is therefore mistaken.

Parmenides used what I have called the *traditional style* in his great discoveries; that is, he explained the world of appearances by hypothesizing a real world behind it, which has been the method of the sciences from the great Ionians to the present day. I propose the thesis that the relation between Part 1 and Part 2 of his poem is an *inversion* of the 'traditional style'. In other words, he used the 'traditional style' when he made his great discoveries, but he inverted it when he decided that the world of appearances was unreal, false, and no more than an illusion or a nightmare – a dream not to be believed.[13]

Although at present I prefer this solution – *the inversion* – it should be made clear that it all depends on the interpretation of one word, and perhaps even on one letter in that word (as explained in the addendum to this essay). If the usual interpretation of this word is dropped, or if the word is emended as proposed in the addendum below, then the 'traditional-style' relationship between Part 1 and Part 2 can be upheld. In this case, Parmenides appears to be even more part of the general tradition which is explained here in the solution to the second problem.

VIII

I end with a remark on the historical consequences. Parmenides' greatest rationalist *elenchus* – the refutation of the reality of movement – made a devastating impression. Zeno, Anaxagoras, Empedocles, the Sophists, even Socrates, and obviously Plato, are some of the witnesses to its influence.

But his greatest followers and opponents are clearly Leucippus and Democritus, the creators of atomism, who inverted his *elenchus* to give an empirical refutation of Parmenides' great cosmology:[14]

There is movement.
We know this from experience.
Thus: The world is *not* full;
there *is* empty space.
The nothing, the void, does exist.
Thus: The world consists of the existing,
of the hard and full *and* of the void:
Thus: The world consists of *'atoms and the void'*.

So the world is dualistic; and it can create all kinds of new things from the combinations of atoms. *Light* may be real: there may be light atoms (photons); it is *night* that is unreal: night is simply the absence of light.

This was not only the result of an empirical refutation of Parmenides' theory: it used Parmenides' theory for its stepwise modification. In my opinion, it was this empirical refutation that created what later was called 'theoretical physics' and today 'mathematical physics'. The presence of Parmenides' apparently absurd theory was of immeasurable use. Here was a theory, and *a theory, even an absurd one, is always better than none.* This is the one and only heuristic: 'Invent a theory! It will be bad, but you can modify it by never-ending criticism.'

Atomism became the first physical hypothesis that was a direct result of a falsifying deductive argument. So what was really new in Parmenides was his axiomatic-deductive method, which Leucippus and Democritus turned into a hypothetical-deductive method, and thus made part of scientific methodology. Therefore Parmenides' philosophy, even if anti-sensualist, belongs, like Anaximander's world and that of Anaxagoras and Democritus, to the philosophy of nature – to speculative natural science.

Parmenides' cosmological poem is thus one of crucial importance in our history. And his work, instead of being mysterious, misconstrued, and historically impossible, now appears as lucid, beautiful, understandable, and historically of decisive importance.

I personally am indebted to Parmenides for giving me the infinite pleasure of knowing of Selene's longing for Helios (DK 28B14–15):

Bright in the night,
With the gift of his light,
Round the Earth she is erring.
Evermore letting her gaze
Turn towards Helios' rays. [15]

Notes

1 See Essay 9, Section 4, note 4.
2 *Moralia, Adv. Col.* 1114b; or DK, I, p. 241, lines 7–11. (See Essay 5, note 3.)
3 Cp. B10.

4 Cp. B14 and B21.

5 The waxing and waning of Selene (the Moon) must be unreal if the Moon is really spherical (as evidenced in note 3); it is an appearance that is a consequence of (a) her spherical shape, and (b) the illumination by Helios, the Sun; this becomes clear once we see that she always turns her shiny side towards him (cp. B14 and especially B15). All this is clearly an astronomical theory explaining the generally observed 'fact' of her waxing and waning.

6 Cp. A1 § 23 and A40a.

7 Cp. A1 § 21 and A44.

8 J. Burnet, *Early Greek Philosophy*, 4th edn (1930), London, 1971, pp. 182f.

9 J. Burnet, *Early Greek Philosophy*, 2nd edn, London, 1908, pp. 208–14.

10 As far as I can make out, the Greek term for a (dark) shadow, *skia* (σκία), is rare in early writing, and it seems to be used more often to mean a shade or ghost, as in Homer, *Odyssey* 10.495, or perhaps in Democritus (DK 68B145), where *skia* is likely to mean the same (a shade, or even a covering up). My hypothesis is that Parmenides uses 'night' (νύξ, B9: 1) for shadow, for darkness, for absence of light, and that his phrase 'light and night' is equivalent to light and darkness (absence of light, shadow). So light and night as the two basic categories of the illusory world of the mortals is a world of the play of lights and shadows (as they play, paradigmatically, on the Moon). Light and night are unreal appearances since reality = (dark and heavy) matter. The unrecognized (νύκτ' ἀδαῆ B8: 59) part of the Moon is recognized by Parmenides as heavy matter. See also Thales (DK 11A5 = Herodotus I.74), where νύξ is an eclipse.

11 G. S. Kirk, J. E. Raven, and M. Schofield, *The Presocratic Philosophers*, 2nd edn, Cambridge, 1983, p. 261.

12 The crucial translation is 'much-erring sense organs'; this is fully justified in view of the examples given by Aristotle, *De Part. Animal*. 1.645b36–646a1. I quote from the Loeb translation: 'Nose, Eye, Face; each of these is named a "limb" (μέλος).' In modernized terms the biochemical state (the 'mixture') which characterizes the sense organs at any one time also determines the state of the intellect, of our knowledge, and of our thought. We just think as the majority of our chemicals command! This describes and ridicules sensualism – the theory that Parmenides hates and of which he is highly contemptuous.

13 Some scholars believe that the relationship of the two parts of Parmenides' poem cannot be that between an explanatory theory of the hidden reality and the phenomenal appearances of this reality for the following reason: the goddess, so they say, declares that the human opinions (or the conjectures), which she intends to develop in Part 2, [are just] positively deceitful lies (ἀπατηλὸν); and this is a relation that is totally different from the one I have described in the text as being more or less traditional. I think myself that the relation between the two parts does transcend drastically the 'traditional [style]', but not for the reason given by those scholars; first, I do not think that ἀπατηλὸν must have so radical a meaning; it could mean 'fallible', or 'non-reliable'. And if not – considering the fact that it is the only word that gives this very radical meaning, it could be emended by changing it to ἀπάτητον, which is used by Democritus (B131) in a perfectly harmless sense. (See further the addendum to this essay.) Parmenides (B8: 52) would then merely claim *novelty* for Part 2 (in agreement with Plutarch). My own reason for claiming that the relation between the two parts of the poem breaks with the tradition is not any shocking falsity of Part 2 but the goddess's simply outrageous claim to truth of Part 1.

14 Strangely enough, precisely this refutation plays its role anew today. I am quoting from a paper by Julian B. Barbour, 'Maximal Variety as a New Fundamental Principle of Dynamics', *Foundations of Physics*, 19, No. 9, 1989, p. 1052: 'Then there is the problem of reconciling quantum mechanics with Einstein's theory of gravitation. Quantization of that theory in the case of a spatially closed universe by the standard methods leads to a "wave function of the universe" that appears to be completely static. Nothing happens at all – there is a complete Parmenidean stasis, in flagrant contradiction of the evidence of our senses.'

15 Or in German translation, where the traditional genders of gods relating to the Sun and the Moon have been inverted to 'Mondgöttin und Sonnengott':

> Leuchtend bei Nacht
> Von dem Licht, das er schenkt:
> So umirrt Sie die Erde.
> Immerzu blickt sie, gebannt,
> Hin auf den strahlenden Gott.

Comments. (1) *Allotrios, alienus* is usually translated by 'alien'. However, its meaning may be explained as 'the opposite of *oikeios*,' i.e. 'homely', 'domestic'. So it may merely mean 'not coming from home' and may not always contain the element of hostility which the English 'alien' seems to carry with it. In the *Odyssey* 17.452, it even characterizes a well-meant gift – although, admittedly, one that was not paid for by the giver! In the present case, Selene is longing for the light that comes to her from her beloved Helios, and *allotrion* merely indicates that her light is *not* produced by herself (*not* homemade!). Since it is a most welcome gift, translating 'with an alien light' would not be quite adequate. (2) My German version retains in its rhythm (although not in its division into five lines instead of two) that of a traditional German elegiac couplet (*Distichon*). In spite of using verse, I have retained that rhythm also in my English version.

ADDENDUM
WITH A NOTE ON A POSSIBLE EMENDATION
AFFECTING THE RELATION BETWEEN
THE TWO PARTS OF PARMENIDES' POEM*

Guthrie, in his brilliant *History of Greek Philosophy*, 1965, vol. 2, p. 4, sees the central problem 'of interpreting Parmenides' quite differently: while the goddess claims Part 1 to be demonstrably true, she claims 'no true reliance' or 'no true certainty' for Part 2. This might make it still possible to regard Part 2 as describing a world of appearance rather than of illusion, of human conjecture or opinion. Yet our text asserts more than the uncertain, hypothetical character of Part 2: it asserts 'unambiguously' (as Guthrie himself says[1]) that the *doxai* of Part 2 are false and even fraudulent.

* Dedicated to my assistant Melitta and her husband Raymond Mew. I am indebted to my friends Ernst Gombrich and Irene Papadaki for having discussed with me the suggestions put forward in the note to this addendum.

'Here is the crux' (Guthrie[2]): why should the goddess at all bother to report brilliant but definitely false and even 'fraudulent' theories? This is the 'central problem' according to Guthrie;[3] in my list of three problems, it corresponds to my third problem.

But it is perhaps not well known to everybody that this famous crux depends upon one single word only: the word *apatēlon* ('fraudulent' or 'deceitful') in B8: 52. There is no other word in our text that could not be interpreted in keeping with the view that the world of Part 2, the Way of Human Opinion, is not a world of uncertain and undemonstrable but serious and possibly true conjectures, the world of Parmenides' own discoveries and conjectures.

Thus if this one word, *apatēlon*, could be interpreted differently, or replaced by another, the relation of the two worlds could be interpreted differently from the way in which it is interpreted above: it would make the text open to an interpretation of reality and appearance in what I call the 'traditional style' and, indeed, closely analogous to Kant.

Now, I think the word can be replaced by a very similar one, *apatēton*, which differs from *apatēlon* only by one letter (and by accents which, however, were not yet in use in Parmenidean times). The word *apatēton* means 'untrodden' or 'very new', 'unusual' or 'so far unused', and so could be, indirectly, Parmenides' claim that his conjectural theory is new. This would be in keeping with the passage from Plutarch's *Moralia* (cited above) and would completely destroy Burnet's (not too satisfactory) position towards my second problem; and it would solve Guthrie's problem. It could be made to cohere with my first central problem and its solution; but it would kill my second problem, and with it, some of the interest of my solution of the first problem.

On the other hand, my two central problems and their solution make the proposed amendment redundant. In either case we can agree with Simplicius, who regards Part 1 'as an account of the intelligible world' and Part 2 'as a description of the sensible';[4] a view condemned by Burnet as an unacceptable 'anachronism'.

Note

The following are six arguments in favour of the proposed emendation of ἀπατηλὸν ('deceitful') to ἀπάτητον ('untrodden' or 'very new' or 'so far unused' or 'unusual': 'unprecedented').

(1) The word proposed occurs in Democritus B131. (Its sense, as here required, is indeed explained by him or by Hesychius: see (6) below.)
(2) A similar usage is found in Parmenides, B1: 27 (ἀνθρώπων ἐκτὸς πάτου).
(3) The metaphor of a trodden or untrodden path or way is always in the

mind of Parmenides, and πάτος, as here cited in (2), is used by him as a synonym of ὁδός – one of the words most frequently used in Parmenides' known fragments.

(4) So the *idea* (ἀ-πάτητος) was present in his mind and, in view of Democritus' usage (and explanation) of the word, we can assume that Parmenides also knew the *word*. (Indeed, he may have coined it.)

(5) The proposed emendation fits the text very well; it fits the sometimes slightly boastful style of the goddess. Moreover, we may assume that Parmenides wanted to expound to his readers his empirical hypotheses: the spherical shape of the Moon and its illumination by the Sun; perhaps the spherical shape of the Earth; and – considering Plutarch's praise quoted in DK 28B10 – very much more; probably also that the tracks (or 'rings' or 'bands') described by the planets on the background of the fixed stars are 'crossing' each other. If so, then no doubt he also wanted to claim novelty for his discoveries; and this is the obvious and fitting place for such a claim. (The claim is foreshadowed in B1: 31f.)

(6) The mistake – if any – of the copyist might have arisen as follows. In the absence of accents (which we may assume), the copyist may have read απατητον with the stress on the last syllable, and may have interpreted it to mean the same as ἀπατητικὸν or ἀπατηλὸν ('fraudulent', 'deceitful'), and he may therefore have assumed that it should better be corrected to ἀπατηλὸν. For the word ἀπάτητον (and even πατητόν) seems to be rarely used, which may have been why the lexicographer Hesychius (and perhaps Democritus himself) explained its meaning: the copyist may not have known the word.

These are my arguments in support of the proposed emendation.

I may perhaps add a somewhat romantic speculation.

The comparative lack of interest in Parmenides' Part 2 may well be due to the word ἀπατηλὸν; for if the goddess's words are admittedly fraudulent or deceitful, why bother with what she says in this part? The mistake (if any) in copying must have been made very early.[5] I like to think that it was commented on by Democritus (who might have received through Leucippus a better text than the texts available at Athens or at Samos), and that Hesychius' citation is the result of this comment.

While the emendation here proposed is designed to solve an awkward problem, it does not even touch on the content of Part 1 and Part 2. I am one of those who look upon the Presocratics as cosmologists; and I interpret both parts of Parmenides' poem as an attempt to solve cosmological problems, foremost the problem of change. Part 1 denies the ultimate reality of change. Part 2 describes cosmological change, similar to Plato's cave, as a play of shadows as practised by children in the days before television: a play of 'light' and 'night' upon the three-dimensional block of unchanging reality. It contains a conjectural cosmology, claimed to be the best (B1: 31f.), in the form of an explanation of how and why men have accepted the world of appearance, of unreal waxing and waning, of birth and death.

This interpretation suggests that the original discovery that inspired Parmenides' poem was his explanatory theory of the waxing and waning of the Moon (and perhaps also of her eclipses) as mere appearances, as unreal, and as due to a play of shadows – 'light and night' – upon an unchanging three-dimensional sphere;[6] a discovery that Part 2 generalizes to *all* change.[7] Thus a proper understanding of Part 1 is impossible without Part 2. For in the presence of Part 2, the existence of an ultimate reality is *needed*: both as an unchanging screen for the display of 'light and night' and as the ultimate limit to the explanatory regress of the (changing or changeable) appearances. It is clear that this reality had to be established 'by reason' or 'by argument'[8] alone, rejecting any appeal to perception or to appearances; not even to those of the moon, now established as an invariant well-rounded sphere,[9] neither waxing nor waning – yet moving, and therefore not truly real.

Notes

1 W. K. C. Guthrie, *A History of Greek Philosophy*, vol. 2, Cambridge, 1965, p. 4.
2 Ibid., p. 6.
3 Ibid., p. 4.
4 John Burnet, *Early Greek Philosophy*, 2nd edn, London, 1908, pp. 208f.; 3rd edn, London, 1920, and 4th edn, London, 1930, pp. 182f. I regard Simplicius' view as inescapable, and I translate fragment B16 accordingly.
5 At any rate before Melissus and Empedocles, DK 31B17: 26.
6 DK 28B14, 15, 21.
7 B10, B8: 50, 8: 55ff., B9.
8 B7: 5.
9 B10: 4.

ESSAY 5

CAN THE MOON THROW LIGHT ON PARMENIDES' WAYS? (1988)

Parmenides' great poem, in which he expounds his view of the world, consists of a kind of prologue or introduction and two main parts, usually called 'the Way of Truth' and 'the Way of Opinion'. In the prologue we learn how Parmenides meets the goddess and that she promises to reveal everything to him: both the 'well-rounded and unshakably certain truth' and the 'opinions of the mortals, which are not true' (B1: 29–30).

1 The problem

The problem in the interpretation of Parmenides' poem to which I here offer a conjectural solution is the following: why, after telling us what the real world is like *in truth*, and after warning us stongly against being misled by the human opinions of appearances, does Parmenides (or the goddess) proceed to describe, at great length, what it is like in *appearance*?

One theory that underlies Parmenides' Two Ways is the traditional view: *only the Gods know. We mortals can only guess.* This is the theory of the fallibility of human opinion. We find it in Homer, in Hesiod, in Heraclitus (B82, 83), Alcmaeon (B1), Xenophanes (B18). So this view of Parmenides is not surprising. What is surprising in Parmenides is the view that *divine knowledge of reality is rational and therefore truthful*, while *human opinion of appearance is based upon our senses, which are not only unreliable but totally misleading*.

Or in other words: the real world of the gods is almost totally different from the world that appears to mortal men.

In order to make our problem clear, it should be explained that in the Way of Truth Parmenides not only describes a reality – a real world – that is obviously totally different from the world we know, but he insists on this difference; moreover, he argues strongly for reason and against the senses.

This essay is dedicated to the memory of my dear wife Hennie. It was written during the summer of 1988 as the first of several renewed attemps at solving the riddle of Parmenides' poem.

97

The defective Way of Opinion describes a world that somehow resembles the world of the Milesian philosophers, and the world of the Pythagoreans. So our problem can be put in the following way:

Why does Parmenides (or the goddess) add a fragmentary second part, a cosmology on more or less traditional lines, to the first part's utterly novel description of reality, which, the goddess says, is the only true one?

2 The facts

It cannot be denied that in his poem Parmenides (the goddess) teaches a Way of Truth and a Way of Opinion. Both of them state cosmologies. The first is said to be *true*; the second is said to be *false*, yet believed by the mortals.

It cannot be denied that – since the mortals believe the False Way (which penetrates everything; B1: 32): it *appears* to them to be true – perhaps Parmenides was (or is) even himself among these mortals.

So it cannot be denied that Parmenides distinguishes, like Kant and Schopenhauer, a *world of reality* from a *world of appearances* (with Parmenides' well-rounded globe corresponding to Kant's 'Thing in itself' or Schopenhauer's Will).

3 The paradox

I agree with John Burnet that these facts are unacceptably paradoxical. They are, as Burnet says, paradoxical because they constitute a sheer impossible anachronism.[1] It is impossible to see the Kant–Schopenhauer distinction of 'Thing in itself', of noumenon and phenomenon, occurring to any philosopher before Plato, and almost impossible to see it occurring before Descartes, Malebranche, Spinoza, or Leibniz, and Locke, Berkeley, or Hume. Indeed, Burnet is right, in my opinion, to stress the historical impossibility that such a thought may have occurred to a philosopher of the early fifth century BC.

However, the paradox remains, since Burnet has no convincing explanation to offer. All he does is to stress that Parmenides clearly says that the Way of Truth (hereinafter called 'Part 1') is alone *true* – and definitely true – and the Way of Delusive Opinion (hereinafter called 'Part 2') is definitely *false*, and not, perhaps, a tentative hypothesis. But he cannot deny that Parmenides (or the goddess) also says that it is, wrongly, believed to be true; and therefore is something like a Kantian or Schopenhauerian 'phenomenon', or 'appearance', in contrast to the 'noumenon'. And it must be said that the view that good, and even the best, hypotheses of science are just such false appearances has been held by many, both scientists and philosophers. So Burnet's view does not at all soften the historical paradox

– the historical incredibility that he constantly denounces (for example in his criticism of Theodor Gomperz[2]).

Burnet seems to believe that the problem may be solved by interpreting the content of Part 2 as attributed to some philosopher whom Parmenides wishes to oppose; and he gives good reasons for choosing the Pythagoreans for this role. But Burnet is mistaken if he thinks that this solves the problem, for Parmenides and the goddess describe Part 2 explicitly (I use Burnet's own translation) as 'the beliefs of mortals' ('Henceforward learn the beliefs of mortals'), and describe it as a world of appearances, as explained above. Although Burnet's theory, that Part 2 is an attack on Pythagoreanism, has its merits, it seems to clash with Plutarch's testimony,[3] which can only have referred to Part 2's delusive opinions; for Plutarch praises Parmenides himself as a cosmologist and scientist.

4   Clarification of the solution to the problem

The general problem in the interpretation of Parmenides' poem is, as stated in Section 1 above, the problem of the relationship of the two parts of the poem. Burnet's unsolved paradox is only part of this problem: when he proposes that Parmenides attacks an opponent in Part 2, then he unconsciously addresses himself to a different aspect of the problem. His solution is, as such, not implausible, despite Plutarch's quoted remark, for Plutarch may, of course, be mistaken in ascribing the ideas of Part 2 to Parmenides himself.

The general problem of the relation between the two parts of Parmenides' poem contains (apart from Burnet's historical paradox) the following question: *Why does the goddess expound Part 2 at all, stressing that it is mistaken?*

Furthermore, the two parts are strongly opposed to each other: while the teaching of Part 1 is demonstrably true, there is 'no true reliance' or 'no true certainty' in Part 2. Yet our accepted text asserts more than the uncertain, hypothetical character of Part 2: it asserts 'unambiguously', as Guthrie stresses, that the *doxai* of Part 2 are false. Our 'central problem' may therefore, according to Guthrie,[4] be formulated this way: *Why should the goddess bother at all to report brilliant but definitely false theories?*

Until recently I thought that the best answer to Guthrie's central problem was: 'Because Part 2 contained Parmenides' own and most brilliant cosmological discoveries, made, perhaps, before his conversion to Part 1, and not to be simply discarded even if found to be untrue'.

But I was never quite satisfied with this answer. And I am now less satisfied with the answer than I was before, because of the dependence of the problem on one single word, ἀπατηλόν (deceitful), in DK 28B8: 52. If this word is omitted from our text or, if possible, replaced by some fitting phrase, then Guthrie's central problem disappears completely. In particular, if the word ἀπατηλὸν ('deceitful') is replaced by the less condemnatory ἀπάτητον (meaning 'untrodden' or 'very new' or 'so far unused' or 'unusual'[5]), then the problem of the relationship between Parts 1 and 2 becomes, essentially, that of the relationship between *knowledge*, as possessed by the gods, and *opinion or conjecture*, as attainable by mortal men; a relationship familiar for example from Xenophanes, even though it is more sharply elaborated in Parmenides than elsewhere. 'Certain truth' or 'true certainty' (Xenophanes DK B34: 1: σαφὲς; Parmenides DK 28B1: 30: πίστις ἀληθής) is beyond us – unless revealed by a goddess: 'For all [our human knowledge] is but a woven web of guesses', of conjectures, of hypotheses.[6]

But the emendation can be done without. We can solve both Burnet's and Guthrie's and, indeed, all the great difficulties of understanding Parmenides' Two Ways by one fundamental historical hypothesis: that Parmenides, deeply interested in cosmology, and possibly still himself a Pythagorean, discovered that the waxing and waning of the Moon was only an appearance, a delusion, and that the Moon was an unchanging well-rounded globe all the time.

Only *this* was true: *change could be an illusion!*

What deceives us, what makes it *appear* that the moon changes? Light and night!

And does it deceive us only once, or several times, or sometimes? No: the unchanging, well-rounded block is *always* the same; and since the deception is again and again renewed in what appears to be the flow of time, time must also be deception, in its turn. For although time may appear to us to flow, it obviously never comes or goes.

So all reality, all being, the All, the real world is unchanging: the firm, the lasting, the everlasting, hard firm matter. But what about appearance? It is unreal, it is nothing: it is *no thing*. It is, like a shadow, both light and night: a mere contrast, rather than a thing. And indeed, the waxing and waning of the Moon is exactly a shadow – a play of shadows of 'light and night', as Parmenides says again and again. Everybody knows that a shadow is unreal, deceptive, untrue. And if this is what a shadow is, then light must also be untrue.

But the unchanging well-rounded block of the Moon is real. It is on its surface that the dance of the shadows plays its unreal game. This also must hold for the universe, for the solid, unchanging firmament, for the adamantine vault of heaven. (One of Parmenides' successors, Empedocles, DK A51, speaks of στερέμνιον . . . οὐρανόν, the solid Ouranos.) This is the well-rounded reality that in itself knows no colours, colour being the unreal, changing result of light and night (as Goethe later taught). So the well-rounded block universe – the 'Thing in itself' – must be like the Moon, the screen upon which the shadows play, upon which the unreal dance of light and night and the colour are projected. The screen itself must be real: lightless and colourless like the real Moon itself. Clearly, reality – the screen – must come first; the unreal second.

Thus the goddess's revelation of the Way of Truth must come first, and the Way of Delusive Opinion must come second, both for logical and for cosmological (physical) reasons: Parmenides *cannot* and must not keep to the order of discovery. He cannot disclose the order of discovery, the move from the falsity of the old to the truth of the new theory: there is no logical path from the refutation of an illusion, of a false view – such as the waxing and waning of the Moon – to the revelation of the truth, of a true theory. There exists no logical bridge leading to the truth from the empirical refutation. Indeed, as he may himself have seen, this is so in every discovery: the new insight is a gift, a revelation from the gods. (It is, for this very reason, only a hypothesis, as Xenophanes boldly admitted in DK B34; but in this admission he was unique among the great discoverers.)

5   Parmenides' proof

It is a frequent experience to find great discoveries interpreted by their discoverers to have a far wider scope than they actually have. My hypothesis is that Parmenides' great discovery of the cause of the phases of the Moon shocked and overwhelmed its initiator, who extended it to the entire cosmos. There is nothing unlikely in such a story.

But arguing for his tremendous new message on empirical grounds was not possible for Parmenides. An *a priori* argument had to be found – a solid proof:

(1) Only what is, is.
(2) The nothing cannot be.
(3) There is no empty space.
(4) The world is full.
(5) Motion and change (which is a kind of motion) are impossible:
(6) There is no room for motion, and thus for change, if the world is full.

This is the goddess's proof: as a proof it is infallible and thus divine. If we look at it as a human achievement, it is staggering. It derives *a priori* the great empirical discovery of the unmoving Moon, and generalizes it. So this discovery is explained, and with it the cosmos! Even for us it is almost as difficult to find a flaw in Parmenides' proof as it is to find a flaw in Zeno's supporting proofs.

Note that Parmenides *had* to give a proof, a compelling logical proof. Without it, his doctrine of the impossibility of change would have been a stillborn paradox. No doubt, he needed it for himself, to convince himself: he had himself been one of the mortals who believed in the reality of the changing world, changing in the light and even in the night.

And note especially that Parmenides' proof is a refutation. It is an *elenchus* (πολύδηριν ἔλεγχον), an obviously much-contested refutation; it is the refutation of the doctrine of the existence of change. Zeno's proofs and Gorgias' proofs are also refutations. And so are most (all?) early mathematical proofs (for example, that of the irrationality of √2), for they are indirect: the *elenchus* rules supreme in the field of the logic of demonstration, or proof. It still rules supreme with Socrates and, I think, with Plato. And indeed the *reductio ad absurdum* is a method of almost absolute proof, in contrast to the axiomatic method, which works with unproved assumptions. And it is in contrast to Aristotle's use of syllogisms, that is, derivations, as proofs – an attempt which (as argued in the Introduction to this volume) drove him to invent induction and which, in despair, he fathered on Socrates because Socrates had used examples – though only for disproof, for the Socratic *elenchus*. In their use of disproof, of refutation, lies in my opinion at least part of the superiority of the Presocratics over Aristotle, though he was a great physicist and an even greater biologist.

6 Parmenides' rationalist *elenchus*

Some enemies of rationalism have tried to claim Parmenides as one of their own. This happened especially in German philosophy (Heidegger is, of course, the leading figure of this group), but also in Anglo-Saxon philosophy, usually by way of interpreting Parmenides as a philosopher of language, more or less in Wittgenstein's manner.

The truth is very different: the Parmenides we know, the Parmenides of the Two Ways, is one of the most radical rationalists who has ever produced a theory of knowledge. His radical brand of rationalism might be described as intellectualism, or even as logicism. He had to adopt this attitude almost by necessity, once he generalized his rejection of the sense-given, of observation, from the Moon to the universe; that is, to everything.

Parmenides' version of rationalism is very simple: if you wish to find the truth, there is only one way: logical proof. In this he is, of course, mistaken; but he is not wholly mistaken, in so far as he applied a method of disproof, of refutation: the *reductio ad absurdum*. Moreover, in rejecting the method of sense-observation, he showed that it led to inner contradictions. (The standard example according to my historical hypothesis would be this: the Moon may be *seen* to wax and to wane; but once you have found that it is the play of light and night upon her surface that produces this deception, then you can even *see* sometimes only with difficulty, her true, well-rounded and existing, though unlit, shape.)

Among the preserved fragments of Part 1, DK B7 shows clearly his enmity towards sense-data empiricism and his inclination towards rationalism. My translation, the last line of which (except for the word 'disproof') I have added to make clearer what is being said, runs like this:

102

Never shall it prevail that things that are not are existing.
Keep back your thought from this way of inquiry; don't let experience,
Much-tried highways, constrain you; and do not let wander your blinded
Eye, or your deafened ear, or even your tongue, along this way!
But by reason alone decide on the often-contested
Argument that I have here expounded to you as disproof.

It is also quite clear that Parmenides' attack on theoreticians of knowledge (who advocate 'the Second Way of discovery') is directed against the sense-data empiricists: they are (B6: 5) 'double headed', that is, bound to contradict themselves (lines 6 to end).

But a most important fragment, DK B16, is usually mistranslated and misunderstood, except possibly by Karl Reinhardt, who does not give a translation but refers to it as full of scorn and irony.[7] Indeed, it is, in my opinion, a scathing parody of the empiricists, who assert that 'Nothing is in our intellect that was not previously in our senses.' My own translation is not only very close to the text, but gives a kind of commentary to it:

What is, at any one time, in the much-erring sense organs' mixture,
That seems genuine knowledge to men. For they take as the same thing
Man's intellecual mind, and his sense organs' varying nature.
'Thought' they call what in this muddle prevails, in each man and all.

Incidentally, this fragment is usually attributed to Part 2 of the poem. I do not deny that it may have belonged there, but I think it more probable that it belonged to an explicit attack on empiricism which once may have found its place somewhere near fragment 6 – perhaps between B6 and B7. (Its present place in Part 2 is due, I think, to its misinterpretation as a serious pro-empiricist passage which one could put, of course, only into the false Part 2.)

Parmenides' greatest rationalist *elenchus* – the refutation of the reality of motion – made a devastating impression. Zeno, Anaxagoras, Empedocles, the Sophists, even Socrates, and obviously Plato are some of the witnesses to its influence. But his greatest followers and opponents are clearly Leucippus and Democritus, the creators of atomism, who inverted his *elenchus* to give an empirical refutation of his cosmology:

> *There is movement.*
Thus: The world is *not* full.
There *is* empty space.
The nothing, the void, does exist.
Thus: The world consists of the existing,
the hard and full, *and* of the void:
Of '*atoms and the void*'.

103

It is dualistic; and it can create all kinds of new things from the atoms. Light may be real: there may be light atoms (photons); night may be simply the absence of light.

This was not only the result of an empirical refutation of Parmenides' theory: it used Parmenides' theory for a stepwise formulation and modification of new theories about the world. The presence of Parmenides' apparently absurd theory, of a theory one can refute, modify, and reevaluate, was of immeasurable use. Indeed, there is no other heuristic. Parmenides' cosmological poem is thus of crucial importance in our history. And his work, instead of being mysterious, misconstrued, and historically impossible, appears as lucid, beautiful and historically fully understandable.

I personally am indebted to him for giving me the infinite pleasure of knowing of Selene's longing for Helios (DK B14–15):

> Bright in the night, with an alien light,
> Round the Earth she is drifting.
> Always she wistfully looks
> Out for the rays of the Sun.

Notes

1 J. Burnet, *Early Greek Philosophy*, 4th edn, London, 1930, pp. 182f.

2 For Burnet's criticism of Th. Gomperz's view on Parmenides, see J. Burnet, *Early Greek Philosophy*, 2nd edn, London, 1908, pp. 208f.

3 DK 28B10. See also Plutarch, *Adv. Colotem*, 1114b–c: 'Thus he [Parmenides] has much to say about earth, heaven, sun, moon, and stars, and has recounted the genesis of man; and for an ancient natural philosopher – who has put together a book of his own, and is not pulling apart the book of another – he has left nothing of real importance unsaid.' (Translated by B. Einarson and P. H. de Lacy, *Plutarch's Moralia*, vol. XIV, London, 1967, pp. 230f.)

4 W. K. C. Guthrie, *A History of Greek Philosophy*, vol. 2, Cambridge, 1965, p. 4.

5 How can the adjective 'untrodden' apply to the order of words? The answer is implicit in a remark by Hermann Fränkel made in 'Studies in Parmenides', where he refers to Pindar (R. E. Allen and D. J. Furley, *Studies in Presocratic Philosophy*, vol. II, London, 1975, p. 2): 'the "path" . . . is at once the course of the song and the course of the ideas', and says that this holds, especially, for Parmenides.

6 Xenophanes, DK B34: 4. (Cp. Essay 2, Section 5.)

7 For details and criticism, see footnote 4 on pp. 408f. of *C. & R.* (I have improved upon the translation since writing this note, see Essay 3, above.)

ESSAY 6

THE WORLD OF PARMENIDES

Notes on Parmenides' poem and its origin in
early Greek cosmology

1   The significance of cosmology

Our Western civilization is a civilization based upon science. It is a
civilization based upon the science founded by Copernicus, Galileo,
Kepler, and Newton. But the science of Copernicus, Galileo, Kepler,
and Newton was the continuation of the cosmology of the Greeks.

It is therefore right to say that our Western civilization was founded by
the Greeks. It is from them too that we have inherited the ideas of truth,
of democracy, of justice, of humanity, and even of the brotherhood of men;
ideas which have become all-important in the political history of Western
civilization. We owe also to the Greeks our Western literature, and this
was, in the beginning, closely related to science and cosmology. Literature
and science both begin with story telling, with myth making, and especially with the making of cosmological myths.

I suggest that story telling or myth making is one of the earliest fruits
of the emergence of specifically human language.[1] Neither self-expression
nor communication is specific to or characteristic of human language: for
animals also express themselves, and communicate with other animals.
What animals appear to be unable to do, and what men can do with
the help of human language, is to tell stories; that is to say, to *describe*
states of affairs: human language can describe actual or possible situations,
actual or possible facts.[2]

This is of the utmost importance. The mere understanding of even the
simplest linguistic description of the simplest fact is an achievement of
the highest order, and it demands an effort of the imagination. Thus the
imagination is stimulated. This leads to creative and imaginative story
telling; of stories, perhaps, that provide an excuse for a failure, or of stories
that exaggerate some success in hunting.

Story telling, which seems to be a specifically human achievement,

*A Henry Dan Broadhead Memorial Lecture delivered at the University of Canterbury, Christchurch,
New Zealand, 7 May 1973.*

creates the problem of distinguishing between *true* and *false* stories. Thus the problem of truth emerges, and the idea of examining a report critically for its truth or falsity. I suggest that it is this critical examination that distinguishes science, which otherwise would consist of typically imaginative explanatory stories or myths.

According to this view, literature and science have a common origin; they both originate in the imaginative explanatory story, the imaginative explanatory myth. What distinguishes them is the predominant part played in science by criticism: by that kind of criticism that is dominated by the regulative idea of truth, by the idea of correspondence to the facts.

Amongst the most important myths are the cosmological myths; that is, the myths that explain to us the structure of the world we live in. It is the critical examination and revision of these cosmological myths that gave rise, in Greece, to early philosophy and to early science.

Like Greek tragedy, in which Broadhead was so intensely interested, Greek cosmological myths and, with them, early Greek science take their themes and their problems from those worlds of thought that were first articulated in the imaginative poetry of Homer and of Hesiod.

To put this in a challenging but hardly exaggerated way: there are just two or three steps that lead from Homer to the early Presocratic philosophers and cosmologists: to Thales, Anaximander, Xenophanes, Heraclitus, and Parmenides, and then on to Democritus, Plato, Euclid, Archimedes, and Aristarchus. And from Euclid, Archimedes, and Aristarchus to Copernicus, Kepler, Newton, and Einstein, there are again only a few steps. So it may be said that Newton and Einstein showed, after almost 3,000 years, that the imaginative dreams of the great makers of myths at the dawn of our civilization were steps towards the truth.

I may add to this that I regard this development as valuable in itself: as valuable not only because it liberates our minds from dogmas and prejudices, but also because it opens new worlds to us – a new reality behind the world of appearances. This I regard as more important than all technological applications.

But these are just generalities. I now come to particulars.

2 The discovery of the Earth and the sky

Cosmology in its narrower sense consists of speculative theories that describe the structure or the ground-plan of the universe. Cosmology in its wider sense also embraces cosmogony, that is to say, speculations about the creation, the origin, and the evolution of the universe. As could be expected, cosmogony plays an important role in early cosmological speculations. Yet cosmogony plays an almost equally important role in twentieth-century cosmology, thanks to the discovery that our universe is not static but expanding and evolving.

There is a striking similarity between the creation myths of the Egyptians, the Mesopotamians, the Greeks, and the Maoris. But there are also some unexpected differences. For while in their creation myths, the Greeks and (according to E. B. Tylor) the Maoris personify the Earth as a goddess, and the sky or the heavens as a god, the ancient Egyptians attributed the opposite sexes to their personifications of the Earth and the sky: the Egyptian myth speaks of the Earth god Geb and the sky goddess Nūt.[3] This inversion of sex is surprising, as the feminine gender for the Earth is suggested by the Earth's bringing forth fruit – a function just as important in Egypt as anywhere else. However, we should perhaps not be unduly surprised, since differences in the attribution of gender are not so rare. In German, for example, as opposed to many other Indo-Germanic languages, the Sun is feminine, and the Moon masculine.

But apart from such variations, some of the stories of Earth and sky are strikingly similar, especially the stories of the Greeks and the Maoris. Thus in the creation myth of Hesiod's *Theogony* we are told[4] how the sky god Ouranos and the Earth goddess Gaia lay locked in an embrace until Gaia's son Chronos forced them apart, thereby creating the gap between the Earth and the sky. This story is surprisingly similar to a creation myth of the Maoris which (according to Tylor[5]) was first written down in the Maori language by Sir George Grey when he was Governor General of New Zealand more than a century ago. This myth is perhaps not as widely known as it deserves to be. It is the story of 'The Children of Heaven and Earth'[6]: 'From Rangi, the Heaven, and Papa, the Earth', the story goes,

> sprang all . . . things, but sky and earth clave together [as in Hesiod] . . . till at last their children took counsel whether they should rend apart their parents or slay them. Then Tane-mahuta, father of forests, said to his five great brethren, 'It is better to rend them apart, and to let the heaven stand far above us, and the earth lie under our feet. Let the sky become a stranger to us, but the earth remain close to us as our nursing mother.'

The continuation of the story is interesting and beautiful; and I think it is superior in all its details to Hesiod's more famous story.

I suggest that what is important about these myths for the further development of a more critical cosmology is the personification of Earth and sky, and the giving of personal names to them. This made it possible later to identify the Earth as a physical body endowed with a definite shape, and it led to the theory of the sky as a hollow, spherical crystal-like body, rotating round the Earth. These steps are far from obvious, and both are most important for the development of cosmology. It is, more especially, far from obvious that the Earth is a physical body of definite shape –

for example, shaped like a disc, as Anaximander said, or, in a step later taken by Parmenides, shaped like a spherical ball. For even in our own day the term 'earth' denotes not only a planet – a physical body – but also the ground under our feet; the land that produces crops; and a muddy kind of material, sometimes like clay, but becoming crumbly when dry. The first step towards viewing the whole Earth as a physical body was taken by the important creation myths that personified it as a goddess.

What is so decisive about this step is the personification, or the giving of a name. It is this that creates an object for further speculation,[7] and ultimately – in Greece – for critical examination. In ancient Egypt and the Near East, this last step does not seem to have been taken. John A. Wilson says repeatedly that the various Egyptian creation myths contradicted each other but that this did not, apparently, bother the ancient Egyptians. 'The Egyptian', he writes, 'accepted various myths and discarded none of them.' And he points out that conflicting stories can be found in peaceful coexistence in one and the same ancient document or inscription.[8]

In Greece we find conflicting stories too, but they belong to different writers and usually to different times. One of the earliest Greek prose writers, Pherecydes of Syros, who is reported to have lived at about 550 BC and is now usually counted among the Presocratic philosophers, wrote a story of the marriage of Earth and sky closely similar to Hesiod's, yet contradicting Hesiod in certain details. 'The gods Zas and Chronos and Chthoniē were for ever', he writes, using the less ordinary name 'Zas' for the sky god Zeus and 'Chthoniē' for the Earth goddess Gaia or Gē, and he continues: 'But Chthoniē was given the name of Gē because Zas gave her the Earth as a gift of honour.' After that, Zas the sky god makes Gē another gift: he gives her as a wedding present a 'wide and beautiful' heavenly cloak, which has sometimes been interpreted as the sky that encompasses the Earth.[9] What is of special interest here is the partial separation between the *personal deities* of the sky and the Earth and the *objects* sky – perhaps represented by the cloak spangled with starry jewels – and earth, which *belong to* the deities and are also *personified by* the deities.

Here we have what may be described as one of the earliest cosmological models: the Earth is a physical object that may become a divine wedding gift; and so may be the sparkling sky, the heavenly cloak or tent,[10] which envelops the Earth.

But a different and in some respects even richer cosmological model can be found, much earlier, in Homer's *Iliad* and in Hesiod's *Theogony*. In book 8 of the *Iliad*[11] we hear how Zeus threatens to throw any disobedient and meddling Olympian god into the deepest pit of Tartarus; and we learn that the deepest pit of Tartarus is as far below Hades as the sky is above the Earth.

This picture of the Earth poised in the middle between the heavens and deepest Tartarus is clarified and elaborated in Hesiod's *Theogony*, where it is said[12] that 'the distance between Heaven and Earth is equal to that between Earth and Tartarus; for an anvil of bronze would take nine days to fall through either space'. This is an estimate of the immensity of the gap between Heaven and Earth; and it also suggests a model with the Earth poised midway between sky and counter-sky.

It will be clear from all this that what we are facing in these stories are theories designed to explain the structure of the universe; and the theory that the distance from Heaven to Earth is equal to the distance from the Earth to the deepest pit of Tartarus can hardly be interpreted in any other way than as the theory that to the hollow vault of the heavens we see spanned above our Earth there corresponds another hollow hemisphere below the Earth; and that these two hemispheres complement each other, forming one complete hollow sphere. In the middle of this model, we have to assume the horizontal Earth, a flat cylindrical disc, dividing the hollow sphere into two hemispheres, one above and one below the Earth.

I regard the cosmological model described by Homer and Hesiod as of the utmost importance. I see it as one of the points from which modern physical science took its departure. Yet Homer and Hesiod were neither scientists nor even philosophers. They are rightly regarded as epic and religious poets.

3 The beginnings of philosophy

Philosophical speculation is assumed to have started with the Ionians: with Thales of Miletus, and his disciple and kinsman Anaximander. And indeed, something very new was added by these two. They added the critical approach or the critical tradition: the tradition of looking at an explanatory myth, such as the model of the universe due to Homer and Hesiod, with *critical* eyes. What early Greek philosophy or early Greek science adds to myth making is, I suggest, a new attitude: the *critical attitude*, the attitude of changing an explanatory myth in the light of criticism. It is this critical examination of explanatory stories, or explanatory theories, undertaken in the hope of getting nearer to the truth that I regard as characteristic of what may be somewhat loosely described as *rationality*. And it is this critical examination that explains the changes in these myths, and the surprisingly rapid development from myth making into what looks very much like science. The theories remain speculative; yet, under the influence of severe criticism, they show a greater and greater degree of truthlikeness. The only way in which this development can be explained is by the conjecture that the critical attitude became a tradition in the Ionian philosophical school.

Thales, accepted by Aristotle as the founder of Greek philosophy, was influenced, according to a suggestion of Aristotle's,[13] by another Homeric tradition: by the Homeric myth of Oceanus. The ocean was the first father of the gods,[14] and this, Aristotle says, is why the gods swear by water or, more precisely, by the river Styx.[15] For 'what is oldest', Aristotle writes, 'is most venerated; and the most venerated thing is that by which one swears'. Whether this explanation is right or not, we are told that according to Thales water is the origin of all things, and that the Earth floats on water.[16] As we know now, a similar explanatory myth was current in ancient Egypt.[17]

What interests me here is the theory that the Earth rests on water, or floats on water, *like a ship* – a theory that appears to have been designed to explain earthquakes, for example.[18]

Thales' theory that the Earth is supported by the ocean is interesting, and from a purely rational point of view it is open to serious immanent criticism: it leads to an infinite regress. For it leads to the question 'What is the ocean supported by?' As Aristotle says,[19] to propose such a theory 'is to forget that the same question may be raised about the water supporting the Earth as was raised [in the first instance] about the Earth itself'.

It seems probable that this is precisely the criticism that was originally raised against Thales' theory by Anaximander, the kinsman and disciple of Thales; and it also seems probable that the incredibly bold and important speculative theory of Anaximander was at least partly inspired by Homer's and Hesiod's model of the universe, which I mentioned before.

For we hear that Anaximander taught that 'The Earth is aloft. It is held up by nothing. It continues in its place because of its equal distance from all things.'[20]

Thus Anaximander belongs, as Aristotle puts it,[21] to 'those who say that the Earth remains at rest because of symmetry'. And Aristotle goes on to say 'For a thing established in the centre [of the universe], with sym-metrical relations to the extremes, has no reason to move up rather than down, or [perhaps] sideways. And since it cannot proceed in opposite directions at the same time, it is forced to remain at rest.'

This theory of an unsupported and freely suspended Earth, kept in its place by the equilibrium of forces that act on it at a distance, is breath-taking in its boldness. It is the first step in the direction of Newton's theory; and in my opinion one might say that without Anaximander's bold theory there might never have been the development of scientific thought that led to Newton, and beyond him. Yet this breathtaking step on the way to modern science was not based upon observation, as so many empiricists have it, but rather upon a critical revision of the mythical poetry of Homer's *Iliad* and of Hesiod's *Theogony* with their imaginative stories of the origin of the Earth and the intrigues of the Olympian gods.

It is very interesting that Anaximander's new model of the universe attributed a spherical shape to the heavens but not to the Earth. For according to Anaximander's theory, the shape of the Earth 'is that of a drum [or of a short cylinder] whose height is one-third of its width'.[22]

(One late report[23] attributes to Anaximander the doctrine that the shape of the Earth is spherical, but it is now generally accepted that this report is mistaken.) The great thinker who first pronounced the doctrine that the Earth had the shape not of a disc but of a sphere, who extended this hypothesis to the Moon, and perhaps to all heavenly bodies, was, it appears, Parmenides of Elea.[24]

4 Parmenides as a cosmologist

Thales and Anaximander lived in Miletus, an old Ionian colony in Asia Minor. Parmenides too was a citizen of a Greek colonial city state. His city, called Elea, was a fairly recently founded colony in southern Italy; it had been founded in 540 BC. Parmenides, who was probably born about 515 BC, seems to have belonged to the first generation born in this colony.

There are many problems about the early philosophers and cosmologists that are unsolved and apparently insoluble, owing to the fragmentary character of our sources; though there is of course always the remote possibility that new finds of papyrus may lead to new solutions. Parmenides, one of the greatest of the early giants of cosmology and philosophy, is at the same time one of those whose work is beset with problems that perhaps will never be solved. This is in spite of our possessing what may well have been a third or even half of the poem of Parmenides, his only work. For Parmenides did not write in prose, as did three of his immediate predecessors. Like Xenophanes, reputed to have been one of his teachers, Parmenides wrote in verse.

Parmenides' poem was written in imitation of the style of Homer and Hesiod, to whom his language often alludes. It described a revelation received by Parmenides from the goddess Dikē.[25] The revelation falls into two distinct parts, as the goddess makes clear. In the First part, the goddess reveals the truth – the whole truth – about what really exists: about the world of reality and of things as they are in themselves.[26] In the Second part, the goddess speaks about the world of appearances, about the illusive world of mortal man. She warns Parmenides at the beginning of the Second part that from now on her words will not be true, but deceitful or even fraudulent, though they will be more like the truth than are other accounts.

This division of Parmenides' revelation into two parts, usually differentiated as 'the Way of Truth' and 'the Way of Opinion', creates the first and greatest unsolved problem about the work of Parmenides. It is strange and difficult to explain why the revelation of the goddess should contain not only a true account of the universe, but also one that is untrue, as she explicitly says. This, I suggest, poses the central problem for the commentator – for those who wish to understand and, if possible, to elucidate Parmenides' work.

In order to understand this problem, we have to look at the two parts of the revelation.

The Second part, called the Way of Opinion (also often called the *doxa*), described by the goddess herself as untrue, and as containing deceitful words, gives an exposition of a cosmology and a cosmogony of the world that appears to mortal men. It is without doubt Parmenides' own highly original work. It is, however, on more or less traditional lines, even though it is emphatically dualistic: instead of assuming *one* building material, as did the Ionian philosophers, Parmenides stresses that the world of appearance, the world of constant change that is our ordinary world, the world of mortal men, needs a duality of building materials; that is to say, it needs two building materials, which are called 'light' and 'night'. As shown in Essay 4 above, he assumes that all things in this world of change are generated by a mixture of light and night. Out of this mixture arise the Earth and the heavenly bodies, supervised by the goddess of necessity, Anankē, who is said to 'steer everything'.[27]

This Second part of the revelation of the goddess, the Way of Opinion – of the habitual opinions of mortal men – is a cosmology more or less on the lines of Parmenides' predecessors, such as Anaximander, Heraclitus, and, perhaps, Pythagoras; yet it contains important original ideas, such as the doctrine of the spherical shape of the Earth,[28] and a theory of the Moon. But the First part of the revelation, the Way of Truth, is not only original, but revolutionary. It is of such originality and boldness that its theory has been described by some commentators as bordering on insanity, and it can be said to be unique in the history of philosophy.[29] Commentators have therefore held that the first part should not be regarded as belonging to the cosmological tradition,[30] and that it is not a cosmology. This seems to me mistaken. If the Second part, the Way of Opinion, is a cosmology, then so must be the First part; for clearly Parmenides looked upon these two parts of the revelation of the goddess as something like two opposites confronting each other. He regarded the First part as telling the truth about reality, about the real world order, the real cosmos; and the Second part as reporting deceptive opinions that describe the world of appearance – the world as it appears to mortal men.

Thus I submit that the Way of Truth contains a cosmology: it reveals the real truth about the real cosmos, the real order of the world, while the Way of Opinion describes what turns out to be a deceptive likeness of the truth, which falls far short of the truth, and thus may be described as an *illusion*.

The cosmology revealed in the First part, the Way of Truth, is simple but grim: it is a dead world, a universe without change or movement. This universe consists of one well-rounded spherical block that is completely homogeneous and structureless. It has no parts: it is one. It has no origin and thus no cosmogony, and it always was and is and always will be at rest, changeless and colourless.

The doctrine of the Way of Truth is utterly different from all pre-Parmenidean cosmologies and also from the cosmology of the Way of Opinion, with which Parmenides wants to contrast it. And yet, there are some aspects of Parmenides' Way of Truth that it shares with the cosmological tradition.

Parmenides was the first who consciously placed reality and appearance in opposition and consciously postulated one true unchanging reality behind the changing appearance. Yet his predecessors also operated implicitly with a very similar distinction, although it was less radical and perhaps not consciously held. Thales said that everything is *Water*; Anaximander said that the *archē*, the origin or principle of everything, is the *Apeiron*, a boundless indeterminate something; his successor Anaximenes said that the principle is *Air*; Heraclitus said that all things are *Fire*; and Pythagoras seems to have said that all things are Numbers and *perhaps* that the principle of the universe is the Number *One*.[31] In saying these things, each of them postulated a hidden true reality behind the appearances. This shows that Parmenides' Way of Truth follows the course of the cosmological tradition, though Parmenides was incomparably more radical than his predecessors.

A similar remark may be made about monism. All the cosmological predecessors of Parmenides just mentioned were monists,[32] with the possible exception of Pythagoras, who may have been a dualist.[33] Parmenides was a monist too, though he was much more radical in his monism than his predecessors; he seems to have accused them of a failure to realize that their systems were not genuinely monistic: that logically they were bound to operate with at least *two* principles – such as light and night – as does the goddess in the Way of Opinion.

A different and perhaps more important point is this. The goddess, by revealing the Way of Truth, offers implicitly a solution to the *problem of change*, a problem that was, also implicitly, encountered by Parmenides' predecessors, and a problem that may be described as the central problem of Heraclitus. The problem may be put as follows. '*How is change possible –* that is, logically possible? How can a thing change without losing its identity? If it remains the same, then it does not change; yet if it does not remain the same, then it is no longer that thing that has changed.'[34] Heraclitus' solution to this problem was that there are no stable things, and that all apparent things are in reality processes, like flames. In reality, there is *only* change. It appears that Parmenides regarded Heraclitus' solution as (logically) inadmissible, as did Aristotle at a later date. Parmenides' own solution, which is very radical and was revealed to him by the goddess in the Way of Truth, was that *change is an illusion*: in reality there is no change. Thus the Way of Truth solves an important problem arising out of the cosmological tradition. The theory of the unchanging block universe is a cosmology.

5 Parmenides was not an ontologist

Many philosophers talk nowadays about ontology, or the theory of being, and many philosophers attribute an ontology to Parmenides. I do not think that there is any such thing as ontology, or a theory of being, or that an ontology can be seriously attributed to Parmenides.

Admittedly, Parmenides attempted to *prove* a non-tautological statement such as 'there cannot be any change'; and admittedly, he tried to *prove* it by deriving it from a tautological statement such as 'only what is (exists), is (exists)'. But we know today that this attempt is impossible, and that a non-tautological statement cannot be validly derived from a tautological one. And so Parmenides' attempt could not succeed.

Thus if we call ontology a theory starting, like Parmenides' theory, from a tautological premise about existence, then such an ontology is an empty theory, from which nothing of interest can be derived: the impossibility of a non-empty ontology is the lesson I should want to learn from Parmenides' valiant attempt.

But even if one does not draw this conclusion, it seems to me clear that Parmenides was not really concerned with a verbal argument about *being*, but with the problem of *change*. And the problem of change is, clearly, not an ontological problem but a cosmological problem. We can explain Parmenides' problem as the problem of whether our world is a changing universe or a dead block universe. And this is not a problem of being, or of the word 'being', or of the copula 'is', but a problem about the character of our world, of our cosmos.

So Parmenides was, in my opinion, essentially a cosmologist; and so far as he made use of an 'ontological' argument, he used it only as an instrument in an attempt to obtain a cosmological result. That his instrument is powerless to achieve this, or any other result, only underlines the weakness of his 'ontology'. But even if an ontology could achieve something interesting, it would not be a valid reason to think that it is the central interest of Parmenides: it would still be for him merely an instrument for deriving cosmological results.

6 Parmenides' new theory of knowledge

As Charles Kahn has forcefully argued,[35] Parmenides regarded his own main achievement as the discovery of *a new way to knowledge*. In other words, he regarded his achievement as belonging to what is nowadays called the theory of knowledge, or epistemology. It may also be called the theory of method. The word 'method' comes, of course, from *methodos* (composed of *meta* and *hodos*) and means 'a way of search' or 'a way of inquiry', which is precisely what Parmenides means by *hodos*, a term that occurs in his poem at least nine times, and has suggested the names 'the Way of Truth' and 'the Way of Opinion' for the two parts of the revelation of the goddess.

What is the *problem of knowledge*, and how does it arise? It always arises from doubt, from uncertainty concerning one's own or other people's claims to knowledge: from the realization that these claims are not well founded; that they are based on insufficient reasons. It arises, in critically minded people, especially when there is a multiplicity of conflicting and competing claims to knowledge. As mentioned before, conflicting stories could exist in Egypt without the consciousness of a clash. But among the more critically minded Greek cosmologists, the multiplicity of conflicting and usually dogmatic claims of the different cosmological theorists led to the question: How can we decide between these conflicting stories? Which story should we prefer?

There are indications that Heraclitus was concerned with this problem of knowledge. He seems to have held that it is the personal quality of the authority who upholds a theory that is decisive: that only the gods, and next to them only the best men – the elite – can attain anything like genuine knowledge or wisdom, while most men are not only acting but also thinking 'as if they were asleep'.

But the most important theorist of knowledge before Parmenides was Xenophanes. Xenophanes questioned the popular theology (also questioned by Heraclitus). He pointed out that people create their gods in their own image; that they turn the gods into human beings;[36] and he developed his own monotheistic theory: an attempt to describe the one God as a unique being, utterly different from men and from the traditional gods – as a kind of unmoved mover, to use the terminology of Aristotle. At the same time he pointed out also that we cannot reach any certainty about the gods and the world, and that all our knowledge remains guesswork, including his own knowledge. To trace this important point I may perhaps repeat my translation of some of Xenophanes' verses.[37]

> But as for certain truth, no man has known it,
> Nor will he know it; neither of the gods,
> Nor yet of all the things of which I speak.
> And even if by chance he were to utter
> The final truth, he would himself not know it:
> For all is but a woven web of guesses.

The word that I have here translated by 'guesses' is the word *dokos*. This word is closely related to Parmenides' term *doxa*, which is usually translated by 'opinion' and may well be translated, even in the poem of Parmenides, as 'guesses' or 'guesswork'.

The verses quoted from Xenophanes are of great importance, not only for our topic, but for the whole history of philosophy. Personally I regard them very highly, for I see in them a kind of anticipation of my own theory of knowledge, according to which all our scientific theories are myths, or in the words of Xenophanes, 'woven webs of guesses'. I hold that scientific theories remain essentially uncertain or hypothetical, although under the influence of criticism they may in time become more and more truthlike; that is, better and better approximations to the unknown – the hidden reality. But even this view was anticipated by Xenophanes, who is remembered for the following verses:[38]

> The gods did not reveal, from the beginning,
> All things to us; but in the course of time,
> Through seeking we may learn, and know things better.

Now given that Parmenides' teaching in the Way of Truth takes the form of a divine revelation of the perfect and certain truth (which Xenophanes regarded as unattainable by mortal man), it seems that Parmenides, though in many respects highly critical, must have been at times inclined towards dogmatism. We may perhaps conjecture even that he was less inclined originally towards self-criticism than was Xenophanes. If we combine this conjecture with the view that Parmenides' Way of Opinion contains a cosmology and cosmogony of considerable novelty, then it seems likely that Parmenides first constructed and accepted the cosmology and cosmogony of the Way of Opinion, and only later became doubtful about it, and in the end rejected it as illusive and deceptive. His doubts, we may conjecture, led him from cosmology to the theory of knowledge. Thus he became convinced that his cosmology was mere illusive opinion or guess-word (*doxa*), and he began to search for the Way of Truth, or for the way to genuine knowledge. This way to genuine and certain knowledge was ultimately revealed to him by the goddess.[39]

Our question now is this: How did the search for the way to knowledge lead Parmenides to his strange theory of the motionless block universe?

I think that we can reconstruct his main steps.

Parmenides' first step, according to this reconstruction, consists of making the distinction between genuine knowledge and mere guesswork or opinion, and it leads to the thesis that genuine knowledge differs radically from mere opinion. This leads to the question of what is essential to genuine knowledge.[40] The answer is that genuine knowledge must be knowledge of what is *true*: genuine knowledge is true belief. But it is more: it is *certain, unshaken, unshakeable and justifiable* conviction,[41] as opposed to 'the [uncertain and shakeable] opinions of the mortals in which there is no true [justifiable and certain] conviction at all'.[42] We do not speak of 'knowledge' if we hit upon the truth by accident. In this case we say (as indeed Xenophanes did say) that we do not *know* but that we are merely guessing.[43] Thus we speak of 'knowledge' only if we can give *sufficient reasons* or *sufficient valid arguments* in support of our assertion;[44] that is, we speak of knowledge only if our assertion can be *justified* or *proved* by argument, by reason. Thus genuine knowledge, which must be fully reliable, and indeed certain, must be proved by reasoning from premises that are certain.

This amounts to Parmenides' second step, his identification of truth with demonstrable truth. (In this he anticipates modern intuitionism; but he deviates from Xenophanes, who taught that we may hit upon the truth without knowing it.)

The third step is then the sharp separation between rational knowledge of demonstrable truth and all other alleged knowledge, such as the deceptive pseudo-knowledge obtained through our senses.[45] This establishes Parmenides' intellectualism or rationalism, and his rejection of experience. Experience is rejected because it can lead only to mere opinion, or to habit: to pseudo-knowledge that is untrue. Experience, habit, and opinion are untrue in the sense that they can never produce *certain* and *demonstrable* truth.

Thus the demand for genuine knowledge becomes a demand for a rational method, a logical method, a method of proof. It seems that Parmenides arrived at this demand for a rational method by a step that had the character of a conversion, of a revelation. I will translate a few of the verses addressed by the goddess to Parmenides;[46] verses in which she tells him not to trust experience and the senses: the eye, the ear, and the tongue; and in which she extols reason.

> . . . don't let experience,
> Much-tried habit, constrain you; and do not let wander your blinded
> Eye, or your deafened ear, or even your tongue, along this way!
> But by reason alone decide on the often-contested argument
> which I have here expounded to you as disproof.

The next step leads to the thesis, clarified by Kahn, that we can *know* a state of affairs only if that state of affairs is a real fact, if it truly exists.[47] Or, as Parmenides puts it: [48]

> For, what can be known is the same as what can be existing.

Thus we can say that Parmenides holds that, in its essence, genuine

117

knowledge is necessarily always knowledge *of* something; of some object that truly exists.[49]

So we arrive at the question: What can we prove, by reason, about this thing that can be known, and must therefore necessarily exist?

It is, of course, of fundamental importance to find out what Parmenides actually said, and to reconstruct and understand the text. But it is also important to reconstruct his main argument from the clear conclusions that he reached, and from some indications he gives of his main steps. I suggest that the deductive proof in the Way of Truth starts with an idea like 'It is' or 'It is the case', or 'It exists', where the 'It' is the thing, presumably a *corporeal* thing, that can be known; and the 'is' or 'exists' turns out, in the light of the conclusion, to imply corporeality. Parmenides' deductive proof may be reconstructed as starting from a tautology, or an analytic statement[50] (as a proof within logic should). The reconstruction is as follows.

Premise:	Only what is truly the case (such as what is known) can be the case, and can truly *be*.
First conclusion:	The non-existing cannot be.
Second conclusion:	Nothingness, or the void, cannot be.
Third conclusion:	The world is full: it is a continuous block without any division.
Fourth conclusion:	Since the world is full, motion is impossible.

In this way, the cosmology of the goddess, the theory of the block universe, is deductively derived from her theory of genuine knowledge.

I may perhaps mention here two of the tenets of Parmenides' theory of knowledge which I regard as mistaken. They are, I think, not essential to his argument, although both do play a part in his argument and an even greater part in Plato's philosophy.

The first is his identification of truth with certain and demonstrable truth. (It seems to be equivalent to Plato's and Aristotle's *epistēmē* and to Brouwer's conception of truth.) In my opinion this is a regression from the position reached by Xenophanes, who knew that we may hit on the truth accidentally without being aware of it.[51]

The second tenet that I regard as mistaken is the doctrine that, just as to the true and unchanging reality there corresponds genuine knowledge, so to the changing appearances there corresponds guesswork or opinion. (This doctrine is more explicit in Plato than in Parmenides.) I think that, on the contrary, we may try to approach the true reality behind the appearances by the method of *doxa* – of guesses, or hypotheses (as does Plato, for example in the *Timaeus*) – and of criticism; that is, by the method of conjectures and refutations.

At first sight, the theory of the motionless block appears indeed to be an almost insane theory. It is therefore worth stressing that it had a tremendous impact on the evolution of physical science.

7 Parmenides and the methods of science

I think that Parmenides can be credited with at least three lasting achievements from the point of view of modern physical and mathematical science.

(1) He was the inventor of the deductive method of arguing and, though indirectly, even of the hypothetico-deductive method, as it is now called.

(2) He was right in emphasizing that the unchanging, or the invariant, may be taken as self-explanatory, and that it can be used as a starting point in explanation. This emphasis led (as Meyerson observed[52]) to the search for principles of conservation, such as the laws of conservation of energy and of momentum, and also to the method of presenting theories or laws of nature in the form of mathematical *equations*: in a process of change, something remains equal to something; some hidden magnitude remains invariant with respect to certain transformations.

(3) Parmenides' theory was the beginning of the so-called continuity theory of matter and, with it, of a cosmological and physical school whose constant rivalry with the Atomistic School in the theory of matter proved extremely fruitful to solutions of the problem of the structure of matter, down to Schrödinger and to modern quantum field theory.

It is most important to realize further that Parmenides' ideas also proved fruitful in being refutable. For we may, as Aristotle suggests, regard Parmenides as the indirect precursor of the Greek cosmological school of the Atomists, of Leucippus and Democritus, who seem to have arrived at their doctrines by way of a point-by-point refutation of Parmenides' conclusion. Thus they turned his deductive system into a hypothetico-deductive system, and falsified it. They accepted the validity of Parmenides' deduction, and also part of the implicit assumption of Parmenides that what is, or what exists, is corporeal in nature: they accepted Parmenides' doctrine of the existence of full and indivisible bodies. But they rightly rejected the truth of Parmenides' conclusion that motion is impossible; and they produced a step-by-step refutation of Parmenides' proof, arguing from the falsity of Parmenides' conclusion to that of his premise,[53] as follows:

(4′)   It is false that motion is impossible, for motion exists.

(3′)   Thus it is false that the world is full, and that it is one large indivisible block. Thus there are many full or corporeal things or small blocks, which are indivisible; that is, many atoms.

(2')   Since it is false that only the full exists, the empty, the void, also exists.

(1')   Thus the allegedly non-existing void does exist.

This means: not only the full exists, but also the empty; and what exist are *atoms and the void*.

This was the first refutation or falsification of a deductive system; and it may be said to mark the beginning of theoretical physics, or even of scientific theorizing in general.

Thus Parmenides with his Way of Truth can be said to be not only the father of the continuity theory of matter but also the grandfather of the atomic theory of matter, the discontinuity theory of matter.

I now turn to the discussion of what I have previously described as the central problem for the commentator of Parmenides' poem.

8   Why is the deceitful Way of Opinion included in the revelation of the goddess?

Charles Kahn, one of the best-informed and most ingenious commentators on Parmenides, says about this problem that he will 'not attempt to resolve the vexing problem of the . . . cosmology offered in the second part of the poem', and that he believes 'that on Parmenides' principles' the problem 'is not really soluble at all'.[54]

In spite of this discouraging remark, I will attempt something like a solution of the problem.

Why does the goddess, the holder of the key to the realm of truth, include in her revelation what is untrue, and even 'fraudulent' (as she puts it herself)? And why does she produce the 'deceitful pattern' of the Way of Opinion?[55]

I propose three closely related replies to this question.

My first reply, which is very simple, does not attempt to explain why Parmenides makes the goddess his speaker in the Second part of his poem. The reply is this. Parmenides could not open the chasm between *reality* and *appearance*, or the Way of Truth and the Way of Opinion, without giving weight to *both* sides of this new distinction. Thus he *had* to give not only a description of the world of true reality, but also one of the world of deceptive appearance.

The second reply is that this new distinction, and Parmenides' unheard-of description of the world of reality, raises at once a question which indeed only the goddess could answer. I mean the question: If this changeless block is the world of reality, how did the world of illusive appearances arise? This is precisely the question that the goddess answers in the Way of Opinion, with its cosmogony.

The third reply, and the most important one of the three, is that the goddess includes the Way of Opinion because of its high degree of approximation to the truth: because of its great truthlikeness. This reply is based on her own words (and thus on Parmenides' own words) about the order or arrangement of the world of mortal men, the world of appearances. For the goddess refers as follows to her intention to discuss the cosmology and cosmogony of the world of appearances:[56]

> Now of that world so arranged to seem wholly like truth I
>   shall tell you;
> Then you will be nevermore led astray by the notions of
>   mortals.

In the interpretation of these verses, everything depends on whether or not I am justified in translating the words *eoikota panta* as 'seem wholly like truth'.[57]

I base my interpretation on the conjecture that Parmenides, using Xenophanes' terminology,[58] alludes to Hesiod's *Theogony*. There the Muses, who play a part analogous to the goddess in Parmenides' poem, explain to Hesiod that not only can they reveal the truth, but they can also say many *false things that resemble the truth* or are *truthlike*.[59]

The fragment from Xenophanes that in its terminology forms a kind of bridge between Hesiod and Parmenides may be translated as follows: [60]

> This, as we well may conjecture, resembles the truth,

where 'resembles the truth' (or 'is like the truth') is a translation of the phrase *eoikota tois etumoisi*, which uses partly the terminology of Hesiod and partly that used later by Parmenides.

I interpret these two verses to mean that the world of appearance that the goddess is about to describe seems wholly like the truth, and thus more like the truth than are any of the traditional stories (or myths) told by mortal men – stories by which mortal men are easily led astray. Thus the goddess, I suggest, says that she will relate the deceitful story, the Way of Opinion, *because of its truthlikeness* – its approximation to the truth, as we might say nowadays. And I suggest that the goddess is perfectly correct: Parmenides' Way of Opinion is indeed a story, a myth, that, as the goddess says, is *false yet truthlike*, in at least three senses.

(1) First of all, appearance is something that *appears* to be true. Thus appearance must resemble the truth in some way.

121

(2) Secondly, the Way of Opinion is false yet truthlike in the same sense in which almost all the best scientific theories of any period are false yet truthlike. Most of them are false because they are, as a rule, imaginative over-simplifications that can be improved on and superseded by the critical method of science. And they are truthlike at least to the extent that they are better approximations to the truth than are the preceding theories. All this holds of the cosmology of the Way of Opinion, which superseded the preceding Ionian cosmologies, at least in its theory of the shape of the Earth, and its theory of the phases of the Moon.

(3) The third sense in which the Way of Opinion is truthlike is more specifically Parmenidean. Parmenides' Way of Opinion resembles in a number of points his Way of Truth, and it may be said even to resemble it more closely than do the earlier cosmologies, in spite of their avowed monism. Although Parmenides' Way of Opinion is a strictly dualistic system, it comes nearer to the strict monism of Parmenides' Way of Truth than could any other pluralistic system, such as, for example, a doctrine of four elements. We must remember that Parmenides suggests that no account of the world of appearance can be genuinely monistic. (In this connection it may be worth mentioning that a dualism of field and matter which resembles a little Parmenides' dualism of light and night has not been superseded in modern physics in spite of Einstein's valiant efforts.) Another similarity between the Two Ways is the significant part played in the Way of Opinion by the sphericity of the Earth, of the Moon, and especially of the sky, and in the Way of Truth by the sphericity of Parmenides' block universe. Moreover, both the spherical sky and the spherical block universe are bound by the fetters of Anankē, the goddess of necessity.[61] Finally there may be something in Aristotle's much-discussed view that there is a correspondence between the role played by light and night in the Way of Opinion and that of being and non-being in the Way of Truth.[62]

I think that the second sense of truthlikeness creates a much more powerful motive for Parmenides to include the Way of Opinion in his poem than does the third sense. Parmenides, I suggest, was right in regarding his scientific discoveries, especially the sphericity of the Earth and the theory of the Moon, as sufficiently important and truthlike to be included in the speech of the goddess.[63]

The solution suggested here to the problem why the Way of Opinion is included in the revelation of the goddess does not clash with her rejection of the Way of Opinion as untrue, false, and deceitful. Not only does the Way of Opinion (even as I interpret it) contain much that is indeed *factually false*, which could make it, as a divine pronouncement, danger-ously deceptive; but even assuming it did succeed in giving a theory of the world of appearance that is *factually true*, it would, quite obviously, be very far from being *logical* or *rational* or *demonstrably* true, that is, true in the

Parmenidean sense. It thus stands in an even stronger contrast to the truth as conceived by Parmenides – that is, to demonstrable truth – than, say, to the Aristotelian and the modern view of truth.[64] (This view, according to which truth is simply correspondence to the facts, was, it seems, also implicitly held by Xenophanes, who in a passage quoted earlier[65] thought it possible that a man may hit on the perfect truth without knowing it.) This modern view differs from that of Parmenides, for whom truth meant true and certain knowledge, knowledge which is fully reliable and justifiable. As I said before, it appears that for Parmenides, truth is confined to demonstrable truth.[66] Thus for Parmenides unjustifiable conjectures are not knowledge, but mere opinion, and therefore also all that we might describe by the phrase 'scientific knowledge': what is not provable is untrue in Parmenides' sense, and any claim that it is *knowledge* is deceitful. Now all we need to assume, I assert, is that he realized that this kind of mere opinion may be nearer to the truth, or further from the truth, more truthlike[67] or less truthlike. This realization, I suggest, encouraged him to let the goddess reveal his new myth, his important scientific discoveries – but with a warning.

In support of the proposed interpretation of Parmenides' poem, I may perhaps refer to some parallel cases. The first and most obvious one is Plato, the author of several myths, such as the Myth of Er and the *Timaeus*, who pointed out that these myths are at best truthlike. But there are also some great modern scientists who made important discoveries that they believed were in reality untenable, but which they did not suppress. I will mention Newton, Einstein, and Schrödinger. Newton's theory of gravitation is a theory of action at a distance. Yet Newton himself rejected action at a distance as 'so great an absurdity that I believe no man who has in philosophical matters a competent faculty of thinking can ever fall into it'.[68] These are strong words – even stronger, perhaps, than those used by the goddess in condemnation of Parmenides' discoveries. (Newton, I think, turned to the theory of the divinity and omnipresence of space – an idea that is perhaps not far distant from the Way of Truth – in order to get over this difficulty.) Einstein regarded his General Theory of Relativity as merely an approximation to a more satisfactory theory: 'In reality', he writes 'the present theory . . . [is] valid only as a limiting case.'[69] Schrödinger, the discoverer of the time-independent *and* the time-dependent wave equations, believed, under the influence of Schopenhauer, that time was an illusion, and with it the world of change and of death, and that the world of true reality was a timeless and deathless spiritual unity.[70] But neither Newton nor Einstein nor Schrödinger suppressed these scientific discoveries, which Newton regarded as absurd, Einstein as a mere approximation to the truth, and Schrödinger as pertaining to a Parmenidean world of illusion.

I suggest that their reasons were similar to the ones that prevented

Parmenides from suppressing the discoveries described in his Way of Opinion. The difference between Parmenides and, say, Schrödinger is in this respect *only* that since Newton, science (= opinion) has become successful and thus less easy to discard.

I will now turn from the philosophical interpretation of Parmenides to a less important psychological conjecture about Parmenides, and I shall end by discussing it briefly as one of several possible sources of inspiration for his poem.

9 A psychological conjecture about Parmenides

Even if my suggestions for solving the central problem 'Why was the Way of Opinion included in the revelation?' should be accepted, there remain a number of unsolved difficulties. One is that in the Way of Opinion, Parmenides chose light and night as the principles or elements from which everything is generated by mixture. This seems to imply, especially, that the colours are blends or mixtures of light and night; that is, of white and black, as in Goethe's theory of colours. Another closely related problem is Parmenides' interesting suggestion that the world of appearance, the world of mortal men, arises out of a linguistic convention.[71] Now, the opposition of *nature* and *convention*, and its equation with the opposition of *truth* and *falsehood*, is traditional in Greek thought, and although it received its authoritative formulation from Parmenides' contemporary Pindar,[72] it may well have arisen with Parmenides himself, even though Parmenides' terminology is quite different, and even though the opposites with which he operates (demonstrable truth and opinion) are more radically opposed to each other than the traditional opposites of 'nature' and 'convention'.

What I am trying to say is that Parmenides' opposites are strange. He operates with the opposition between a world of truth or reality, and a world of appearance that is a sham world, invented not even by the senses but by the tongue:[73] by human name-giving, by the largely arbitrary conventions that constitute human language.

This strange aspect of Parmenides' theory, and the connected problem of his doubts about the reality of our world, the world of our experience, seem to demand a psychological explanation. They seem to point at what Freud might have described as a neurosis – as a rejection of what Freud called the 'reality principle'. By the way, I am not a Freudian, and I even think that Freud's description of the world of the human mind may indeed be regarded as largely due to a convention or invention – a very influential convention indeed.

I am not in favour of the still somewhat fashionable method of psycho-analysing philosophers or poets (though I do not object to the psycho-analysing of psychoanalysts). But I was impressed by a suggestion about Goethe communicated to me in 1969 by a former graduate student of mine from Canterbury, Dr Noel Bradley, whom I first met in Christchurch in 1937. He suggested that Goethe may have been totally colour-blind, and that this may explain the strange theory in his *Theory of Colours* that colours are blends of white and black – that is, that all colours are shades of grey. Bradley also informed me that he had found, in his experience as a clinical psychologist, that colour blindness may lead to the adoption of a sceptical attitude towards the reality of our everyday world; to a disbelief in the truthfulness of men; and to a belief that what men tell you contains a strong element of arbitrary convention.

All this seems quite plausible; and it suggested to me that Parmenides too may have been totally colour-blind. This conjecture is not only wild but, of course, untestable. Nor is it really needed for solving any of the problems of interpreting Parmenides. Yet it seems to me to fit the poem, and to be unexpectedly persuasive. Parmenides mentions colour only once, in the Way of Truth, where he says that change of motion and change of colour are unreal, and that they are human inventions or rather conventions, arising out of the conventional giving of names, the conventional use of words.[74] Moreover, Parmenides' theory of knowledge implies of course that colour is unreal in the sense that it belongs to the world of visual appearance, which for Parmenides is an unreal world of linguistic convention. Thus Parmenides' thesis, at the very beginning of his Way of Opinion, that the world of illusion is the product of light and night (of the human acceptance or convention to regard these *two* as real while only *one* – the dark world of heavy matter – is real) implies that colours are (if anything) mixtures or blends of black and white, as they would appear to a man who is colour-blind.[75]

Perhaps the most suggestive aspect of this psychological or rather physiological conjecture is this, that it would explain the psychological background of Parmenides' ambivalent attitude towards the world of experience: his total rejection of it, combined with his inclusion of it in the revelation of the goddess; who at the same time issues a solemn warning that she is using words that are deceitful.

10 Summary of these notes on Parmenides' poem

Parmenides appears to me as one of the strangest but also as one of the greatest of all philosophers. I regard him as a cosmologist, as the author of the theory of the sphericity of the Earth, which corrected and completed Anaximander's model of the universe, and as the author of the theory of the sphericity of the Moon and of its shining by borrowed light, and of its phases. These discoveries are crucially important signposts on the way of inquiry that leads on to Aristarchus, Copernicus, Newton, and Einstein. But they are dwarfed by Parmenides' discoveries in the theory of knowledge. He was the founder of the tradition that all cosmology and all science are a search for the hidden reality, the Thing in itself behind the world of appearances (a tradition that may well be described as anti-positivistic).[76] He built the first deductive system describing the universe, whose refutation led to the foundation of physics. At any rate, it was the most important contribution to theoretical physics ever made, since it became the basis of working with mathematical *equations* in physics. He also initiated the continuity theory of matter and he became, more indirectly, responsible for the theory of 'atoms and the void', leading to modern atomic theory.[77]

With the cosmology of the Way of Opinion and even with his cosmogony, Parmenides greatly influenced Plato, especially the Myth of Er in the *Republic*, and also the *Timaeus*, which became one of the epoch-making works on cosmology. His influence on Plato's theory of knowledge was immense. In his insistence on rational proof he may have gone too far. But he was right in his stress on critical rational thought[78] and in his criticism of the theory that the senses are sources of genuine knowledge.

11   Concluding remarks

I suggest that scientific theories are inventions that differ from myths mainly in the adoption by science of the critical approach. The critical approach exerts something like an evolutionary selection pressure upon the theories and so encourages their evolution towards greater truthlikeness. This view is part of the theory of knowledge that I try to uphold. It has led me to look out for the similarities between myths and theories, especially among the early scientists, and also for the marks of the critical approach that is so highly developed in Parmenides (though in some respects he is a dogmatist).

This critical attitude is characteristic of what has been so well described as the Greek miracle. How did this miracle arise?

I think that a miracle such as this can never be fully explained. There cannot be a satisfactory explanation of creativity. But I think that a very partial explanation of the critical attitude is possible, and of considerable interest. The critical attitude is partly, I suggest, the product of the *clash of different cultures*.

Homer describes culture clash, though hardly consciously. Some of the early philosophers such as Thales and Pythagoras were, as tradition tells us, great travellers and students of Egyptian and oriental wisdom. The Ionian philosophers in Asia Minor were in contact with the civilizations of Phoenicia and Mesopotamia and some of the great men of Greece, especially Herodotus, were fully conscious of the significance of culture clash.[79] The much-travelled Xenophanes, born in the Ionian city of Colophon, consciously uses the clash between the theologies of different tribes or nations, in order to explain his critical approach to the traditional theology and also his own monotheistic theology, which deviates so markedly from all traditions.

Notes

1 Cp., for example, *C. & R.*, pp. 38 and 126; and *O.K.*, pp. 347f.

2 For a more detailed discussion see *C. & R.*, pp. 129f., 134f., 295ff., and *O.K.*, pp. 119–22, 235–40.

3 See John A. Wilson, 'Egypt', in *The Intellectual Adventure of Ancient Man*, by H. Frankfort, Mrs. H. Frankfort, J. A. Wilson, and T. Jacobsen, Chicago, 1946. Reprinted by Pelican Books under the title *Before Philosophy*, Harmondsworth, 1949; see p. 63.

4 Hesiod, *Theogony* 116–38.

5 E. B. Tylor, *Primitive Culture*, London, 1871, vol. I; see pp. 322–5, which is based upon Sir George Grey's *Polynesian Mythology*, London, 1855, pp. 1–15.

6 Quoted from Tylor, op. cit., p. 322.

7 The idea that the giving of a name may create an object (or rather a pseudo-object, i.e. one in the world of appearance) by an act of linguistic convention was first put forward by Parmenides; see the fragments of Parmenides in DK 28B8: 38; 53; B9: 1; B19: 3; see also B8: 17.

8 See Wilson, op. cit., p. 59 for the quoted passage, and pp. 59–70 for the plurality of Egyptian cosmogonical theories. Other examples may be found in Erik Iversen, 'Fragments of a Hieroglyphic Dictionary', *Historisk-filologiske Skrifter*, vol. 3, no. 2, The Royal Danish Academy of Sciences and Letters, 1958, pp. 9–13.

9 See DK 7B1 and B2. In B2 the cloak or mantle is embroidered with the Earth and Oceanus. But Robert Eisler, *Weltenmantel und Himmelszelt*, Munich, 1910, vol. 2, pp. 376f., gives reasons for identifying it with the heavens.

10 See Eisler, ibid., pp. 592f.

11 *Iliad* 8: 13–16; cp. DK 7B5.

12 *Theogony* 720–5.

13 Aristotle, *Metaphysics* 983b20f.

14 *Iliad* 14: 202, 246.

15 *Iliad* 2: 755; 14: 271; 15: 37f.; *Odyssey* 5: 185f.

16 Aristotle, *Metaphysics* 983b21; *De Caelo* 294a28.

17 See *Before Philosophy*, referred to in note 3 above, p. 54.

18 Cp. Seneca, DK 11A15; Aristotle, *De Caelo, loc. cit.*, and Essay 1, Section III above.

19 Aristotle, *De Caelo* 294a32f.

20 Hippolytus, *Refutatio* 1.6.3 (= DK 12A 11).

21 Aristotle, *De Caelo* 295b12–16.

22 DK 12A10.

23 DK 12A1 (= Diogenes Laertius II.1f.); see Charles H. Kahn's comments in

his *Anaximander and the Origins of Greek Cosmology*, New York, 1960, 1964, p. 56.

24 For Kahn's defence of the view that Parmenides was the first to assert the sphericity of the Earth, see note 63 below.

25 For a defence of this view, see *C. & R.*, pp. 405f.

26 That what Parmenides describes is a revelation that he has received is rightly stressed by Jaap Mansfeld in his most thoughtful book *Die Offenbarung des Parmenides und die menschliche Welt*, Assen, 1964.

   Concerning 'Things in themselves', which is, of course, an allusion to a similarity with Kant, severely castigated by Burnet as an anachronism, see the discussion in note 76 below. I completely agree, however, with Burnet's now generally accepted view that Parmenides was not an idealist and that his Things in themselves have to be regarded as corporeal.

27 DK 28B12: 3 (*'daimōn hē panta kubernai'*); see also A37 (p. 224, lines 8–9). Compare Heraclitus, DK 22B41 (*'ekubernēse panta dia pantōn'*), and B64.

28 This attribution is defended in note 63 below.

29 In this I agree with G. E. L. Owen, 'Eleatic Questions', *Classical Quarterly* N.S. 10, 1960, pp. 84–102.

30 Cp. ibid., p. 101, and the comments by Alexander P. D. Mourelatos, *The Route of Parmenides*, New Haven, 1970, p. xiv.

31 But Pythagoras may have been a dualist, for according to some reports the Number *One* was regarded by him as both odd and even; the odd belonging to the principle of the limited and the even to the principle of the unlimited. (See also note 33 below.) All theologies, and especially Xenophanes' doctrine of the *One God*, may, of course, also be regarded as postulating a hidden reality behind appearances.

32 For Heraclitus' monism see especially DK 22B50. Xenophanes' monism comes nearest to that of Parmenides; see especially DK 21B23–6.

33 This is suggested by the Pythagorean table of opposites. (But see text to note 31 above.)

34 The passage in quotation marks is taken, with a slight variation, from Essay 1, end of Section VIII above; see also *C. & R.*, p. 80.

35 Charles H. Kahn, 'The Thesis of Parmenides', *Review of Metaphysics* 22, 1969, pp. 700–24; see especially pp. 704ff. and 710. Cp. *C. & R.*, pp. 164f. and (2nd and later edns) pp. 405–13.

36 See the quotation from DK 21B16 and 15 in Essay 2, Section 4 above, and the Addendum to this essay, pp. 136f.

37 DK 21B34. For my translation, see *C. & R.*, pp. 26 and 153. For Xenophanes' criticism of popular theology, see DK 21B15 and 16, Essay 1, Section XII, and Essay 2, Section 4 above.

38 DK 21B18. For my translation, see Essay 1, Section XII above and *C. & R.*, p. 26.

39 The following argument in support of the conjecture that the Way of Opinion was conceived by Parmenides prior to his revelation is admittedly weak but perhaps not without all force. Parmenides says of himself right at the beginning of his poem that he was, apparently prior to receiving the revelation, an 'experienced man' (*eidota phōta*; see DK 28B1: 3), using a term which otherwise he seems to use exclusively for *(pseudo-)knowledge from sense experience* (cp. B6: 4; B10: 1 and 5). This might be interpreted (especially in view of the last two references) as meaning that prior to receiving the revelation Parmenides had been experienced in the Way of Opinion; that is, that he had been a cosmologist and cosmogonist in the traditional manner. However, I would

not mention such an argument from verbal usage but for the fact that there are, in my opinion, stronger arguments to the same conclusion.

40 I regard this search for essences as dangerous, as I have explained elsewhere. (See, for example, *C. & R.*, chapter 3, and *O.K.*, chapter 5; in chapter 2 of the latter volume a distinction is made between 'knowledge' in its more severe sense, knowledge that is certain, and 'scientific knowledge', which is hypothetical and belongs to Parmenides' *doxa* or opinion.) But the Parmenidean quest for the essence of knowledge, and the Parmenidean solution, dominated Plato and, with him, the whole history of the theory of knowledge.

41 DK 28B1: 29.

42 DK 28B1: 30; regarding the insertion 'shakeable', contrast line 30 with line 29 and compare the 'erring' and 'unsettled' pseudo-knowledge (*plankton noon*) in B6: 6.

43 See Xenophanes, DK 21B34, quoted in the text to note 37 above.

44 DK 28B6: 1: 'Necessary it is that what can be known exists truly.' See also B8: 7–8: 'Growth I will not allow you to know or make known by assertion. Nothing can be known or made known by words that is not truly existing.'

45 See DK 28B7 (quoted in the text to the next note), and especially B16. Fragment B16 and its significance are discussed in *C. & R.*, pp. 408–13, and again in more detail in Essay 3, Section 6 above.

46 DK 28B7; for the translation see *C. & R.*, p. 165.

47 Mourelatos writes on p. 743 of his criticism of Kahn ('Comments on "The Thesis of Parmenides"', *Review of Metaphysics* 22, 1969, pp. 735–44): 'I suggest that the *esti* of Parmenides fr. 2 is the "is" of the formula "it is —" (e.g. "it is air," "it is fire," "it is number and the unlimited").'

This does not seem to me different from Kahn's position. And the main thing is that from any such assertion like 'it is air', it follows, in Aristotelian as well as Russellian logic, that it exists:

'*a* is air' entails 'there is an x such that x is air', which further implies 'there is an x such that $x = x$' and further 'there is an x', or 'it exists'.

In other words, the existential meaning follows (in any 'normal' logic with a non-empty universe of discourse) from what Kahn and Mourelatos call the veridical meaning, *without any muddle*. And all this holds for 'There is an x such that x is known.'

My view is that Kahn may be right that the subject of Parmenides' 'it is' is something like 'that which can be known', and Mourelatos may be right too; but the essential step in the proof of Parmenides is: 'what is not cannot exist', where 'what is not' is clearly identified with what the atomists later called 'the void', that is, empty space. For only in this way could Parmenides arrive at the conclusion that what in reality exists is the undivided, immobile, all-comprehending and unique full body. Thus we find in the end, by logical rather than linguistic means, that 'it is' must have meant, for Parmenides, 'it is corporeal' (indeed like 'it is air' or 'it is fire'). All this was very clearly understood and criticized by the atomists.

48 DK 28B3. For the translation see J. Burnet, *Early Greek Philosophy*, 4th edn, London, 1930 (where the fragment is numbered 5, as in the early editions of Diels), p. 173, especially footnote 2. I deviate from Burnet in translating *noein* by 'can be known' (rather than 'can be thought'), following the important clarification in Kahn, op. cit., p. 703, note 4, where Kahn refers to von Fritz. Two similar passages, I suggest, may be translated as follows. First, fragment B2: 1–2:

> Come, then, and you mark well my words, for I will now tell you
> All the ways of search that there are and can lead you to knowledge.

(More literally, 'that there are for knowing'.) Secondly, B8: 34 may be translated:

> Knowing is of the same thing for the sake of which knowledge exists.

(Cp. Burnet, op. cit., p. 176.) This can perhaps be put very freely: 'Knowing is always the same as knowing that which exists.' Anyone who reflects critically on these last formulations is led almost at once to the question: 'Can we perhaps know something that does not exist?' This is precisely what Parmenides denies: he denies that the non-existing can exist or be known or be made known or be described. It is unknowable (*anoēton*: B8: 17; compare also B8: 16, and B2: 3–8). Thus I suggest that we translate B2: 7–8 as follows:

> For, you can never know that which is not truly existing,
> Nor can you ever describe it . . .

For B16 (which treats of pseudo-knowledge) see the Addendum to this essay, and Essay 3, Section 6 above.

49 Parmenides was in my opinion far from being a forerunner of language analysis; nor did he want to give a conceptual analysis (as suggested by Mourelatos, *The Route of Parmenides*, for example p. 217). He was, rather, a cosmologist, and an epistemologist. Note that the verbs of knowing (especially *noein* and *ginōskein*; see the reference in the preceding note to Kahn's clarification) are used both transitively and intransitively. And note that in DK 28B16 *noos* and *noēmo* do not refer to genuine knowledge and are used absolutely, without an object. Parmenides, I suggest, based his epistemology on the thesis that in line with this verbal usage, genuine knowing or genuine knowledge is always *essentially* transitive. It is always *of* something which, whenever there is genuine knowledge, must truly exist. I suggest that Parmenides uses 'knowing', if genuine knowledge is intended, always with this essential meaning in mind; and it appears (cp. Kahn, 'The Thesis of Parmenides', p. 713, note 18) that he also uses various verbs for speaking or saying (such as *phanai* and *phrazein*) in a very similar way: they may be interpreted as 'naming [something]', or 'making [it] known by words', or 'pointing [it] out' or 'describing [it]'; as a rule they are used in an essentially transitive sense. Compare DK 28B1: 23; B2: 6–8 (see note 48 above); B6: 1; and B8: 34.

In believing that Parmenides remains in the cosmological tradition even in the Way of Truth, I agree with Kahn ('The Thesis of Parmenides'). Excellent suggestions about the relation of Parmenides' poem to the theories of Anaximander can be found in Howard Stein, 'Comments on "The Thesis of Parmenides"', *Review of Metaphysics* 22, 1969, pp. 725–34; see especially pp. 733f. It may be added that what may have made Parmenides give up the cosmology of the Way of Opinion was a doubt about Anaximander's theory of the unsupported position of the Earth. Failing to find a more satisfactory theory, and unwilling to return to Anaximenes' or Thales' or similar views, he might have decided that the fault was the existence of a void, and that only a block was in accordance with reason.

50 Since I think, with Cornford and Guthrie, that Parmenides did start with a tautology (which was then given content by identifying what is not with the void) I think also that W. K. C. Guthrie, *A History of Greek Philosophy*, vol. II, Cambridge, 1965, pp. 15–17 is essentially right, and that Mourelatos, *The Route of Parmenides*, text to note 19 on p. 274, is mistaken. Kahn, in 'The Thesis of Parmenides', also mentions tautologies such as the law of non-contradiction (p. 708), at least as steps in the argument. (See also p. 711: 'This claim would generally be regarded as non-controversial. It calls for no argument . . .'.)

51 This view of Xenophanes' is implicit in DK 21B34, quoted in the text to note 37 above.

52 See Emile Meyerson, *Identity and Reality*, London, 1930, pp. 231 and 253 (and *C. & R.*, p. 80, note 21). In these two passages, Meyerson refers to causation and identity in connection with Parmenides. If for 'cause' we substitute 'causal laws', and further, 'differential equations' and 'conservation laws', then we come to something like the view here described in the text.

53 This point-by-point reply to Parmenides is preserved in Aristotle, *De Generatione et Corruptione* 316a14ff.; compare my *C. & R.*, p. 83, note 34.

54 Kahn, 'The Thesis of Parmenides', p. 705.

55 The translation 'deceitful pattern' (*kosmon apatēlon*: DK 28B8: 52) is due to Guthrie, *A History of Greek Philosophy*, vol. II, p. 50.

56 DK 28B8: 60–1; for another attempt at a translation, see Essay 9, Section 4, where I also refer to Xenophanes (DK 21B35), discussed in the text to note 60 below, and where I also translate some other lines of Parmenides' (DK 28B1: 31–2). These I now regard, in the light of the discussion in Mourelatos, *The Route of Parmenides*, Chapter 8, as in need of revision (in particular, 'delusive opinion' should, I now believe, be replaced by 'delusive appearance'). Line B8: 61 could be more literally but, I think, less smoothly translated as follows:

Then at no time can you be led astray by the notions of mortals.

57 Mansfeld, op. cit., pp. 146f., whose discussion of *eoikota panta* is particularly thorough, and who (like myself) takes *panta* as an adverb to *eoikota*, suggests a translation like 'wholly fitting [the two elements]'.

58 Apart from the references in Plato and Aristotle, the only evidence so far available that Parmenides knew Xenophanes and was strongly influenced by him is the following: (a) Xenophanes had a spherical God, and one God; Parmenides has a spherical 'exists', and one 'exists'; (b) there is evidence of culture clash in both Xenophanes and Parmenides: one God and many stories of god, one truth and many opinions, are found in both; (c) Parmenides' terminology: Parmenides uses certain terms, which Xenophanes does not use as technical terms, as if they were technical terms. (I have found that some of my students do the same with terms which I happened to introduce in a non-technical way.) The evidence about Parmenides being acquainted with Heraclitus is similar (see further the Addendum to this essay).

59 See *Theogony* 27, where the Muses 'say plainly' that they can tell many lies that are *like the truth* (such as imaginative stories; compare *Odyssey* 19.203) but that they can also (in a more didactic manner) reveal the truth.

Thanks to Mansfeld, op. cit., p. 146, note 3, I find that my suggestion that DK 28B8: 60 should be compared not only with Xenophanes B35 but also with *Theogony* 27 was anticipated by F. M. Cornford, *Principium Sapientiae*, Cambridge, 1952 (see p. 119, note 2 and text); Cornford, however, does not interpret *eoikota* by 'like the truth' but by 'plausible', and his interpretation is incompatible with mine. Mansfeld argues (op. cit., pp. 146f.) against Cornford by asserting that *eoikota* needs some object of reference (*Ergänzung*). This does not seem to me quite convincing, in view of the evidence discussed in Addendum 1 to Essay 1 above. Moreover, for an absolute use of *eoiken* etc. see countless Platonic passages, for example the typical passage *Republic* 334a, usually translated 'it seems so' with the obvious meaning 'it seems like the truth'.

Cornford, referred to by Mansfeld, seems to have connected *eoikota* in B8: 60 with *Theogony* 27. Thus Edwin F. Dolin Jr, 'Parmenides and Hesiod', *Harvard Studies in Classical Philology* 66, 1962, pp. 93–8, compares (p. 94) *Theogony* 26–8 with Parmenides B1: 24 and 26–30, but not with B8: 60. The same holds for Hans Schwabl, 'Hesiod und Parmenides', *Rheinisches Museum für Philologie* 106, 1963, pp. 134–42. And similarly Alexander P. D. Mourelatos emphasizes, *The Route of Parmenides*, p. 33, that the 'double account given by Parmenides' goddess seems to have as its prototype the claim of the Hesiodic Muses that they can speak both "truth" and "lies"'. But again, Mourelatos does not stress the truthlikeness of the lies, nor does he refer to the prototype of Parmenides' *eoikota* in Hesiod and Xenophanes; and thus he does not discuss the possibility that it may mean 'like the truth' (cp. Mourelatos, *The Route of Parmenides*, pp. 230f.). For the whole problem of truthlikeness, see the addenda to Essay 1, Essay 9, Section 4, and *C. & R.*, pp 232–7. See also the remarks on truth and verisimilitude in *O.K.* ch. 2, sections 6–11.

60 DK 21B35. See Essay 1 above, and points 4–6 of Addendum 2 to that essay.
61 Compare especially DK 28B10: 5–6 with B8: 30f. and B8: 42f.

Another similarity between the Two Ways may be this. Giorgio de Santillana suggested in his brilliant and challenging *Taft Semple Lecture* 'Prologue to Parmenides', University of Cincinatti, 1964, p. 18 (see also note 76 below) that Parmenides' *stephanas*, the garlands, or wreaths, or crowns (Cicero) may be interpreted as the spatio-temporal representations or diagrams of stellar orbits. According to this interpretation the various ('scattered') observed positions of the fixed stars and also of the planets were intuitively seen by Parmenides to be continuous and co-present. Now, if this is correct, it may perhaps be connected with DK 28B4, where the Way of Truth supplies something like an epistemological basis for A37 and B12: 1, which belong to the Way of Opinion. B4 may be translated as follows:

Look, in the light of reason, at things afar as if present!
For, what is is not torn from what is: it is holding together,
Neither scatt'ring itself through the world, according to order,
Nor being placed in positions nearby.

If we accept de Santillana's interpretation, as I am inclined to do, then Parmenides' crowns or wreaths can still be regarded as suggested by, and developed from, Anaximander's circles or wheels, and as a correction or rationalization of these wheels in the light of the doctrine of the sphericity

of the heavenly bodies; or as a further approximation to the truth. (For the
wheels or 'rings', see Kahn, *Anaximander*, especially pp. 57–62 and 85–92.)

62 See Aristotle, *Metaphysics* 986b34–987a1 (= DK 28A24). And the discussion
in Guthrie, op. cit., vol. II, pp. 71–6.

63 Some authorities attribute the discovery of the sphericity of the Earth to
Pythagoras. But the argument of Kahn, *Anaximander*, pp. 115–18, which
strongly supports its attribution to Parmenides, has convinced some outstanding scholars such as Guthrie, in his *History of Greek Philosophy*, vol. II, p. 65,
note 1. Kahn analyses the testimony of Theophrastus preserved in two passages of Diogenes Laertius, who reports that Theophrastus said of Parmenides
that he was 'the first to apply the name "cosmos" to the heavens, and the
name "spherical" to the Earth' (DL VIII.48–9). Diogenes notes that some other
authorities (no doubt lesser ones; one seems to have been Favorinus) attributed
the priority to Pythagoras. In a later passage (DL IX.21) Diogenes simply
says, no doubt under the influence of Theophrastus, that Parmenides 'was the
first to state that the Earth is spherical'. (He adds 'and situated in the centre of
the universe'; but this was, of course, stated before by Anaximander.) At any
rate, we know almost nothing about the cosmology of Pythagoras, and there
can be little doubt that Parmenides was the first who publicly announced the
sphericity of the Earth (perhaps influenced by Xenophanes; see the pseudo-
Aristotelian treatise *On Melissus, Xenophanes, Gorgias*). As to the theory of the
Moon and its borrowed light, DK 28B14 and 15 seem to me decisive, and
transmitted by a good authority (Plutarch):

> Bright in the night with an alien light round the Earth she is erring,
> Always she wistfully looks round for the rays of the Sun.

Moreover, the repetition of Parmenides' description by Empedocles (DK
31B45) is good evidence. Thus the attribution of the discovery to Anaxagoras
seems to be mistaken; the mistake is easily explained if we credit Anaxagoras
with the theory of the eclipses.

It may be mentioned incidentally that the sphericity of the Moon (mentioned in DK 28B10: 4) follows almost immediately (by observing the
shapes of the phases) once it is realized that the Moon is always looking in
the direction of the Sun (B15) and shines by borrowed light (B14). The
significance of this discovery for Parmenides' Two Ways is now further
expounded in Essays 3 and 4 above.

64 For Tarski's theory of truth, see, for example, *O.K.*, pp. 44–7.

65 See the text to note 37 above.

66 See the text to note 48 above.

67 That Parmenides realized this follows clearly from DK 28B8: 61, quoted
above in the text to note 56.

68 See *C. & R.*, pp. 106f. and notes 20f.

69 See Albert Einstein, *The Meaning of Relativity*, 6th edn, Princeton, 1956, p. 123.

70 See Erwin Schrödinger, *My View of the World*, Cambridge, 1964, especially pp.
92ff.

71 See DK 28B8: 38 and 53, B9: 1, and B19: 3. See also Essay 9, Section 4.

72 Cp. *O.S.*, vol. I, chapter 5 (and notes 3, 10, 11, 12, and 28 to that
chapter).

73 In DK 28B7: 5, Parmenides may refer to the tongue in the first instance as a
sense organ. But in view of the importance of name-giving, in B8: 38 and 53;
B9: 1 and B19: 3, the reference may also be to speech.

74 See DK 28B8: 41. I translate B8: 38–41 (cp. Mourelatos, *The Route of Parmenides*, p. 181, note 37):

> Whole it is, and unmoving. To it all the names have been given
> Men have laid down by agreement, trusting them to be truthful.
> 'Coming to be' or 'passing away' or 'to-be-and-to-be-not',
> Names such as 'change of place' or 'change of visible colour'.

The word here translated as 'visible' may also mean 'bright' and perhaps even 'luminous'; but as it is closely related to *phainein*, it seems possible that the phrase is used ambiguously or that it contains an allusion to 'apparent colour'.

75 The world then assumes the character of a black-and-white photograph which contains, of course, intermediate shades. This world is an illusion, just as a cinema (black-and-white) love story is an illusion: there is only the material screen.

76 Burnet describes any such allusion to Kant as an 'anachronism'. (See his *Early Greek Philosophy*, pp. 183f., including his footnotes.) I suggest, on the contrary, that with his clear opposition between *appearance* and *reality*, Parmenides may be described as a precursor of Kant. For with this opposition, Parmenides created a tradition that was developed by Plato and to which Kant alludes whenever he uses the Platonic opposition between *phainomena* and *noumena*. The main differences between Kant's position and Parmenides' position are two. (1) Kant regards *noumena* as in neither space nor time, while Parmenides' Thing in itself is in space: it fills the *finite* space (in contradistinction to the infinite space of Melissus attributed to Parmenides by de Santillana, op. cit.). (2) After Newton, a theory of the phenomenal world could hardly be denied the *status of a science* (*epistēmē* – a term introduced by Plato as a near equivalent of Parmenides' Way of Truth; Plato's term *doxa* is the same as Parmenides' term). This is why Kant attempted an *a priori* proof of Newton's theory of the phenomenal world. But in this he was mistaken: Newton's theory, like the whole of natural science, belongs to Parmenides' *doxa* rather than to *epistēmē*. (See my *C. & R.*, pp. 93–5.) But, as Xenophanes saw, our guesses, our *doxa*, may be true, even if not demonstrably true.

In this connection it is interesting that Aristotle (*De Caelo* 298b22ff.) attributes to Parmenides a typically Kantian ('transcendental') argument when he writes of Parmenides and of Melissus that they were 'realizing for the first time that such [unchanging] entities have to be postulated if knowledge and understanding are to be possible'.

77 Two remarks are pertinent here: (1) Leucippus' and Democritus' theory of *atoms and the void* is consciously dualistic, as is the Way of Opinion; no doubt Leucippus (for whose relation to Parmenides see especially DK 67A8, one of the rare reports to distinguish him from Democritus) accepted Parmenides' argument that a world of change cannot be monistic. (2) This dualism has remained characteristic of atomic theory: under the influence of Faraday and Maxwell, it became a dualism of fields and particles. The continuity theory, which takes the Way of Truth as its point of departure, may be said to have *monistic* tendencies. Descartes saw the physical world as full of matter in motion; Einstein as a four-dimensional field without discontinuities – as a kind of four-dimensional Parmenidean block universe.

78 Parmenides, if I am right, directed his criticism at the claim of the cosmologists, including probably himself, to have discovered truth (which he inter-

prets as certain and demonstrable truth). He was conscious of the fact that his arguments against sensualism were critical ones – a critical 'much-contested disproof'. See DK 28B7, especially line 5, translated in *C. & R.*, p. 165; see text to note 46 above.

79 See Herodotus III.38, referred to in *O.S.*, note 3 to Chapter 5, p. 233.

ADDENDUM
A HISTORICAL CONJECTURE ABOUT THE ORIGIN OF PARMENIDES' COSMOLOGY

I propose that the reason why Parmenides made his goddess add an elaborate cosmology to her Way of Truth is that he was himself the author of this interesting and highly original version of a cosmology on traditional lines going back to Anaximander, Heraclitus, Xenophanes, and others.

I conjecture that Parmenides became acquainted with Heraclitus only after he had more or less completed his own cosmology; for Parmenides' cosmology appears to be more like Anaximander's cosmology completed.

A problem remaining to be solved is: Was Parmenides' cosmology free of Xenophanes' influence? I do not think so: it is possible that the full impact of Xenophanes' scepticism dawned on both of them only after both had worked out the spherical theory.

Here is one reconstruction:

1   Parmenides writes the fragments from B10 onwards (without B16[1]);
2   Xenophanes works out his theology without sphericalness; discussions with Parmenides;
3   Parmenides comes under the influence of Xenophanes' scepticism;
4   Xenophanes accepts Parmenides' spherical theory of the Earth and the cosmic bodies and applies it to theology;
5   Parmenides realizes the full consequences of scepticism;
6   Parmenides comes under the influence of Heraclitus' problem of change;
7   Height of Parmenides' crisis;
8   Conversion to rationalism: 'whatever is, truly exists' is an irrefutable proposition.

The historical origin of Parmenides' cosmology may perhaps then be sketched as follows.

This addendum is based on two letters written to Arne F. Petersen, sent from Brandeis University on 12 and 24 November 1969. {The critical remarks on Karl Reinhardt's dating of Xenophanes, Heraclitus, and Parmenides, now included in Section 2 of the present text, are from a non-annotated footnote perhaps prepared for, but not included in, the 3rd revised edition of C. & R. *(1969).Ed.}*

(1) One of our main but not very reliable sources, Diogenes Laertius, calls Parmenides a pupil of Xenophanes. Diogenes adds, however, that 'Parmenides did not follow Xenophanes meekly' (or that he 'did not rely on Xenophanes'), but that 'according to Sotion, he associated also with Ameinias the Pythagorean'. It may have been Ameinias with whom Parmenides studied first. (On Ameinias' death, Parmenides 'built a shrine to him . . . it was Ameinias and not Xenophanes who led him to adopt a contemplative approach', writes Diogenes.[2])

So under the influence of his first teacher, Ameinias, Parmenides may have written a first version of a cosmology that combined, and transcended, ideas of Anaximander, Pythagoras, Pherecydes, and perhaps Hesiod. It was a most important and original work, since Parmenides did what Anaximander had left undone.

Although we have only a few fragments left of this cosmology, and a few not very reliable reports, it seems clear that it must have contained some new and important cosmological hypotheses. The most important of these was, I suggest, formulated in fragments B14 and B15 about the Moon which J. Beaufret (*Le Poème de Parménide*, Paris, 1955, p. 8) called 'one of the most beautiful stanzas in Greek':

> Bright in the night with an alien light
> Round the Earth she is erring.
> Always she wistfully looks round
> For the rays of the Sun.

In these lines is clearly formulated the theory that the phases of the Moon are to be explained by her borrowed light; and it is thereby implied that the Moon is a spherical body, for only so can her phases be explained. (This can easily be checked with the help of any spherical clay model.)

This theory of the shape of the Moon and of her phases was one of the great breakthroughs of astronomy: Anaximander was far removed from it. It led to the theory that the Sun was also a spherical body (rather than the opening of a tubular chariot wheel filled with fire, as Anaximander taught). The circular movement round the Earth was explained by Parmenides in a similar way to Anaximander's: the tubular wheel was replaced by a crown, or a wreath, too dark (or too transparent) to be visible, on which the rotating heavenly body was fixed.[3]

(2) It is here that the influence of Xenophanes' monotheism may have come in. For that there was such an influence seems to me very likely (among other reasons are striking terminological similarities). While Heraclitus was what we call nowadays a relativist, Xenophanes believed in

absolute truth. But he taught (in fragment B34) that certainty – certain truth – was not for mortal men:

But as for certain truth, no man has known it,
Nor will he know it; neither of the gods
Nor yet of all the things of which I speak.
And even if by chance he were to utter
The perfect truth, he would himself not know it.
For all is but a woven web of guesses.

These verses mean that truth is absolute and objective. But certainty, certain truth, is unattainable by us; and thus we can never know, for knowledge entails certainty. According to Xenophanes, all that appears to be human knowledge is only guesswork; it is conjectural knowledge.

The verses quoted here from Xenophanes are, I think, his own resigned comments upon his very new and very original theology. I think they show an extraordinary degree of rational self-criticism; for his new theology must have struck him at first as a revelation, as a message authorized by God himself. To realize that it was merely his guess was a unique act of self-control in the interest of truth. Here are Xenophanes' fragments (B23; B26; B25 and 24) in my almost literal translation:

One God, alone among gods and alone among men, is the greatest,
Neither in mind nor in body does he resemble the mortals.
Always in one place he remains, without ever moving.
Nor is it fitting for him to wander now hereto now thereto.
Effortless he swings the All, by mere thought and intention.
All of him is sight; all is knowledge; and all is hearing.

It is often reported of Xenophanes that he identified God with the universe, and it seems that this report goes back to a remark in Aristotle's *Metaphysics* (986b20–5). I do not believe that Xenophanes made this identification. For as we have seen,

Effortless he swings the All by mere thought and intention.

Here the word I translated by 'the All' means, clearly, 'the heavens' or 'the universe'; and as, obviously, he swings it relative to the Earth, which does not move, as he himself does not move, he cannot be identified with the moving All, the heavens. (However, the verses have also been interpreted in a different and, I believe, unacceptable way.)

In his work *Parmenides und die Geschichte der griechischen Philosophie* (1916;

2nd edn, Frankfurt-am-Main, 1959, pp. 221f.) Karl Reinhardt defends the (revolutionary) theory that Heraclitus was younger than, and influenced by, Parmenides. He also conjectures that Xenophanes was a popularizer of Parmenides' ideas.

Though Reinhardt puts forth his arguments with great force, he does not consider the at least equally powerful counter-arguments. For assume his conjecture to be true; then Xenophanes (born in 570 BC) has to be credited (a) at a date when he was quite old, with an understanding and appreciation of Parmenides' totally revolutionary way of thinking; (b) with a completely independent, and unprecedented, application of this new theory to new problems of cosmology and theology; and (c) with producing a highly original sceptical-critical twist to the new theory.

All this contradicts Reinhardt's central argument, which consists of elaborate and almost circumstantial evidence, convincingly presented and attempting to prove that Xenophanes could have been neither a serious nor an original thinker. The above-sketched counter-argument seems to me completely destructive of Reinhardt's point and to re-establish the traditional view with renewed force: the existence of an Eleatic School founded by Xenophanes. For Reinhardt's argument that the two, Parmenides and Xenophanes, were closely connected is unanswerable.

What has been said so far has important implications for Reinhardt's attempted inversion of the traditional view that Heraclitus preceded Parmenides; a second of Reinhardt's arguments put forth with great force, and perhaps even stronger than the first one just mentioned, maintains that Xenophanes was older than Parmenides, while there are certainly some well-known difficulties in the early dating of Heraclitus. Not only the known date of Elea's foundation in 540, but also Plato's way of comparing Heraclitus and Empedocles (who was clearly younger than Parmenides) in the *Sophist* 242d speaks for making these two nearly contemporaneous; however, if we assume that the later fragments of Heraclitus were written when he was an old man in, say, 473 (three years before Socrates was born) and Empedocles' poem, say, about 445, then Plato's remark (making Empedocles come in quick succession after Heraclitus) would be even more natural than a similar remark nowadays comparing Descartes and Locke.

Reinhardt has shown clearly that there is some dependence between the views of Heraclitus and Parmenides. But again, he makes Heraclitus dependent on Parmenides. But if we say that Socrates was 22 when Parmenides came to Athens, this would mean that Parmenides was born in, say, 513 and reached the age of 35 at the time when Heraclitus wrote his book. There is then every possibility that Parmenides might have argued against Heraclitus: in spite of what he says in the proem, it was hardly the work of a very young man. (Of course, the revelation which he describes in the proem may antedate his writings.)

(3) Xenophanes thus convinced Parmenides that his earlier efforts to develop a new cosmology could not produce truth but only opinion ('a woven web of guesses', as Xenophanes had it), and this was a great shock to Parmenides. It caused a crisis in his thinking, and for a time diverted his interest from cosmological (or scientific) speculation to epistemological speculation: *what can we know? How can we know?*

This led him to a sharp distinction between reason and the senses: his cosmological speculations were, to be sure, attempts to *explain* (rationally) the world of our senses. Therefore reason must be a better instrument than the senses, for we can (like Xenophanes) challenge our cosmological and theological speculations, designed to explain the world of our senses.

This crisis is solved by a revelation: if only we decide to adhere solely to the guidance of reason – of rational argument – then we can obtain knowledge about the real world: about existence. We have, however, to renounce that pseudo-knowledge, that opinion, which tells us how *the world of our senses* is organized; even in its best form, it must be renounced; even in the form in which Parmenides himself had put his cosmology.

(4) It seems that Xenophanes also taught that the shape of his one God is spherical: there is almost unanimity on this point among the traditional witnesses. (See W. K. C. Guthrie, *A History of Greek Philosophy*, vol. I, Cambridge, 1962, pp. 376f.) If this is true, we may conjecture that he arrived at this idea when learning about Parmenides' early discovery of the spherical shape of the Earth. Xenophanes certainly taught that 'gods are not born' (B14), which in the context means 'not created'.

(5) Once his naive faith in his early discoveries had been shaken Parmenides could not proclaim them as science or knowledge or truth; but he was too good a scientist to throw them away altogether. He knew that he had come nearer to the truth than had other mortals before him or at his time. Therefore he gives a full account of his discarded, or renounced, cosmology – under the guise of an example, of the best possible example from the Way of Opinion – the one false cosmology nearest to the truth; even nearer than any other mortal so far had reached.

The goddess explains it all as due to one vital mistake: while in the Way of Truth she tells us that existence must be *one* and undivided, she now shows that by positing *two* (real things) instead of one reality, and giving them names (such as 'light' and 'night', both of which are not real, as is matter) – name-giving is, of course, conventional – we are already on the wrong way, on the slippery slope to sensualism, conventionalism, and untruth.

Together with Pindar, his contemporary, Parmenides introduced into Greek thought the famous opposition:

Nature or Truth *versus* Convention or Untruth.[4]

This important distinction is the result of *culture clash*. Xenophanes' reference in fragments B16 and B15[5] makes it quite clear how great a role is played by culture clash in the awakening of critical, i.e. argumentative, thinking. What is first discovered is that the laws and the gods of different peoples are a bit different: they are *conventional*; they are not the truth (which must be *one*), but consist of *many* differing conventions.

In this way, multiplicity ('manyness', as it were) becomes an indicator of untruth and conventionality. Similarly, different peoples hold many different opinions on almost all subjects under the Sun – prone as they are to occupy themselves with the phenomenal world, the world of the senses – but all this is only opinion, sheer convention. And *naming* is conventional. (We may interpret this to mean that the vocabulary of the various languages of the various peoples are conventional.)

Now, the minimum 'manyness' is two: thus a dualistic world picture is conventional *and* is the first step towards the abyss of untruth. So by deviating from the (monistic) way of truth even by one step we are bound to end in untrue opinion. The first step of our intellectual fall is described, and analysed, by the goddess, who tells us 'how it was *bound* to happen' – that is, 'how delusive (or conventional) opinion was bound to win through' once the smallest concession to conventionalism was made.

This means leaving behind the whole of conventional thought, which is infected by sense and by convention. It means rising to a higher plane, to a superhuman level. Thus he describes his revelation as a journey to the goddess Dikē, who then reveals to him the truth. She also tells him the story of the intellectual fall of man: for she cannot tell the story to be renounced simply as such: she must reveal the truth, and thus she tells the story of '*how* it was that delusive opinion was mistaken for reality, and thus became victorious, and penetrated everything'. In this way, she can then tell Parmenides' own early cosmology – not as truth, of course, but as a superior form of human opinion: it is a better *approximation* to the truth – more truth*like* – than all other notions of mortals; but still it is false.

During his epistemological crisis, as told here in (3) and (4) above, I conjecture that Parmenides read (or heard of) Heraclitus and in this way became acquainted with *the problem of change*. Thus his rationalism solved two problems – that of truth, and the *cosmological* problem of change; which contributed to its revelatory character.

(6) In order to reconstruct the problem situation in which Parmenides must have been when he experienced the revelation of the goddess, described in his poem, we should start from the assumption that all her main points must have been revealing answers to a great riddle. I assume here that the riddle was purely intellectual. However, it must have had an emotional aspect.

I suggest, tentatively, that the riddle can be expressed by what we may call 'the Heraclitean problem':

How is change possible?

It can also be put as follows: if any thing changes, it is certainly a different thing after the change from what it was before the change. And yet, it must be *the same* thing: it must remain even identically the same thing, or else we could not say that it has changed. So the very possibility of change involves the contradiction that the thing after it has changed is, at the same time, identical and non-identical with the thing before the change. On the other hand, any change turns a thing into its opposite. So opposites are identical, as Heraclitus teaches:

'They all are the same, the living and the dead, those who are awake and asleep, young and old. For these turn into those and those into these.' (B88) 'The cold becomes warm, the warm cold; the moist dry, the parched wet.' (B126)

The idea of the identity of opposites is applied by Heraclitus in order to obtain other paradoxes:

'God is day and night, winter summer, war peace, satiety hunger.' (B67) 'Connected are wholes and non-wholes, homogeneity and heterogeneity, unity and duality, all becomes one and one becomes all.' (B10) 'We are and we are not.' (B49a) 'The way up and down is one and the same.' (B60) 'Good and evil are the same.' (B58)

Now, these paradoxes of Heraclitus appeared to Parmenides, I suggest, as logically inescapable, and yet as intolerable. But he found a sudden enlightenment: another paradox, but one that is rationally defensible even if it clashes with all we seem to know from experience:

Opposites need not and do not exist.
Movement does not exist.
All is one, one unchanging and undifferentiated unity.

Everything else is an illusion, due to the much-erring senses of mortal men; or an invention (or, perhaps, a linguistic convention) made by them: at any rate, it is a Delusive Opinion of the mortals. It is the senses that

141

seduce and mislead us: they make us see double, hear double, and think double. And they make us mistake our much-erring senses and the muddle they produce for genuine thought, for true reason.

The mortals believe, of course, that all their knowledge is due to sense perception; and that was in part even Xenophanes' view as it comes out in fragment B34. But the goddess warns Parmenides (B7) not to allow himself to be seduced by this much-used highway:

Never shall it prevail that things that are not are existing.
Keep back your thought from this way of inquiry; don't let experience,
Much-walked highways, seduce you; and do not let wander your blinded
Eye, or your deafened ear, or even your tongue, along this way!
But by reason alone decide on the often-contested
Argument which I have here expounded to you as disproof.[6]

But although genuine knowledge is not the product of sense perception, for the much-erring mortals it holds indeed that nothing is in their much-erring intellects that has not been previously in their much-erring senses. As the goddess says about the mortals:

What is, at any one time, in the much-erring sense organs' mixture,
That seems established knowledge to men; for they take as the same thing
Man's intellectual mind, and the sense organs' nature or content.
'Thought' is called what in this muddle prevails, in each man and all.

This fragment, B16, is, I think, one of the most important ones of the poem.[7] It scorns and ironizes the empiricist view that *'Nothing is in the intellect that has not been previously in the senses.'* And I suggest that an empiricist formula, an empiricist summing up like this either preceded Parmenides or arose (perhaps in the form of Protagoras' *homo mensura* principle) by opposing Parmenides' scorn, or by not grasping it.

(7) If I am wrong and Xenophanes did identify the universe with his God, then there can be no doubt that Parmenides was influenced also by this idea; for then the very strange and very abstract doctrine,

The universe is unmoving, ungenerated, spherical, and is emphatically ONE,

which he arrived at during the height of his crisis, could be found not only in Parmenides' Way of Truth, but also in Xenophanes. At any rate I think – and so thought many Greek philosophers from Plato on (*Sophist* 242c–d) – that the similarity between Parmenides' teaching and that of Xenophanes is very striking indeed, and even more so if Xenophanes did not teach the doctrine I have ascribed to him in (2) above but another one where 'the universe' is identified with 'God'.

So it may well be that Parmenides found his new message, his Way of Truth, in Xenophanes' new monotheistic theology; either by reading it or, more probably, by listening to a recitation of it.

But what struck him as an utterly new and, indeed, as a divine revelation was not so much the message, but the insight that his *new message can be proved, by reasoning alone*, at least that part which asserts that change is impossible.

It can be proved, deductively, from the nature of being, from the nature of existence.

It was, for all I know, the first deductive theory of the world, the first deductive cosmology: one further step led to theoretical physics, and to the atomic theory.

(8) If I am right, then Parmenides' central problem is the problem of change. This view conflicts with the prevalent doctrine, for what has usually been taken to be his problem is the problem of being. I do not think that this is so. The problem of being is, I believe, just a consequence of his having to defend the impossibility of change. This leads, first, to the rejection of sense experience, and next to the need to rely on purely rational arguments. And it is this need that, in its turn, leads to the theory '*Only what is, is*': the theory from which a rational proof of a never-changing block universe is obtained.

If my view is right, then Parmenides is, fundamentally, a cosmologist, as his predecessors were, rather than an 'ontologist'; a cosmologist, as he himself was when he developed a theory that went far beyond Anaximander's (which he may have known from reports by Xenophanes[8]); a cosmologist, as was Heraclitus, who challenged him by proposing to him the problem of change. And a cosmologist like Xenophanes who, with his unheard-of monotheism, his globular God who never moves, might have given him a hint for the unheard-of solution to his central problem.

Only if Parmenides looked at the Way of Truth as a cosmology – an unheard-of cosmology – is its connection with his false (but second-best) Way of Delusive Opinion at all understandable. And only if that Way of Delusive Opinion is indeed his own theory – rejected by himself but once seriously proposed – is there a point in his letting the goddess preserve it, both as the second-best theory, and as a warning.

So it seems to me. But, of course, this too is all 'a woven web of guesses'.

Comment on the historical conjecture

Burnet once said (see Essay 4, Section II) that we must not (as Th. Gomperz did) interpret Parmenides as a Kant before Kant: we must not interpret the Two Ways as *Reality versus Appearance*. But this is exactly what we must do. The difference is in the main that Kant was a post-Newtonian Parmenides, and that after Newton the world of appearance could no longer be renounced, or denounced, as mere delusion: the world of *doxa*, of appearance, had become the realm of scientific 'truth'.

Parmenides could not, once his naive faith in his early discoveries had been shaken, proclaim them as science or knowledge or truth; but he was too good a scientist to throw them away altogether. He knew he had come nearer to the truth than had other mortals.

There are many examples in the history of thought (and of science) of a similar attitude: Bohr's correspondence arguments; Schrödinger's Schopenhauerianism; Einstein's attitude to general relativity (of which he was highly critical); even Newton's attitude towards action at a distance and Kepler's dislike of the area law may all be mentioned as cases where great scientists published some work in whose truth they did not believe though they rightly felt that they had made a step towards greater truthlikeness.

If we take *eoikota* in Parmenides (DK B8: 60) as a term first used in the sense of 'truthlike' by Xenophanes as argued above, then what Parmenides (or the goddess) says is that one of the reasons for writing the Way of Opinion is the superior truthlikeness of its cosmology.

We must, however, take it that Parmenides sincerely renounced the Way of Opinion and his erstwhile cosmology – just as Schrödinger renounced the world of appearance – the world described by natural science, in spite of his great contributions to science, and his great interest in science. As just remarked about Kant, my thesis is that the difference between Parmenides and, say, Schrödinger is in this respect *only* that since Newton, science (= opinion) had become successful and thus less easy to discard.

So much for the time being on the relationship between Parmenides' Two Ways. I think my conjecture throws some light on the Way of Truth (in which there are allusions to a Third Way). The main point is the thesis 'there is only *one* truth', which may have misled Parmenides. But in the main, there is more to the Way of Opinion – I mean, more truth – than most people believe. At any rate, it was the most important contribution to theoretical physics ever made, since it became the basis of working with mathematical *equations* in physics.

Notes

1 Fragment B16 should be placed as early as possible after fragment B8, perhaps after fragment B9, possibly even before B8.
2 Diogenes Laertius IX.21.
3 DK12 A18; A11; and A21.
4 See F. Heinimann, *Nomos und Physis*, Darmstadt, 1965, pp. 10f, where support is given to Karl Reinhardt's suggestion that the opposition between

nomos ('convention') and *physis* ('nature') goes back to Parmenides' antithesis between *doxa* and *well-rounded truth*.

5 See Essay 1, Section XII.

6 Disproof (*elenchus*) is also Socrates' favoured form of argument. (See the Introduction and Essay 10, Sections IV–IX.)

7 It is astonishing how this fragment has been misunderstood by commentators (except, perhaps, Karl Reinhardt) and how the translators have failed to make any sense of it. (See Essay 3, Section 6.)

8 I conjecture that Xenophanes knew Anaximander's cosmology, and that he even defended it against Anaximenes when he wrote what is now preserved as fragment B28. [See Essay 2, Section 2. Ed.]

ESSAY 7

BEYOND THE SEARCH FOR INVARIANTS

What unites philosophers of science – if anything does – is an insatiable interest in ideas and in their history. I mean, of course, *abstract ideas*: those things in whose existence Berkeley did not believe, although, being a great philosopher of science, he was as fascinated by them as any of us. Abstract ideas, that is, theories, hypotheses, conjectures, and other 'notions', in every state of their development, from groping and confused ideas to clearly and sharply formulated ones, are the things on which we feed, and on which we thrive.

1   Parmenides and modern science

Ideas, products and contents of thoughts, exert an *almost* omnipotent[1] influence over human minds, and over the direction that the further evolution of ideas may take. This is quite obvious as far as religious ideas are concerned: the ideas of Buddhism or Christianity may rule over us, colouring not only our language but our thinking, every step we take, and even every observation. Yet few philosophers or scientists are aware (despite the work of Emile Meyerson, or Charles Kahn's *Anaximander*) of the influence exerted by some of the oldest ideas of Greek philosophy and Greek science upon our most advanced scientific theories: upon classical physics and chemistry, relativity, quantum theory, genetics, and even molecular biology.

I shall attempt here to show you the almost unlimited power still exerted over Western scientific thought by the ideas of a great man who lived about 2,500 years ago: Parmenides of Elea.

These ideas of Parmenides determined the aim and methods of science as the search for invariants. But I shall attempt to show you that these

Opening Address to the International Colloquium on the Philosophy of Science, Bedford College, London, 11 July 1965. The original title was 'Rationality and the Search for Invariants'. {Section headings to the present essay have been proposed by Mr David Miller, who also made numerous suggestions for the stylistic improvement of the text throughout the collection. Ed.}

146

truly portentous ideas of Parmenides suffered a kind of breakdown almost as soon as they were conceived, leading to what I shall call a *Parmenidean apology*, and that this breakdown was portentous too; for Parmenidean ideas in modern science have also broken down, again and again, and their breakdown has led to typical Parmenidean apologies. And I shall attempt to show you that since, say, 1935, these ideas have been breaking down again, perhaps more radically than ever before. Yet so deeply and unconsciously do they pervade our ways of thinking that very few people (the only one I know of is David Bohm[2]) have made any conscious effort to replace them.

Since, according to my story, Parmenides' ideas have had so powerful a grip upon the evolution of scientific ideas, it goes without saying that I am not only an admirer of Parmenides, but also (as was Meyerson) highly appreciative of his influence. Indeed, admiring or appreciating the ideas of both 'classical' and 'modern' physics is, according to my story, almost the same thing as appreciating the influence of Parmenidean ideas.

Nevertheless, I shall try, throughout this story, to speak critically of this influence; and I shall try to make a contribution towards transcending it. For I am deeply convinced that, in science, criticism of ideas is second in importance only to the production of new ideas; and that it is the critical attitude towards its most cherished ideas – their criticism *sub specie veritatis* – that distinguishes science from most other intellectual activities.

I suggest that, as philosophers, we have a very special critical task – the task of swimming against the tide. Thus we should try, in spite of our critical attitude, to help and support any neglected idea, however unpromising, and especially any *new* idea; for *new ideas are rare*; and even if there is only a little truth in some of them, they may perhaps indicate an intellectual need, or perhaps some confusion within the set of ideas that we have uncritically accepted so far.

And I suggest that we should try to continue to swim against the tide, even after the new idea has become accepted, and particularly if it should become a powerful dogma, a ruling ideology. In other words, we should be ready to criticize almost any idea that has been accepted, and we should fight that widespread tendency to follow the lead of some ruling fashion and to climb on to the intellectual bandwagon, whether it is a philosophical bandwagon, or a so-called paradigm, or an influential scientific fashion.

2 Scientific inquiry – an unending quest

The attempt to swim against the tide may sometimes lead to unexpected situations. For example, a philosopher or scientist may be struck by the calamity that his own ideas become fashionable. An experienced swimmer against the tide will, however, know what to do should he ever find himself in this envied yet unenviable position. He will simply continue his favourite exercise, even if it means swimming against the tide of his own followers. Thus Isaac Newton, as we all know, described action at a distance, perhaps a bit too severely, as a theory that only a philosophical nitwit could accept[3] – in spite of his loyal follower Roger Cotes. Karl Marx is credited with the splendid remark 'Moi, je ne suis pas marxiste!' – if he ever made it, it was surely his best. Charles Darwin never ceased to fight for the doctrine of evolution, yet he never ceased to stress that variability and selection were merely two of the most important factors contributing to its explanation. Albert Einstein said that he could imagine for relativity 'no fairer destiny . . . than that it should point the way to a more comprehensive theory'.[4] And P. A. M. Dirac closes his book *The Principles of Quantum Mechanics* with the following paragraph on the difficulties of his theory:[5]

> The difficulties, being of a profound character, can be removed only by some drastic change in the foundations of the theory, probably a change as drastic as the passage from Bohr's orbit theory to the present quantum mechanics.

3 Parmenides' teaching of the Two Ways

Even Parmenides, whom one might easily mistake for the most dogmatic of all great philosophers (as Charles Kahn rightly stresses, he claims 'absolute certainty' for his doctrine), adopts, perhaps unconsciously, a somewhat similar attitude. For his poem is written in *two* parts. In the first part, the Way of Truth (or more fully, the Way of Inquiry that Alone Leads to Truth), he discloses the revelation, received from 'the goddess', of the real world, the world of knowledge and truth. But this is followed by a second part, the Way of Illusion (the *Doxa*, or the Way of Delusive Opinion), in which he adds the goddess's revelation of the origin of error, of the fatal mistake made by mortals, and of its necessary consequence: the emergence of a whole world of illusion.[6]

Thus we are first given the certain truth, the only truth, and the whole truth. (Like Wittgenstein at the end of the preface to the *Tractatus*, Parmenides might have written: 'the *truth* of the thoughts here communicated seems to me unassailable and definitive'.) This truth is based on the thesis '*it* [the knowable, the object of knowledge, the real world] *is, or exists*', so that it cannot not exist.[7] Parmenides (or the goddess) asserts that, beyond speaking of,[8] and knowing,[9] what exists, no speech or knowledge (that is, thought) is possible: 'What can be said, and what can be known, must be what *is* (what is the case, what exists, what is real).'[10] Indeed, he might well have quoted Wittgenstein: 'Whereof one cannot speak [and thus whereof one cannot think] thereof one must be silent.'[11] Yet like Wittgenstein, he found himself speaking about the unspeakable.

For having proved, in the Way of Truth, that it was impossible for the existing to change or to evolve,[12] he proceeded, in the Way of Illusion, the second part of his poem, to discuss in detail the world order (*diakosmos*) of change, the world order that did not exist – except in the delusions of erring mortals.[13] Thus he eagerly passed on to his audience that the goddess revealed to him also

> . . . how it was that delusive opinion,
> forcing its way through all things, was destined to pass for the real.[14]

Of this world of illusion Parmenides gives a marvellous and highly original description, incorporating for the first time (as far as we know) the borrowed light of the Moon, the identity of the Morning and Evening Stars, and, it seems, the spherical shape of the Earth.

Why did Parmenides (or the goddess) include this second part, the revelation of the mistake made by erring mortal men, a mistake that led them by necessity along the way of error and illusion to the belief in something non-existent, a world order of illusion of sense, of change, of genesis and destruction?[15]

The goddess gives two reasons.

The first reason is that she wishes to give the true logical explanation of this fatal mistake: how it arises, and how it brings about with necessity the illusion of the genesis, or cosmogony, of a world order that in truth is non-existing, though its deceptive description sounds wholly like the truth.[16]

The second and equally important reason is that by her explanation she wishes to fortify the faith, the conviction, of the recipient of her revelation against the danger of being perverted by the unfounded conventional claims to knowledge: the claim that we know from our senses[17] that this world of change does exist, and that it is the seat of awful demonic or divine powers.[18] Against these seductively deceptive claims she wishes to make her disciple secure, so that he would not be unduly impressed and wrongly carried away by any false claims to knowledge, but would be able to understand why they are mistaken and yet so deceptively truthlike. Thus he

> . . . will be nevermore led astray by the notions of mortals.[19]

By 'the notions of mortals' Parmenides meant to allude, somewhat contemptuously, to the claims to knowledge of traditions and conventions: of common sense, of Greek religion, of cosmogonies such as Hesiod's.[20] Most probably he also had in mind the cosmologies of the Ionian and early Italian philosophers; and almost certainly, in my opinion, the cosmology (and logic) of Heraclitus.[21]

4 A Parmenidean anticipation of critical rationalism

Interpreted in this way, the function of the second part of Parmenides'
poem is to strengthen the impact of the first. And yet, I think it reveals an
uneasiness, a lack of certainty: Parmenides *felt the need* to explain our world
of error and illusion, even if only to combat and to transcend it; *he felt, and
admitted, the need* to make his reader secure against false claims to knowledge. He clearly did not admit (in anticipation of Marx's saying) that he
was no Parmenidean. But he felt the need to prop up his case by what I
may perhaps call a '*defensive attack*'; and this I think can only mean that he
felt, however unconsciously, that there was something weak in his Way of
Truth, in spite of its great logical strength. This diagnosis of Parmenides'
Second Way as a defensive attack, as an apology – a '*Parmenidean apology*' as
I will call it – is supported by the fact that his great pupil Zeno also made
use of defensive attacks – indeed, perhaps the most searching and ingenious defensive attacks known in the history of philosophy.

The relationship between Parmenides' Two Ways has always puzzled
philosophers. I think that it is, on the face of it, perfectly straightforward:
the goddess always speaks the truth, even when she warns her listener that
she will now end her true account of existence[22] in order to tell him how
error and illusion were fated to arise;[23] and she still speaks the truth when
she explicitly warns him that her account of the world that arises out of
error and consists of illusions will be highly deceptive and truthlike,
because she will show how it arose, from a basic mistake, almost with
logical necessity.[24]

But though this is no doubt what the words of the poem tell us, there
remains that symptom that I have described as a 'defensive attack' or a
'Parmenidean apology': *the attempt, in brief, to reconcile a world of appearance
with the world of reality*, by *explaining* the world of appearance or, quite
literally, *by explaining it away*, as a delusion. This, I assert, is a symptom of
weakness. The implicit admission that an apology is needed is an unintended and probably unconscious concession that there may be more than
meets the eye in that world of illusion.

It was this symptom I had in mind when I said earlier that the ideas of
Parmenides suffered some kind of breakdown almost as soon as they were
conceived.

I shall try to show that this breakdown is not only symptomatic, but
typical; and that, in the long sequence of philosophical ideas and physical
theories that Parmenides engendered, down to our own day, there is also a
long sequence of similar breakdowns. If I am right in this, then the story I
am going to tell may be able to throw some additional light on the
problem of the relationship between the Two Ways of Parmenides –
and, at the same time, on the greatness of this great mind. For it shows,
I think, that Parmenides was less dogmatic and, at least unconsciously,

more self-critical than one may be inclined to admit at first. That Parmenides was a *rationalist* – that he believed in the critical use of logical argument, that is, in the use of refutation[25] – is obvious enough. If I am right, he was, in spite of his fundamentally dogmatic approach, not quite as far from being a '*critical rationalist*' as one might think.

Giorgio de Santillana in his spirited book *The Origins of Scientific Thought*, and in a fascinating lecture, 'Prologue to Parmenides', has given strong and attractive arguments in support of two interesting theses which, in spite of much that can be said in their support do not, on balance, appear to me acceptable.[26]

The first of these two theses is that Parmenides' 'being' is (his version of) Euclidean three-dimensional space – in fact, pure (and therefore 'empty') space. I agree that Parmenides' being is spatially extended; and de Santillana's argument that it is an attempt to correct the Pythagorean discrete geometry of points seems to me attractive. But Parmenides says that the world is *full*; and he says even that it has a *middle* and is firmly held within *limits*, or within widely extended (*megalōn*, B8: 26; cp. B1: 13) fetters. This seems to me decisive – even though I am well aware of the fact that the text can be explained away.

The second of de Santillana's theses, which also seems to me hard to accept, is even more attractive than his first; and the evidence against it seems to me less strong. It concerns the relation between the Way of Truth and The Way of Opinion, and may be summed up as follows. The Way of Truth is mathematics (geometry), which is certain; the Way of Opinion is physics, which is *conjectural opinion*. The traditional view that in Parmenides *doxa* (or *dokeō*) means 'illusion' rather than 'conjecture' (as it does in Xenophanes) is according to de Santillana due to 'the idealistic philosophers', especially Plato and Aristotle.

I wish I could accept this view: it would fit my own view that Parmenides was something like a critical rationalist. Yet it seems to me that two arguments speak, on balance, against it, even though I could myself marshal many suitable uses of the words *dokeō* and *doxa*. One of the arguments is that these uses, apart from those in Xenophanes, come especially from Plato (who is held by de Santillana to bear the main responsibility for the misinterpretation of Parmenides); yet, especially in the *Timaeus* (see, for example, 27d–28d), Plato himself propounded, with unmistakable allusion to Parmenides, an epistemological view concerning the physical world that is almost identical with the one that de Santillana ascribes to Parmenides. Plato, however, appears to hold this view as an urgently necessary *adjustment* of Parmenides' too rigid interpretation of the *doxa*. This makes it difficult to explain Plato's view of Parmenides by Plato's own idealistic deviation from Parmenidean realism, as suggested by de Santillana.

But the main point is again Parmenides' text. It seems only too clear that Parmenides' epistemological opposition between Truth and *doxa* (*dokeō*) is much more severe than that of Xenophanes (B34 and 35): he constantly opposes the *doxa* to *true belief* (while Xenophanes admits that mortals may hold, accidentally, some true opinion, although they would not *know* it), and he emphatically declares that, according to truth, a world of motion, of change, and of plurality, is *impossible*. So when the genesis of this impossible world is explained, it is explicitly described as *due to a mistake*. These passages are, I feel, decisive, and there is no need to quarrel about the question whether the goddess characterizes her own description of this impossible world of change as 'a *deceptive* order of my words' (which seems to me the correct rendering) or as 'a *tricky* order of my words' (as de Santillana suggests). I cannot but feel that the tendency of the text is unmistakable: the *doxa* are the delusions of the mortal, which must be explained (and explained away). Just as Reason is opposed to the senses (which are utterly rejected in B7), so Truth is opposed to *doxa*. Thus the *doxa* are rejected also – and in no uncertain manner. They are delusions in Parmenides and his immediate successors rather than conjectures; and they are restored to the status of conjectures by the idealist Plato.

A use of the term *doxa* that is clearly Parmenidean in this sense, together with what I believe to be an allusion to Parmenides (B8: 60–1), may be found in Empedocles (B132), who can hardly be dismissed as a Platonic idealist. (See note 20 below, where the passage from Empedocles is quoted and discussed.)

(After finding – in 1986, cp. the Addendum to Essay 4 above – that the word ἀπατηλὸν = 'delusive' is most likely a copying mistake for ἀπάτητον = 'untrodden', 'very new', etc,. my view on *doxa* has to some extent approached that of de Santillanas.)

5 Knowledge without foundations

What I call the *attitude of the critical rationalist* goes somewhat beyond the attitude of cherishing ideas and their critical discussion: the critical rationalist is (unlike Parmenides) aware that he can never *prove* his theories but can, at best, refute some of their competitors. Thus the critical rationalist never tries to *establish* a theory about the world: he does not believe in 'foundations'. Yet he may believe – as I do – that if we produce many competing ideas, and criticize them severely, we *may*, if we are lucky, get nearer to the truth. This method is the method of *conjectures and refutations*; it is the method of taking many risks, by producing many (competing) hypotheses; of making many mistakes; and of trying to correct or eliminate some of these mistakes by a critical discussion of the competing hypotheses. I believe that this is *the* method of the natural sciences, including cosmology, and I think that it can be applied also to philosophical problems; yet I once believed that arithmetic was different, and that it could have 'foundations'. As far as arithmetic is concerned, my former colleague, Imre Lakatos, converted me four or five years before the first version of this essay was written to the opposite belief: I owe to him my present view that it is not only the natural sciences (and, of course, philosophy) but also arithmetic that has no foundations. Yet this does not prevent us from always trying, as Hilbert suggested,[27] 'to lay the foundations at a deeper level as it becomes necessary with any edifice if we add to its height', as long as we mean by 'foundations' something that does not guarantee the security of the edifice, and that may change in a revolutionary way – as it may in the natural sciences.[28]

Despite its lack of (secure) foundations, our knowledge can *grow* – and it can grow in height only if it grows in depth: it grows by producing new problems, of new depth, which stimulate new tentative solutions; that is, new ideas; and it grows by the critical discussion of these ideas. Nothing in our intellectual life is exempt from this process of criticism and error elimination.

Though I call this view 'critical rationalism', or sometimes simply 'rationalism', I am aware, of course, that there are many other views that may be called 'rationalism', and I shall also call by this name views that differ considerably from my own; for example the somewhat less critical doctrine of Parmenides. I say this partly to avoid misunderstanding, and partly to indicate that I do not care much for 'a precise terminology'. Words do not matter. What we should discuss are not words, but *problems and theories about the world*, as Parmenides did.

6 Realism

Like Parmenides I am a realist: I am interested in *problems and theories about the world*. If, in addition to critical rationalism, I may confess to a second faith, it is *realism*.

My faith in realism and my faith in critical rationalism are not, however, commitments, but merely conjectures, since I am quite ready to give them up under the pressure of serious criticism. Yet with respect to realism I feel very near to Parmenides. For should I have to give up realism I think I should lose all interest in ideas, since the only reason for my interest is my desire to learn something about the world, and for this we need ideas, especially theories about the world. It seems to me almost miraculous that we have learnt so much about the world, even though all this knowledge is conjectural, and beset with unsolved problems, which constantly remind us how little we know. Next to art, or even equal to it, science – that is, producing and testing theories *about the world, about reality* – seems to me to be the greatest creative enterprise of which men are capable.

7 Rationality and the search for invariants

Thus far my personal confession of a conjectural faith may be summed up by the two slogans 'critical rationalism' and 'realism'. I felt that I had to state these early, in order to avoid misunderstanding. For, as I have said, my topic is no less than an attempt to criticize a closely related version of rationalism; a version of rationalism that has determined the limits of Western science, and especially of Western physical science, for the last twenty-four centuries; limits that many rationalists believe to be indeed the proper limits of all rational science.

The limits of rationalism I have in mind are drawn by the (post-) Parmenidean doctrine that *science is strictly limited to the search for invariants: the search for what does not change during change*: for what remains constant, or invariant, under certain transformations.

As against this version of rationalism I shall propose, *very* tentatively, the conjecture that though the search for invariants is admittedly one of the most important of all scientific tasks, it does not constitute or determine the limits of rationality, or of the scientific enterprise.

But my plans for this essay go beyond this. After my remarks on the history of my problem, I shall try to argue that there was, and still is, something valuable in at least some of the irrationalist attacks on rationalism; something important has been seen by those irrationalists who spoke of 'creative' or 'emergent' evolution. I have no intention of making any concessions to irrationalism, and certainly none to vitalism. But I believe that one should always be ready to learn and to accept suggestions – especially from the camp of one's enemies.

So much by way of introduction. I now proceed to my historical remarks.

8 Early ideas of opposites and change

The naive or commonsense view of the world that we find in Homer or Hesiod and, I should say, is still widely accepted is this: all kinds of changes are going on in our world, but certain things such as mountains or stars are quite stable. Other things, such as the phases of the Moon or the seasons, change *regularly*. Of course, there are lots of things that change irregularly, which may be explained as owing to the whim or temper of some demon or deity. Yet in early oriental and Greek religion, the whims of the gods show a tendency to become subject to law, to justice, to regularity: chaos gives way to cosmos, to a world order; the seasons become linked with the regularities of the starry heavens; and even the whimsical planets, the wandering gods, are suspected of being ruled by law.

In his wonderful book *Anaximander and the Origins of Greek Cosmology* Charles Kahn has shown in great detail how the cosmogony and cosmology

154

of Anaximander developed and transformed these early ideas. Anaximander's unbounded and inexhaustible *Apeiron* is the origin and starting point, the 'principle' (*archē*) of the world, the imperishable power that gives birth to all things. (Anaximander's map of the heavens, like his map of the Earth, must have pictured the universe as organized in a system of concentric circles.[29]) From the *Apeiron*, there 'emerge the opposing principles whose interaction constitutes the world'.[30]

The idea of *opposites or contraries* is a very old one: hot and cold, moist and dry, day and night, summer and winter, and many others, are conceived as active powers fighting each other. Opposites play an important role in many primitive views of the world. Their confrontation is strife, or *war*. This shows that the role played by the opposites, the opposing powers, is closely connected with the social or political theory of the natural world, or with the early identification of the social order and the order of nature, or of normative laws and natural laws.[31]

All this is to be found in Anaximander; and under his influence, the idea of opposites developed into a primitive *theory of change*: change is conceived as qualitative change, as the temporary victory of one of a pair of opposing powers over the other.

Thus the idea of change, and even a theory of change linked with the doctrine of opposites, were in existence before Heraclitus. But it was Heraclitus, I believe, who first saw, though only intuitively, what may be called the paradox of change or, simply, the *problem of change*.

9　The problem of change

The problem of change, and of understanding change, is a strange and perplexing problem, and one that it is difficult to make people aware of. Whether they are physicists or philosophers, it was solved for them so long ago that they take it for granted that there cannot be much in it. (Nor are they aware that the various solutions offered are incompatible.)

The problem may be put as follows. All change is change of something. There must be a *thing* that changes; and that thing must remain, while it changes, *identical with itself*. But if, we must ask, it remains identical with itself, how can it ever change?

The question seems to reduce to absurdity the idea that any particular thing can change.

A green leaf changes when it becomes brown; but not if we replace it with a brown leaf: it is essential for change that the changing leaf remains the same during change. But it is also essential that it becomes something else: 'it was green, and it becomes brown; it was moist, and it becomes dry; it was hot, and it becomes cold.'[32]

Aristotle said, much later, that what remains identical is the matter (*hylē*) or the substance (*ousia*).[33] But our problem arises also for immaterial, abstract 'things', such as situations – say, in war. In war 'the situation has changed' may (for example) mean that the enemy's advance has been turned into a retreat. There is no 'matter' or 'substance' here to serve as the subject of change.

I believe that it was a thought such as this that led Heraclitus to his solution of the problem of change.

Heraclitus' solution is: 'Everything is in flux, and nothing is at rest.'[34] It is a denial of 'things' that change (or, we may say, it is the placing of 'thing' in quotes). *There are no things – there are only changes, processes.* There is no leaf-as-such, no unchanging substratum that is first moist and then dry; there is rather the process, the drying leaf. 'Things' are an illusion, a mistaken abstraction from reality. All things are like flames, like fire. *A flame may look like a thing, but we know that it is not a 'thing' but a process.*

Thus what appears to our senses as a thing is a comparatively slow or (as Heraclitus puts it) 'measured' process; it is like a situation in war that does not change, owing to the balance (the 'tension') of the opposing forces.

All this applies to ourselves. We may appear to ourselves as things, if we look at ourselves superficially. But if we look a little deeper, we find that we are processes; and that, if the processes stop, that is the end of us. This, it seems, was the original insight that led to Heraclitus' discovery: 'I searched myself',[35] he tells us. And what he found was not a thing, but a process: a burning fire, a flame. We are the more alive, the more fully ourselves, the more we are *awake*. If we are *asleep*, if our life processes are reduced, our souls are hardly any longer a living fire – we are almost dead.

Thus there are no things, but only processes; or rather, *one world process* in which all the individual processes merge: 'All things are one', Heraclitus says, and 'God is day and night, winter and summer, peace and war, satiety and hunger' – all the opposites, this is the meaning – 'and He changes . . . .'[36]

Thus for Heraclitus, rest is a state of change: 'In changing it is at rest', he says.[37] But this is only an instance – though an extreme one – of the doctrine that day and night, winter and summer – in short, all the opposites – are identical.

For they are merely the constitutive aspects of *the self-identical process or change* that replaces the self-identical thing, and consists in linking one of some pair of opposites with the other. None of them can exist without the other, or without the process, the change, that unites them.

10 Parmenides' logical resolution of the problem of change

Now we come back to Parmenides; for it was he who replied to Heraclitus and, with his reply, given in the Way of Truth, laid down the metaphysical framework for almost all serious thinking in Western science and philosophy.

Parmenides answered Heraclitus simply by applying the original argument to the whole world (which, according to Heraclitus, was *one* world process). The world, reality, that which we want to understand, the subject of our discourse, *exists in truth*.[38] Whatever else reality may be, since there is only *one* reality – or, as Heraclitus says, since reality is *one* – it must remain identical with itself during change. Thus the old problem arises again: *change is paradoxical*.

This paradox, according to Parmenides, constitutes a *logical* impossibility. *The existence of change can be logically disproved*. The disproof follows from the premise: 'It is.'[39] This may be interpreted: 'The knowable exists.' Or in a tautological form: 'What is, is.' Or else, equally tautologically: 'What exists, exists.' This is the premise. The argument can be put in several ways; for, as Parmenides himself remarks:[40]

> Where to begin is all the same to me:
> I shall return thereto in time again.

I will here restate, almost literally, some of Parmenides' arguments:[41]

(1) We start from our premise '*It is*'.
(2) We are now faced with the '*decision*' (*crisis*): '*It is or it is not.*' (The 'or' here is to be interpreted as *exclusive*; and there is no third possibility.[42])
(3) 'It is not' is impossible. This follows from (1) and (2), and can also be expressed as: *Nothingness cannot exist*.
(4) *All is full of the existing.*
(5) *It is all continuous and one, for the existing is everywhere in perfect contact with the existing.* (There cannot be any 'pores'.[43])
(6) The existing is throughout one and the same (*homoion*) and *indivisible*. This leads to what I regard as *the main theorem*:
(7) *The existing is motionless*: self-identical and resting in itself, it remains firmly where it is.

Proof: Since the existing is indivisible (6) and all is full of it (4), there is no space for movement.

The argument may be summed up as follows:[44]

> *Only what is, is.*
> *Nothingness cannot exist.*
> *The world is full.*
> *Motion is impossible.*

(8) The full world of Parmenides was, according to what the poem says, *corporeal*.[45] It was a *motionless block universe*.

157

11 The atomist critique of Parmenides' solution

Parmenides' theory of the block universe was the first deductive cosmology. One might even call it the first deductive system of theoretical
physics. I do not wish to discuss here the purely verbal question whether
Parmenides himself should or should not be regarded as the first theoretical physicist. It is enough that he became the father, or perhaps the
grandfather, of all theoretical physics, and, more especially, of the atomic
theory.

The atomic theory arose, as almost every empirical theory does, from an
empirical refutation of its predecessor.[46]

Parmenides had derived an *empirically testable* conclusion: the conclusion
that motion is impossible.

Yet this conclusion is clearly refuted by experience; and so the refutation
of the conclusion can be used, step by step, to refute part of the original
position. As usual in such empirical refutations, the refuted system is
retained as far as this is possible.

The refutation may be put as follows:

Motion is a fact. Therefore motion is possible. Therefore the world
cannot be *one* full block; rather, it must contain both many blocks – it
must be divisible – *and* nothingness; that is, empty space. Nothingness or
empty space is thus not non-existent. The full blocks are *in* empty space.

The blocks remain Parmenidean – that is, full and *unchangeable*; they
were first called 'the existing' or 'the full' and soon afterwards 'indivisibles'
or 'atoms'. The empty space was called 'the non-existing', and later 'the
void'. Thus we arrive at a world consisting of *atoms and the void*.

This was how atomism emerged. We know how successful it became.
But by far its greatest success was that it could offer a solution to
Parmenides' original problem: atomism provided a straightforward *solution
to the problem of change – a rational theory of change*. And the solution was
this.

All change, including qualitative change, is due to spatial movement;
more especially, to the movement of the unchangeable full atoms in the
unchangeable void.

Thus all change is sheer rearrangement. Parmenides' teaching was
accepted at least in two all-important points: the really existing, the
atoms, never changed. Consequently there could be no intrinsic change,
no intrinsic novelty. There could only be *new arrangements* of what was
intrinsically always the same thing. Kahn has seen this very clearly.
According to Parmenides, Kahn writes, 'the generation of something
essentially new was considered an impossibility'.[47]

This theory of change, that all change is movement – a theory due to
Leucippus and Democritus – remained the basis of theoretical physics for

more than 2,000 years. It is mainly – but by no means exclusively – in this form that Parmenidean rationalism not only survived, but continued to dominate Western science. It still does.

12   Parmenides' rationalist research programme

Before proceeding, I wish to raise an important question.

The result of Parmenides' theory – that reality is one unchangeable block, and that the changeable world of mortals is an illusion – is not only unacceptable. Not only does it clash with common sense; it is clearly absurd. Accordingly, Parmenides was scoffed at by the few who took any notice of his bold theory. Some, we hear, even called him a madman. And yet, this madman succeeded in throwing a spell upon us sceptical and reluctant rationalists; upon Western theologians as well as upon Western scientists. How can we explain this? Wherein lies Parmenides' achievement?

Parmenides, I believe, was a *cosmologist*, and a *metaphysical realist*. This fundamental attitude he inherited from his predecessors; in the main from Anaximander. And he inherited too the most important attitude of searching for a *world behind this world* – a real world behind this world of appearance.

But what was new in his approach? I shall deal with this question under two headings: (1) Epistemology and logic; (2) Methodological consequences.

(1)   Epistemology and logic

Parmenides was not the originator of epistemological thought: he was preceded by Xenophanes, Alcmaeon, and Heraclitus.[48] Heraclitus, like Alcmaeon, began his book with a kind of epistemological preface or proem, albeit a sketchy one compared with that of Parmenides. (Thus there started a tradition of epistemological prefaces that is still alive; most probably owing to its having been reinforced by Plato's epistemological preface to the *Timaeus*, in which he is heavily indebted to Parmenides.)

But though Parmenides did not originate epistemology, he was the first to make it *the centre of philosophical thought*. He was the first to announce a rationalist programme. *Reason, rather than sense.* Pure thought, critical logical argument, rather than common sense, plausibility, experience, and tradition.[49]

There was argument before Parmenides. But for all we know it was little articulated. It was implicit in the attempts to improve upon the theories propounded by one's predecessors, or by tradition. For example, Xenophanes' criticism of anthropomorphic thinking in theology is, clearly, highly argumentative. And yet, we do not know of any fully articulated argument before Parmenides. His rationalism produced the first discursive logical reasoning. And it was critical reasoning – refutation. His proofs are proofs by *reductio ad absurdum*: they reduce the assumptions to absurdity.[50]

Thus he inspired Zeno: it took just one generation for logical reasoning to reach the very height and depth of subtlety. And although I do not think that Parmenides' 'being' is Euclidean space (or any other space),[51] I fully agree with A. Szabó[52] that the origin of the method which culminated in Euclid's axiomatics can be found in the dialectic of the Eleatic School.

Apart from the achievement of Anaximander (and possibly that of Thales), there is nothing quite as significant in the history of Western thought as this breakthrough from darkness to light (so Parmenides describes it in his proem), the invention of articulated critical argument.

(2) Methodological consequences

The consequences of this breakthrough were momentous, especially the methodological consequences.

Parmenides was the first to assert explicitly the existence of a theoretical world of reality behind the phenomenal world of appearance; a reality created by argument and utterly different from the phenomenal world. And he was the first to formulate something like a criterion of reality. (He equated the real with the invariant, the unchanging.)

In addition he was the first to formulate, though (I believe) by way of attack, the empiricist dogma: 'There is nothing in the intellect of the mortals that was not previously in their senses.'[53]

He also gave something like the first formulation of the (in my opinion invalid) distinction between primary and secondary qualities.

Within methodology proper, he invented the first deductive system and he introduced the method of multiple competing theories and also the method of evaluating competing theories by critical discussion.

He introduced determinism (in an extremely severe form), and linked explanation to logical deduction.

More or less unintentionally, he also introduced the first falsifiable deductive theory. At any rate, he certainly acknowledged the task of explaining appearances; and he saw the need to link the explanation of appearances with the theory of the reality behind the appearances.

Behind all this there lay hidden the following more specialized ideas of scientific method:

The invariant needs no explanation: it can be used as an explicans.

Rational science is the search for invariants.

Out of nothing, nothing can arise.

The immense variety of appearances must have *one* (or at any rate very few forms of) reality behind them. Thus we arrive at the conservation laws (and at ideas like 'substance', 'mass', and 'energy').

Since the real remains identical with itself, science can be expressed in terms of equations. Change of appearance is ruled by unchanging reality.

Parmenides' cosmology together with his epistemology, logic, and methodology may be said (a little arbitrarily) to embody a *metaphysical research programme*; the term is to remind us that it all flows from, or is implicit in, his more or less intuitive metaphysical cosmology, his metaphysical view of the world. It can be described as a research programme because it suggests not only new problems for investigation but also what kind of solutions to these problems would be felt to be satisfactory, or acceptable.

The function of such a comprehensive research programme is in some respects very similar to the function that Thomas Kuhn attributes to those dominant scientific theories that he has unfortunately called 'paradigms': a research programme, if it becomes dominant, exerts a directing influence upon scientific research. However, research programmes do not form part of science in the way that Kuhn's dominant theories do. They are metaphysical, epistemological, and methodological in character.

The Parmenidean research programme became in time more and more articulated. In this way it developed first, by arousing opposition, into the atomistic research programme; and secondly, again by arousing opposition, into the research programme of the continuity theory of matter. Ultimately it developed into scientific theories of the structure of matter, especially into modern atomic theory.[54]

13   The legacy of Parmenides' search for truth

If what I have said so far gives a more or less adequate picture of Parmenides' achievement and immediate influence, then we can understand his hold over his successors, from Zeno and the Eleatic School to Empedocles, the atomists, and Plato. Parmenides, I said, was a rationalist. But he was also a man of intuitions; like many scientists, he combined 'mysticism and logic'.

The atomists, more especially, retained much of Parmenidean thought. They even retained his doctrine that qualitative change and intrinsic or essential novelties are illusions: illusions of mortal men, so constituted that they are deceived into reliance upon their sense organs, and seduced into mistaking the content of their senses (which is that of their sense organs) for 'intellectual thought' and for 'knowledge'. Parmenides formulates this idea in a devastatingly ironical attack on the sensualist theory of knowledge:[55]

> What is, at any one time, in the much-erring sense organs' mixture,
> That seems genuine knowledge to men. For they take as the same thing
> Man's intellectual mind, and his sense organs' nature or mixture.
> 'Thought' they call what in this mixture prevails, in each man and all.

I conjecture that this anti-empiricist fragment was the stimulus that created, in response, the famous empiricist dictum: 'There is nothing in our intellect (or in the human mind) that was not previously in our senses.' For Parmenides' fragment can be interpreted to say that so-called 'human knowledge' is erroneous because 'Nothing is in the mortals' (much-erring) intellect that was not previously in their much-erring senses.' The empiricist response may first have come from Protagoras. For his 'Man is the measure' (*homo mensura*) doctrine was directed against all those (Heraclitus, Xenophanes, Parmenides) who credited only the gods with knowledge but insisted that men could only guess (Xenophanes) or err (Parmenides). Against these, Protagoras pointed out that we have to take human knowledge as our measure in matters of knowledge.

By contrast, Empedocles and especially the atomists accepted the view of Parmenides: our sense organs, they said, are too dull to allow us to observe the movements and the spatial rearrangements of the real things — which, for the atomists, were the unobservable, the atoms. Owing to the dullness of our senses, the atomists said, most of these movements and rearrangements appear to us only as *qualitative* change, which, as in Parmenides, is an illusion. Only Parmenidean rational thought can help us to transcend this illusion, and to interpret it as the result of atoms moving in the void.

Thus the early atomists were, like Parmenides, opposed to our relying on our senses. They also took over Parmenides' theory from the Way of Opinion, according to which what happens to our sense organs is that they get mixed up with our environment. (Not, of course, with 'the light and the dark', or 'the hot and the cold', as in Parmenides' Way of Opinion; but with atoms that emanate from the things that are composed of them.)

But Democritus (according to Galen[56]) realized that, without sense experience, the problem of improving upon Parmenides would never have arisen, so that there would never have arisen an atomic theory refuting Parmenides' cosmology and explaining by the movement of the atoms what Parmenides took to be illusions. This led him to the famous dialogue between Reason and the Senses, as transmitted by Galen:

> *Coloured – by convention; sweet – by convention; bitter – by convention.*
> *But in truth – atoms and the void.*

Against this reasoning, he – Democritus – imagined the senses to speak thus:

Poor intellect! You take your credentials from us and want our downfall? Casting us down you fall yourself!

Thus the Two Ways of Parmenides became the way of reason and the way of the senses: rationalism and empiricism. They also gave rise to the distinction between primary and secondary qualities – between spatial shape or extension (which is real and objective) and colour and sound (which are subjective and hardly better than illusory); a distinction that plays so important a role in Galileo and his successors.

14   The atomist theory of change

Were we to measure the success of a physical theory by the time it lasts, then atomism and its theory of change would certainly be the most successful of all physical theories. For atomism, including its theory of change, survived in physics until about thirty years ago.[57] (In chemistry and molecular biology it is still alive.) It survived the distinction between atoms and molecules; it survived the break-up of the atoms into elementary particles, electrons and protons. It survived the transmutation of atoms and the discovery of the neutrino and of the positron. It survived even Schrödinger's attempt to explain matter as a wave motion. And it began to be seriously threatened only with pair creation and pair destruction, and with the discovery of many new elementary particles that *change intrinsically*, turning one into another, and thus exemplifying what at this moment still seems to be intrinsic or essential change.

But when this happened, Einstein's equation $E = mc^2$ had already provided us with a powerful defence against intellectual defeat. Although physics, for the first time since Leucippus, had no theory of change, we could comfort ourselves with the thought that in all these intrinsic changes and transmutations, energy, which is the same as inert and heavy mass, remains conserved (in conjunction with momentum). So there is something that remains identical with itself even during intrinsic changes – the amount of energy and momentum – which is the essential invariant of change. This fact made us somewhat insensitive to an intellectual blow that otherwise we might have felt strongly – the threatened disintegration of the atomists' theory of change, of the solution to the great problem set by Heraclitus and Parmenides.

15   The Parmenidean theory of invariants

Meanwhile the Parmenidean legacy, and the corresponding research programme, had grown, though perhaps invisibly: the programme became
enshrined in certain general principles, which were taken as trivially true.
Thus arose the principle that a real thing can never come out of nothing –
ex nihilo nihil fit; a principle that soon became a *theory of causality*, or of
causal determinism: everything must have an adequate or equal cause – *causa
aequat effectum*.

These principles mean, of course, again that there is no real change. If
the cause equals the effect, then this equality shows that there really is no
change, no intrinsic variation, but that something remains identical with
itself throughout the causal process. It is in this way that Parmenidean
rationalism led to the theory of invariants, and to the theory that all
explanation of change must *explain change away* (as Emile Meyerson puts
it[58]), not necessarily as an illusion, but at any rate by pointing to that
reality that does not change during change. Consequently this unchanging
reality is not itself in need of explanation. So there must be laws of all
change, and these laws must be expressible in the form of equalities; that
is, as *equations*. And there is but *one* reality behind, and explaining, the
immense variety of experiences (or at any rate very few forms of reality).

In the field of science this leads, among other things, to the conservation
laws (and to ideas like *substance*, and *mass*, and *energy*); and in the philosophy
of science we are led to the so-called *principles* of *causality* and of *the uniformity
of nature* (and what I have called *philosophical determinism*[59]). Anti-militarists,
anti-conformists, and empiricists, like John Stuart Mill, tried to force nature
into uniform, against all the evidence of experience, which told us that
though two guardsmen may appear to be indistinguishable, two cows or
two dogs are usually quite easily distinguished by their owners, and that the
occurrence of identical twins is a rarity rather than a commonplace.

Yet long before the principle that the cause must equal the effect was
accepted by Western scientists (and by Western empiricist philosophers),
it was accepted, with slight though significant modifications, by Western
theologians.

16   Parmenidean roots of continuity and discontinuity
theories of modern physics

The Parmenidean research programme at an early date split into *two main
forms*: the *discontinuity* theory of the atomists – atoms separated by the void
– and the *continuity* theory of a full (yet changing) world, due to Empedocles, Plato, and Aristotle.[60] In its original and simplest form the continuity theory or vortex theory explained all motion as like that of
tea-leaves carried along by the tea in a cup. It always remained a strong
competitor of atomism. Descartes and Huyghens were continuity theorists,

164

while Gassendi and Newton were in the atomist tradition. These two competing dominant theories have remained almost equal in power: and there were attempted mergers from Leibniz to Faraday and Maxwell, Lorentz, Einstein and Schrödinger, with atomism somewhat in the lead. During the middle ages it was Aristotle's continuity theory that dominated Western theology. Yet more important than this somewhat technical aspect of Parmenidean physical theory was the metaphysical principle, accepted in spite of its difficulties for theology, that the cause must equal – or *at least* equal – the effect.

I may perhaps quote Arthur Lovejoy.[61] Though he does not refer to Parmenides, he says that it was

> the doctrine of most mediaeval European metaphysics that all the 'perfections', or positive attributes, of the creatures must be possessed by the First Cause – even though it was found necessary to assert with equal emphasis that this Cause and its creatures have no attributes in common . . . ; the preformationist principle . . . left undiminished the abundance and diversity of nature and did not exclude quantitative and qualitative change from the natural order, but [it] placed behind these a supersensible cause in which all this abundance and diversity were declared to be in some fashion antecedently or eternally contained.

According to this theory, everything that exists has existed, in some form or other, in God, as one of his 'perfections'. Thus even the creation has made no essential change: it only transformed *some* of the pre-existing intrinsic perfections of the Creator into his creation. Thus the cause either equals the effect or is greater than the effect (in which case it is not only prior to the effect, but outlasts the effect); yet the effect is always present in the cause. This means that, in reality, nothing happens; or at any rate, nothing that can make an essential difference: no intrinsic novelty can emerge. Thus with all its abundance and diversity, the mediaeval world is still the offspring of Parmenides' block universe.

Its descent from Parmenides is also very marked in the Cartesian doctrine of a world full of continuous matter in motion (*vortices*), in which the amount of motion is preserved; and it is very clear in most forms of determinism; in Spinoza, for example, or in a somewhat different form in Leibniz. Take Leibniz's pre-established harmony: everything is put into the world by God from the beginning. One wonders what his pre-established clocks are for; their Creator, one fears, must get bored if he sees them going on to perform *precisely* as he made them perform.

Yet Parmenides' idea reached, I think, its highest fulfilment in the continuity theory of Einstein. (I may perhaps mention that I discussed this point with Einstein, and that he agreed with my characterization of his theory as Parmenidean.) Einstein's deterministic cosmology is that of a four-dimensional Parmenidean block universe.[62]

The space-time continuum of general relativity (perhaps even more so than that of special relativity) has sometimes been interpreted as a space, a geometry, that incorporates time. Objective, physical time has been said to be assimilated to the space coordinates. Together with these, it displays the whole content and history of the universe at once, as it were. It forms, as Hermann Weyl puts it,[63]

> a four-dimensional world in which space and time are linked together indissolubly. . . . [It is only our] consciousness that passes on in one portion of this world [and] experiences the . . . piece which comes to meet it and passes behind it, as *history*, that is as a process that is going forward in time.

Elsewhere, Weyl writes: 'The objective world simply *is*, it does not *happen*. Only to the gaze of my consciousness . . . does a section of this world come to life as a fleeting image in space which continuously changes in time.'[64]

Thus change is an illusion, according to this description of Weyl's. There is no change in the four-dimensional objective reality, but only in the way in which our consciousness – the opinion of the mortals – experiences things. It is an illusion attributable to the fact that the events ordered along each of our (time-like) world lines are experienced consecutively by our consciousness.

17 The reality of time: remarks on a modern version of the problem of change

I have reached here a crucial point: the modern form of the problem of the *reality of change*, which may also be called the problem of the *reality of time* (and which is closely related to that of the *arrow of time*, or the *direction of time*). It is a problem where I feel that I am swimming against a veritable spring tide. It seems to me that, with the exception of G. J. Whitrow, the most influential philosophers of physics who have recently written on this subject are to be found in a very different camp, though they hold widely differing views among themselves. There are some of the greatest physicists in that other camp: Boltzmann, Weyl, Schrödinger, and the greatest of all, Einstein. The main question of the reality of time is the question whether the fundamental temporal relations of before and after are objective or merely an illusion.

I am strongly convinced (a) that change and therefore time (which is involved in the physical theory of change) are objective; (b) that no good arguments have been offered against this view (Gödel's construction of a time machine would be a very strong argument if his premises for it were valid); (c) that the idealistic theory of time is irrefutable, but criticizable.

In order to expound the problem as simply as possible, we may start from Newtonian mechanics. Here we have a three-dimensional space, which may be characterized by three space coordinates, and a one-dimensional time, characterized by a time coordinate. Together, they form a four-dimensional manifold.

A realist may be doubtful about calling this manifold 'real'; for clearly, space and time are abstractions. He will, however, say that the spatio-temporal *relations* between real events are real; and he will say that the theoretical system – geometry plus chronometry – of the potential or virtual relations between possible events may be called part of physics, that is, part of our conjectural theories of reality.

These conjectural theories are of our own making (and in so far 'ideal'); but the realist will insist that they are part of our attempt to describe and understand as well as we can the physical reality, the system of events, the system of changes.

Now, it is very convenient, even in Newtonian mechanics, to *represent* the time coordinate by a space coordinate. (This is done in every temperature or pressure curve.) Such a spatial representation of the time coordinate has, however, no direction – any more than the space coordinates have – unless we give it a direction, by marking an arrow pointing, say, in the direction from the 'past' to the 'future'.

Now let us look at a spatial representation of a time coordinate before it has been so marked (see Figure 1).

The suggestion has been made, by Clausius and others, that there is a universally valid law, the law of increasing entropy (or 'the second law of thermodynamics') that can be represented by a curve as in Figure 2, *provided we mark first the direction of time*, as running from left to right.

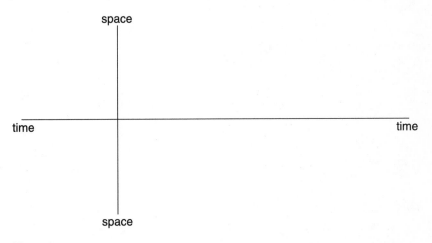

Figure 1

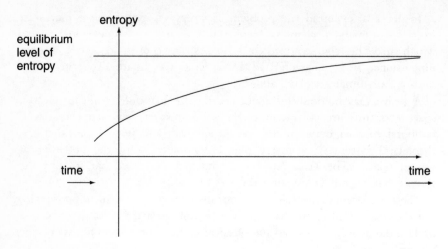

Figure 2

Eddington later suggested that we may take the universal increase of entropy as an objective, physical, indicator of the direction of time, or the arrow of time. It is interesting that Eddington made this suggestion long after the great battle between Boltzmann and Zermelo, which ended with Boltzmann's admission that the curve of statistical mechanics had a very different shape – that of rare occasional downward statistical fluctuations from a maximum entropy or maximum probability equilibrium value (see Figure 3).

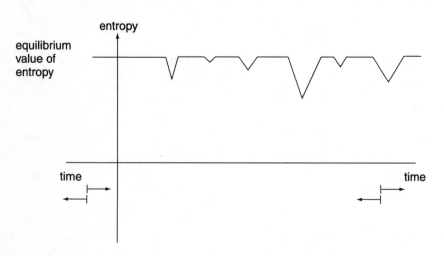

Figure 3

This entropy curve does not change its character if we invert the direction of time: it does not indicate which way 'the arrow of time' should point.

Ludwig Boltzmann, the great physicist and realist, for a time believed that he had been able to deduce, from the molecular theory of gases, a curve of entropy increase like our first curve. Under the criticism of Loschmidt, Poincaré, and especially Zermelo, he gave this theory up, and admitted that the curve was more like our second curve; that is, symmetrical or insensitive with respect to an inversion of the direction of time.

Accordingly, there was still the law of entropy increase to be explained. In this desperate situation, Boltzmann very tentatively suggested, as a way out, a staggeringly bold theory, described by himself as a speculation. The theory can be expressed, slightly distorting our second curve, as in Figure 4.[65]

That is to say, the time coordinate itself has no arrow, no direction; but whenever there is a major fluctuation in some part of the world, then any live organism, any observer, will *experience* a direction of time: he will experience that the future lies in the direction of entropy increase. This explains the 'second law'.

To quote Boltzmann himself:[66]

> For the universe as a whole the two directions of time are indistinguishable, just as in space there is no up and down. However, just as at a certain place on the earth's surface we call 'down' the direction towards the centre of the earth, so a living being that

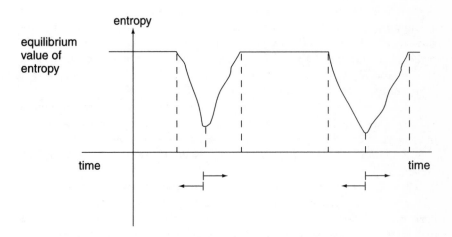

Figure 4

finds itself in . . . a [non-equilibrium region of the] world . . . can characterize the direction of time as going from less probable to more probable states (the former will be the 'past' and the latter the 'future'), and by virtue of this characterization he will find that this . . . region, isolated from the rest of the universe, is 'initially' always in an improbable state.

At first sight, this theory of Boltzmann's may easily be thought to be inconsistent. It becomes consistent only if one takes the time coordinate, like any space coordinate, as having *objectively no direction*. There is nothing like an objective past or an objective future; there is no objective before or after. Time, whatever it may be, becomes like space at least in so far as it forms just one dimension in a four-dimensional manifold which we may call 'objectively co-present', in the sense that no part comes objectively before or after another. (Of course, the phrase 'objectively co-present' is merely another term for 'objectively timeless' in the sense that relations of 'before' or 'after' are no longer regarded as objective. It may help to introduce 'just for the moment', the idea of another auxiliary yet 'genuinely temporal' time dimension – a fifth dimension – and regard the four-dimensional space-time manifold as *at rest*, and therefore '*co-present*', in this five-dimensional world; we shall soon be able to discard the auxiliary fifth dimension.) I shall call this view of Boltzmann's, for brevity's sake, '*the geometrization of time*' (or 'the spatialization of time') without implying that there is no time left in the theory, only space: there *is* a coordinate that is a *time* coordinate, but there is no objective 'before' or 'after'.

Boltzmann's suggestion is admirable and breathtaking in its boldness. But it implies that, objectively speaking, *change is an illusion*. It therefore amounts to giving up his two main tenets: philosophical realism; and the explanation, by way of statistical mechanics and probability theory, of entropy increase with increasing time. For by explaining the direction of time as the direction of entropy increase, the increase of entropy in time becomes a tautology that does not need, and is not open to, a physical explanation. Thus Boltzmann's suggestion, for all its boldness, is *ad hoc*; it is not only *ad hoc* – it amounts to a theoretical suicide.

Boltzmann himself said of this theory: 'Obviously, no one would regard such speculations as important discoveries'. My impression is that he was not happy about this speculation because he felt – no doubt rightly – that it was *ad hoc*. The theory that change is an illusion is a Parmenidean apology.

It is not very surprising that few physicists took Boltzmann's suicidal *ad hoc* speculation seriously: those who were ready to accept Boltzmann's derivation of the entropy law felt that a weaker assumption of Boltzmann's (called by him 'assumption A'[67]) was sufficient: that our own world, or part of the world, found itself some time ago in a state of severe disequilibrium; so severe that it is still very far from equilibrium, though moving towards it. This assumption about an initial state of our part of the world, together with Boltzmann's theory, explained the observed tendency towards an entropy increase, and thus the 'second law'.

This was also the view adopted in the famous monograph on Boltzmann's statistical mechanics by Paul and Tatiana Ehrenfest. As Tatiana Ehrenfest puts it in her preface to the English translation (1959):[68]

> The very important irreversibility of all observable processes can be fitted into the picture in the following way. The period of time in which we live happens to be a period in which the H-function of the part of the world accessible to observation decreases [i.e. the entropy function increases]. This coincidence is not really an accident, since the existence and the function of our organisms, as they are now, would not be possible in any other period. To try to explain this coincidence by any kind of probability considerations will, in my opinion, necessarily fail.

It will be seen that neither Boltzmann nor the Ehrenfests gave anything resembling a mechanical or statistical explanation of the second law. What they gave were *ad hoc* attempts to explain away the failure of the enterprise. It is interesting that Boltzmann's bold, 'suicidal' *ad hoc* speculation which declared all change to be an illusion was not even mentioned by the Ehrenfests, no doubt because their own 'explanation' (which also goes back to Boltzmann) achieved about as much with less radical means. In fact, Boltzmann's Parmenidean apology, and even the theoretical breakdown that gave rise to it – the breakdown of his attempt to give a mechanical theory of the 'second law' – were largely forgotten; for example by Born (see below).[69] Schrödinger, who, for metaphysical reasons, believed in the ideality of time, was one of the few who not only remembered it but saw in it a philosophically most important result of physical theory – indeed, the philosophically most important and intrinsically most beautiful of all physical theories.[70]

18 Parmenidean three-dimensional space and modern relativity theory

Minkowski's emphasis on the indissoluble unity of space and time placed that part of Boltzmann's *ad hoc* speculation that geometrizes or spatializes time at the core of the theory of relativity; so that many, though not all, physicists believed it to be an intrinsic part of the theory. The objective co-presence of the spatio-temporal manifold was accepted as part of relativity by Hermann Weyl and Kurt Gödel, for example; Schrödinger passionately believed in it; and Einstein was certainly much inclined to adopt the same interpretation, though he was far from dogmatic about it.

So after twenty-four centuries, we still have Parmenides' Two Ways – the way of the well-rounded truth, and the way of appearance or illusion. Parmenides' own well-rounded truth seems to have been something like a three-dimensional Riemannian curved universe; Einstein's is, of course, four-dimensional.

Historians of science or philosophy who are reluctant to attribute to a great thinker like Parmenides a doctrine as severely unempirical as the illusionary character of the world of change (and a doctrine as difficult to accept as the doctrine that consciousness is the only thing in the universe that actually undergoes change) may perhaps be less reluctant when they see that great scientists, such as Boltzmann, Minkowski, Weyl, Schrödinger, Gödel, and above all Einstein, have seen things in a similar way to Parmenides, and have expressed themselves in strangely similar terms.

19   Are there limits to rationality?

Thus Einstein, one of the greatest and most revolutionary thinkers of all time, was a Parmenidean. He often called himself a Spinozist, which is not so very different; and when challenged, he admitted his – tentative – Parmenidean faith.

Was Einstein right? Is this the true faith? Are the Parmenidean limits of thought the true limits of rationality? Was Meyerson right when he said, as I mentioned before, that 'to explain is to explain away', and that all rational explanation consists in finding that hidden unchanging reality that establishes the identity of cause and effect?

The possibility that Parmenides' apparently crazy idea, the denial of the reality of change, may indeed define the true *limits of all rationality and of all science*, and confine us to the search for what is invariant, must be taken seriously. It must be taken the more seriously as it was often attacked by all kinds of enemies of rationalism, who talked of dialectical evolution, or of creative evolution, or of emergent evolution, or of 'becoming', without, however, producing a serious theory of 'becoming' – one that could be rationally, that is, critically, discussed.

I think that to take this Parmenidean approach seriously means to criticize it seriously.

To this end, I intend to proceed as follows. I shall first say a few words about alternative interpretations of relativity theory; and I shall then try to point out that the Parmenidean approach has repeatedly broken down in other parts of physics without destroying the rationality of science. Finally I shall try to argue in favour of a non-Parmenidean research programme.

20   Relativity theory and indeterminism

It has sometimes been denied that any serious physicist has ever held the theory of the block universe, and that fighting this theory is a fight against windmills. The main value for our discussion of the quoted passage from Boltzmann is to show that this is not so: as pointed out above, Boltzmann's *ad hoc* speculation is consistent only if we assume that an objective physical time coordinate, in itself directionless, can, in different parts of the universe, be *experienced* as having different directions. But this entails not only the subjective character of the direction of time, but also that the time coordinate is in *some* sense either 'timeless' or 'co-present'. In brief, it geometrizes or spatializes time, in the sense explained above.

That Schrödinger passionately believed in Boltzmann's Parmenidean *ad hoc* speculation I know for certain. That Weyl upheld it seems to me clear from the quotations given (though some people say that he expressed himself only metaphorically). That Einstein was, to say the least, attracted by this interpretation, and ready to defend it, I also know for certain. Thus we have before us more than windmills.

Now, as the passage quoted from Tatiana Ehrenfest shows, there is no need to take Boltzmann's *ad hoc* speculation too seriously. For we have to admit *in any case* that his most admirable statistical mechanics failed to establish the arrow of time (or the phenomenological entropy law) as he had hoped. In order to explain the phenomena – the observed increase of entropy – *some* additional assumption is needed. But we need not make it as strong as Boltzmann's speculation: the much weaker assumption proposed by Ehrenfest is sufficient. This assumption involves a perfectly reasonable conjecture about the conditions under which organisms can live. Yet reasonable as it is, it is not a part of statistical mechanics; any more than Boltzmann's speculation is. With this, we may discard Boltzmann's highly metaphysical *ad hoc* speculation which geometrizes or spatializes time.

Much more important are the arguments from relativity; for both the special and the general theory, each in its way, and the special theory perhaps more strongly, suggest that space and time are closely linked together.

Assume that there are two inertial frames, F_1 and F_2, in relative motion, fitted with the two marks M_1 and M_2, which mark points at rest in F_1 and F_2 respectively; and that M_1 and M_2 coincide (more or less precisely) at an instant of time t, which may be assumed to be the same instant of time (say 11.10) according to the clocks of both F_1 and F_2.

Then there will be always events $e, e', e'', \ldots$ in the world all of which happen in F_1 before t, and in F_2 after t. This will be so according to any consistent general definition of simultaneity and consequently of 'before t' and 'after t'.

This is a very serious blow to the commonsense view of time, and necessitates an adjustment of this view: it shows that there is a common-sense *theory* of time, and that this (let us say Newtonian) *theory* has to be corrected in the light of the critical findings of Einstein. Thus time and space relations do not have exactly the properties we naively assume. More especially, the commonsense idea of *one universal time*, which orders all events in distant physical systems in various states of motion, has to be abandoned.

However, *no element of subjectivity is thereby introduced*. If a universal and consistent definition of simultaneity is adopted, then *it holds for any inertial frames F_1 and F_2 (and thus objectively) that* 'before t in F_1' and 'after t in F_1' will not in general coincide with 'before t in F_2' and 'after t in F_2', and it will hold objectively *however* these characterizations are related.

Thus it is a mistake to think that relativity introduces necessarily an 'observer' and 'subjective' temporal relations dependent upon the observer: the so-called 'observer' is just a symbol, a metaphor, standing for the more abstract 'inertial frame'. No subjectivity, no consciousness, enters the theory.

What the theory implies is that any time measurement will in a definite way depend on the *state of motion*, that is, on the inertial system in which the clock used for the measurement is at rest. It will depend, accordingly, on time *and space*. Time is no longer separable from motion and thus from space: *space and time are linked together*.

This result, however, can be interpreted in different ways. It need not be interpreted as establishing something like a geometrization or spatialization of time. On the contrary, we are free to interpret it in the opposite way: as something like a partial temporalization of space: we must beware of being misled by the convenient *graphical representation*, or the *spatial picturing*, of time. All the theory tells us is that there is a four-dimensional manifold, and that time-like world lines are not 'absolutely' time-like in the Newtonian sense.

An interpretation of general relativity in which this aspect – the possibility of 'temporalized' space – is implicit has been given by John Archibald Wheeler, who has for years stressed the *dynamic* character of Einstein's alleged geometrization of the world: he describes Einstein's theory as 'geometrodynamics'. By this, I think, he wishes to stress that Einstein's geometry is a changing geometry – a geometry that interacts with itself and *changes* its state under the influence of earlier states.

All that I wish to say here is that *we are not committed* by relativity to any interpretation like the block universe favoured by Weyl, and, under the influence of Boltzmann's speculation, by Schrödinger.

One important point is that the block universe interpretation, and any similar interpretation, commit us to *metaphysical determinism*. By this I mean a determinism like the one that assumes an omniscient deity (with or without *the deity*) knowing all future events, so that what happens in the future is fixed, whether by natural laws or by chance – events subject either to probabilistic rules, or to no rules at all: even a partly chaotic universe may be conceived of as metaphysically deterministic. In a theatre, chaos on the stage may be minutely determined (by the director); and if filmed, it will obviously be determined every time it is reproduced, even if it was not planned by any director.

All I will say here on the subject of metaphysical determinism is that it appears to me contrary to common sense. And while commonsense views have to give way if there are strong rational arguments against them, they should not be given up (though opposite views ought to be tried out) unless the rational arguments are strong. They do not seem to me at all strong in the matter of determinism.

I think we should, in accordance with common sense, assume that at any instant of time t_n, the future of t_n is essentially *open*: it is alterable by us, and partly – but only partly – foreseeable by us. It is also partly determined, both in the sense of scientific predictability and in a meta-physical (or perhaps ontological) sense; but *only partly*. (Any system that is not wholly determined is, of course, to be described as indeterministic.)

If we look upon the future as open in this sense, then all interpretations of physics that regard time or change in any other way appear not only metaphysical but *arbitrary*. They are, as are all forms of idealism, *irrefutable*. An idealist who (like Berkeley or Schopenhauer) asserts that the world is his idea, or his dream, cannot be refuted. But he cannot claim scientific status for his thesis: it is untestable. Similarly the thesis of the spatializa-tion of time is untestable – unless, indeed, we can build a time machine, an idea that, I believe (in contradistinction to Gödel), leads to insurmount-able logical difficulties.

Thus there do not seem sufficient grounds to give up the commonsense view of the world as metaphysically indeterministic and thus as incom-patible with the spatialization of time.

In addition to these somewhat negative arguments, which all say that there is nothing in relativity to make us accept a block universe, there is another and stronger argument against any theory of the subjectivity of time, that is, any theory that links the problem of the reality of time, or of its direction, with human consciousness.

Anybody who upholds a Parmenidean or block-universe view of objec-tive reality must, of course, introduce a subjective theory of time that makes time, and change, illusions of our consciousness. Thus illusion or consciousness becomes an adjunct to the real world. But this creates immense difficulties – and gratuitous difficulties. For the illusion of change is, in its turn, a *real* illusion: we *do* experience change. But this means that our consciousness does, in fact, change. How can we accom-modate this change in an objectively changeless world? The problem seems to me insoluble; and if not insoluble, at any rate, a gratuitous pseudo-problem. If there is *any* change in the world, even changing illusions, then there is change. (A cinema film exists all at once, but in order to create in us the illusion of motion or change, it must run through a projector – that is, it must move, and change.) And if there is change in the world, then Parmenideanism has to be given up, or radically adjusted.

Of course, it goes without saying that the *experience* of change depends not only upon a changing environment but also upon our consciousness, just as the *experience* of size or shape or colour does. But consciousness seems to be reasonably good in decoding (with the help of theories or conjectures) the facts of our environment that are important for us, including change. To do so, we need theories; and so we develop them – for example the marvellous theory of space-time invented by Newton and revolutionized by Einstein.

With this, I conclude the discussion of the most radical form (a continuity theory, of course, rather than an atomistic one) of Parmenideanism in modern physics. I shall now proceed to sketch the emergence of some non-Parmenidean aspects of physics, in order to show that we need not fear that they lead to a breakdown of rationality.

21   Appearance of non-Parmenidean aspects in physics

Everything connected with the law of increasing entropy is anti-Parmenidean, though this may become clear – as in the case of Boltzmann's *ad hoc* speculation – only through the appearance of a Parmenidean apology, as Meyerson was clearly aware.

Any Parmenidean or near-Parmenidean physics must obviously be reversible in time. But Carnot and Clausius (and common sense) demanded that we should take note of irreversibility. Our own lives and deaths should teach us that some, if not all, natural processes are in fact irreversible.

Isaac Newton saw this long before Clausius and entropy. He taught that the universe was perishable; and because of this teaching he was accused of impiety by the scholastics among his contemporaries. The imperfection of the Creation, they said, reflected the wisdom and perfection of the First Cause, the Creator of the universe. The story is well told by Newton's friend, Pemberton:[71]

> I think it not improper to mention a reflection made by our excellent author upon these small inequalities in the planets' motions; which contains under it a very strong philosophical argument against the eternity of the world. It is this, that these inequalities must continually increase by slow degrees, till they render at length the present frame of nature unfit for the purposes

it now serves [Newton, *Optics*, p. 378]. And a more convincing proof cannot be desired against the present constitution's having existed from eternity than this, that a certain period of years will bring it to an end. I am aware this thought of our author has been represented even as impious, and as no less than casting a reflection upon the wisdom of the author of nature, for framing a perishable work.

Pemberton then proceeds to defend Newton. The defence is extremely reasonable, though highly anti-Parmenidean.[72] He writes:

> The body of every animal shows the unlimited wisdom of its author no less, nay in many respects more, than the larger frame of nature; and yet we see, they are all designed to last but a small space of time.

Thus Newton did not believe in reversibility, in spite of the obvious reversibility of Newtonian dynamics; and his arguments were sound. In fact, they might nowadays be described as thermodynamic arguments; for he appealed, among other things, to the friction that results from the tides.

Laplace discarded Newton's somewhat imperfect Creator altogether. By his doctrine of a fully deterministic and in principle fully predictable world he introduced Parmenides into Newtonian dynamics, and confirmed his status in it (and in Einstein's theory) for over a century. Laplace's whole work in mechanics and mathematics seems to have been motivated by this problem.

Now, it is of some interest to observe that the (Newtonian) mechanics of continuous media and the (classical) theories of fields have to do with systems that are extended; not only over a spatial region but also, essentially, over a temporal region. (The boundary conditions are to be given, in principle, for every instant of time, and even for approximation purposes for a considerable span of time.) Thus the Laplacean idea that initial conditions for *one* instant of time determine the behaviour of a (closed) mechanical system for all time is mistaken (even for closed or separated systems); this idea only holds for the mechanics of mass points.

Accordingly the Laplacean programme was superseded, in fact by Young's and Fresnel's theory of light (one might even argue, by Huyghens' principle): a grid has to be extended in space – in principle infinitely – and it can be used for spectroscopy only if the *process*, the incidence of light upon the grid, is uninterruptedly extended in time, in principle infinitely. Thus within *classical physics* the idea of momentary states collapses: while a gas, or even a 'continuous body', may perhaps be regarded in classical physics as approximated by a system of mass points, this is not true in the classical (wave) theories of light. (It also does not hold generally for structures such as flutes or violins.[73])

The collapse of the universal applicability of the very idea of momentary physical states furnishes us with the physical background for a theory that regards consciousness as extended in time. (This extension is often called 'the specious present'.) Indeed, we could not see (or react to) *colours* if our consciousness consisted of a sequence of strictly momentary states.[74]

This gives also an indication of why the traditional distinction (which goes back to Parmenides' Two Ways) between primary and secondary qualities has to be abandoned. Spatially extended *physical surfaces* are more than mere accumulations of point-particles since they interact with light as grids do (that is, in a holistic manner)[75] and are therefore physical wholes extended in time as well as space. More or less the same holds for all processes that form the objective physical basis of the so-called 'secondary qualities'. These processes - the interaction of surfaces with light (where colour-invariant properties and other optical properties of the surfaces become important) - are as 'primary' in character, from a physical point of view, as the (temperature-dependent) molecular processes that determine the rigidity and the shape-invariance of solid material systems. Similarly, *experiences* of objective 'primary' and 'secondary' qualities are also quite of the same character: both kinds of experiences depend on the interpretation or the decoding by an organism of physical processes (signals) in which the organism is using theories discovered by processes of selection rather than instruction. Perhaps it would be best to speak of physical ('primary') processes and of the correlated mental ('secondary') processes.

The temporal extension of the factors determining physical states limits severely, within classical physics, detailed predictability and detailed testing, except in the very special case of a separated system of mass points not interacting with any field. It is therefore linked with the idea of *partial* rather than full determination – that is, of indeterminism (or 'chance', at least in some of the senses of this term).[76]

22   Maxwell's demon

Since Daniel Bernoulli and Laplace the theory of chance has been waiting on the threshold of physical theory. It invaded it with the kinetic theory of gases (later to develop into statistical mechanics) of Clausius, Maxwell, Boltzmann, Planck, Gibbs, and Einstein; and in spite of powerful resistance it all but absorbed the theory of thermodynamics, founded by Sadi Carnot.

There can be no doubt about the fundamental anti-Parmenidean character of thermodynamics and the original programme of the kinetic theory (statistical mechanics). But the kinetic theory contained, from the very start, the seeds of conflict between Parmenidean and anti-Parmenidean tendencies: it was an attempt to explain away anti-Parmenidean thermodynamics in terms of Parmenidean atomic principles in the form of equations. Its main aim was, at least for a long time, to reduce to these essentially *reversible equations* the essentially *irreversible inequality* of the thermodynamic law of entropy (as Clausius christened the 'second law of thermodynamics': historically this was the first law, going back to Carnot, and it might be called the Carnot–Kelvin–Clausius principle). Clausius interpreted the entropy law as a sentence of death on the universe ('thermal death'); clearly a radically anti-Parmenidean idea. This death sentence was taken very seriously for a long time, although the law of entropy increase obviously does not in general apply to open systems,[77] as shown by many counterexamples. (In this connection we should keep in mind that in the days of Clausius, and before general relativity, cosmology had only advanced from the closed world to the infinite universe, and not yet from the infinite universe to the closed world.)

The tension between Parmenidean and anti-Parmenidean tendencies within the kinetic theory made itself felt first when Clerk Maxwell, in 1871, discovered his famous 'sorting demon', the first great puzzle of the kinetic theory.

As is well known, Maxwell's demon breaks the entropy law by inserting a diaphragm into a box filled with gas and fitting a shutter to a tiny hole in the diaphragm. He closes the shutter whenever a fast molecule approaches from the left or a slow one from the right. By thus sorting the molecules he causes the gas on the left to get hotter and that on the right cooler; and so the entropy of the system decreases.

Maxwell's demon is no longer young, but he is still going strong. Although innumerable attempts have been made on his life, almost from the day he was born, and although his non-existence has frequently been proved, and explanations of his non-existence have frequently been given, he will no doubt soon celebrate his hundredth birthday in perfect health and vigour. I for one feel confident that he will survive us all, and that all the proofs and explanations of his non-existence will, as fast as they are produced, be exposed as inconclusive.

One of the most recent and most ingenious proofs *and* refutations of the non-existence of Maxwell's demon is due to Professor Dennis Gabor, who constructed a model showing that the demon *can* exist according to classical physics but not according to quantum physics.[78] Gabor's demon is sufficiently clever to evade any classical disproof of his existence; which would show, as Gabor points out, that the second law is false in classical physics and becomes valid only in quantum physics.

Gabor's model of a Maxwell demon is not generally accepted (as Gabor told me); which illustrates, in the most striking fashion, how very open the whole question still is, after almost a century of intensive study.

179

I agree with Gabor that we can construct a Maxwell demon who *is* clever enough to manage a classical physical system; but I do not feel convinced that quantum theory can defeat a demon *that* clever. For clearly his wits will suffice for sufficiently large molecules (even on the assumption that classical physics is not valid and quantum physics valid); and this should suffice to ensure the demon's success.

The possibility of his success is, I hold, an immediate consequence of Einstein's first paper on Brownian motion.[79] In this paper, Einstein says very clearly that 'classical thermodynamics [that is, the second law] can no longer be looked upon as applicable with precision to bodies even of a size that makes them distinguishable in a microscope'. And he shows that on a diaphragm permeable by a liquid (or a gas) an osmotic pressure will be exerted, not only by a *solute* but by *any* 'small suspended particles', always assuming that the diaphragm is impermeable by them.

But this means that we can construct a Maxwell demon and build a perfectly practicable though extremely inefficient perpetual motion machine of the second kind, as follows.

Inside a glass cylinder we place a piston with small holes through which air can pass easily. (It is assumed that the piston is prevented by mechanical obstructions from reaching the very ends of the cylinder.) Then we insert on the left of the piston *one* little balloon that is too big to pass through the holes. According to Einstein's calculations, there will be an osmotic pressure driving the piston to the right.

If we wish to reverse the movement of the piston, we need only play the role of Maxwell's demon, a role that is here very easy: we fit the piston with a Maxwell hole and shutter; the hole must be big enough to let the balloon pass. We then wait until the balloon drifts through the hole, from the left to the right of the cylinder, and close the shutter. The excess pressure will then be to the right of the piston.

This mechanism can be simplified: we can omit the shutter, and need not take any action whatever, provided we ensure that the Maxwell hole is small compared with the diameter of the piston, so that the balloon will pass through the hole only very rarely. In this case the direction of the pressure will change after some finite time; although, of course, (on the average) only after a very long time.

Those who know some of the history of information theory will see at once that my perpetual motion machine (which works automatically and without any information input) refutes a famous thought experiment published by Leo Szilard in 1929.[80] Leon Brillouin says about Szilard's experiment that it showed 'for the first time the connection between information and entropy'.[81] I fear that this will have to be done again. (I do not, of course, criticize Shannon's formula, which I discuss in more detail in Section 28 below.)

These considerations show also that a suspicion very tentatively expressed in a paper published in 1957 may well be correct.[82] It is the suspicion that 'a gas or liquid in a closed circular tube . . . fitted with a *one-way valve*' (spring-loaded with a very weak spring) would 'constantly circulate through the tube', though of course extremely slowly.[83] One might even put it more drastically: if you can wait long enough – a few billion years – your flat tyre will blow up.

As the above construction shows, we can have a Maxwell demon working automatically, without any information input. This is quite interesting because it destroys a typical Parmenidean apology.

For according to Maxwell (and Szilard), if we had the demon's intelligence, skill, and knowledge – which we cannot have, being poor erring mortals – we could ourselves break the entropy law; which means that we could establish reversibility and, with it, re-establish the power of Parmenides in physics.

Now, this amounts to saying that the anti-Parmenidean irreversibility is due to our being not fully informed: we are not Maxwell demons, but erring mortals. Thus the failure of Parmenideanism – of Parmenides' Way of Truth – is explained, as it was explained by Parmenides himself, as (at least partly) due to our ignorance – to a failure of human information. So we still have Parmenides' Two Ways – the Way of Truth, or reversibility, of a world in which cause and effect are equal and nothing intrinsically new can ever happen, and a world of irreversibility and of evolution. According to von Neumann,[84] this second world, the World of Appearances (though not exactly of illusions) owes what existence it has at least partly to the peculiar limitations and activities of mortal men.

Regarded in this way, Maxwell's demon foreshadows what has been called by Heisenberg 'the difficulty of separating the subjective and objective aspects of the world', a difficulty due to the fact that 'it is not possible to decide, except arbitrarily, what is . . . part of the observed system, and what . . . of the observer's apparatus'.[85] In the modern disintegration of the Parmenidean research programme for physics we meet at every step a Parmenidean apology. Some part or other of his Way of Opinion always turns up as an explanation of the observed non-Parmenidean world of change – as a Parmenidean apology for the imperfection of the changing world. The Parmenidean apology of the modern physicist is that the observer or 'the subject' (as Heisenberg first put it) necessarily invades the world of objective physics, and subjectivizes it. Thus the apology appeals, as did that of Parmenides, to the ineradicable ignorance of mortal men.

23   Boltzmann's defence of atomism

It is a pity that I cannot recount here at length the marvellous and tragic story of Ludwig Boltzmann, the Viennese apostle of Clerk Maxwell who hammered out the details of Maxwell's kinetic theory of gases and brought it near to completion.[86] One of the greatest intellects of his time, a great physicist, a philosopher of originality who described clearly the hypothetico-deductive method, and a scholar of the highest standards, Boltzmann saw his achievements threatened, and even partly destroyed, by the Parmenidean paradox that beset the kinetic theory. Boltzmann's kinetic theory of entropy was attacked from all sides; and indeed, it was shaky. Boltzmann thought at first that he could give a strict derivation of the entropy law from mechanical premises; but in 1877, replying to a criticism of Loschmidt's,[87] Boltzmann gave up this programme, replacing it by a programme of showing that 'since there are infinitely many more uniform than non-uniform distribution states' (that is, infinitely more equilibrium distribution states than non-equilibrium ones), the occurrence of a system changing from an equilibrium state to a non-equilibrium state 'can be regarded as impossible for practical purposes'. Boltzmann graciously acknowledged that 'Loschmidt's theorem seems . . . to be of the greatest importance since it shows that the second law is intimately connected with probability theory, whereas the first law is independent of it.'[88]

This was the birth of the probabilistic form of the kinetic theory; that is, of statistical mechanics proper (though, as Boltzmann points out, 'Clausius, Maxwell and others have said repeatedly before that the theorems of gas theory have the character of statistical truths'[89]). The results were eminently fruitful. But the Parmenidean paradox rose again, and at a moment when the atomic theory was violently attacked from all sides and especially by Mach and Ostwald; and Poincaré remarked in 1893 that he was sceptical of any derivation in which 'reversibility is found in the premises and irreversibility in the conclusion'.[90]

At this moment, in 1896, Boltzmann suffered a severe intellectual defeat at the hands of an unknown young physicist, Ernst Zermelo. Zermelo's papers,[91] which in essence repeated the Loschmidt argument in a refined form based on a theorem of Poincaré's, were not particularly clear; nor were they free of misunderstanding. This was especially so in the case of the first paper, to which Boltzmann replied more or less on the lines of his reply to Loschmidt: that the kinetic theory of entropy gives only a probabilistic derivation, though one with absolutely tremendous odds (which Boltzmann calculated) in favour of an entropy increase. To this Zermelo replied by pointing out, not too clearly, and again mixing in some irrelevances, that the probability considerations, according to Poincaré's theorem (whose truth Boltzmann admitted), must be reversible also; in brief, the entropy curve (Boltzmann's H-curve) must be symmetrical with respect to time.

This new yet obvious argument was admitted by Boltzmann at once, although on reading the reply one feels that it must have been a terrible blow. But Boltzmann, rightly, did not surrender the atomic theory, which was the real aim of the attacks of his opponents. He pointed out that all is well if we make the 'assumption A (which is of course unprovable) that the universe, . . . or at least a very large part of it which surrounds us, started from a very improbable state, and is still in an improbable state'; in other words, he made the assumption later restated by Tatiana Ehrenfest (and quoted above). And he then proceeded to offer that bold *ad hoc* speculation that I have discussed at length – that the direction of time is a subjective illusion, determined by the direction of entropy increase. This, as we have seen, implies the spatialization or 'co-presence' of all points of the time coordinate.

As I showed above, this does indeed mean abandoning the programme of deriving the entropy law from mechanics: even a statistical derivation is given up. The essential premises – whether 'assumption A' or the *ad hoc* speculation – are no longer within the theory. This surrender was probably not clearly seen by Boltzmann; at least, he did not state it. But he must have felt it. He also felt, and stated correctly, that the atomic-statistical theory was more important than the phenomenological entropy law (a position that, though true, was treated by Zermelo and Mach with scorn and contempt). Poincaré, the greatest physicist among Boltzmann's contemporaries – he was only ten years younger than Boltzmann – was among his opponents, and Mach's enmity, as Boltzmann's eminent pupil Flamm reports,[92] was bitter. All the attacks were directed against Boltzmann's belief in atomism.

In 1898 Boltzmann wrote:[93]

> I am conscious of being only one individual, weakly struggling against the current of the time. But it still remains in my power to do something to ensure that one day, when the theory of gases is revived, not too much will have to be rediscovered.

Eight years later – at a moment when, as we now know, the 'current of the time' was turning – Boltzmann committed suicide. As Flamm says, he died a martyr of his ideas.[94]

24 Resolution of the paradox of the second law of thermodynamics

Boltzmann was the victim of a paradox. The solution of the paradox is simple. He stated it repeatedly; but it was felt, wrongly, to be *ad hoc*. It is this.

Although kinetic and statistical theories set out to provide a derivation of the entropy law, they cannot succeed because the empirical and phenomenological entropy law is false. The result that is actually derived from the theory is a better approximation to the truth than is the empirical law.

Boltzmann did say so; but he did not say that this was far from paradoxical. He did not say that Newton tried to derive Kepler's and Galileo's
laws, but instead derived something better. He did not see that it is *one of
the greatest achievements of a theory if it does not yield the results it was expected to
yield, but some better results (that is, results nearer to the truth), even if these results
have not yet found any empirical corroboration.*[95]

The deviations from the entropy law that Einstein successfully derived
from statistical mechanics (in his papers on Brownian motion) in the year
before Boltzmann's death were actually contemplated by Boltzmann in his
second reply to Zermelo.[96] There he wrote:

> I assert only that the mechanical picture agrees with [the entropy
> law] . . . in everything that can actually [now] be observed. The
> fact that it *suggests the possibility of certain new observations – for
> example, of the motion of small particles in liquids and gases . . . does not
> seem to provide any basis for rejecting the mechanical theory,* . . .

It did provide the basis for the first victory of the mechanical theory:
Wilhelm Ostwald was converted by the excellent agreement between the
quantitative predictions of Einstein's and Smoluchowski's theory of Brownian motion and the observations made to test these predictions.

25   Schrödinger's version of Boltzmann's theory

Mach too saw that Boltzmann's mechanical 'interpretation of the second
law' would lead to 'a violation' [*Durchbrechung*] of this law; but he found
that this was too absurd to be seriously contemplated. Boltzmann's 'interpretation of the second law in terms of mechanics', he writes,[97]

> seems to me rather *artificial*. If one reflects on the fact that there is
> no real correlate to the *increase of entropy* in a purely mechanical
> system [except the increase of disorder], then one can hardly resist
> the conviction that a violation of the second law should be
> possible – even without the help of a demon – if it were true
> that such a mechanical system forms the *real* basis of thermal
> processes.

In contrast to Mach's view that Boltzmann's ideas are 'highly artificial',
it seems to me that they are very natural. It seems to me as natural that gas
molecules show an inherent tendency to get mixed up as it is that a crowd
in the centre of a city shows such a tendency. Moreover, it seems to me
perfectly natural to make use of a statistical theory if we wish to explain
this tendency. This, of course, does not imply that an intuitive view (such
as mine) is true; or that, even if it is true, we can derive it from any

particular system of assumptions, even if these should also be true in their turn.[98]

As we have seen, Boltzmann was unable to derive from statistical mechanics this 'tendency of the molecules to get mixed up', though he had first thought that he could do so: he needed, unexpectedly, some additional assumption – his 'assumption A', or his Parmenidean *ad hoc* speculation that time is an illusion.

This *ad hoc* speculation was felt by Schrödinger to be not only an essential part of Boltzmann's physical theory, but the most beautiful theory of physics altogether, because in this theory mechanism transcends itself and yields a metaphysical result establishing the ideality of time, and thus idealism.

For this reason Schrödinger resisted any attempt to find an indicator, other than entropy, of the direction of time: this would be an attempt to destroy the most beautiful theory of physics, he said to me accusingly (because I had made such an attempt[99]). And in one of his last books he wrote: 'the statistical theory of heat must be allowed to decide by itself high-handedly, by its own definition, in which direction time flows'.[100] To this he added: 'This has a momentous consequence for the methodology of the physicist. He must never introduce anything that decides upon the arrow of time, else Boltzmann's beautiful building collapses.'[101]

Thus for Schrödinger objective time has no direction in contrast to experienced time, which has a direction towards a state of increased entropy or probability (here indicated in Figures 3 and 4 in Section 17). Earlier he had made a suggestion that would enable us to define ('high-handedly') the direction of time on the basis of a reformulation of the entropy law and of Boltzmann's 'suicidal' *ad hoc* speculation.[102] (Obviously he did not see that this reduced the content of the H-theorem to a trivial consequence of a 'high-handed' definition.) Schrödinger's suggestion was that we reformulate the entropy law as follows. We start from a time coordinate t that is 'directionless' in the sense that the direction of increasing numerical values of t is completely arbitrary (cp. Figure 3 in Section 17 above). We assume that we can determine the entropies S_1 and S_2 of two partial systems of the universe (called 'branch systems' by Reichenbach), systems 1 and 2, at two important instants t_A and t_B, such that *between* t_A and t_B the two systems are separated, whereas *outside* this interval they interact. Schrödinger calls the entropies of the two systems at these instants S_{1A} and S_{2A}, S_{1B} and S_{2B}; and he then states a new entropy law (E), which he expresses by the formula

(E) $(S_{1B} - S_{1A})(S_{2B} - S_{2A}) \geq 0.$

This formula does not assert an increase of entropy along t, but merely a parallel development in both systems. (The entropy increases in both systems, or else it decreases in both systems.)

Now we may if we like proceed to give a direction to time by defining (as Boltzmann did) t^* as a new time coordinate so chosen that the entropy S_1, and in view of (E) therefore also S_2, will increase with increasing t^*; this will be by definition the direction from 'past' to 'future'.

The only significant difference between Schrödinger's formulation and Boltzmann's *ad hoc* speculation is this: Schrödinger is able to formulate (E) – his new entropy law, which follows from the usual law – independently of any direction of time. Thus he avoids an objection to which Boltzmann might be said to be open: that the entropy law is non-empirical because it follows from the *definition* of the direction of time. In Schrödinger's theory the *usual* entropy law follows, by contrast, from (E), in conjunction with the definition; and (E) itself may be considered as its empirical nucleus.

This may be regarded as an improvement of Boltzmann's *ad hoc* speculation; but the main difficulty of Boltzmann's formulation is not touched. It is this.

The basic idea of the Boltzmann-Schrödinger theory is that there must be some small and some exceedingly big fluctuations of the entropy down from the equilibrium value, and that the direction of time from 'past' to 'future' is the direction of increasing entropy. But this at once invites an obvious objection: only very big fluctuations can be used thus to characterize the direction of time; for if we allow every small fluctuation to invert the arrow of time, then we run (as is easily seen) into contradictions: we are quite sure that the atomic clocks do not run backwards and forwards if the atoms are in a fluctuating gas; and that the life cycle of microorganisms is not disturbed if their environment fluctuates. Thus the question arises: *how big* do the spatial extension and the size of the deviation from equilibrium of the fluctuation have to be to be able to determine the direction of time? It seems clear to me that this question is (a) *unanswerable* and (b) bound to lead to *inconsistencies* near the crucial value, however chosen, of the size of the fluctuations just big enough to affect the direction of time. (Schrödinger assumes *very* big subsystems 1 and 2, separated through *very* long periods of time; but I cannot see the theoretical relevance of this assumption.)

Yet quite apart from this obvious objection, the central question is whether (E), in contradistinction to the usual entropy law (Boltzmann's H-theorem), can be derived from Boltzmann's statistical mechanics.

At first sight one may think that this is possible. For the main argument against the derivability of the entropy law is that (as Poincaré remarked) irreversible conclusions cannot be derived from a reversible theory such as statistical mechanics. Now, it is clear that this objection does not touch (E), which is a weakened corollary of the entropy law. But doubts are raised by further scrutiny. For we can, of course, only hope, at best, to derive (E) *with high probability*; and clearly, the equilibrium case in which the left-hand side of (E) very nearly *equals* zero (with any desired degree of precision) will be the overwhelmingly probable one. But this is only the equilibrium case, and for this the game is not worth the candle, since for the equilibrium case we can derive with overwhelming probability the usual entropy law from Boltzmann's theory, even if the time coordinate has an arrow.

The consequence of Boltzmann's theory for the more interesting case – when non-equilibrium states are considered – can be formulated (following a suggestion of Boltzmann's[103]) in this way: if we draw any two lines, below and parallel to the equilibrium level, then for any small interval ϵ between these lines, there will be, given sufficient time, a denumerable infinity of fluctuations that at least reach this interval; and among these fluctuations, *almost all* will have their peak (the lowest entropy reached) within the interval. Thus the relative probability of a fluctuation transcending any given interval, given that it has reached the interval, will be zero.

This formulation, essentially due to Boltzmann, is like (E) in assuming no directed time coordinate. Yet it seems to me preferable to (E). For (E), as I shall now show, cannot be generally valid, even with high probability, and especially not for very big systems 1 and 2, and for very long periods of time between A and B. For assume a directed time, and assume that a system, 1 + 2, fluctuates widely (which may mean, for example, that a part of the system becomes hotter and another part cooler) and that 1 and 2 become separated at the instant A that occurs during the fluctuation but before its peak (some minimum entropy of 1 + 2) is reached; and let 1 and 2 rejoin at some later time. Especially if the fluctuation is a big one, it is extremely probable, from what has been said, that at least one of the partial systems (say system 1) will, after the separation, at once start to move towards equilibrium. From our assumption that the fluctuation of 1 + 2 has not reached its peak, it follows then that the other system (system 2) will move on towards the peak of the fluctuation (that is, to the minimum entropy). Thus we should get a diagram like Figure 5, using a time coordinate with an arrow (the dips [the 'entropy valleys'] are simply deviations from equilibrium).

Now we may assume that at time A, when they become separated, 1 and 2 are approximately equally far from equilibrium. If we bring the two systems together at any time B or B' before C (that is, the instant when 2 returns to the entropy level it had at A), then $S_{1B} - S_{1A}$ will be positive because 1 has moved towards equilibrium, whereas $S_{2B} - S_{2A}$ will be negative, because at B it has not yet regained the level of entropy it had at A. Thus (E) *will not hold*. There seems to me no reason whatever why systems separated during a big fluctuation (assuming there are any big fluctuations) should not behave like this; on the contrary, this behaviour is

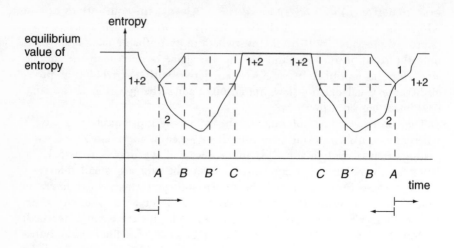

Figure 5: In this figure, the special case of $AB = BB' = B'C = CB' = B'B = BA$ is shown. In general, however, these intervals would not be equal.

infinitely more probable (given that the entropy of $1 + 2$ continues to decrease after separation) than an increase in entropy in *both* systems. Of course, if we wait beyond C before we bring the separation to an end, then (E) will be satisfied. But there seems no reason why we should wait. It seems to me therefore hopeless to try to derive (E) from statistical mechanics; though, of course, (E) must be true at least as often as the entropy law in its old thermodynamic formulation, since (E) follows from the latter.

Despite my unbounded admiration for Schrödinger I tried (first in 1956) in a series of letters to *Nature* to show, with the help of some examples, that *we can characterize the direction of time independently of entropy increase*. The asymmetry I tried to point out was one that affects the realizability of *initial conditions*, in contradistinction to an asymmetry of the theories or laws.[104]

If such an asymmetry exists, it must suffice to characterize the direction of time; and so (as Schrödinger admitted) it would make it impossible to impress a direction upon time by either Boltzmann's or Schrödinger's method, since there would not be available a neutral or undirected time coordinate upon which an entropy fluctuation could impress a direction. (We must remember that according to Boltzmann and Schrödinger every sufficiently big fluctuation will impress – as shown in Figure 4 in Section 17 – *two opposite directions* on two stretches of the otherwise neutral time coordinate, both of them running away from the low of the entropy, that is, from the peak of the fluctuation, towards the high entropy and equilibrium level.)

What would we lose if I am right? We would lose a powerful method of metaphysical explanation that allows us to *explain* (by a huge fluctuation) first, the fact that our world is in disequilibrium; secondly, the law of entropy increase; and thirdly, the apparent direction of time; indeed a method of explanation so powerful that it can explain almost anything.[105] What we would gain if I am right is the reality of change.

While, in 1956, I tried to show only that the *initial conditions* of certain ordinary non-entropic phenomena show an inherent direction of time that can be characterized in purely physical terms, L. L. Whyte boldly suggested in 1955 (that is, one year earlier) that we should look for *theories* or *laws* that are irreversible in time.[106] There seems no reason not to believe that such laws do exist; in fact, the inherent direction in the asymmetry of realizable initial conditions would be very hard to explain otherwise. Since 1956, indications have been accumulating that suggest that we may find these laws soon – if we have not found them already in the laws of 'weak decay interaction'.

All this would affect the Boltzmann–Schrödinger idea of the illusion of change and time; but though it might perhaps lead to minor modifications of statistical mechanics, it clearly does not essentially affect its basic ideas.

26   The conversion of modern physics to Boltzmann's theory

Schrödinger was a confirmed Parmenidean. (He interpreted Parmenides' *'one being'* as thought or consciousness.[107]) Yet in spite of the devotion to Boltzmann's ideas that he shared with Einstein, Schrödinger was, like Einstein in his younger years, and many other physicists of that generation, deeply impressed by Mach's positivistic or sensualistic epistemology, and (as I myself was until recently) unaware of Boltzmann's anti-positivistic theory of science. In fact, Schrödinger realized what Mach, the anti-metaphysician, failed to realize – that Mach's epistemology, developed consistently, should lead to the metaphysical idealism in which Schrödinger believed.

Mach himself seems to have come to his epistemology from a very different side: from his dissatisfaction with atomism and all other *theories of the structure of matter*. He found all these theories unsatisfactory because of their highly speculative character and their scanty experimental support. (We should remember that even in 1902 Poincaré believed that the atomic and continuity theories of matter could not be experimentally distinguished, and that no experiment could establish – or even favour – the existence of atoms.) In this unsatisfactory situation Mach reflected on the epistemological basis of the theories of matter, and was led to his famous

Analysis of Sensations.[108] As a result he adopted a philosophy of science hardly different from Berkeley's: he discarded matter as a metaphysical idea, like the idea of 'substance'.[109] (Of course, all theories of matter are, in origin, metaphysical – more precisely, Parmenidean.) But Mach was not a Berkeleian by inclination. *He adopted the non-existence of matter as a physical theory*: it *explained* the inconsistencies that beset most theories of matter (especially if a radical empiricism is presupposed).[110] Thus he saw in Boltzmann's troubles a strong confirmation of his own physical theories, and he considered thermodynamics the most adequate, because most phenomenological, of all physical theories.

Thus Mach, like Berkeley, had adopted Parmenides' second Way, discarding the first Way altogether. There was no thing in itself, no object of knowledge – only a world of appearance; only a 'world thus arranged to seem wholly like truth' (DK 28B8: 60). It seemed wholly like truth simply because there was no other world of truth.

But shortly before his death Mach seems to have been converted to the reality of atoms. Approximately eight years after Boltzmann's death Mach was shown by Stefan Meyer, in the Vienna Institute for Radium Research, the scintillation of α-particles. 'Now I believe in the reality of atoms', he said. As Meyer reports, his 'whole view of the world had changed within a few minutes'.[111]

The adherents of the Vienna Circle of logical positivism and of the Mach Association (*Verein Ernst Mach*) used to say that systems of metaphysics are merely the ghosts of departed scientific theories: scientific theories that have been abandoned. It is interesting how well this description fitted their own Machist philosophy. Machian positivism is a short-lived physical theory that, according to some, was even abandoned by its founder, the hero of positivism, shortly before his death (see, however, the discussion of this incident in J. T. Blackmore's excellent biography of Mach[112]).

Thus all Boltzmann's great enemies were converted, or at least deeply shaken in their disbelief of his theory. Zermelo translated Willard Gibbs' masterpiece in 1905 and wrote a preface full of admiration – though with reservations regarding the derivation of the entropy law.[113] Poincaré wrote in 1905 about statistical mechanics: 'All this Maxwell and Boltzmann have explained; but the one who has seen it most clearly . . . is Gibbs.'[114] Poincaré also saw, in the same year in which Einstein published his first paper on Brownian motion (one year before Boltzmann's death), that Brownian motion was 'contrary to Carnot's principle' (the entropy law); and he added: 'we see, under our eyes now motion transformed into heat . . . now heat, inversely, changed into motion [thus violating the second law] and that without any loss, since the movement lasts forever'. (Thus he realized the existence of a perpetual motion machine of second order.) 'We need no longer', Poincaré continued, 'the infinitely keen eye of Maxwell's demon: our microscope suffices.'[115]

I will now sum up the situation as it existed between, say, 1897 and 1904. Boltzmann, Poincaré, Zermelo, Mach, and Ostwald realized the untenability of Boltzmann's earlier belief that the (irreversible) entropy law can be derived from the reversible equations of statistical mechanics. At first all these physicists, except Boltzmann, interpreted this as a refutation of statistical mechanics and Boltzmann's programme, and of the atomic theory of matter (or 'materialism', as they all sometimes called it) that Boltzmann continued to uphold. By about 1902 Poincaré believed in the statistical mechanics of Boltzmann and Gibbs,[116] and thus presumably in atomism: he was also, it seems, the first to be converted by Brownian motion – thanks to precisely the kind of fluctuation, violating the entropy law, whose possibility Boltzmann had admitted when he was sorely pressed by Zermelo's attack, and whose observability he had then regarded as a remote possibility. Mach had looked upon this admission of Boltzmann's as an admission of defeat,[117] and so far as I know he was always an opponent of the kinetic theory (even if he was shaken in his disbelief in the atomic theory[118]). Ostwald was converted by the success of Einstein's theory of Brownian motion. Zermelo seems to have accepted the kinetic theory before 1904 (or 1905 at the latest) with reservations concerning the derivability of the entropy law.[119] In this he was, of course, correct; for the entropy law is, as all participants realized, underivable. Indeed, it is not generally valid: fluctuations such as those in Brownian motion do occur.[120]

As shown by Schrödinger's attempt to find a substitute for the entropy law derivable from Boltzmann's (or Gibbs'[121]) theory – at least with very high probability – there was, in 1950 anyway, no formulation of the entropy law that satisfied him; and (as explained in the previous section) I do not think that Schrödinger succeeded in supplying a satisfactory formulation. Moreover, it is quite clear that neither Boltzmann's nor Gibbs' statistical mechanics can as such explain even the thermodynamic observations: at least an assumption like Boltzmann's 'assumption A' must be invoked, that is to say, a cosmological assumption outside statistical mechanics. In order to explain this cosmological assumption away, Boltzmann proposed, very tentatively, his bold Parmenidean *ad hoc* speculation which reduces all change to illusion; a speculation that, to my knowledge, only Schrödinger adopted in all seriousness. (Since then, some others have adopted Schrödinger's views.)

Thus we have, it seems, neither a sharp formulation of the entropy law at our disposal nor, of course, its valid derivation from statistical mechanics. Nevertheless, the tremendous power of this theory is unquestionable; and the validity of a substitute of the entropy law stating that, of all the fluctuations from equilibrium of an ideal gas that have reached any given level, almost all will be immediately succeeded in time by a state that is nearer to equilibrium, seems derivable from Boltzmann's theory;[122] also, that if the gas happens to be in a state of low entropy, the probability that it will be followed by a state of higher entropy is very nearly certainty, and consequently far greater than the probability that it will be followed by a state of still lower entropy. (All this holds for closed systems only; an electric kettle and the surrounding kitchen are thus approximately a closed system after the kettle has been switched off.)

In spite of the unquestioned victory of the ideas for which Boltzmann fought and died, one cannot say that the situation is wholly satisfactory even now.

27 Another Parmenidean apology of modern physics: the subjectivist interpretation of probability

There is still another way of looking upon the matter: another Parmenidean theory that is widely accepted. One of its most forceful presentations so far was given in 1949 by Max Born.[123] Schrödinger's paper on irreversibility was in fact provoked by Born's book. For this reason, and because of the generally representative views developed in this book, I will now discuss some of its arguments.

I have already had occasion to refer to an important critical analysis of Boltzmann's theory (also containing some interesting historical remarks) by Paul Ehrenfest, a former pupil of Boltzmann's, and Tatiana Ehrenfest. (It was published in 1911.) They described not only the successes of Boltzmann's theory but, almost equally forcefully, its failures. Yet these failures seem to have been repressed by some of their readers, and Max Born, then one of the greatest living physicists (he died in 1970), surprisingly refered to their work, I suppose from memory,[124] as one that managed 'to . . . clear up the matter beyond doubt'.[125]

The point is of considerable interest because Born's interpretation of Boltzmann (which he believed was shared by the Ehrenfests) contains one of the most important and influential Parmenidean apologies of contemporary physics: *the interpretation of probability theory as a theory of our ignorance.*

That this interpretation does not play any role either in the Ehrenfest monograph or in Boltzmann's work illustrates, I believe, how much it is taken for granted, and therefore (unless explicitly opposed) read by some physicists into other people's work.

It is intuitively very plausible to say that whenever we possess *knowledge*, certain knowledge, we do not need probability theory; so that having to apply probability theory to a problem shows the uncertainty of our knowledge in the field, and so establishes the fact of our ignorance, and the relevance of this fact to the problem we wish to solve. This argument is plausible and convincing, and even Einstein used it.[126] It is a point where I think that he was mistaken.

For probability theory does not enter physics *because* of our ignorance (a fallibilist like myself will take our ignorance for granted), but because of the nature of our question – *of the problem we want to solve.*

Consider a university entrance examination. Here we know with the greatest precision imaginable how many candidates have passed in each subject, and how many have failed; and we know, in addition, the names of the candidates. Yet we may also wish to possess, in addition to this precise knowledge, a kind of overall picture; for example because we wish to compare the results of different years. For such a purpose we need statistics: averages, percentages. And for calculating these, or at least for processing the results of the calculation, we may need a statistical theory.

Now, it may be said that all this *and more* is contained in the original precise knowledge, and that, if faced with a choice between the precise knowledge and the statistical knowledge, we should always prefer the former because it entails the latter. Let us first admit this for the sake of the argument. It remains true, nevertheless, that there are certain problems for whose solution the more precise knowledge is useless unless it is statistically processed.

But there are more interesting problems for which the detailed knowledge of individual cases does *not* contain the statistical information in which we are interested. These problems arise unfailingly in connection with *statistical laws*, or *macro laws*, and their explanation and testing.

To make this clear, let us assume that we possess sufficiently powerful measuring devices and computers to ascertain 'precisely' (whatever this may mean) the positions and momenta of all the molecules of a gas in some container, and to calculate their future positions and momenta for any time ahead. (We shall also have to know a lot about the walls of the container, but for simplicity's sake we will neglect this aspect.) Let us assume that we have defined what we mean by the 'temperature' and the 'pressure' of the gas, and that we can calculate these by averaging over our precise information; and also that they will remain constant for the initial conditions we have ascertained.

Now we may wish to solve the problem of what will happen to the temperature and pressure *whenever* we allow ten molecules to escape from the container (say by opening a valve). *This turns out to be an essentially statistical problem.* No answer can be found by 'precise' methods, simply because we have not precisely *specified the conditions under which the ten molecules will escape.* Even if we have names for all the molecules, and specify which of them we shall allow to escape, our problem remains insoluble by purely dynamical methods (indeed, the possible solutions are of the power of the continuum). Only if we have data for the precise conditions under which the removal of the ten molecules takes place can we begin our calculations, and *perhaps* find what everybody knew before – that the temperature and pressure will be slightly lowered after the removal, but so little that thermometers and pressure gauges will fail to register the difference. (I say *'perhaps'* because this will not be the result in all cases, but merely in almost all cases – which introduces a typical probability concept; it may well happen that in a precisely specified case, temperature and pressure will start to oscillate wildly.)

Yet all this leaves us still with a single case rather than a law. It was simply not our problem, for we wanted to know what will happen *in general* if we remove ten molecules. In the attempt to deduce a general prediction concerning the variation of temperature and pressure, no amount of knowledge of the positions and momenta of the molecules in one or in many containers will help. Rather, we have to apply the methods of *statistical* mechanics, with their characteristic estimates of the probabilities (measures of *sets*) of the realization of conditions of certain *kinds*.

It is thus *not* our lack of detailed information or knowledge but the *kind of problem* we wish to solve that leads us to have recourse to probability theory.

To give another example, a similar one, we might imagine that we know enough about the conditions of radium atoms to predict of a certain atom that it will disintegrate within the next three seconds; but this would not necessarily help us to determine the statistical rate of disintegration of radium. Similarly, knowledge sufficient to enable us to predict whether a man whose appendix has just been removed in an English hospital will survive the next three hours will not provide us with a knowledge of the mortality rate of English hospital patients in the first three hours after the removal of their appendices.

The general result of these considerations is this. Probabilistic or statistical problems demand probabilistic or statistical knowledge and probabilistic or statistical methods.

I am painfully conscious of being, with this thesis of mine, in disagreement with many great physicists. (I think that they sometimes overlook that we often work with probabilistic hypotheses of equidistribution.) Max Born, for example, explains the contradiction between Boltzmann's *H*-theorem and Liouville's theorem by saying that Boltzmann's collision integral represents the situation 'roughly'; and he explains that 'roughly' means here 'after some reasonable averaging'. And he goes on to say: *'This averaging is the expression of our ignorance of the actual microscopic situation.* Boltzmann's theorem says that . . . *mixing mechanical knowledge with ignorance of detail* leads to irreversibility.'[127]

But it is not the crudity of our knowledge or the roughness of our ignorance that leads to averaging and to statistics, but the character of our problem. It is the problem that decides what instrument we are going to use. It takes a stout axe to deal with a rough block; and it takes a statistical theory to deal with a rough average, as Born calls it. (As mentioned before, I have been unable to find either in Boltzmann or in the Ehrenfest monograph anything like the view that Born believes to be theirs; but the view is widespread none the less.)

The subjectivist interpretation of probability, which makes the applicability of probability a consequence of our ignorance, is one of the most important Parmenidean apologies of our time. It originates from Parmenides' determinism: the determinist can hardly explain chance in any other than a subjectivist way – as an illusion due to our ignorance.

28 Some critical remarks on the subjectivist interpretation of information theory

The subjectivist interpretation of the theory of probability has led to a subjectivistically interpreted mathematical theory of information, founded by Claude Shannon. This theory *may* be interpreted as a theory of *channels* transmitting *sequences of signals* (information); sets of such sequences; *sources* of information (and their '*memory*'); *input* and *output* of the channel; *channel noise*; codes and their powers of compression; the probability of recovering the input from the (coded) output under certain specified conditions; and other such objective ideas.

I am giving these examples in order to show that *information theory may be interpreted objectivistically*. But it is, essentially, an application of probability theory; and if probability theory is interpreted subjectivistically, information theory will also be so interpreted.

An important idea of mathematical information theory is that of the '*uncertainty*' of an experiment for whose outcome a discrete probabilistic distribution is given. 'Uncertainty' means here the manner in which the distribution differs from a '*certain*' distribution, that is to say, from a distribution that attributes to one possible outcome of an experiment the probability 1 and to all other outcomes the probability 0. Clearly, the distribution furthest removed from this will be the uniform distribution – the one that distributes to each of the n possible outcomes (we are dealing with *finite* distributions, that is, with a finite n) the probability $1/n$. This shows that, as long as we interpret 'probability' objectivistically, the 'uncertainty' of the outcome of an experiment, or of a probability distribution, will also have to be interpreted *objectivistically*. A very useful mathematical measure of this 'uncertainty' introduced by Shannon has, interestingly enough, exactly the same mathematical form as Boltzmann's expression for entropy. This is unexpected, but intuitively understandable; for both can be interpreted as probabilistic measures of disorder. A random sequence of 0s and 1s in which both have the probability 0.5 will be more disordered than a random sequence in which the probability of 0 equals 0.9 and that of 1, accordingly, 0.1; for the latter will consist of many 0s, with only here and there a 1 or two.[128] This may be shown by the two sequences:

```
0110001110101001000001011110011 . . .
0000000010000000000000100000100 . . .
```

Clearly there is a sense in which the first of these is more disordered than the second.

Thus we have *two* distinct ideas of disorder: randomness (or probabilistic independence)[129] and 'uncertainty'. Both admit of degrees; and for both we can define a mathematical measure. Entropy measures the second kind of disorder, not the first.

These remarks are intended to make clear that there exists an objectivist interpretation not only of Shannon's theory in general but in particular of the idea of 'uncertainty', as it occurs in this theory. Thus what I am (by implication) opposing here is not information theory but its subjectivist interpretation.

This subjectivist interpretation has been linked with the subjectivist interpretation of statistical mechanics, which assumes that statistical mechanics is motivated by our ignorance and asserts, besides, that its results – such as Boltzmann's entropy theorem (the *H*-theorem) – *require for their derivation an assumption of ignorance* ('mixing mechanical knowledge and ignorance', as Max Born says).

The alleged link between thermodynamic entropy and the subjectivist idea of uncertainty is very simple. It is asserted (a) that both entropy and uncertainty are measures of our ignorance or lack of information; (b) that *negentropy* is therefore a measure of the knowledge or information that we possess; and (c) that Maxwell's demon can invert the law of entropy increase only if in doing so he utilizes and spends his knowledge (negentropy), so that he puts into the system (at least) as much negentropy as he obtains from his activities. Moreover, it is asserted that in order to obtain his knowledge, he has to work, and thus to increase the entropy of some part of his environment. So he obtains his knowledge at the cost of an entropy increase. This is assumed to be at least equal to his knowledge (negentropy). As a result we can assert finally that the following sequence occurs, where the arrow means 'produces': *entropy increase* → *negentropy (or information) increase* → *entropy decrease.*

This theory seems to me to be utterly mistaken. It goes back to a paper of 1929 by Leo Szilard (further developed mainly by von Neumann, Gabor, and Brillouin) to which I have already referred; a paper that I criticized in 1957[130] and (I believe more decisively) in Section 22 above, where I have tried to show that a Maxwell demon exists who is a variant of Szilard's demon, but who does not need to do any work, or to expend any information.

At any rate, the subjectivist interpretation of information theory with its negentropy theory of the information possessed by Maxwell's demon – which, in some radical forms, explains even physical entropy production as the consequence of human nescience – seems to me completely *ad hoc*. Moreover, it is a typical Parmenidean attempt to let our ignorance play a constructive role in the physics of appearances. In opposition to these views I believe that the Sun will continue to produce entropy, and that hot air will continue to escape from overheated lecture rooms, even if there are no intelligences at work to provide the required amount of nescience.[131]

Entropy is not itself an invariant, and it is therefore outside the Parmenidean picture, as Meyerson realized. But it may, I think, be boldly asserted that it is a problem of physics rather than of biology or of psychology.

29 Indeterminism in quantum physics viewed as a breakdown of Parmenideanism

My next example of a breakdown in Parmenideanism is quantum mechanical *indeterminism*. It appears, as usual, together with a Parmenidean apology.

I am myself an indeterminist. And I *do* agree that quantum mechanics is a statistical, and an indeterministic, theory. It is a statistical theory because it developed under the pressure of an essentially statistical problem: the problem of the intensities of the spectral lines, which are interpreted in terms of photons and transition probabilities.

But Heisenberg explains the probabilistic character of quantum theory as due to our ignorance. He first gave a causal explanation of the breakdown of causality: it is due to the fact that we, the mortals, the observers, interfere with (that is to say, act causally upon) physical objects while we measure them; and that we thereby disturb them in a manner that makes us ignorant of their actual state. This implies that if there were no meddling physicists about, the world would be properly Parmenidean, and that it is really us, and our ignorance, the erring opinions of the mortals, that are responsible not only for the 'reduction of the wave packet', but for the breakdown of the Parmenidean Way of Truth, and thus of causality. Or as Dirac puts it: 'Causality applies only to a system which is left undisturbed. If a system is small, we cannot observe it without producing a serious disturbance. . . . *Causality will still be assumed to apply to undisturbed systems.*'[132]

I shall not say more here about Heisenberg's argument because I have analysed it in considerable detail in the appendix on imaginary experiments in my *L. Sc. D.*, and elsewhere.[133]

30 Other anti-Parmenidean developments of modern physics

I shall say only very little about the two most important anti-Parmenidean developments in recent years: the breakdown of the electromagnetic theory of matter and, connected with it, the most important of all: the discovery of a host of new unstable 'elementary particles'.

The electromagnetic theory of matter dominated physics at least from 1907 to 1932. Einstein believed in it till his death; and so did Eddington, with his theory of protons and electrons. Dirac too believed in it for a long time. It was an automatic part of the Copenhagen interpretation.[134]

But, strangely enough, this dominant theory has long been overthrown without anybody's commenting on the overthrow. At first there were Parmenidean apologies for the neutrino (an imaginative but imaginary invention), for the positron (a hole) and for the neutron (a proton *cum* electron); but when the number of elementary particles increased, a dominant theory of physics passed away unsung. If I were pressed to explain why its disappearance was so little discussed I should offer the conjecture that there was simply no Parmenidean apology at hand for its rejection.

Nor do I know of a Parmenidean apology for the adoption of the new unstable particles. The new particles, and especially the fact that they can decay into very different particles, represent the theoretically most important discovery since Democritus. For they have destroyed the fundamental research programme of physics – the atomistic theory of change. We have qualitative change now, and though it can be partly described quantitatively, there does not seem to be any prospect for its explanation by, or reduction to, the movement of particles in the void. (Incidentally, the void disappeared much earlier, to be replaced by fields – but this could be interpreted as an addition to the atomistic programme, rather than as a refutation of it.)

Moreover, this most important of anti-Parmenidean developments was connected with the discovery of new kinds of forces – the first since electromagnetism – of which especially the *'weak interaction forces'*, responsible for the decay of certain kinds of particles, promise *to base the direction of time upon laws*, rather than upon initial conditions only; which would bear out the hopes for a new research programme, and the prediction of its possibility, made by L. L. Whyte.[135]

31 Non-Parmenidean explanations of the expanding universe

My last example of a deviation from the Parmenidean Way of Truth I will take from cosmology – from the conflict between the two main competitors in the explanation of the expanding universe: I mean the steady state theory and the big bang theory.

It is clear that the fact to be explained – the expanding universe – is anti-Parmenidean in the highest degree; and as a consequence, neither of the two cosmologies can be Parmenidean.

Yet, at least in the past, the main criticism levelled by the adherents of each theory against the other was the accusation of irrationality: of a deviation from Parmenideanism.

Of course, they do not use these terms. Rather, the steady state theory is accused of irrationalism and of a deviation from the true scientific method because it gives up one of the identity laws – the law of conservation of mass–energy–momentum. The accusation obviously presupposes Parmenideanism.

On the other hand, the defenders of the steady state theory feel, quite rightly, that they are quite as good Parmenideans, and perhaps even better ones, than the explosionists. For what could be less Parmenidean than the original big bang? Clearly, it is more rational and Parmenidean to assume that the overall structure of the universe does not really change – even if we have to pay for this adherence to Parmenideanism with something like matter creation. For is not this matter creation a steady one? And can we not almost say, with Parmenides, that in the world at large, no intrinsic change occurs?

32 Summary of the deviations from the Parmenidean programme

Let me sum up my story. We have seen at least six deviations (of course, all heretical or conjectural) from the Parmenidean programme: imperfection (Newton); irreversibility; quantum-theoretical indeterminism, and the invasion of probability; the breakdown of the electromagnetic theory of matter; the breakdown of the atomistic theory of change over the transmutation of elementary particles; and the new cosmologies. Most of them were accompanied by Parmenidean apologies, which abound in modern physics; but these apologies are redundant, since it has turned out very clearly that science need not perish, or cease to progress, even if it does deviate from the Parmenidean version of rationalism. Admittedly, these developments have created a strong longing, a real need, for some great new constructive ideas. But this is all to the good: perhaps the demand will stimulate the supply. (As mentioned earlier, David Bohm has made a most interesting contribution towards a new theory of change.)

But it is for the philosopher of science, I think, to combat the lapses into subjectivism and irrationalism that, I suggest, are due to an obviously unwilling and therefore repressed abrogation of an unconsciously held belief. The nescience theory of irreversibility or the theory that irreversibility and even change are illusions; the theory that indeterminacy can be explained by ignorance due to the interference of the observer or apparatus with the object of observation; these, I think, are lapses in a field in which the philosopher of science, as much as the physicist, may have a say.

What he should say, I think, is that no such excuses are needed for a deviation from the Parmenidean programme. With the breakdown of the Democritean theory of change the Parmenidean programme has turned out to be too narrow, in spite of the tremendous services it has rendered (and no doubt will continue to render) to rational science. This, I think, is the lesson to be learnt from the more recent development of modern physics. We should try to broaden the rationalist framework.

33   A lesson from non-Parmenidean economics

I may perhaps briefly mention that the first science to achieve a major breakthrough by giving up its originally Parmenidean programme was economics. Parmenidean economics is the doctrine that all economic exchange is a *zero-sum game*; or in other words, that in every exchange between you and me, your gain must be my loss. This primitive theory, based on what might be called '*the principle of the conservation of wealth*', was the basis of mercantilism. It is at the root of the Marxist theory that the accumulation or increase of wealth among capitalists must be matched by an increase of misery among workers. Thus Marx retained in this politically most revolutionary and important of his doctrines an already quite obsolete piece of Parmenidean economic theory – in spite of his pointedly anti-Parmenidean dialectic. Nevertheless, something like this is still widely believed, and its influence can still be felt in the struggle for the greatest slice in the division of the national cake.

The real progress in economic theory started with the surrender of this Parmenidean prejudice. It started when Adam Smith made it clear that in a voluntary exchange, as a rule *both parties are gainers and nobody is the loser*. This anti-Parmenidean discovery is still, I believe, the most important lesson we can learn from economics.

With this, I conclude my historical argument for a conscious broadening of the rationalist programme. I speak of broadening the programme, for I do not, of course, intend to suggest that we should give up the search for invariants. I suggest, rather, that we should not only continue this search, but *at the same time*, consciously try to go beyond it.

34   Beyond the search for invariants: towards a logical theory of understanding

Of course, we cannot give up either Parmenidean rationality – the search for reality behind the phenomenal world, and the method of competing hypotheses and criticism – or the search for invariants. But what we ought to give up is the identification of the real with the invariant. In order to see what may be the possible consequences of this, let us look at a Parmenidean 'table of opposites', in the style of the famous Pythagorean table. I put on the left what may be called 'Parmenidean Ideas or Categories' (or the Way of Truth) and on their right their anti-Parmenidean opposites (or the Way of Opinion):

Necessity	Chance
Perfection	Imperfection
Precision	Approximation
Reversibility	Irreversibility
Repetition	Variation
Things	Processes
Invariance	Emergence

The ideas (or 'categories') listed in this table are not meant to represent anything definite. They are only *labels*, to serve as reminders of certain theories and certain problem situations. Given this warning, we rationalists might consciously admit, I think, the existence in this world of all the non-Parmenidean ideas. Quite apart from the almost trite fact that we should remember that what appears as a thing (including an elementary particle) is always a process, we should admit the significance of Chance, Imperfection, Approximation, Irreversibility, Variation, and transcending Invariance, even of Emergence.

I shall not say much here about the last four of these opposites; for I have said quite a bit about Irreversibility already, and as to Repetition versus Variation, it may be sufficient to remind you that, at least since Darwin, the problem of (precise) Repetition or reduplication versus imprecise repetition or Variation or mutation should have been recognized as of fundamental importance in almost all biological phenomena.

The inclusion of the category of Emergence may seem somewhat suspect to rationalists, and it is, I admit, in need of a defence. I shall not undertake this defence here because I have dealt with it elsewhere. [136] Yet I might mention that philosophers of science can hardly do without a theory that can account for the emergence, and the significance, of novel ideas and theories (that is, for their 'creative evolution').

Thus I shall confine myself here to some remarks on the distinction between things and processes, and the relation of this distinction to the ideas of Chance, Imperfection, and Approximation.

The vague distinction, much stressed by Whitehead, between things and processes may perhaps be related in physics to the distinction between the mechanics of mass points and that of continuous media, or between particle theories and field theories. That field theories show a lesser degree of determinism than a (Laplacean) mechanics of mass points (because boundary conditions have to be 'given' for all time) has been mentioned above;[137] as has the part played by the idea of Chance in modern physics, which is usually combined with the idea of probabilistic independence, such as the independence of two consecutive penny tosses. But not only does Chance or perfect independence play a part in modern physics – so also does approximate or partial or imperfect independence: I need remind you only of Einstein's and Smoluchowski's theory of Brownian motion, or of the importance of the theory of Markov chains and random walks. Thus Imperfection (including imperfect independence) enters together with Chance.[138]

But the ideas of Imperfection and Approximation might be further exploited. To illustrate this, I will refer to the part played by the theory of *resonance* in modern physics (and thus again to field theory). *Almost all interaction* can be described in terms of resonance – from the interaction between atoms emitting and absorbing *light*, to that interaction that binds them together as molecules and crystals, and thus even to those 'mechanical' interactions based on the (relative) impenetrability of solids. (It should be noted that this 'resonance' does not commit us to a wave-theory or to a quantum-theoretical 'dualism of particle and wave': it is fully compatible with a pure particle interpretation.)[139]

But *resonance* is almost never perfect (though it is perhaps almost perfect in the case of the coherent light of lasers and masers).[140] For example, the finite width of spectral lines indicates the imperfect or approximate equality of the emitted frequencies.

We see here that the idea of Approximation (which at first seems only to refer to degrees of knowledge and ignorance, or perhaps to the growth of our knowledge) plays also a more objective role: it is needed in physics to explain such phenomena as the width of spectral lines, or the beats that result from the approximate equality of acoustical frequencies, or the limited stability of radioactive atoms (which can obviously be measured by their half-life).

The almost universal Imperfection of all resonance phenomena is connected with the spatio-temporal properties of our universe: to be in perfect resonance, the distance between two oscillators would have to be a precise multiple of their wave-length; which is impossible if the oscillators are in relative motion, or are themselves extended physical systems rather than mass points. Moreover, the relativity of simultaneity makes anything like perfect resonance impossible (since resonators are not inertial systems: two resonators, especially if their frequency is high, must, even if they are located in the same inertial system, change their hyperplane of simultaneity; *and they cannot do this simultaneously.*

Thus Imperfection may be a major building block of our so obviously non-Parmenidean world. In fact, it seems likely that a world in perfect resonance could not exist – in the sense that nothing could ever happen in such a world: it would indeed be a Parmenidean world.

On the other hand it may well be the case that imperfect resonance and imperfect interference could explain much of the non-Parmenidean character of our world, and that they could do so without forcing us to surrender any of our Parmenidean victories. It might be of help not only in a general theory of change, interaction, and irreversibility, but perhaps even in the theory of evolution.

If there is anything in this programme and in the idea of imperfect resonance, then it might be presented, strangely enough, as a return from the philosophy of Parmenides to the even older one of Heraclitus, who wrote:[141]

> Things brought together are whole and not whole, agree
>   and disagree, are in tune and out of tune. . . .
> What disagrees [with itself] agrees with itself: a union
>   or harmony is due to recoil or tension, as in the
>   bow or in the lyre.

I suggest that what cannot, in all likelihood, be explained by the Parmenidean method of invariants is the problem of change and of time itself, and especially the problem of the arrow of time. The Heraclitean problems of change, of variance, and of conflict seem to transcend the method of invariants. This is why Parmenides denied change. (And this is why some people deny that there can be a problem here.)

But does not this praise of a Heraclitean programme indicate a readiness to adopt irrationalist doctrines such as vitalism or Bergsonianism?[142] I do not think so.[143] The trouble with these theories is that they have no explanatory power; nor have they been fruitful research programmes.

On the other hand, these irrationalists have sometimes seen *problems* that Parmenidean rationalists did not want to see, and were too easily inclined to dismiss as pseudo-problems.

But we should never be afraid of problems; and the best method of avoiding irrationalism is, I believe, to return to the ancient postulate that we must always *try to understand*.

Thus we must return to the postulate of *understanding as well as possible* what we are doing in science. Quantum theorists have been unnecessarily pessimistic about understanding, because they inclined to the view that understanding is limited to what can be pictured or represented by classical mechanical models. Yet I believe that we can develop a *logical theory of understanding* – and of different degrees of understanding – that shows that understanding is quite independent of pictures and models: a theory of *rational* understanding based upon a purely logical rather than a psychological idea of problem solving; and applicable to the most abstract scientific problems, and to the boldest and most novel scientific theories.

Of course, such a theory would be (a) a theory of problems and their solutions, and (b) a theory of the different levels of problems, and of why certain solutions are better than others. I understand a physical or biological theory if I know how it functions; if I know its virtues (its preferability to others); and if I know the problems it solves and cannot solve, and the new problems it suggests. As we see, understanding may have levels. This is why we may speak of 'deeper' understanding, or of deepening our understanding.[144]

This rational theory of understanding, I believe, will make it possible for us to tackle problems that in the past have been often left to the irrationalists. I think that rationalists should no longer avoid these problems but should face them in the spirit of Heraclitus and Parmenides; of Boltzmann, of Darwin, and of Einstein.

Notes

1 I am alluding to Freud's theory of the 'omnipotence of thought', by which, however, he meant the omnipotence of wishes. What I mean is, rather, the omnipotence of theories; sometimes even of theories in which nobody really believes.

2 See David Bohm, 'Space, Time, and Quantum Theory, Understood in Terms of Discrete Structural Processes', *Proceedings of the International Conference on Elementary Particles*, Kyoto, 1965, pp. 252–87.

3 See Newton's letters to Richard Bentley, of 17 January 1693 (1692–3), and especially that of 25 February of the same year, in which he writes: 'that one body may act upon another at a distance . . . is to me so great an absurdity that . . . no man who has in philosophical matters a competent faculty of thinking can ever fall into it.' See also *C. & R.*, pp. 106f. (On other occasions Newton expressed himself somewhat differently.)

4 A. Einstein, *Relativity: The Special and General Theory*, London, 1920, p. 77. I have slightly modified the translation.

5 P. A. M. Dirac, *The Principles of Quantum Mechanics*, 4th edn, Oxford, 1958, p. 310. Since then Dirac has expressed himself even more radically.

6 Referring to DK 28B6: 2–3, Karl Reinhardt suggested in his fascinating (though I believe often unacceptable) *Parmenides*, Frankfurt-am-Main, 1916, 1959, pp. 35f., that there may have been more than two 'ways of inquiry' (*one* way of truth and two mistaken ways). This suggestion is rejected by L. Tarán, *Parmenides*, Princeton, 1965; see especially his detailed discussion on pp. 59–61. But Tarán's own suggestion cannot, I think, reconcile DK 28B6: 3 with the next extant line, B6: 4, for the latter can only mean, in the context, 'but [I] also [hold you back] from this [further way of inquiry]', and is followed unambiguously by a brief anticipation of the Way of Illusion. Accordingly, the phrase '*I hold you back*' in B6: 3 must have the same meaning as its implied continuation in B6: 4: it is impossible that it means in 6: 3 'I hold you back *momentarily*' (Tarán, op. cit., p. 61, line 5) and in 6: 4 '. . . *permanently*'. Tarán's attempt to avoid this conclusion has no basis in the text; in fact, it is contradicted by the text.

A very satisfactory solution (which implicitly solves Tarán's difficulty and adopts essentially Reinhardt's three ways) is given by W. K. C. Guthrie, *A History of Greek Philosophy*, vol. II, Cambridge, 1965. He points out (p. 21) that 'the thought [DK 28B6: 2–3] is uncomfortably condensed' and that the second of the three ways (which is here the first *false* way), though not explicitly stated by Parmenides, is implied. (It is clearly stated in B7: 1.) Thus when the goddess asserts in B6: 2 '[*the*] *nothing is not*' or '*nothingness does not exist*' (Kahn translates: 'there is nothing which is not'; I suppose the clearest interpretation is '*there is nothing at all which is not*'), and then warns us in B6: 3 against '*this* first [wrong] way', we have, Guthrie points out, to take '*this* way . . . *ad sensum* to be the way of thinking that [the] "nothing" *can* exist'. (Incidentally the suspected yet unlikely omission after line 3 might easily have said something like this: 'For this first wrong way is the impossible opinion that nothingness can exist'; but there is no need to assume this.) The second of the wrong ways would then be here the opinion (B6: 8; cp. B8: 40) that 'to be and not to be are the same'. But since it follows from this that 'the non-existent exists' or perhaps 'some non-existent is' (B7: 1), the first wrong way is reducible to the second; which explains why Parmenides may distinguish, fundamentally, between only two ways, the first (right) and the second (wrong) way, as in B2: 5 or B8: 15–18.

7 DK 28B2: 3. (The assertion is repeated in B6: 1; 8: 2; 8: 15–18, and 8: 36.) The suggestion that the (semantical or extra-linguistic) subject of 'is' (= 'exists') is 'the knowable, the object of knowledge', I have derived from a most interesting but so far unpublished paper on Parmenides by Charles H. Kahn, which he has kindly allowed me to make use of, and in which this suggestion is supported by a detailed and critical textual analysis. He has also helped me with some critical comments. (Kahn's 'The Thesis of Parmenides' has since been published in *Review of Metaphysics*, 22, 1969, pp. 700–24.)

8 Parmenides uses three terms in the main when speaking of 'speaking in a serious sense' (that is, as opposed to merely using one's tongue, DK 28B7: 5): one is *legein* (DK 28B6: 1) with its suppletive forms of *eirein* (B2: 1; 7: 6); the others are *phrazein* (B2: 6; B2: 8; B6: 2); and *phanai* (B1: 23; B8: 8). Now, it is important to note that all these are used by Parmenides in the (transitive) sense of speaking *of*, or *about*, something; reporting something (cp. Xenophanes DK 21, B8: 4); recounting something (cp. *Odyssey* 14: 197); or pointing to, pointing out, referring to, something (cp. *Iliad* 23: 138; *Odyssey* 11: 22), and thus of making something known (B8: 8). This explains why, since we have to speak *of* something, we cannot speak of nothing: nothingness is unspeakable. (A not very significant exception seems to be B1: 23, where *phato* (from *phanai*) is apparently used in the sense of 'spoke as follows' [Kahn], though possibly the sense is 'made known, revealed, the following words [and the truth!] to me'.) On *legein* and *phrazein* see also Guthrie, *A History of Greek Philosophy*, vol. II, pp. 19f. with footnote 1 on p. 20.

9 Kahn points out convincingly (see note 7 above) that the verb often translated by 'thinking' (*noein*) has in Parmenides' poem, and in early Greek usage generally, a sense of *apprehending something*, which is close to our word 'knowing': we know (*of*) *something* – the something that to start with is the quite unspecified object of discourse; in brief *the knowable*. (This corresponds closely to what I say in note 8 above about speaking *of something*; and if we use 'thinking', it should be in the sense 'thinking *of something*'.) See also note 19 below, and my translation of *gnōmē* in B8: 61 as 'notion' or '(alleged) knowledge'. Cp. K.

von Fritz's study 'Nous, Noein, and their Derivatives in Pre-Socratic Philo-sophy', *Classical Philology*, 40, 1945, pp. 223–42, and 41, 1946, pp. 12–34.

E. Hoffmann, *Die Sprache und die archäische Logik, Heidelberger Abhandlungen zur Philosophie und ihrer Geschichte*, 3, Tübingen, 1925, p. 11, says that Parmenides never uses *noein* (knowing) by itself, but always in conjunction with *legein* (saying). (This was accepted by Georg Misch, *The Dawn of Philosophy: A Philosophical Primer*, ed. in English by R. F. C. Hull, London, 1950, p. 318.) However, it is not true of fragments B3: 1 and B4: 1, while it is true of B6: 1, where the emphasis is on *legein*: 'One must say *and* think that only being exists.'

10 DK 28B2: 7. (Cp. also B6: 1; B3; and B8: 34.) The paraphrase 'what is the case' originates with a suggestion of Kahn's.

11 See the last sentence of Wittgenstein's *Tractatus*, and the second and third paragraphs of his preface. Parmenides agrees with Wittgenstein that one can speak meaningfully only *about something*. But Parmenides differs from him in identifying this something with the real or existing 'state of affairs' (as Kahn points out). Consequently one cannot but *speak the truth*.

12 This is the main argument of DK 28B8: 13–38; see also note 41 below.

13 DK 28B6: 4–9; B7; B8: 39–41 and 51–61 (the deceptively truthlike *diakosmos* of change is mentioned in B8: 60; see also note 24 below); and fragments B9–B19. See especially the double occurrence of the idea that *the mortals have adopted the convention or habit (katatithēmi)* of inventing *names of opposites*; in B8: 38–40 they did so with the names of 'coming into being' and of 'perishing', relying on the mistaken opinion that these (mere) names denote some truth; and in 8: 53 they did so with the names 'fire' (or 'light') and 'night', relying on the mistaken opinion that these two names denote opposites that are, necessarily, *one unity* (according to the identity of opposites asserted by Heraclitus). The mistake made, it is implied in both passages, is that opposites can exist; and thus especially *that being and not-being can both exist* (cp. B6 and 7). But from this would follow, for Parmenides, that they both exist and do not exist: the non-existence of being follows from the existence of nothing, since 'it [= the knowable] is not' would mean 'nothing exists *at all*'; and *vice versa*, the non-existence of nothing follows from the existence of being, since 'it is' means 'it is altogether and completely'. (Cp. the end of note 6 above.)

14 DK 28B1: 31–2.

15 DK 28B6: 4–9; B7; B8: 53–5; B16.

16 DK 28B1: 31–2 (see note 14 above); and B8: 51–2 and 60. Cp. also Essay 9, note 10, and Addendum 1 to Essay 1 in this volume.

17 DK 28B7, and B16.

18 DK 28B10, and B12.

19 DK 28B8: 61. More literally, perhaps, we may translate: 'So that no notion [no alleged knowledge, no convention, no name-giving] of the mortals will ever carry you away beyond the truth.' (Cp. *Iliad* 5: 236; *Odyssey* 12: 353; and add there '*para*' to the meaning, in the sense of 'across' or 'beyond' or 'wrongly'.) However, even the usual way of taking *parelasso* as 'outwit' or 'get unduly (or wrongly) the better of' (as in *Iliad* 1: 132) is quite acceptable, provided that it is realized that the goddess has not the slightest interest in instructing Parmenides how to win an intellectual tournament. (See also note 20.) She is interested solely in the *purely epistemological* question of *certain and secure knowledge* which she wants to make safe against over-persuasion and invalid though highly deceptive arguments, derived from sense, common sense, convention, and the description of a truthlike world order.

20 Regarding the religious element that may be contained in the term *doxa*, and against which (according to my interpretation) the goddess warns Parmenides, I find most interesting the following passage by Empedocles in DK 31B132 (for similar ideas see B2, 3, 23, and 114): 'Wretched (or awed) is he whose heart is weighed down [cp. *Iliad* 18: 463] by some sinister superstition (or by some nightmarish delusion) regarding the gods.' Here the context makes it clear that the sense does not change if we translate *doxa* more neutrally by 'opinion' or 'belief' or 'notion' rather than by 'superstition' or 'delusion'.

21 The more often I read Parmenides the more I am impressed by the extreme closeness of his poem to the fragments of Heraclitus; I am tempted to say, in almost every word he writes. There are no other philosophers who almost continually dwell on the problem circle: change; change implies the existence of opposites; also the identity of opposites; and the world is one unity. In the Way of Illusion (DK 28B8: 50–60), Parmenides seems to argue: if fire, which is the same as *light*, is to play the almost divine role it plays in Heraclitus, it ought to have *night* as its opposite (night = dark = dense and heavy = earth [= ashes?]). If we agree to *name* (and thus wrongly to accept the existence of) these two opposites, *light* and *night* (of which Heraclitus incorrectly named one only, and of which a Heraclitean identity of opposites, that is, 'a unity', has no rightful or proper status although light can *'mix'* with night), then we make that fatal mistake which is our fall from intellectual grace; for given these (non-identical though mixable) opposites, we are committed to change, becoming, and the whole cosmogony of a world of illusion.

22 DK 28B8: 50–1. What may be a repetition of a play on words is perhaps worth drawing attention to since 'the evidence that Parmenides . . . had Heraclitus especially in mind, is cumulative', as Guthrie says, *A History of Greek Philosophy*, vol. II, p. 32. Heraclitus, in a fragment in which Dikē plays an important part – B28 – uses a play on the words *'dokeonta . . . dokimōtatos'*. Parmenides uses in B1: 31–2 *'dokounta . . . dokimōs'*, in a passage that might be a reply to Heraclitus' appeal to Dikē.

23 DK 28B8: 51f. and 60; cp. also B1: 31–2; B6; B7; and B16.

24 DK 28B6; B8: 53f. Cp. *C. & R.*, pp. 236f. and Essay 9, Section 4.

25 DK 28B7: 5. See note 49 below.

26 Giorgio de Santillana, *The Origins of Scientific Thought*, Chicago, 1961, and 'Prologue to Parmenides', The University of Cincinnati, 1964, pp. 1–49. (Delivered as the *Louis Taft Semple Lecture* on 28 March and 1 April 1963.)

27 See David Hilbert, 'Axiomatisches Denken', *Mathematische Annalen* 78, 1917, pp. 405–15 (also in his *Gesammelte Abhandlungen*, Berlin, 1935, vol. III, pp. 146–56). It must be mentioned however, that Hilbert connected this process of laying deeper foundations with a demand that we should try *to guarantee the security of the edifice*. I do not agree with this demand: I believe that security and certainty are false gods, and that the quest for certainty (if taken seriously) must lead us to abandon science and to confine ourselves to tautologies – as Parmenides did (in his Way of Truth), if my analysis below is correct.

28 Cp. *L. Sc. D.*, last paragraph of Section 30, p. 111.

29 The Planisphere of Bianchini (Plate II A in Charles H. Kahn, *Anaximander and the Origins of Greek Cosmology*, New York, 1960) presents a late, eclectic symbolism and an elaborate system of celestial reference that was probably unknown to the Greek astronomers. But the general scheme of concentric circles and intersecting radii, focused upon the polar constellations of the Dragon and the Bears, must have been characteristic of all Greek planispheres and globes, including Anaximander's. Such a pattern of rings and radii is

identical with the cross section of Anaximander's cosmos sketched by Hermann Diels in his article on the cosmos of Anaximander ('Über Anaximanders Kosmos', *Archiv für die Geschichte der Philosophie* 10, 1897, p. 236; reprinted in H. Diels, *Kleine Schriften zur Geschichte der antiken Philosophie*, Darmstadt, 1969, p. 21), and Diels himself remarked on the parallel between this plan and Anaximander's map of the Earth. (For a detailed discussion of the Planisphere of Bianchini, see F. Boll, *Sphaera*, Leipzig, 1903, pp. 299–346.) Comparable zodiac schemes are known from Egyptian monuments as well as from Greek astronomical manuscripts.

30 See Kahn, *Anaximander*, p. 236; for the *opposites*, see also pp. 130ff.

31 Cp. *O.S.*, Chapter 5, 'Nature and Convention', especially Section ii. The language of the theory of nature is, most obviously, taken largely from that of society, and especially also from *war*. *Archē*, 'principle' or 'origin', is derived from *archō* ('to lead, rule, govern, command'); *kosmos* means 'order' (order as an attractive or interesting whole, including a battle order); *kata kosmon* means 'according to order', which may be a human or a cosmic law; *chreōn* = that which an oracle declares (or decrees) as 'what is necessary'; thus *kata to chreōn* = 'according to what is right and due' or 'according to fate' or else 'according to (natural or cosmic) necessity': the discovery of the distinction between 'nature' (equated to objective truth) and human convention (custom, man-made social order, man-made opinion, fiction, illusion), a distinction that appears also in Parmenides' contemporary, the poet Pindar, is largely the result of Parmenides' distinction between truth on the one hand and, on the other, human conventional error, which breeds illusions.

32 See Essay 1, Section IX.

33 Cp. Aristotle, *Metaphysics* 1069b3ff., and 1070a5.

34 I am well aware of the fact that this passage from Plato's *Cratylus* 402a (cp. DK 22A6) has been under fire for a long time, especially from G. S. Kirk, but I find the reasons unconvincing. I still think that the interpretation of Heraclitus' theory of change that I gave in 1945 in my *O. S.*, Chapter 2 (cp. 5th edn, 1966, pp. 11ff. and 20ff.) is correct, though of course I have developed my views since; in the main, by emphasizing the conjecture that the *problem of change is Heraclitus' central problem*. (See Essay 1, Section IX and *C. & R.*, p. 159, with note 5; p. 79, with note 19, etc.) This emphasis is perhaps the only point on which I somewhat disagree with the beautiful and convincing interpretations of W. K. C. Guthrie, *A History of Greek Philosophy*, vol. I, 1962, pp. 403–92 or of Hermann Fränkel, *Wege und Formen frühgriechischen Denkens*, Munich, 1955, pp. 237–83.

35 DK 22B101. Cp. G. J. Whitrow, *The Natural Philosophy of Time*, London, 1961, who says on p. 113 (after an apposite reference on the preceding page to Descartes): 'mind . . . is purely a "process" and not a "thing"'.

36 DK 22, end of B50; the second fragment is B67. On the latter fragment, and especially its final verses (not quoted here), see Fränkel, op. cit., pp. 237–50.

37 DK 22B84a.

38 Cp. my reference to Kahn's paper in note 7 above.

39 (Added 1982.) I have now been able to make some use of an excellent book by Charles Kahn, *The Verb 'Be' in Ancient Greek*, Dordrecht, 1973; unfortunately I have been unable to rewrite my whole treatment of Parmenides in the light of this great work.

40 DK 28B5. This remark shows considerable intuitive insight into the aimed-at tautological character of Parmenides' premise.

41 The theorems and proofs here numbered (1)–(8) are all taken from DK 28B8.

They will be found in the following lines of B8: (1) in lines 15–16; (2) in 16–18; (3) in 8–9; (4) in 4 and 24; (5) in 5, 24, and 25. The argument that the existing is ungenerated, imperishable, and unviolated is to be found in lines 3–15 and 46–8; some support for (6) is in lines 22-4; and for the whole argument in lines 42–4 and 49; (7) in lines 26–33; (8) in lines 30–3 and 42–9.

42 It is important to realize, as does Kahn in his paper on Parmenides mentioned in notes 7 and 9 above, that Parmenides' two propositions 'It is' and 'It is not' (or 'The existing exists' and 'The existing does not exist') are, indeed, contradictories and not contraries. 'It is' and 'It is not' cannot be both true together, and they cannot be false together: exactly one of them must be true and one false. This is indicated by Parmenides' insistence that we have here a '*crisis*' or 'decision'. (Parmenides' argument has been recently criticized as invalid by G. E. R. Lloyd, in his interesting book *Polarity and Analogy: Two Types of Argumentation in Early Greek Thought*, Cambridge, 1966, pp. 103–7, mainly because 'the "propositions" that Parmenides expresses are not contradictories' (p. 104) but contraries. Now, it is quite true that '*opposites*' are usually contraries rather than contradictories; but there is no reason why this should hold for Parmenides' ontological opposites, 'It is' and 'It is not'; and though Parmenides was not, of course, a logician, the intuitive implicit logic of his argument is, at least in this point, unassailable.)

43 'There cannot be any "pores"' is, of course, not in Parmenides: the 'pores' are my own allusion to Empedocles. But the fact that in B8: 45 (cp. B8: 23–5) Parmenides alludes to something like weak spots (or 'pores') within the existing (which he says cannot exist) gives support, I think, to my interpretation in theorem (8).

44 Cp. *C. & R.*, p. 80. It may be remarked that although in B8: 41 change other than motion (change of colour) is explicitly distinguished from change of place (motion), no separate argument refuting the possibility of such change seems to occur in the extant fragments. See also Fränkel, op. cit., the interesting note 2 on p. 206.

45 The evidence for theorem (8), '*The full world is corporeal*' (or 'material', though not in the Aristotelian sense of 'matter'), apart from a remark in note 43 above, corresponding to Parmenides' argument (from the word 'Since' on), is found in B8: 30–3 and 42–9. (It should be noted that B8, line 45, mentioned in note 43, forms part of this passage.) Yet the non-corporeality of Parmenides' 'being' or 'existent' seems to be widely accepted, for example by L. Tarán, *Parmenides*, Princeton, 1965, pp. 193f. (Were it not question-begging I might be tempted to call the tendency of ascribing non-corporeality to Parmenides' 'being' as 'unhistorical'. There was, one might retort, Melissus. But it seems to me decisive that Melissus came after Parmenides and, most probably, even after Zeno.)

46 The story is well told by Aristotle in *De Generatione et Corruptione* 325a ff. As I see it, this development is *not* a consequence of my general thesis that our knowledge grows, as a rule, by our discovery that we have made a mistake, or unconsciously accepted a mistaken theory. For my theory is a logical theory or a methodological rule (a normative theory), that we ought to search for cases that might count as refutations. So my methodology does not claim to be an empirical theory; and although it can be criticized, of course, it is not in its turn empirically refutable. (See my *Realism and the Aim of Science*, Totowa, New Jersey, 1983, pp. xxxi–xxxv.)

47 See Kahn, *Anaximander*, p. 236. Aristotle (*De Caelo* 298b) attributes to

Parmenides a typical Kantian 'transcendental' argument when he writes of Parmenides (and Melissus) that 'they were . . . realizing for the first time that such [unchanging] entities had to be postulated if knowledge and understanding were to be possible'.

48 Xenophanes' epistemology seems to precede Heraclitus. If so, it appears to be the first ever attempted. [Cp. Essay 2.] His thinking is not only the most original of all, but seems to me completely acceptable. The aim is truth, which is correspondence with the facts. But nobody who has found the truth – even the most perfect theory – can know for certain that he has found it: all our knowledge 'is but a woven web of guesses'. Alcmaeon says that only the gods know for certain; men are confined to draw [uncertain] inferences; that is, guesses; though we are alone able not only to perceive, but to understand (DK 24B1–1a). Heraclitus also denies that man alone can reach the truth – even if it is revealed to him by one who has reached it (DK 22B1).

49 See especially B7, which is translated in Essay 6, Section 6.

50 The text to notes 41–5 exhibits the method of indirect proof (or proof by *reductio ad absurdum*).

51 He thinks in terms of bodies, I suggest (see note 45 and text), rather than space. That his bodies are three-dimensional may be admitted; but this does not mean that they fill a three-dimensional nothingness. (See also my reference to de Santillana in Section 4 above.)

52 See Essay 9, Section 6.

53 See text to note 55, and *C. & R.*, p. 165, second quotation, which (as suggested by Reinhardt, *Parmenides*, 1916, p. 77) may have been intended to be scathingly ironical. (Cp. Essay 3, Section 6.)

54 My text here refers to the two great traditions in cosmology and the theory of matter: the *discontinuity theory of atomism* ('atoms and the void') and the *continuity theory* ('there is no void') founded by Parmenides and continued by Empedocles. These two traditions led to Heisenberg and Bohr on the one hand and to Descartes, Faraday, and Einstein, de Broglie and Schrödinger on the other. (The great fight ended only when it was superseded by the great 'quantum muddle', as I have called it.) The existence side by side of these two traditions shows the inadequacy of Kuhn's fashionable thesis that there is at any time just *one* paradigm in science (defined, so to speak, by a Parmenidean oneness). See also the text to note 60.

55 DK 28B16. See *C. & R.*, pp. 409–13, and Essay 3 of this volume for an elaborate defence of translating *melea* by 'sense organs' rather than 'body' (Guthrie uses 'limbs', Tarán uses 'body'), which was called even by Xenophanes (but also by others) *sōma* (B15: 4) and *demas* (B15: 5 and B23), while Aristotle calls each of the various sense organs *melos*. In his *De Partibus Animalium* 645b35–646a1 (Loeb edition, pp. 104ff.) we read: 'Examples of parts are: Nose, Eye, Face; each of these is named a "limb" or a "member".' From this translation (*melea* = sense organs) and Parmenides' often-repeated anti-sensualism, as well as from the context in which Theophrastus quotes the fragment, everything that I assert about this fragment follows almost 'with necessity'. I prefer *ekastos* to mean 'at each time' (*ekastote* in Herodotus I. 128), since the content of the sense organs is not only much-erring, but may change at any moment. Karl Reinhardt (*Parmenides*, 1916, p. 77) noticed that fragment B16 is meant as a scathing attack on mere human knowledge. (He translates '*meleōn polyplanktōn*' as '*den vielirrenden Organen*' – 'the much-erring organs'.)

56 Galen, *De Med. Emp.* (DK B125), a fragment edited by H. Schöne, 'Eine

Streitschrift Galens gegen die empirischen Ärzte', *Sitzungsberichte der königlichen preussischen Akademie der Wissenschaften zu Berlin*, Jahrgang 1901, Bd II, p. 1259. (Some scholars think that the dialogue, which Galen attributes explicitly to Democritus, is Galen's own invention.)

57 [Counted from 1965, the approximate date of this Essay. Ed.]

58 Emile Meyerson, *Identité et réalité*, Paris, 1908, 2nd edn 1912, pp. 250 and 470; English translation by Kate Loewenberg, *Identity and Reality*, London, 1930, pp. 227 and 415.

59 See *O.K.*, pp. 219–22.

60 See above, note 54. In *De Caelo* 306b5, Aristotle criticized Plato for holding a continuity theory (a theory of a full world) even though the shape of his atoms prevented them from being packed tightly, without holes between them; the passages are referred to in *C. & R.*, p. 88, note 44. This criticism seems to me to be valid; but on the other hand we should pay tribute to Plato's atomism for preparing the way for both the molecular theory and the theory of subatomic structures.

61 See Arthur O. Lovejoy, 'The Meanings of "Emergence" and its modes', *Proceedings of the Sixth International Congress of Philosophy* (Harvard, September 1926), London, 1927, pp. 20–33.

62 See my *Open Universe*, Totowa, New Jersey, 1982, pp. 89–92.

63 H. Weyl, *Space–Time–Matter*, London, 1922, p. 217.

64 H. Weyl, *Philosophy of Mathematics and Natural Science*, Princeton, 1949, p. 116.

65 The arrows indicate regions in which life may occur and time may be experienced as having the indicated direction. See also my *Unended Quest*, Glasgow, 1976, p. 159.

66 L. Boltzmann, *Vorlesungen über Gastheorie II*, Leipzig, 1898, p. 257; English translation, with minor amendments from, S. G. Brush, *Lectures on Gas Theory*, Berkeley and Los Angeles, 1964, p. 447.

67 L. Boltzmann, 'Zu Hrn. Zermelo's Abhandlung "Ueber die mechanische Erklärung irreversibler Vorgänge"', *Annalen der Physik*, 3, 60, 1897, p. 392; English translation by S. G. Brush in *Kinetic Theory 2*, ed. S. G. Brush, Oxford, 1966, p. 263.

68 Paul and Tatiana Ehrenfest, *The Conceptual Foundations of the Statistical Approach in Mechanics*, translated by M. J. Moravsik, Ithaca, 1959 (first published in German 1912), p. xi. Tatiana Ehrenfest's preface was written long after Paul Ehrenfest's suicide.

69 M. Born, *The Natural Philosophy of Cause and Chance*, Oxford, 1949; 2nd edn, Oxford, 1964, p. 59. (See also note 123 below.)

70 E. Schrödinger, 'Irreversibility', *Proceedings of the Royal Irish Academy*, 53a, 1950, p. 191. I criticized Schrödinger's views in a lecture to the Oxford University Science Society (20 October 1967). See also my *Unended Quest*, note 263 and text.

71 Henry Pemberton, *A View of Sir Isaac Newton's Philosophy*, London, 1728, p. 180. (The reference to Newton's *Optics*, London, 1721, p. 378, is a footnote of Pemberton's.)

72 Pemberton, op. cit., p. 181.

73 Sound waves in the air (but not necessarily in a solid) may be interpreted as consisting of very small processes that accumulate so as to form waves (of increasing and decreasing *density*). Light waves react with grids in interactions, which ideally are infinitely extended in space and time. I suggest that the interaction of sound waves in the air with a violin (or even with a tuning fork:

the action of the whole fork upon its molecules) and the interaction of light waves with structures like grids may be seen as cases of *downward causation*, to use a term introduced by Donald Campbell. (See also *S. I. B.*, pp. 14f.)

74 Hobbes concluded from the fact that seeing a colour is a process that may take time (the colour remaining the same) that light must be a process that goes on through time like a vibration (Thomas Hobbes, *Tractatus Opticus*, Editione integrale di Franco Alessio, in *Rivista critica di storia della filosofia*, Anno XVIII, Fasc. II, 1963, pp. 147–288; see also Hobbes, *De Corpore*, in *Elements of Philosophy. The English Works of Thomas Hobbes*, vol. 1, London 1839; 2nd reprinting, Darmstadt, 1966, p. 79.

75 A grid (like a prism) acts upon a time-extended light wave by reflecting the various colours (monochromatic rays) at different angles. But the capacity of the grid to do this depends essentially upon the *size* of the grid: a small grid is a bad grid, or in any case, it does not work as well as one that is an extension of it. So the grid is an example of holism in physics (see my *Poverty of Historicism*, London, 1957, pp. 82f.), and at the same time an example of downward causation. (As mentioned in note 73, a good example of downward causation is the functioning of a tuning fork: if one cuts its prongs so as to change its tune one causes all its molecules to vibrate in a different way from before.)

76 Cp. my *Quantum Theory and the Schism in Physics*, Totowa, New Jersey, 1982, Section 3, especially the sixth thesis, pp. 54–60. Here it is emphasized that Heisenberg's indeterminacy formulae are an immediate consequence of the classical principle of harmonic resolving power (that is, classical wave theory); but this in its turn is an expression of the essential spatio-temporal extendedness of fields, as discussed here.

77 The reason is that the entropy produced in an open system can be exported according to the Onsager equation.

78 Dennis Gabor, *M.I.T. Lectures*, 1951, referred to in L. Brillouin, *Science and Information Theory*, New York, 1956, pp. 168 and 179–82.

79 A. Einstein, 'Die von der molekularkinetischen Theorie der Wärme geforderte Bewegung von in ruhenden Flüssigkeiten suspendierten Teilchen', *Annalen der Physik* 4, 17, 1905, pp. 549–60; English translation by A. D. Cowper, in A. Einstein, *Investigations on the Theory of the Brownian Movement*, ed. R. Fürth, London, 1926, 1956, pp. 1–18. (I have slightly amended the translation.)

80 Cp. Leo Szilard, 'Über die Entropieverminderung in einem thermodynamischen System bei Eingriffen intelligenter Wesen', *Zeitschrift für Physik* 53, 1929, pp. 840–56.

81 Cp. Brillouin, op. cit., p. 176.

82 Cp. my paper 'Irreversibility; or, Entropy since 1905', *The British Journal for the Philosophy of Science* 8, 1957, pp. 151–5.

83 Note my actual wording and the context. What prevents the machine from working is, of course, friction. Note that my idealization is, however, much less excessive than that accepted by Szilard and Brillouin. (In the paper mentioned in note 82 I also criticized severely Szilard's paper of 1929.)

84 John von Neumann, *Mathematical Foundations of Quantum Mechanics*, Princeton, 1955, pp. 419–21 (German edn., Berlin, 1932, pp. 223f.). According to von Neumann (who only sharpens the views of Bohr and Heisenberg), an atom has no position or momentum unless we have measured its position or momentum. Thus there is a world of things in themselves that is turned into a world of appearances by our interference: therefore we can know only the world of appearances.

85 Werner Heisenberg, *The Physical Principles of the Quantum Theory*, New York, 1930. The first quotation is from p. 65; the second from p. 64. (I have replaced the translators' words 'other than' by 'except'.)

86 A part of the story is now retold in my *Unended Quest*, sections 35 and 36.

87 J. Loschmidt, 'Über den Zustand des Wärmegleichgewichtes eines Systems von Körpern mit Rucksicht auf die Schwerkraft', *Sitzungsberichte der kaiserlichen Akademie der Wissenschaften zu Wien* 73, 1876, pp. 128 and 366. Boltzmann replied in 'Bemerkungen über einige Probleme der mechanischen Wärmetheorie', *Sitzungsberichte . . . Wien* 75, 1877, pp. 67–73. Cp. Boltzmann's *Wissenschaftliche Abhandlungen* 2, Leipzig, 1909, pp. 116–22. This paper was soon followed by 'Über die Beziehung zwischen dem zweiten Hauptsatze der mechanischen Wärmetheorie und der Wahrscheinlichkeitsrechnung, respective den Sätzen über das Wärmegleichgewicht', *Sitzungsberichte . . . Wien* 76, 1877, pp. 373–435 (cp. Boltzmann's *Wissenschaftliche Abhandlungen* 2, 1909, pp. 164–223) in which Boltzmann formulated the relation between entropy and probability. Loschmidt's criticism consisted of pointing out that kinetic theory cannot entail the entropy law; for if it did, then an inversion of the velocity vectors of a system would return it to its initial state of lower entropy.

88 Boltzmann, 'Bermerkungen', p. 72; cp. Boltzmann's *Wissenschaftliche Abhandlungen* 2, 1909, p. 121.

89 L. Boltzmann, 'Entgegnung auf die Wärmetheoretischen Betrachtungen des Hrn. E. Zermelo', *Annalen der Physik* 3, 57, 1896, p. 773. (Cp. Boltzmann's *Wissenschaftliche Abhandlungen*, 3, 1909, p. 567.) See the English translation in *Kinetic Theory 1*, ed. S. G. Brush, Oxford, 1966, p. 218.

90 H. Poincaré, 'Le méchanisme et l'expérience', *Revue de Métaphysique* 1, 1893, pp. 534–7 (the quotation is on p. 537).

91 E. Zermelo, 'Ueber einen Satze der Dynamik und die mechanische Wärmetheorie', *Annalen der Physik* 3, 57, 1896, pp. 485–94; and 59, 1896, pp. 793–801.

92 E. Broda, *Ludwig Boltzmann*, Vienna, 1955, p. 27.

93 From the foreword, dated August 1898, to the second volume of Boltzmann's *Vorlesungen über Gastheorie*; see Brush's translation, *Lectures on Gas Theory*, p. 216.

94 See Broda, op. cit., pp. 27f.; the words on Maxwell and spectroscopy, on p. 39.

95 See my paper 'The Aim of Science', *Ratio* 1, 1957, pp. 24–35, now in *O.K.* (1972), pp. 191–205.

96 L. Boltzmann, 'Zu Hrn. Zermelo's Abhandlung "Ueber die mechanische Erklärung irreversibler Vorgänge"', p. 397; cp. Boltzmann's *Wissenschaftliche Abhandlungen*, 3, 1909, p. 584. (The translation and the italics are mine.) Cp. also p. 243 of *Kinetic Theory 2*, ed. S. G. Brush. Oxford, 1966.

97 E. Mach, *Die Prinzipien der Wärmelehre historische-kritisch entwickelt*, Leipzig, 1896, p. 364. (The italics are Mach's.)

98 Intuition is invaluable: there is no creativity without it. But it is often wrong, and is never reliable.

99 In a number of letters to *Nature*: 'The Arrow of Time', 177, 1956, p. 538; 'Irreversibility and Mechanics', 178, 1956, p. 382; 'Irreversible Processes in Physical Theory', 179, 1957, p. 1297; and 181, 1958, pp. 402f.. (This series of letters was continued after the publication in 1958 of Schrödinger's book, *Mind and Matter*; see also note 100 below.)

100 E. Schrödinger, *Mind and Matter*, Cambridge, 1958, p. 86. (This book

consists of the Tarner Lectures, delivered at Trinity College in October 1956. In a later edition, printed together with *What is Life?*, (Cambridge, 1967), the quotation appears on p. 164).

101 The passage is added in brackets; and since Schrödinger particularly drew my attention to it, referring to our previous debate, I suppose that he added it as a kind of reply to my letters to *Nature*. However this may be, I feel unable to agree with him. From a methodological point of view, our task is to criticize and, if possible, refute the view that the statistical theory can decide 'high-handedly' (Schrödinger's excellent characterization) upon the direction of time. And a methodology that makes it the task of physicists to preserve some theory (however beautiful) would turn this beautiful theory into a religious dogma.

102 Cp. E. Schrödinger, 'Irreversibility', *Proceedings of the Royal Irish Academy* 53, 1950, pp. 189–95.

103 In Boltzmann's second reply to Zermelo (cited in note 96 above), especially pp. 397f.

104 If you have some oscillation going on within a small region *R*, there will be waves *emanating from R* in time: a kind of arrangement (of initial conditions) easy to realize. If you wish to realize the time reversal of these expanding waves, you have to generate waves coming towards *R* and being absorbed in *R*. But this is a process difficult to realize, except by reflection of an expanding wave on a spherical mirror (which would be a very special case): in all other cases, it could be achieved only by a huge set of distant oscillators working coherently – a still more special and improbable arrangement of initial conditions. So the *expanding* wave may be used to characterize time's arrow. (See my letter 'The Arrow of Time', *Nature*, 177, 1956, p. 538.)

105 See *L. Sc. D.*, Section 67, entitled 'A Probabilistic System of Speculative Metaphysics'.

106 L. L. Whyte, 'One-Way Processes in Physics and Biophysics', *British Journal for the Philosophy of Science* 6, 1955, pp. 107–21.

107 E. Schrödinger, *Nature and the Greeks*, Cambridge, 1954, pp. 25f., and *My View of the World*, Cambridge, 1964, pp. 92f.

108 E. Mach, *Contributions to the Analysis of Sensations*, Chicago, 1897. First German edition: *Beiträge zur Analyse der Empfindungen*, Jena, 1886. Mach hoped to solve the psycho-physical problem and, indeed, his work founded 'neutral monism', as Russell called it. (See also *S. I. B.* especially Section 53, pp. 196–9.)

109 Cp. my paper 'A Note on Berkeley as Precursor of Mach and Einstein' (first published in *British Journal of Philosophy of Science* 4, 1953, pp. 26–36), *C. & R.*, chapter 6, pp. 166–74.

110 This is perhaps corroborated by the following passage from his *Prinzipien der Wärmelehre*, Leipzig, 1896, p. 363: 'One may, for example, very well have strong reservation with regard to the metaphysical concept of "matter", without finding it necessary to *eliminate* the valuable concept of "*mass*": we can continue to work with the latter concept in much the same way as I did in "*Die Mechanik*", just because one has realized that this concept need not be taken to entail more than that an important equation [viz. the law of conservation of mass] is satisfied by it.'

111 Stefan Meyer, *Festschrift zum 40jährigen Bestand des Wiener Institutes für Radiumforschung*, 1950; quoted in Broda, op. cit., p. 84.

112 John T. Blackmore, *Ernst Mach: His Life, Work and Influence*, Berkeley, 1972, pp. 321f. (My own view of the undoubtedly true reports of Meyer, Przibram,

and Chmelka is that Mach was shaken, but that he was too old to change his mind permanently on a point that was so important for him.)

113 Josiah Willard Gibbs, *Elementary Principles in Statistical Mechanics*, New York, 1902; German translation by E. Zermelo, Leipzig, 1905. Unaware of Gibbs' work, Einstein developed almost simultaneously the principal features of statistical mechanics (see *Ann. d. Phys.* 4, 9, 1902, pp. 417–33; 11, 1903, pp. 170–87; 14, 1904, pp. 354–62; and 34, 1911, pp. 175f.) and at once proceeded to apply his results to blackbody radiation and to Brownian motion (cp. note 115; see also Max Born, in *Albert Einstein: Philosopher-Scientist*, ed. P. A. Schilpp, Evanston, Illinois, 1949, pp. 163ff.; Martin J. Klein, *Science*, 157, 1967, pp. 509ff.; and Martin J. Klein, in *Albert Einstein: Historical and Cultural Perspectives* (ed. G. Holton and Y. Elkana), Princeton, New Jersey, 1982, pp. 39ff.). (I am indebted to Troels Eggers Hansen for the precise references in this note, and also in notes 114–5.)

114 H. Poincaré, *La valeur de la science*, Paris, 1907, pp. 182f.; English edition, New York, 1958, p. 97.

115 *La valeur de la science*, p. 184; English edition, p. 98. It may be worth noting that a mathematical (quantitatively testable) theory of Brownian motion was first given by Einstein in 1905 (see *Ann. d. Phys.* 4, 17, 1905, pp. 549–60; cp. note 113 above). See further M. v. Scholuchowski, *Ann. d. Phys.* 4, 25, 1908, pp. 205f. and *Krakauer Berichte*, 1913, pp. 418f.; and also A. Einstein, *Ann. d. Phys.*, 33, 1910, pp. 1294f., where a 'mathematical (quantitatively testable)' theory' of opalescence is stated.

116 Poincaré, *La valeur de la science*, pp. 182f; English edition, p. 97. See also Poincaré, *Thermodynamique*, Paris, 1908, p. 450.

117 Mach, *Die Prinzipien der Wärmelehre*, p. 363.

118 See note 112 above.

119 J. W. Gibbs, *Elementary Principles in Statistical Mechanics*, Chapter 12.

120 The following remarkable understatement in the Ehrenfests' monograph of 1911 is worth quoting here (English edition, p. 94, note 155): 'It is worth remarking in this connection that the Brownian motion is much more compatible with kinetic ideas than with the dogmatic formulation of the second law.' (See note 68 above.)

121 Schrödinger explained in his *Statistical Mechanics*, Cambridge, 1946, the reason for the superiority of Gibbs' treatment over Boltzmann's.

122 This symmetry of the fluctuation with respect to time is, of course, totally different from the following alleged but mistaken identity: 'the probability that a state of low entropy is followed by a state of higher entropy is identical with the probability that a state of high entropy is followed by a state of lower entropy' (*The Encyclopedia of Philosophy*, ed. Paul Edwards, New York, 1967, vol. I, p. 336, the article on Boltzmann). However, even a non-expert might know that the heat of a hot body tends to dissipate; and it is immensely improbable that a body may collect heat from its cooler surroundings and so get hotter. Boltzmann fully succeeded in explaining this trite fact by showing that the dissipation is highly probable, and the opposite highly improbable; his difficulty was only this: to show that this fact can be *derived from the laws of mechanics* (which are symmetrical with respect to time reversal).

123 Born, *Natural Philosophy*, pp. 58f (cp. note 69, above).

124 Ibid., preface: 'I had to . . . improvise.'

125 Ibid., p. 59.

126 Einstein raised the point with me twice in his letters. See my *L. Sc. D.*, p.

459 (with footnote). I took it up at our meeting in 1950; and he then agreed.

127 Born, loc. cit. (Italics mine.)

128 *L. Sc. D.*, p. 163.

129 That is, the condition that allows us to operate with the special multiplication theorem $p(xy) = p(x) \, p(y)$.

130 See my 1957 paper in *Nature* mentioned in note 99 above, and more especially the paper mentioned in note 82 above.

131 *British Journal for the Philosophy of Science*, 8, 1957, p. 155.

132 P. A. M. Dirac, *The Principles of Quantum Mechanics*, 4th edn, Oxford, 1958, p. 4. (The italics are mine.)

133 *L. Sc. D.*, Appendix *xi, Section 3. See also my paper 'Quantum Mechanics without the Observer', in M. Bunge (ed.), *Quantum Theory and Reality*, Berlin–Heidelberg–New York, 1967, pp. 7–44, and my *Quantum Theory and the Schism in Physics*, Totowa, New Jersey, 1982, pp. 15–30.

134 See the paper mentioned in note 133, especially pp. 8f.

135 L. L. Whyte, 'One-Way Processes in Physics and Biophysics', *British Journal for the Philosophy of Science* 6, 1955, pp. 107–21.

136 See, for instance, *Of Clouds and Clocks: an Approach to the Problem of Rationality and the Freedom of Man* (The Second Arthur Holly Compton Memorial Lecture, Washington University, 1965). Now in *O.K.*, Chapter 6.

137 In Section 21.

138 It is interesting to see that Hume, the great opponent of apriorism, denied on *a priori* grounds the existence of anything intermediate between pure chance and complete lawlike determination, contrary to the everyday experience of the vagaries of the weather (which we find combined with some degree of predictability) and contrary to our present views in physics and, indeed, in practically all sciences. Thus Hume asserted in his *Treatise* (see P. H. Nidditch's new edition of Selby-Bigge, Oxford, 1978, p. 171) that there cannot be anything intermediate between chance and causation: 'as the mind must either be determin'd or not to pass from one object to another, 'tis impossible to admit of any medium betwixt chance and an absolute necessity.' This is wrong. Take a physical situation with n logical possibilities. The simplest case will be an equidistribution, with each of the n possibilities having the probability of $1/n$. From this, we have a steady intermediate rise to necessity by 'loading' one of the n possibilities, so that its probability rises to, say, $3/2n$; to $2/n$; and so on until it reaches 1; while the probabilities of the other $n-1$ possibilities decrease. (See also A. I. Khinchine, *Mathematical Foundations of Information Theory*, New York, 1957, pp. 2f.)

139 See especially the work of Alfred Landé, and his emphasis on Duane's particle theory of *apparent* wave phenomena (which may constitute 'resonance').

140 The relationship between coherence of light and irreversibility seems to be in need of further investigation. The problem was investigated by Max von Laue (*Ann. d. Phys.* 4, 20, 1906, pp. 365ff; 23, 1907, pp. 1ff. and 795ff; and *Phys. Zeitschr.* 9, 1908, pp. 778ff.), who showed that it is possible *to increase the temperature difference of two* (or more) *coherent rays of light* without making any use of any compensating (entropy-increasing) process.

141 DK 22 B10 and B51.

142 Some excellent quantum physicists have recently made attempts to reintroduce some kind of vitalism. Especially well known is the attempt of Eugene

Wigner to show that biology must transcend physics because biological reproduction contradicts the quantum-mechanical theorem (alleged by Wigner) that the probability of the existence of a self-reproducing unit is zero. (See the essay 'The Probability of the Existence of a Self-Reproducing Unit', in E. Wigner, *Symmetries and Reflections – Scientific Essays*, London, 1970, p. 93, footnote.)

143 See my *Quantum Theory and the Schism in Physics*, pp. 159f.

144 I have often told my classes that, after a lecture, a student may leave with the comfortable feeling of having understood every word, while another student may feel that he has understood nothing. Yet the first *may* be unable to comment on the contents of the lecture while the second *may* be able to say *why* he did not understand it, and thereby show a deeper understanding than that of the lecturer. And a third student may even solve the second student's problems.

ADDENDUM
A NOTE ON OPPOSITES AND EXISTENCE IN PRESOCRATIC EPISTEMOLOGY

I

The idea of *opposites or contraries* – hot and cold, moist and dry, light and darkness, being and nothingness, generation and destruction, growth and diminution, limited and unlimited – conceived as acting powers fighting one another is a very old one. It can be found in many primitive views of the world. Their confrontation is strife, war. This idea is developed further by Heraclitus, who, I believe, was the first to see the great and fundamental *problem of change*, discussed in the preceding essay.

His predecessors had, of course, seen change and had tried to explain it. But they had not realized its problematic character; and, as Charles Kahn has pointed out, they had allowed the changing corruptible world to emerge from a living and life-giving but incorruptible and eternal principle (*archē*) such as Anaximander's *Apeiron*, which, although it gives birth to changing things, 'does not change into something other than itself',[1] while the warring opposites are perishable and can change one into the other: the stronger of the opposing forces can overpower and eat up or absorb the weaker. Ultimately, Anaximander taught, each of the opposites must 'perish into its source';[2] it must return into the *Apeiron*: 'Whence is the generation of things, thereto their destruction takes place, according to what is right and due; for they make amends and give reparation to each other for their offence, according to the ordinance of time.'[3] This, Kahn explains, means: 'according to the everlasting cycle which includes not only the seasons but all other rhythmic patterns of growth and diminution'.[4] Among these patterns we may include the patterns of war or strife,

217

as well as the give and take of human relations, and their order; an order that imposes penalties for any transgression.

These ideas of Anaximander, Kahn observes, form the background of Western cosmological thought.

II

Of Anaximander's successors before Parmenides I shall briefly mention two whose influence on Parmenides seems to me unmistakable: Xenophanes and Heraclitus.[5]

Xenophanes is important in this context mainly as *the father of epistemology* – the first to reflect on the limitations of our knowledge. He describes his own cosmological and theological thought, which owes much to Anaximander, as 'a web of guesses'. He stresses that 'certain truth' is beyond the reach of man, and asserts the conjectural character of all *human knowledge*, which he opposes to *divine knowledge*. And he made the discovery that human ideas of gods and the world are utterly unreliable because they are vitiated by anthropomorphism. In spite of this severely critical approach, Xenophanes was not a sceptic, but something like a critical rationalist; for he believed that we can, with our guesswork, our conjectures, make progress towards the truth.[6]

Heraclitus mentions Xenophanes with contempt. Yet, like Xenophanes, his thought moves within the framework of Anaximander; moreover, like Xenophanes he is an epistemologist, and his epistemological ideas are closely related to those of Xenophanes: the contrast between divine wisdom and the guesswork of mortal men (which can improve) is retained, but modified. It becomes a contrast between divine wisdom (in which, he claims, he himself participates, being wide awake) and the obtuseness of 'the other men'[7] who are hopelessly asleep. It seems clear that in his epistemology, Heraclitus wishes to correct Xenophanes; which tends to show that it was Xenophanes who made Heraclitus epistemologically conscious. It is interesting that the epistemological problem – the problem of knowledge, of understanding, of wisdom – has become so important for Heraclitus that he begins his book by announcing his claims to knowledge and by denouncing 'the other men'. This epistemological preamble created a tradition. In Parmenides, his proem becomes a weighty part of his work. An immediate descendant of this can be easily identified in the epistemological introduction of Plato's *Timaeus*. The tradition is enforced in various ways by Aristotle; and it can be traced down to many modern epistemological or methodological prefaces to textbooks in the physical, biological, and social sciences.

But epistemology was not Heraclitus' main contribution. It was not his main problem. As shown in the preceding essay, I think that Heraclitus' greatness lies in the fact that he discovered the central problem of the physical sciences and of cosmology: *the problem of change*. Of course, I do not say that Heraclitus discovered change, or that he was the first to notice its cosmological role. What he discovered was the paradoxical character of all change. He saw that there was a problem – almost a logical problem: *how is change possible?* It is essential to the idea of change that the thing that changes retains its identity while changing, and yet, if it changes, it cannot retain its identity.

Not all philosophers take this problem seriously: some are conditioned by a long tradition that solves the problem in terms of self-identical substance (its potentiality for changing, actualization of the changing substance). Few physical scientists take the problem seriously, because thanks to Parmenides, Leucippus, and Democritus, physics has been for a long time in possession of a very successful theory of change: all change, including qualitative change, is due to movement. So we have lost the sense of the problem of change. This, I think, is the reason why so few people agree that it could ever have been a fundamental problem of cosmology; and why so few believe that it was Heraclitus' great problem.

What was Heraclitus' solution?

Like his predecessors he saw change mainly as qualitative – as the change from one of a pair of *opposites* to the other: what is moist becomes dry. And indeed, the *opposites* play an enormous part in Heraclitus' thinking: they determine the structure of change, and indeed of the whole world.

We can state Heraclitus' solution in the form of seven theses.

(1) There are no things that change: it is wrong to conceive the world as consisting of a collection of *things* – even of *changing things*. The world does not consist of things but of *processes*.

(2) What *appear* to our senses as things are more or less 'measured' or 'steady' processes – opposing forces that keep each other at bay, in equilibrium.

(3) We ourselves *appear* to ourselves as things – unless we search ourselves. 'I searched myself',[8] says Heraclitus; and what he found was not a thing, but a process, like a burning flame. Fire, the flame, if it burns steadily, looks to the obtuse, to those who are half asleep, who do not search themselves, like a thing – a changing thing. But it is not a thing. It is a process.

(4) Though there are more or less separable processes, all processes are interlocking. They are not separable (and countable) as are things. The whole world is *one* world process.

(5) Thus there are no things that have to remain paradoxically self-identical during change. But the processes, that is, the changes, are self-identical; and this includes the *opposites*, which characterize each change and all change: *the opposites are identical* because they can exist only as poles of a contrast, that is, together; or as poles of a change, constituting the

changing process as such: 'the same thing is living and dead, waking and sleeping, young and old. For these things when changed are those, and those things when changed are these. . . . Cold things grow hot, hot cold; moist dry, dry moist.'[9]

(6) This holds for the total process, the whole world: 'In changing it is at rest',[10] because in changing it is self-identical, *and* because of *the identity of opposites*, which applies even to the opposites called 'change' and 'rest'.

(7) Thus Heraclitus says of God that he is, like the cosmos, the identity of 'all the opposites':[11] 'God is day and night, winter and summer, war and peace, satiety and hunger.' (Like Anaximander, Heraclitus identifies God with a cosmic principle.)

To sum up, Heraclitus solves the paradox of the self-identity of things during change by *a theory of things* that explains things as the misunderstood, or misinterpreted, appearances of often invisible processes. Processes, and especially the world process, are self-identical changes, involving opposites that are thus at the same time opposed and identical.

I do not pretend that all this is entirely clear and lucid. (Heraclitus himself loves paradoxes.) But it allows us to attribute to Heraclitus a fundamental problem, and a brilliant and revolutionary theory as its solution; and it gives what seems to me a coherent interpretation of the fragments and of Heraclitus' relation to Parmenides.[12]

III

Like Xenophanes and Heraclitus, Parmenides stands clearly in the tradition of Anaximander (and probably also of Pythagoras). It seems to me that there are many signs that he stands under the influence of Xenophanes.

Like Xenophanes he distinguishes guesswork or opinion from divine knowledge. But he develops Xenophanes' criticism of the anthropomorphism of human knowledge into the theory that the human commonsense interpretation of the world is a human delusion.

But the decisive influence seems to come from Heraclitus. Parmenides, I suggest, gives a point-for-point refutation of Heraclitus, the antilogia to Heraclitus' logos. He beats Heraclitus with his own logical weapon: the identity of opposites.

Like Heraclitus, Parmenides begins with an epistemological introduction. He largely accepts Heraclitus' 'correction' of Xenophanes' epistemology: divine knowledge, truth, is opposed to false claims to knowledge of mortal men; and, like Heraclitus, he claims participation in divine knowledge. We have here the epistemological opposites that come from Xenophanes:

Divine knowledge	Human (erroneous or) fallible opinion
Truth	Appearance, seeming, illusion

But Parmenides outdoes Heraclitus in operating more precisely and consciously with these opposites. Moreover, he beats Heraclitus at once on his own ground: *these* opposites at least are *not identical*. This non-identity is clearly implied in Heraclitus' preamble, and pervades all he says.

He further sharpens another pair of epistemological opposites that can be found in Heraclitus:

Reason   Sense (perception)

Heraclitus would have to admit the superiority of reason. Moreover, he clearly implies that the two are not identical. But he fails to draw a sharp line (opposition?) between them – thereby violating his usual method.

Parmenides' sharp opposition of reason and sense perception is a momentous step. European thought has been dominated by it ever since.

This concludes Parmenides' epistemological introduction. Though dependent on Xenophanes and Heraclitus, Parmenides may be said to be the true founder of epistemology; and ever since, epistemology has remained at the heart of philosophy.

When we proceed to cosmology, we find that Parmenides again operates with opposites. The fundamental pair is

Being (= what is)   Nothingness (= what is not),

a pair that Heraclitus never thought of. Had he thought of it, he might have asserted the identity of these opposites. Parmenides proceeds to prove (a) that they cannot be identical, and (b) that Heraclitus (or anybody who believes in change) will, in contradiction to the logical refutation, have to assert that they are identical.

Opposites are, in general, contraries rather than contradictories. This means that two opposites or contrary assertions such as

Socrates exists   Socrates does not exist

are partly compatible: they can be *false* together – but not *true* together. If we try to hold both these contraries true, we are led to the ontological consequence: Socrates does not exist. Thus in the case of an ontological predicate like 'exist', the two contraries cannot be true together. Any attempt at assuming them true together leads to an absurdity. In the case of an ontological predicate, contraries operate like contradictories: their disjunction is a tautology, and only one of the pair of contraries can be true. [13]

221

Notes

1 Charles H. Kahn, *Anaximander and the Origins of Greek Cosmology*, New York, 1960, p. 238.
2 Ibid., p. 196.
3 DK 12B1. Cp. Kahn, op. cit., pp. 166 and 196; see also the preface to the second printing, 1964.
4 Kahn, op. cit., p. 196.
5 I shall say nothing of Pythagoras, whose influence is more difficult to assess.
6 DK 21B18.
7 DK 22B1.
8 DK 22B101.
9 DK 22B88; B126.
10 DK 22B84a.
11 Hippolytus' comment on the fragment DK 22B67.
12 About Heraclitus more is to be found in Essay 1 above. Of all recent presentations of Heraclitus I find myself most closely agreeing with that of W. K. C. Guthrie, *History of Greek Philosophy*, Cambridge, 1962, vol. I, pp. 435f. (excepting one point: I do not believe in the identification of logos and fire: I think the *logos* is Heraclitus' 'account', that is, his theory, which includes the forces that control the fire). But I fear that Guthrie would not accept my conjecture concerning the central problem of Heraclitus, though he may accept part of what I have described as its solution.
13 Some people may protest, with Kant and Russell, that 'exists' is no predicate, and that there are no ontological predicates. But this is a mistake. Let E be 'exists'. Then we can define $Ex \equiv (x = x)$. In other words, E is the universal predicate, and $-E$ is the empty predicate, both relative to some universe of discourse. Now, if s is a constant (a name), '$-Es$' means 's does not belong to the universe of discourse', or ' "s" is an empty name' (' "s" names no element of the universe of discourse'). Thus if 's' is short for 'Socrates', we indeed get the result: from Es & $(-Es)$ follows $-Es$, so that Socrates is not an element of our universe of discourse, or of the existing things according to our assumed ontology.

ESSAY 8

COMMENTS ON THE PREHISTORIC DISCOVERY OF THE SELF AND ON THE MIND–BODY PROBLEM IN ANCIENT GREEK PHILOSOPHY

1   The history of our picture of the universe

Human thought in general, and science in particular, are products of human history. They are, therefore, dependent on many accidents: had our history been different, our present thinking and our present science (if any) would be different also.

Arguments like these have led many people to relativistic or to sceptical conclusions. Yet these are far from inevitable. We may accept it as a fact that there are accidental (and of course irrational) elements in our thought; yet we may reject relativistic conclusions as self-defeating and as defeatist. For we may point out that we can, and sometimes do, learn from our mistakes, and that this is the way science progresses. However mistaken our starting points, they can be corrected and thus transcended; especially if we consciously seek to pin down our mistakes by criticism, as we do in the sciences. Thus scientific thought can be progressive (from a rational point of view), irrespective of its more or less accidental starting points. And we can actively help it along by criticism, and so get nearer to the truth. The scientific theories of the moment are the common product of our more or less accidental (or perhaps historically determined) prejudices, *and* of critical error elimination. Under the stimulus of criticism and of error elimination their truthlikeness tends to increase.

Perhaps I should not say 'tends'; for it is not an inherent tendency of our theories or hypotheses to become more truthlike: it is rather the result of our own critical attitude, which admits a new hypothesis only if it looks

This essay is a reprint from K. R. Popper and J. C. Eccles, The Self and Its Brain: An Argument for Interactionism *(1977), 3rd edn, London, 1990, Part I, Chapter 5, Sections 43–7. (Minor adaptations and notes containing references distinguish the present text from the original.)*

like an improvement over its predecessors. What we demand of a new hypothesis before allowing it to replace an earlier one is this.

(1) It must solve the problems which its predecessor solved at least as well as did its predecessor.

(2) It should allow the deduction of predictions which do not follow from the older theory; preferably predictions which contradict the old theory; that is to say, crucial experiments. If a new theory satisfies (1) and (2), then it represents possible progress. The progress will be actual if the crucial experiment decides in favour of the new theory.

Point (1) is a necessary demand, and a conservative demand. It prevents regression. Point (2) is optional and desirable. It is revolutionary. Not all progress in science has a revolutionary character, although every important breakthrough in science is revolutionary. The two demands together ensure the rationality of scientific progress; that is, an increase in verisimilitude.

This view of scientific progress seems to me to be strictly opposed to relativism and even to most forms of scepticism. It is a view that allows us to distinguish science from ideology, and to take science seriously without overrating or dogmatizing its often dazzling results.

Some of the results of science are not only dazzling but unfamiliar and quite unexpected. They seem to tell us that we live in a vast universe, consisting almost wholly of space empty of matter and filled by radiation. It only contains a little matter, most of it in violent agitation; also a vanishingly small amount of living matter; and a still smaller amount of living matter endowed with consciousness.

Not only are vast amounts of space empty of any living matter, according to present scientific views, but also vast periods of time. We can learn from molecular biology that the origin of life from lifeless matter must be an event of extreme improbability: even under very favourable conditions – themselves improbable – life, it seems, could originate only after innumerable and long sequences of events, each of them nearly but not wholly successful in producing life.

One cannot say that this picture of the universe, as it is painted by contemporary science, strikes us as familiar or as intuitively quite satisfactory (though it is certainly intellectually and intuitively exciting). But why should it? It may well be true, or near to the truth: we should have learnt by now that the truth is often strange. Or else it might be far from the truth – we may in an unexpected way have misread the whole story, or rather, what we regard as the evidence supporting our story. Still, it is improbable [1] that there has been no increase of verisimilitude in the critical evolution of the story. There is, it appears, inanimate matter; life; and consciousness. It is our task to think about these three, and their interrelations; and especially also about the place of man in the universe, and of human knowledge.

224

I may mention in passing that the strangeness of the scientific picture of the universe seems to me to refute the subjectivist (and the fideist) theory of probability, and also the subjectivist theory of induction or, more precisely, of 'probable belief'. For according to this theory, the familiar thing, the thing to which we are accustomed, should also be the rationally and scientifically acceptable thing; while in fact the evolution of science corrects and replaces the familiar by the unfamiliar.

According to our latest theories, these cosmological matters could hardly look more unfamiliar; a fact that shows, incidentally, how far science has moved away, under the pressure of criticism, from its beginnings in anthropomorphic myths. The physical universe bears – or so it seems – several independent and consistent traces of having originated in a violent explosion, the 'first big bang'. Moreover, what seem to be the best of our contemporary theories predict its ultimate collapse. These two terminal events have even been interpreted as the beginning and the end of space *and time* – though obviously when we say such things we hardly understand what we are saying.

The strangeness of scientific theory, as compared with a more naive view, was discussed by Aristotle, who said (*Metaphysics* 983a11), alluding to the proof of the incommensurability of the diagonal with the side of the square:

> The acquisition of knowledge must establish a state of mind right opposite to that from which we originally started our search. . . . For to those who have not yet grasped the reason it must seem a marvel that there should be something [that is, the diagonal of the square] that cannot be measured, not even by the smallest unit.

What Aristotle appears not to have seen was that the 'acquisition of knowledge' may be an unending process, and that we may *continue* to be surprised by the progress of knowledge.

There could hardly be a more dramatic example of this than the story of the development of the theory of matter. From the Greek *hylē*, which we translate by 'matter' and which often means 'firewood' in Homer, we have progressed to what I described in *S. I. B.*, Section 3, as the self-transcendence of materialism. And some leading physicists have gone even further in their dissolution of the idea of matter. (Not that I am prepared to follow them in this.) Under the influence of Mach, a physicist who believed neither in matter nor in atoms, and who proposed a theory of knowledge reminiscent of Berkeley's subjective idealism, and under that of Einstein – who was a Machian when young – idealistic and even solipsistic interpretations of quantum mechanics have been put forward by some of the great pioneers of quantum mechanics, especially by Heisenberg and by

Wigner. 'Objective reality has evaporated', wrote Heisenberg.[2] As Bertrand Russell puts it: 'It has begun to seem that matter, like the Cheshire Cat, is becoming gradually diaphanous until nothing of it is left but the grin, caused, presumably, by amusement at those who still think it is there.'[3]

My remarks on the history of thought will be very sketchy. This would be unavoidable even if telling the story were my main purpose; but it is not. My main purpose is to make the present problem situation concerning the relation of mind and body better understandable by showing how it arose out of earlier attempts to solve problems – and not only the mind–body problem. Incidentally, it should illustrate my thesis that history ought to be written as a history of problem situations.[4]

2 A problem to be solved by what follows

One of my main aims in writing on the ancient history of the mind–body problem is to show the baselessness of the doctrine that this problem is nothing but part of a modern ideology and that it was unknown in antiquity. This doctrine has a propagandist bias. It is suggested that a man who has not been brainwashed by a dualist religion or philosophy would naturally accept materialism. It is asserted that ancient philosophy was materialist – an assertion which, though misleading, contains, a grain of truth; and it is suggested that those of us who are interested in the mind, and in the mind–body problem, have been brainwashed by Descartes and his followers.

Something on these lines is suggested in the brilliant and valuable *Concept of Mind* by Gilbert Ryle;[5] and it is even more stongly suggested in a broadcast in which Ryle speaks of 'the legend of the two theatres' (p. 77), which he describes as a 'fairly new-fangled legend'.[6] He also says that 'For the general terms in which the scientists [the allusion is to Sherrington and Lord Adrian] have set their problems of mind and body, we philosophers have been chiefly to blame' (p. 76). For 'we philosophers' one must read here 'Descartes and the post-Cartesian philosophers'.

Views like this are not only to be found in an outstanding philosopher (and a student of Plato and Aristotle) such as Ryle, but they are widespread. William F. R. Hardie, author of *A Study in Plato* (1936) and *Aristotle's Ethical Theory* (1968), examines in a recent article two books and eight articles on Aristotle, of which he says: 'In most of these articles [and books] what is being said or suggested in different ways is that Aristotle, for better or worse, had no concept of consciousness or not one corresponding closely to ours.'[7] Hardie examines with great care the best of the articles, and concludes – not totally unexpectedly – that Aristotle

226

was not a Cartesian. Yet Hardie makes it clear (pp. 409f.) that, if 'being "conscious" or having a "mind" [is] what distinguished animals from plants or what distinguished men from other animals', then Aristotle, 'who gave us the terminology ("psychology", "psychical", "psychophysical", "psychosomatic") which we use to mark' this distinction, cannot be said to have 'neglected' the distinction. In other words, even though Aristotle may not have had a term corresponding precisely to our 'consciousness' in its very wide and somewhat vague sense, he had no difficulty in speaking of the various kinds of conscious events.

Nor did Aristotle have any doubt that body and mind interact – though his theory of this interaction was different from the ingenious but inconsistent (and thus untenable) detailed elaboration which Descartes gave to interactionism.

In the brief historical sketch that constitutes this essay I shall try to argue in favour of the following views.

(1) Dualism in the form of the story of the ghost in the machine (or, better, of the ghost in the body) is as old as any historical or archaeological evidence reaches, though it is unlikely that prior to the atomists the body was regarded as a machine.

(2) All thinkers of whom we know enough to say anything definite on their position, up to and including Descartes, were dualist interactionists.

(3) This dualism is very marked, in spite of the fact that certain tendencies inherent in human language (which originally was, apparently, appropriate only for the description of material things and their properties) seem to make us inclined to speak of minds or souls or spirits as if they were a peculiar (gas-like) kind of body.

(4) The discovery of the moral world leads to the realization of the special character of the mind. This is so in Homer (see *Iliad* 24, which recounts, as the climax of the whole poem, the visit of Priam to Achilles in which moral and humane considerations play a decisive role); in Democritus; and in Socrates.

(5) In the thought of the atomists, one finds materialism, interactionism, and also the recognition of the special moral character of the mind; but they did not, I think, draw the consequences of their own moral contrast between mind and matter.

(6) The Pythagoreans, Socrates, Plato, and Aristotle tried to transcend the 'materialist' way of talking about the mind: they recognized the *nonmaterial character of the psyche* and tried to make sense of this new conception. An important speech attributed to Socrates by Plato in the *Phaedo* (see Section 4 below) deals explicitly with the moral explanation of human action in terms of ends, and decisions, and contrasts this with the explanation of human behaviour in terms of physiological causes.

(7) Alternatives to interactionism arose only after Descartes. They arose

because of the special difficulties of Descartes' elaborate interactionism and its clash with his theory of causation in physics.

These seven points obviously indicate a very different view from the one which seems so widespread at present. To these seven points I shall add an eighth:

(8) We know that, but we do not know *how*, mind and body interact; but this is not surprising since we have really no definite idea how physical things interact. Nor do we know how mental events interact, unless we believe in a theory of mental events and their interaction which is almost certainly false: in associationism. The theory of the association of ideas is a theory which treats mental events or processes like things (ideas, pictures) and their interaction as due to something like an attractive force. Associationism is therefore probably just one of those materialist metaphors which we almost always use when trying to speak about mental events.

3   The prehistoric discovery of the self and of the world of mind (World 2)

The history of the theories of the self or of the mind is very different from the history of the theories of matter. One gets the impression that the greatest discoveries were made in prehistoric times, and by the schools of Pythagoras and of Hippocrates. More recently, there has been much critical activity, but it has hardly led to great revolutionary ideas.

The greatest achievements of humanity lie in the past. They include the invention of language and of the use of artificial tools for making other artefacts; the use of fire as a tool; the discovery of the consciousness of self and of other selves; and the knowledge that we all have to die.

The last two of these discoveries seem to depend on the invention of language, and so perhaps may the others. Language certainly looks the oldest of these achievements, and it is the one most deeply rooted in our genetic make-up (although, of course, a specific language has to be acquired from tradition).

The discovery of death, and the sense of loss, of bereavement, must also be very old. From the old customs of burial, reaching back to Neanderthal man, one is led to the conjecture that these people were not only conscious of death, but that they also believed in survival. For they buried their dead with gifts – most likely gifts they thought useful for the journey to another world and to another life. Moreover, R. S. Solecki reports that he found in the Shanidar cave in northern Iraq the grave of a Neanderthal man (perhaps of several) who apparently had been buried on a bed of twigs, decorated with flowers.[8] He also reports that he found the skeletons of two old men, one of them 'a very handicapped individual', the other 'a

228

rehabilitation case'.[9] It appears that they were not only tolerated, but helped by their family or group. It seems that the humane idea of helping the weak is very old, and that we must revise our ideas of the primitivity of Neanderthal man, supposed to have lived in the period from 60,000–35,000 years ago.

Much speaks, it seems, for the conjecture that the idea of surviving death entails some kind of dualism of body and mind. No doubt the dualism was not Cartesian. Everything speaks for the idea that the soul was regarded as extended: as a ghost or a spectre – as a shade with a physical shape resembling the body. This, at any rate, is the idea which we find in our oldest literary sources, especially in Homer, in sagas and in fairy tales (and also in Shakespeare).

It is, in a sense, a form of materialism, especially if we accept the Cartesian idea that matter is characterized by (three-dimensional) extension. Nevertheless, its dualistic character is clear: the ghostlike soul is *different* from the body, it is *less* material than the body, it is finer; more like air, like vapour, like breath.

In Homer, we have a plurality of words for the mind or the soul, and for its functions, the 'processes of consciousness', as R. B. Onians calls them: feeling, perceiving, thinking, scorning, anger, and so on. [10]

I shall refer here to only three of these words.[11] (Their use in Hesiod is similar.)

Of the foremost importance in Homer is *thymos*, the stuff of life, the vaporous breath soul, the active, energetic, feeling and thinking material related to blood.[12] It leaves us when we faint or, with our last breath, when we die. Later this term is often restricted in meaning, so as to mean courage, energy, spirit, vigour. By contrast, *psyche* in Homer (although sometimes used as a synonym of *thymos*) is hardly a principle of life, as it is in later authors (Parmenides, Empedocles, Democritus, Plato, Aristotle). It is, in Homer, rather the sad remainder which is left over when we die, the poor unintelligent shade, the ghost that survives the body: it is 'not concerned in ordinary consciousness'; it is that which 'persists, still without ordinary consciousness [or ordinary life] in the house of Hades . . . the visible but impalpable semblance of the once living' body.[13] Thus when Odysseus in the eleventh book of the *Odyssey* visits the underworld, the dark and gloomy house of Hades, he finds that the shades of the dead are almost completely lifeless until he has fed them with blood, the stuff which has the power of restoring a semblance of life to the shade, the *psyche*. The scene is one of utmost sadness, of despairing pity for the state in which the dead survive. For Homer, only the living body is a fully conscious self.

The third term, *noos* (or *nous*, in the decisively important passage *Odyssey* 10.240 to be discussed presently), is usually quite well translated into English as 'mind' or 'understanding'. Usually it is mind with an intention, a purpose (in German *Absicht*; see *Odyssey* 24.474). Onians (*op cit.*, p. 83) characterizes it well as 'purposing consciousness'. It involves, as a rule, an understanding of a situation, and it sometimes means, in Homer, conscious intelligence, or even intelligent consciousness of self.

In view of the fact that it has been sometimes denied, by implication, that a (dualistic) idea of mind occurs before Descartes, which would make my ascription of this idea to Homer grossly unhistorical, I wish to refer to a passage (*Odyssey* 10.240) which to me appears as absolutely crucial for the prehistory and the early history of the mind–body problem.

It is the story of a magical transformation of the body, a metamorphosis which leaves the mind unchanged, one of the oldest and most widespread topics of fairy tales and folklore. In this, almost the oldest extant literary document of our Western civilization, it is explicitly stated that the magical transformation of the body leaves the self-identity of the mind, of consciousness, intact.

The passage, in the tenth book of the *Odyssey*, describes how Circe smote some of the companions of Odysseus with her wand: 'They had the head, and voice, and bristles, and the body (*demas*[14]) of swine; but their mind (*nous*) remained unchanged, as before. So they were penned there, weeping.' Clearly, they understood their frightful situation, and remained conscious of their self-identity.

This, I think, is clear enough; and we have every reason to interpret the many magical metamorphoses of classical antiquity and of other fairy tales accordingly. Thus the conscious self is not an artefact of Cartesian ideology. It is the universal experience of mankind, whatever contemporary anti-Cartesians may say.

Once this is seen, it is also seen that mind–body dualism is in evidence everywhere in Homer,[15] and of course in later Greek authors. This dualism is typical of the very ancient tendency to think in polar opposites, such as the antithesis 'mortal–immortal'.[16] For example, Agamemnon says of Chryseis (*Iliad* 1.113–15): 'Know you, I prefer her to Clytemnestra, my wedded wife, as she is no whit inferior to her, either in body or its bearing, or in her mind[17] or in its accomplishments.' The opposition, or dualism, of body and mind is quite characteristic of Homer (see note 14 above); and since the mind is usually conceived as material, there is no obstacle whatever to the obvious doctrine of mind–body interaction.

Concerning dualism, it should be made clear that the opposition or polarity of body and mind must not be exaggerated: 'my mind' and 'my body' may well occur as synonyms of 'my person', although they are rarely synonyms of each other. An example may be found in Sophocles, when Oedipus says 'My mind (*psychē*) bears the weight of my and your sorrows' and, at another place, 'He [Creon] has been cunningly plotting against my body (*sōma*).' In both cases, 'my person' (or simply 'I') would do as well in English, or even better; but in the Greek as well as in English we could not replace in either case the one expression (*psychē*) by the other (*sōma*).[18] That we cannot always do this holds for Homer or for Sophocles as well as for ourselves.

Concerning what I have just said about interactionism – the interaction of a material soul with a material body – I do not wish to imply that the interaction was conceived in a mechanistic way. Consistent mechanistic thinking becomes prominent only very much later, with the atomists, Leucippus and Democritus, although there were, of course, plenty of skilled users of mechanics before. There was much that was not well understood, neither in mechanical nor in other terms, in Homeric times and for a long time after, and that was interpreted in a crudely 'animistic' way, such as the thunderbolt of Zeus. Causation *was* a problem, and animistic causation was something bordering the divine. And there was divine action on both bodies and minds. Infatuation, such as Helen's, and blind anger and pigheadedness, such as Agamemnon's, were attributed to the gods. It was 'an abnormal state which [demanded] a supernormal explanation', as E. R. Dodds (op. cit., p. 9) puts it.

There is an abundance of important evidence that supports the hypothesis that dualistic and interactionist beliefs concerning body and mind are very old – prehistoric and of course historic. Apart from folklore and fairy tales, it is supported by all we know about primitive religion, myth, and magical beliefs. There is, for example, shamanism, with its characteristic doctrine that the soul of the shaman may leave the body and may go on a journey; in the case of the Eskimos, even to the Moon. The body is meanwhile left in a state of deep sleep or coma, and survives without food. 'In that condition he is not thought, like the Pythia or like a modern medium to be possessed by an alien spirit; but his own soul is thought to leave its body' (Dodds, op cit., p. 140). Dodds gives a long list of prehistoric and historic Greek shamans;[19] of the prehistoric ones, only legends are left, but they are sufficient evidence for dualism. The story of the Seven Sleepers of Ephesus probably belongs to this tradition, also perhaps the theory of metempsychosis or reincarnation. (Among the shamans of historical times, Dodds counts Pythagoras and Empedocles.)

Interesting from our point of view is the distinction, due to the social anthropologist E. E. Evans-Pritchard,[20] between witches (male or female) and sorcerers. His analysis of the ideas of the Azande led him to distinguish witches from sorcerers according to whether or not conscious intention plays a part. According to Zande views, witches have inherited special innate supernatural powers to harm others, but they are completely unconscious of their dangerous potentialities. (An evil eye may be an example of such a potentiality.) By contrast, sorcerers have acquired the techniques of handling substances and charms by which they can intentionally harm others. This distinction appears to be applicable to numerous, though not all, primitive African cultures.[21] The applicability shows the existence of a widespread primitive distinction between conscious intentional actions and unconscious and unintended effects.

Myths and religious beliefs are attempts to explain to ourselves theoretically the world we live in – including, of course, the social world – and how this world affects us and our ways of living. It seems clear that the old distinction between soul and body is an example of such a theoretical explanation. But what it explains is the experience of consciousness – of intelligence, of will, of planning and of carrying out our plans; of using our hands and feet as tools; and of using artificial, material tools, and of being affected by them. These experiences are not philosophical ideologies. The doctrine of a substantial (or even a material) soul to which they lead us may well be a myth: indeed, I conjecture that the substance theory as such is a myth. But if it is a myth, it may be understood as the result of grasping the reality and effectiveness of consciousness and of our will; and grasping its reality leads us first to conceive of the soul as material, as the finest matter, and later to conceive of it as a non-material 'substance'.

I may perhaps finally summarize the major discoveries in this field which, it appears, were made by primitive man and prehistoric man (and partly by Neanderthal man, who is generally classified as prior and distinct from our own species, and more recently conjectured to have mixed his blood with *Homo sapiens*).

Death and its inevitability are discoverd; the theory is accepted that the states of sleep and of unconsciousness are related to death and that it is consciousness or spirit or mind (*thymos*) which 'leaves' us at death. The doctrine of the reality and therefore the materiality and substantiality of consciousness – of the soul (or mind) – is developed, and further, the doctrine of the complexity of the soul or mind: desire, fear, anger, intellect, reason or insight (*nous*) are distinguished. Dream experience and states of divine inspiration and possession and other abnormal states are recognized, also involuntary and unconscious mental states (such as those of 'witches'). The soul is regarded as the 'mover' of the living body, or as the principle of life. Also, the problem of our lack of responsibility for unintentional acts or acts committed in abnormal states (of frenzy) is grasped. The problem of the position of the soul in the body is raised, and usually answered by the theory that it pervades the body yet is centred in the heart and the lungs.[22]

Some of these doctrines are no doubt hypostatizations, and they have been, or may have to be, modified by criticism. Others are mistaken. Yet they are nearer to modern views and modern problems than the pre-Ionian and even the Ionian theories of matter,[23] though admittedly this may be due to the primitive character of our modern views about consciousness.

4   The mind–body problem in Greek philosophy

It is sometimes asserted that the Greeks were aware of a soul–body problem, but not of a mind–body problem. This assertion seems to me either mistaken or a verbal quibble. In Greek philosophy, the soul played a role very similar to that of the mind in post-Cartesian philosophy. It was an entity, a substance, which sums up the conscious experience of the self. (It may be said to be a hypostatization – almost unavoidable and possibly justified – of conscious experience.) Moreover, we find as early as in fifth-century Pythagoreanism a doctrine of the incorporeality of the soul; and several concepts (for example *nous* and *psychē*) in several authors sometimes correspond very closely to the modern concept of mind. (Remember also that the English concept 'mind' has often to be translated into German as *Seele*, which is also the translation of 'soul'; a sympton of the fact that 'mind' and 'soul' are not so different as the assertion at the beginning of this section indicates.) Although the use of certain terms may often be indicative of the theories held, and of the views taken for granted, this is not always so: theories which are closely similar or even identical are sometimes formulated in very different terminologies. Indeed, some of the main changes after Homer regarding mind and body are terminological; and they do not run parallel with changes in theory. [24]

In what follows, I will briefly sketch the history (I) of the material soul from Anaximenes to Democritus and Epicurus (including that of the location of the mind); (II) of the dematerialization or spiritualization of the mind, from the Pythagoreans and Xenophanes to Plato and Aristotle; (III) of the moral conception of the soul or mind, from Pythagoras to Democritus, Socrates, and Plato.

I

In Homer the material soul of the living body was a vaporous breath. (It is not quite clear how this breath-soul was related to intelligence or under-standing or mind.) In the Ionian philosophical tradition from Anaximenes down to Diogenes of Appolonia it remains very nearly the same: the soul consists of air. [25]

As Guthrie points out, *psychē* meant for a Greek thinker of the fifth century BC 'not only *a* soul but soul; that is, the world was permeated by a kind of soul-stuff which is better indicated by the omission of the article'. [26] This certainly is true of the materialist thinkers of the time: they regarded soul as air (and the soul as a portion of air) because air is the finest and lightest of the known forms of matter.

As Anaxagoras, who perhaps no longer believed in a material mind, puts it (DK 59B12), 'Mind (*nous*) . . . is the most rarefied of things and the purest; it has all the knowledge with respect to everything, and it has the greatest power. And all that has life (*psychē*), the biggest [organisms] and the smallest, all these mind rules.' Whether or not Anaxagoras believed in a material mind, he certainly distinguished sharply between mind and all other existing (material) substances. For Anaxagoras, mind is the principle of motion and order, and therefore the principle of life.

Even before Anaxagoras a more exciting though still a materialist interpretation of the doctrine of soul – of the soul stuff – was given by Heraclitus, the thinker who of all materialists was perhaps furthest removed from mechanical materialism for he interpreted all material substances and especially the soul as material *processes*. The soul was *fire*. That we are flames, that our selves are processes, was a marvellous and a revolutionary idea. It was part of Heraclitus' cosmology: all material things were in flux: they were all processes, including the whole universe. And all were ruled by law (*logos*). 'The limits of the soul you will not discover, not even if you travel every road: so deep is its *logos*' (DK B45). The soul, like fire, is killed by water: 'It is death for souls to become water' (DK B36). Fire is for Heraclitus the best and the most powerful and the purest (and no doubt also the finest) of material processes.

All these materialist theories were dualist in so far as they gave the soul a very special and exceptional status within the universe.

The schools of medical thinkers were also certainly materialist *and* dualist in the sense here described. Alcmaeon of Croton, who is usually regarded as Pythagorean, seems to have been the first Greek thinker to locate sensation and thought (which he seems to have sharply distinguished) in the brain. Theophrastus reports 'that he spoke of passages (*poroi*) leading from sense organs to the brain' (Guthrie, *A History of Greek Philosophy*, vol. I, p. 349; DK A5, p. 212, line 8). He thereby created a tradition to which the School of Hippocrates adhered, and Plato; but not Aristotle, who, adhering to an older tradition, regarded the heart as the common sensorium, and thus as the seat of consciousness.

The Hippocratic medical treatise *On the Sacred Disease* is of the greatest interest. Not only does it assert with great emphasis that the brain 'tells the limbs how to act', but also that the brain 'is the messenger to consciousness (*sunesis*) and tells it what is happening'. The brain is also described as the interpreter (*hermēneus*) of consciousness. Of course, the word *sunesis*, here translated by 'consciousness', can also be translated as 'intelligence' or 'sagacity' or 'understanding'. Yet the meaning is clear – and so is the fact that the author of the treatise discussed at length what we should call the mind–body problem, and mind–body interaction. (*On the Sacred Disease*, especially chapters XIX and XX.) He explains the influence of the brain by the fact that 'it is the air that gives it intelligence' (chapter XIX); thus the air is interpreted as soul, as with the Ionian philosophers. The explanation is that 'when a man draws breath into himself, the air first reaches the brain'. (It may be worth mentioning that Aristotle, who was greatly influenced by the medical tradition yet gave up the connection between air and soul, retained the connection between air and the brain, and regarded the brain as a mechanism for cooling by means of air – as a kind of air-cooled radiator.)

The greatest and most consistent of the materialist thinkers was Democritus. He explained all natural and psychological processes mechanically, by the movement and the collision of atoms and by their joining or separating, their composition or dissociation.

In a brilliant essay 'Ethics and Physics in Democritus', first published in 1945–6, Gregory Vlastos discusses in considerable detail the mind–body problem in Democritus' philosophy.[27] He points out that Democritus, himself a writer of medical treatises, was arguing against the professional tendency to make 'the body the key to the well-being of both body and soul'. He points out that a famous fragment of Democritus' (DK B187) should be interpreted in this sense. The fragment says:

> It is fitting for men that they should make a *logos* [= law, or theory] more about the soul than about the body. For the perfection of the soul puts right the faults of the body. But bodily strength without reasoning does not improve the soul.

Vlastos points out that 'the first axiom of this *logos* of the soul' is the principle of responsibility: the soul, not the body, is the responsible agent. This follows from the principle of physics 'that the soul moves the body'.

In Democritean atomic physics, soul consists of the smallest atoms. They are (according to Aristotle, *De Anima* 403b31) the same atoms as those of fire. (Clearly, Democritus was influenced by Heraclitus.) They are round and 'best able to slip through anything and to move other things by their own movement'.

The small soul atoms are distributed throughout the body in such a way that atoms of soul and body alternate (see Lucretius, *De Rerum Natura* III. 371–3). More precisely, 'the soul has two parts; the one, which is rational (*logikos*), is located in the heart, while the unreasoning part is dispersed throughout the whole body' (DK 68 A105). This is no doubt an attempt to solve certain aspects of the mind–body problem.

Like Socrates, who taught (cp. the *Apology*) 'Care for your souls', so did the mechanical materialist Democritus: 'Men don't get happiness from bodies or from money, but by acting right and thinking wide' (DK B40). Another ethical fragment is 'Who chooses the goods of the soul chooses the more divine; who chooses those of the body chooses the more human' (DK B37; cp. Vlastos, op. cit., pp. 382f.). Like Socrates, his contemporary, he teaches: 'He who commits an act of injustice is more unhappy than he who suffers it' (DK B45).

One can describe Democritus not only as a materialist but as a monistic atomist. But owing to his moral teaching he was also a kind of dualist. For although he plays a major part in the history of the materialist theory of the soul, he also plays an important part in the history of the moral conception of the soul and its contrast with the body, to be treated below under (III). Here I will only briefly mention Democritus', Epicurus', and Lucretius' theory of dreams (*De Rerum Natura* IV), from which we see that the materialist theory of the soul did not neglect conscious experience: dreams are not given by the gods but consist of memories of our own perceptions.

II

We have just seen that the Homeric idea of the soul as breath – as air, or as fire: as a very fine corporeal substance – survived for a long time. So Aristotle was not quite correct when he said of his predecessors (*De Anima* 405b11): 'Almost all of them characterize the soul by three of its attributes: [the power of] movement; sensation; and incorporeality.' The last term should be weakened to 'comparative incorporeality' to make this quite correct; for some of his predecessors thought that the soul was a fine body.

However, Aristotle's slip is excusable. Even the materialists, I suggest, were dualists who habitually contrasted the soul with the body. I suggest that they all saw in the soul or in the mind the *essence* of the body.

There are, obviously, two ideas of essence: a corporeal essence and an incorporeal one. The materialists, down to and beyond Democritus, regarded the soul or spirit of man as analogous to the spirit of wine – or the spirit of wine as analogous to the soul. (See *S. I. B.*, Part 1, Section 30, note 2.) Thus we come to a (material) soul substance like air. But another idea, due, I suspect to Pythagoras, or to the Pythagorean Philolaus, was that the essence of a thing is something abstract (like number or the ratio of numbers).

Perhaps transitory, or already within the tradition of incorporeality, is Xenophanes' monotheism. Xenophanes, who brought the Ionian tradition to Italy, emphasizes that the mind or the thought of God is the divine essence; though his God is not conceived in the likeness of man (DK B23, 26, 25, 24):[28]

> One god, alone among gods and alone among men, is the greatest,
> Neither in body does he nor in mind resemble the mortals.
> Always in one place he abides: he never is moving;
> Nor is it fitting for him to change now hereto, now thereto.
> Effortless he swings the world by mere thought and intention.
> All of him is sight; all is knowing; and all is hearing.

Mind is here identified with perception, with thought, with the power of will, and with the power of acting.

In the Pythagorean theory of immaterial hidden essences, *Numbers*, and relations between numbers such as 'ratios' or 'harmonies', take the place of the substantial 'principles' of Ionian philosophy: the *Water* of Thales, the *Unlimited* of Anaximander, the *Air* of Anaximenes, the *Fire* of Heraclitus. This is a very striking change, and it is best explained by the assumption that it was Pythagoras himself who discovered the numerical ratios which underlie the concordant musical intervals: [29] on the monochord, an instrument of one string which can be stopped with the help of a movable bridge, one can show that the octave corresponds to the ratio of 1:2, the fifth to the ratio of 2:3, and the fourth to the ratio of 3:4 of the length of the string.

Thus the hidden essence of melodic or harmonic concords is the ratio of certain simple numbers 1:2:3:4 – even though a concord or harmony as experienced is clearly not a quantitative but a qualitative affair. This was a surprising discovery. But it must have been even more impressive when Pythagoras discovered that a right angle (clearly another qualitative affair) was connected with the ratios 3:4:5. Any triangle with sides of these ratios was rectangular.[30] If, as it seems, it was Pythagoras himself who made this discovery, then the report is likely to be true that 'Pythagoras spent most of his time upon the arithmetical aspects of geometry' (Diogenes Laertius VIII. 11f.).

These reports explain the background of the Pythagorean theory that the hidden essences of all things are abstract. They are numbers; numerical ratios of numbers; and 'harmonies'. Guthrie *A History of Greek Philosophy*, vol. I, p. 301) puts it as follows: 'To the Pythagoreans *everything* was an embodiment of number. They included what we should call abstractions like justice, mixture, opportunity.' It is perhaps interesting that Guthrie writes here 'embodiment'. Indeed, we feel still that the relation of the essence to that of which it is the essence is like the relation of the soul or the mind to the body.

Guthrie has suggested (ibid., pp. 306f.[31]) that there were in fact two theories of the soul which went under the name 'Pythagorean'. The first, the original theory, probably due to Pythagoras himself, or perhaps to Philolaus the Pythagorean, was that the immortal soul of man was a harmony or attunement of abstract numbers. These numbers and their harmonious relations precede and survive the body. The second theory, put by Plato in the mouth of Simmias, a pupil of Philolaus, was that the soul is a harmony or attunement of the body, like the harmony or attunement of a lyre (it should be noted that the lyre is not just a physical, World 1 object but also a theory-impregnated, World 3 object; and so is its proper attunement or harmony). It must perish with the body, as the harmony of the lyre must perish with the lyre. The second theory became popular, and was extensively discussed by Plato and Aristotle.[32] Its popularity was clearly due to the fact that it offered an easily grasped model of mind–body interaction.

We have here two related but subtly different theories; two theories which may be interpreted as describing 'two kinds of soul' (Guthrie, *A History of Greek Philosophy*, vol. I, p. 317), an immortal and higher kind of soul, and a perishable and lower kind of soul; both are harmonies. There is historical evidence for the existence of both theories, of Pythagoras' theory and of Simmias' theory. But to my knowledge, they have not been clearly distinguished before Guthrie's searching and brilliant discussion of Pythagoras and the Pythagoreans.

The question should be raised of how the theory which we may with Guthrie describe as Pythagoras' theory (in contradistinction to Simmias' theory) envisages the relation of soul (harmony, ratio of numbers) to body.[33] We may conjecture that the answer to this question could have been similar to a theory – a Pythagorean theory – that can be found in Plato's *Timaeus*. There the formed or shaped body is the result of a pre-existing form that impresses itself on unformed or indefinite space (corresponding to Aristotle's first matter).[34] This form would be of the nature of a number (or a numerical ratio, or of a triangle). From this we might conclude that the organized body would be organized by a pre-existing harmony of numbers which therefore could also outlast the body.

The philosophers who followed the Pythagoreans (including 'Simmias') in proposing a theory of the soul and/or of the mind which interpreted them as incorporeal essences were (possibly) Socrates and (certainly) Plato and Aristotle. They were later followed by the Neo-Platonists, by St Augustine and other Christian thinkers, and by Descartes.

Plato proposed, at different times, somewhat different theories of the mind, but they were always related to his theory of forms or ideas in a way similar to that in which Pythagoras' theory of the mind was related to his theory of numbers or ratios. The Pythagorean theory of numbers and their ratios can be interpreted as a theory of the true nature or essence of things in general, and so can Plato's theory of forms or ideas. And while, for Pythagoras, the soul is a ratio of numbers, for Plato, the soul, though it is not a form or idea, is 'akin' to the forms or ideas. The kinship is very close: the soul is, very nearly, the essence of the living body. Aristotle's theory is again similar. He describes the soul as the 'first entelechy' of the living body; and the first entelechy is, more or less, its form or its essence. The main difference between Plato's and Aristotle's theory of the soul is, I think, that Aristotle is a cosmological optimist, but Plato rather a pessimist. Aristotle's world is essentially teleological: everything progresses towards perfection. Plato's world is created by God, and it is, when created, the best world: it does not progress towards something better.

Similarly, Plato's soul is not progressive; if anything it is conservative. But Aristotle's entelechy is progressive: it strives towards an end, an aim.

It seems to me probable that this teleological theory – the striving of the soul towards an end, the good – goes back to Socrates, who taught that acting for the best purpose, and with the best aim, follows with necessity upon knowing what is best, and that the mind, or the soul, was always trying to act so as to bring about what is best. (See also Socrates' auto-biographical remarks in the *Phaedo*, 96a ff., especially 97d, which I am inclined, following Guthrie vol. III, pp. 421ff., to regard as historical.[35])

Plato's doctrine of the world of essences – his theory of forms or ideas – is the first doctrine of what I call World 3. But (as I have explained in section 13 of *S. I. B.*) there are considerable differences between my theory of World 3, the world of products of the human mind, and Plato's theory of forms. However, Plato was one of the first (together, perhaps, with Protagoras and Democritus) to appreciate the importance of ideas – of 'culture', to use a modern term – for the forming of our minds.

As to the mind–body problem, Plato regards this problem mainly from an ethical point of view. Like the Orphic-Pythagorean tradition, he regards the body as a prison of the soul (it is perhaps not quite clear how we can escape from it through transmigration). But according to Socrates and Plato the soul, or mind, or reason *ought* to be the ruler of the body (and of the lower parts of the soul: the appetites, which are akin to the body, and liable to be ruled by it). Plato often points out parallelisms between mind and body, but he accepts an interactionism of mind and body as a matter of course: like Freud he upholds the theory that the mind has three parts: (1) reason; (2) activity or energy or liveliness (*thymos*, often translated by 'spirit', or by 'courage'); and (3) the (lower) appetites. Like Freud he assumes a kind of class struggle between the lower and the higher parts of the soul. In dreams, the lower parts may get out of control; for example our appetites may make a man dream (*Republic*, beginning of book IX, 571d ff.) of marrying his mother, or of 'any foul deed of blood' (such as parricide, James Adam adds). It is clearly implied that such dreams arise from the action of our bodies on 'the beastly and savage part' of the soul; and that it is the task of reason to tame these parts, thereby ruling the body. The interaction between mind and body is due to forces which Plato regards here, and in some other places, as similar to *political* forces rather than to *mechanical* forces: certainly an interesting contribution to the mind–body problem. He also describes the mind as the pilot of the body.

Aristotle too has a theory of lower (irrational) and higher (rational) parts of the soul; but his theory is biologically rather than politically or ethically inspired. (But he says, in the *Nicomachean Ethics* 1102b10 ff., probably alluding to the dream passage in Plato, that 'the dreams of good men are better than those of ordinary people'.)

239

Aristotle's ideas anticipate, in several respects, biological evolution. He distinguishes the nutritive soul (found in all organisms including plants) from the sensory soul and the soul which is the source of motion (only found in animals) and the rational soul (*nous*), which is to be found only in man, and which is immortal. He frequently stresses that these various souls are 'forms' or 'essences'. But Aristotle's theory of essence is different from Plato's. His essences do not like Plato's belong to a separate world of forms or ideas. Rather they are inherent in the physical things. (In the case of organisms, they may be said to live in the organism, as its principle of life.) The irrational souls or essences of Aristotle may be said to be anticipations of modern gene theory: like DNA they plan the actions of the organism and steer it to its *telos*, to its perfection.

The irrational parts or potentialities of Aristotle's sensory and moving souls have much in common with Rylean dispositions to behave. They are, of course, perishable, and they are altogether similar to Simmias' 'harmony of the body' (though Aristotle has much to say in criticism of the harmony theory). But the rational part, the immortal part of the soul, is different.

Aristotle's rational soul is, of course, conscious of its self, like Plato's (see, for example, the *Posterior Analytics* 99b20 to the end, with the discussion of *nous*, which here means intellectual intuition). Even Charles Kahn, who is prepared to stress the differences between the Aristotelian notion of soul and the Cartesian notion of consciousness, arrives, after a brilliant and most careful investigation, at the conclusion (which I regard as almost obvious) that Aristotle's psychology *does* possess the notion of the consciousness of self.[36]

In this context I will refer only to one important passage which at the same time shows Aristotle's realization of the interaction between our physical sense organs and our subjective awareness. In Aristotle, *On Dreams* 461b31, we read:

> If a man is unaware that a finger is being pressed below his eye, not only will one thing *seem* to be two, but he will think that it is two; whereas, if he is not unaware [of the finger being pressed below his eye], it will still appear to be two, but he will not think that it is two.

This is a classical experiment to demonstrate the reality of conscious awareness, and of the fact that sensation is *not* a disposition to believe.[37]

III

In the development of the theory of the soul or the mind or the self, the development of ethical ideas plays a major role. It is, in the main, the changes in the theory of the survival of the soul which are most striking and important.

It must be admitted that in Homer and in some other myths of Hades the problem of the reward and punishment of the soul for its unusual excellence or for its moral failures is not always avoided. But in Homer, the status of the surviving soul of ordinary people who have never done much evil is terrible and depressing. Odysseus' mother is just one of them. She is not punished for any crime. She suffers merely as part of the condition of being dead.

The mystery cult of Eleusis (and perhaps what is called 'the Orphic religion') led to a change in this belief. Here was a promise of a better world to come – if the right religion with the right rituals was adopted.

For us post-Kantians, this kind of promise of a reward does not seem to be a moral motivation. But there can be little doubt that it was the first step on the way to the Socratic and the Kantian point of view in which the moral action is done for its own sake; in which it is its own reward, rather than a good investment, a price paid for a promised reward in the life to come.

The steps in this development can be seen clearly; and the developing idea of a soul, a self, which is the responsible acting person, plays a most important part in this development.

Possibly under the influence of the Eleusian mysteries and of 'Orphism', Pythagoras taught the survival and the reincarnation of the soul, or metempsychosis: the soul is rewarded or punished for its action by the quality – the *moral* quality – of its next life. This is the first step towards the idea that goodness is its own reward.

Democritus, who in many respects was influenced by the tenets of the Pythagoreans, taught like Socrates (as we have seen earlier in this section) that it is worse to commit an act of injustice than to suffer it.[38] Democritus, the materialist, did not, of course, believe in survival; and Socrates seems to have been an agnostic with respect to survival (according to Plato's *Apology*, though not according to the *Phaedo*[39]). Both argued in terms of reward and punishment – terms unacceptable to moral rigorism of a Kantian kind. But both far transcended the primitive idea of hedonism – of the 'pleasure principle'. (Cp. *Phaedo* 68e–69a.) Both taught that to commit an act of injustice was to debase one's soul; in fact, to punish one's self. Both would have accepted Schopenhauer's simple maxim 'Do not hurt anybody; but help everybody as well as you can!' (*Neminem laede; immo omnes, ut potes, juva!*) And both would have defended this principle by what, in essence, was an appeal to self-respect, and the respect of other individuals.

Like many materialists and determinists Democritus did not seem to see that materialism and determinism are, in fact, incompatible with their enlightened and humanitarian moral teaching. They did not see that, even if we look upon morality not as being God-given, but as being man made, it is part of World 3: that it is a partly autonomous product of the human mind. It was Socrates who first realized this clearly.

Most important for the mind–body problem are two comments, probably genuinely Socratic, which are reported in the *Phaedo*, the dialogue in which Plato describes the last hours in prison and the death of Socrates. The two comments to which I am alluding occur in the passage in the *Phaedo* (96a–100d) that is famous for containing some autobiographical remarks by Socrates.[40] The first comment (96b) is one of the crispest formulations of the mind–body problem in the whole history of philosophy. Socrates reports that when he was young he was interested in questions such as these:

> Does the hot or the cold bring about the organization of animals by a process of fermentation, as some say? Do we think with our blood, or with air, or with fire? Or is it none of these but, rather, the brain that produces the sensations – hearing, sight, and smell; and do memory and opinion arise from these? And does demonstrative knowledge (*epistēmē*) derive from firmly established memory and opinion?

Socrates makes it clear that he soon rejected all such physicalist speculations. Mind, or thought, or reason, he decided, always pursued an aim, or an end: it always pursued a purpose, doing what was best. Upon hearing that Anaxagoras had written a book in which he taught that the mind (*nous*) 'orders and causes all things', Socrates was most eager to read the book; but he was severely disappointed. For the book did not explain the *purposes* or the *reasons* underlying the world order, but it tried to explain the world as a machine driven by purely mechanical *causes*:

> It was [Socrates says in the second of the two comments, *Phaedo* 98c–99a] . . . as if somebody would first say that Socrates acts with reason or intelligence; and then, in trying to explain the causes of what I am doing now, should assert that I am now sitting here because my body is composed of bones and sinews . . . and that the sinews, by relaxing and contracting, make me bend my limbs now, and that this is the cause of my sitting here with my legs bent. . . . Yet the real causes of my sitting here in prison are that the Athenians have decided to condemn me, and that I have decided that . . . it is more just if I stay here and undergo the penalty they have imposed on me. For, by the Dog . . . these bones of mine would have been in Megara or Boetia long ago . . .

242

had I not thought it better and nobler to endure any penalty my
city may inflict on me, rather than to escape, and to run away.

John Beloff rightly calls this passage a 'superb affirmation of moral
freedom in the face of death'.[41] But it is meant as a statement distinguishing sharply between an explanation in terms of physical causes (a World 1
causal explanation) and an explanation in terms of intentions, aims, ends,
motives, reasons, and values to be realized (a World 2 explanation that also
involves considerations of World 3: Socrates's wish not to violate the legal
order of Athens). And it makes clear that both kinds of explanation may
be true, but that so far as the explanation of a responsible and purposeful
action is concerned the first kind (the World 1 causal explanation) would
be absurdly irrelevant.

In the light of some modern developments we can well say that Socrates
considers here certain parallelist and identity theories; and that he rejects
the claim that a causal physicalist explanation or a behaviourist explanation of a human action could possibly be equivalent to an explanation in
terms of ends, purposes, and decisions (or to an explanation in terms of the
logic of his situation). He rejects a physicalist explanation not as untrue,
but as incomplete and as lacking any explanatory value. It omits all that is
relevant: the conscious choice of ends and means.

Here we have a second and very different comment on the mind–body
problem, even more important than the previous one. It is a statement in
terms of responsible human actions: a statement within an essentially
ethical context. It makes it clear that the ethical idea of a responsible
moral self has played a decisive part in the ancient[42] discussions connected
with the mind–body problem, and the consciousness of self.

The position here taken by Socrates is one that any interactionist must
subscribe to: for any interactionist, even a full explanation of human bodily
movements, *taken purely as physical movements*, cannot be provided in purely
physical terms: the physical World 1 is not self-contained, but causally
open to World 2 (and through it, to World 3).[43]

5 Conjectural versus ultimate explanation

Even for those who are not interested in history but mainly in understanding the contemporary problem situation, it is necessary to go back to
two opposed views on science and on scientific explanation which can be
shown to be part of the tradition of the Platonic and the Aristotelian
Schools.

The Platonic and the Aristotelian traditions can be described as objectivist and rationalist (in contrast to the subjectivist sensualism or empiricism which takes as its starting point sense impressions and tries to
'construct' the physical world out of these). Almost[44] all the forerunners

of Plato and Aristotle were rationalists in this sense: they tried to explain the surface phenomena of the world by postulating a hidden world, a world of hidden realities, behind the phenomenal world. And they were right.

Of course, the most successful of these forerunners were the atomists, Leucippus and Democritus, who explained many properties of matter, such as compressibility, porousness, and the changes from the liquid state to the gaseous state, and to the solid state.

Their method can be called *the method of conjecture or hypothesis*, or that of *conjectural explanation*. It is analysed in some detail in Plato's *Republic* (for example 510b–511e), in the *Meno* (86e–87c), and in the *Phaedo* (85c–d). It consists, essentially, in making some assumption (we *may* have nothing to say in its favour) *and seeing what follows*. That is to say, *we test our assumption or our conjecture by exploring its consequences*; aware of the fact that in doing so, we can never establish the assumption. The assumption may or may not appeal to us intuitively; intuition is important, but (within this method) never decisive. One of the main functions of the method is to explain the phenomena, or 'to save the phenomena'.[45]

A second method which in my opinion ought to be sharply distinguished from the method of conjecture or hypothesis is *the method of the intuitive grasp of the essence*; that is to say, *the method of essentialist explanation* (the intuition of the essence is called, in German, '*Wesensschau*'; this is Husserl's term[46]). Here 'intuition' (*nous*, intellectual intuition) implies infallible insight: it guarantees truth. What we see or grasp intuitively is (in this sense of 'intuition') the essence itself. (See, for example, Plato's *Phaedo*, 100c; and Aristotle's *Posterior Analytics*, especially 100b.) The essentialist explanation allows us to answer a 'what is' question, and (according to Aristotle) to state the answer in a *definition of the essence*, a formula of the essence. (Essentialist definition, real definition.) Using this definition as a premise we can then try, again, to explain the phenomena deductively – to save the phenomena. However, if we do not succeed, then it cannot be the fault of our premise: the premise must be true, if we have properly grasped the essence. Moreover, an explanation by the intuition of the essence is an *ultimate explanation*: it is neither in need nor capable of any further explanation. By contrast, any conjectural explanation can give rise to a new problem, to a new demand for an explanation: the 'why?' question can always be reiterated, as even small children know. (Why did daddy not come home for lunch? He had to go to the dentist. Why does he have to go to the dentist? He has a bad tooth. Why does he have a bad tooth?) It is different with 'what is' questions. Here an answer may be ultimate.

I hope I have made clear the difference between conjectural explanation – which, even if guided by intuition, always remains tentative – and, on the other hand, essentialist or ultimate explanation – which, if guided by intuition (in another sense), is infallible.

244

There are, incidentally, two corresponding methods of criticizing an assertion. The first method ('scientific criticism') criticizes an assertion by drawing logical *consequences* from it (perhaps from it in conjunction with other, unproblematic assertions), and by trying to find *consequences which are unacceptable*. The second method ('philosophical criticism') tries to show that the assertion is *not really demonstrable*: that it cannot be derived from intuitively certain premises, and that it is itself not intuitively certain.

Almost all scientists criticize assertions by the first method; almost all philosophical criticism I know proceeds by the second method.

Now, the interesting thing is that the distinction between the two methods of explanation can be found in the works of Plato and of Aristotle: both the theoretical description of the two methods is there, and also their use, in practical examples. But what is missing, from Plato right down to our own day, is a full consciousness that the methods are two: that they differ fundamentally; and, even more important, that only the first method, conjectural explanation, is valid, and feasible, while the second is just a will-o'-the-wisp.

The difference between the two methods is more radical than a difference between two methods that lead to what have been termed 'knowledge claims'; for only the second method leads to knowledge claims. The first method leads to *conjectures* or *hypotheses*. Although these may be described as belonging to 'knowledge' in an objective or World 3 sense, they are not *claimed* to be known or to be true. They may be *conjectured* to be true; but this is an entirely different thing.

Admittedly, there exists an old traditional movement against essentialist explanation, starting from ancient scepticism; a movement that influenced Hume, Kirchhoff, Mach, and many others. But the members of this movement do not distinguish the two kinds of explanation; rather, they identify 'explanation' with what I call 'essentialist explanation' and they therefore reject explanation altogether. (They recommend instead that we take 'description' to be the real task of science.)

Over-simplifying things (as we always have to in history), we can say that, in spite of the existence of the two kinds of explanation, clearly recognized at some places by Plato and Aristotle, there is an almost universal conviction, even among the sceptics, that only the essentialist type of explanation is really an explanation, and that it alone is to be taken seriously.

I suggest that this attitude is almost unavoidable in the absence of a clear distinction between World 2 and World 3. Unless this distinction is clearly made, there is no 'knowledge' except in the subjective or World 2 sense. There are no conjectures or hypotheses, no tentative and competing theories. There is only subjective doubt, subjective uncertainty, which is almost the opposite of 'knowledge'. We cannot say of two theories that the one is better than the other – we can only believe in the one and doubt the other. There can be, of course, different degrees of subjective belief (or of subjective probability). But as long as we do not recognize the existence of an objective World 3 (and of objective reasons which may make one of the competing theories objectively preferable or objectively stronger than another though none of them may be known to be true), there cannot be different theories or hypotheses of different degrees of objective merit or preferability (short of outright truth or falsity). As a consequence, while from the point of view of World 3, theories *are* conjectural hypotheses, for those who interpret theories and hypotheses in terms of World 2 beliefs there is a sharp division between theories and hypotheses: theories are known to be true, while hypotheses are provisional and at any rate not yet known to be true. (Even the great William Whewell – who in some ways comes near to the point of view here advocated – believed in the essential difference between a hypothesis and a finally established theory: a point of agreement between Whewell and Mill.)

It is interesting that Plato almost always stresses, when he comes to relate a myth, that the myth has only verisimilitude, not truth. But this does not affect his belief that what we seek is certainty, and that certainty is to be found in the intellectual intuition of essences. He agrees with the sceptics that this may not (or not always) be available. But the method of conjecture is, it seems, regarded by all parties not only as tentative but as a provisional *stop-gap for something better*.

One of the most interesting incidents in the history of science is due to the fact that this view is held even by Newton. His *Principia* may be described, I believe, as the most important of all works of conjectural or hypothetical explanation in history, and Newton clearly realized that his own theories in the *Principia* were not essentialist explanations. Yet he never rejected, and implicitly accepted, the philosophy of essentialism. Not only did he say 'I do not feign hypotheses' (this particular remark may well have been meant 'I do not offer *speculations* about possible ultimate explanations, as does Descartes'), but he agreed that essentialist explanations are to be searched for and that they would, if found, be final, and superior to his attraction at a distance. It never occurred to him to give up his belief in the superiority of an essentialist explanation to his own type of explanation (which he wrongly believed to be based on induction from the phenomena rather than on hypotheses). In contradistinction to some of his followers, he admitted that his theory was not an explanation; and he merely claimed that it was 'the best and safest method first diligently to investigate the properties of things . . . and [only] then to seek hypotheses to explain them'.[47] In the third edition of the *Principia* (1726), Newton added to the beginning of Book III at the end of the Rules of Reasoning in Philosophy, 'Not that I affirm gravity to be essential to bodies', thus disclaiming that the force of gravity could be taken as an essentialist explanation.[48]

To sum up, Newton, probably the greatest master ever of the method of conjectural explanations which 'saved the phenomena', was of course right in appealing to the phenomena. He wrongly believed himself to have avoided hypotheses and to have used (Baconian) induction. He rightly believed that his theory might be explained by a deeper theory, but he wrongly believed that this would be an essentialist explanation. He also wrongly believed that inertia was essential to matter – an inherent *vis insita* of matter.[49]

Notes

1 'Improbable' in the sense of *O.K.*, pp. 101–3.

2 W. Heisenberg, 'The Representation of Nature in Contemporary Physics', *Daedalus*, 87, 1958, pp. 95–108.

3 B. Russell, 'Mind and Matter', in *Portraits from Memory*, New York, 1956, p. 145.

4 See especially *O.K.*, Chapter 4.

5 G. Ryle, *The Concept of Mind*, London, 1949.

6 G. Ryle, 'The Physical Basis of Mind', in P. Laslett (ed.), *The Physical Basis of Mind*, Oxford, 1950, pp. 75–9.

7 W. F. R. Hardie, 'Concepts of Consciousness in Aristotle', *Mind* 85, 1976, pp. 388–411.

8 R. S. Solecki, *Shanidar*, New York, 1971, pp. 246f.

9 Ibid., p. 268. Samples of the soil were analysed eight years after the discovery by a French palaeobotanist, a specialist in pollen analysis, Mme Arlette Leroi-Gourhan, who made this staggering discovery.

10 R. B. Onians, *The Origins of European Thought*, London, 1954.

11 For two further words (*phrēn* or *phrēnes* and *eidōlon*) see notes 14, 17 and 24 below.

12 Onians, op. cit., p. 48.

13 Ibid., p. 94.

14 In Homer *demas* (in later writers, from Hesiod and Pindar on, often *sōma*), the body, the frame or stature of men, is often opposed to the mind, for which various terms are used, for example *phrēnes*; see note 17 below, and *Iliad* 1.113–15; cp. also *Odyssey* 5.211–13. See further *Iliad* 24.376f., with the contrast of body (*demas*) and mind (*noos*); *Odyssey* 18.219f., with the contrast of bodily size (*megethos*, here used as a synonym for *demas*, as can be seen from 251) and mind (*phrēnes*); *Odyssey* 17.454, where bodily shape (*eidos*) is contrasted with mind (*phrēnes*). In *Odyssey* 4.796, a *phantom* (*eidōlon*, similar to the Homeric *psychē*) is clad by the goddess into a body (*demas*). Cp. the opposition of phantom or mind (*eidōlon*) and body (*sōma*) in Pindar quoted in note 24 below; and *C.&.R.*, pp. 409f.

15 Interesting Homeric passages from the *Iliad* indicating dualism (of course, a materialistic dualism) are, for example, the golden girl robots (see *S. I. B.*, part I, section 2, note 1), who are clearly described as *conscious* robots: they have understanding or mind (*nous*) in their hearts (cp. *Iliad* 18.419). See also *Iliad* 19.302; 19.339; and 24.167; passages in which overt speech is contrasted with concealed thought; and also 24.674, where Priam and the herald are going to sleep in the forecourt of Achilles' hut, 'their minds heavy with cares'.

(E. V. Rieu, in the Penguin Classics edition, 1950, translates very freely but very well 'with much to occupy their busy minds'.)

16 Cp. G. E. R. Lloyd, *Polarity and Analogy*, Cambridge, 1966.

17 Here the term *phrēnes* (according to Onians originally in Homer the lungs and the heart) is used for 'mind'; see Onians, op.cit., Chapter 2).

18 See Sophocles, *King Oedipus*, lines 64 and 643; cp. E. R. Dodds, *The Greeks and the Irrational*, Berkeley and Los Angeles, 1951, p. 159, note 17.

19 See also K. Meuli, 'Scythia', *Hermes*, 70, 1935, pp. 121–76.

20 E. E. Evans-Pritchard, *Witchcraft, Oracles and Magic Among the Azande*, Oxford, 1937.

21 S. F. Nadel, 'Witchcraft in Four African Societies: An Essay in Comparison', *American Anthropologist*, N.S. 54, 1952, pp. 18–29.

22 See Dodds, op.cit., Chapter 1, p. 3, on Agamemnon's apology (*Iliad* 19.86ff.); and compare Sophocles, *Oedipus at Colonus*, lines 960ff.

23 See further Essay 1.

24 For Homer *psychē* (or *eidōlon*) meant phantom or shade; later *psychē* assumes a meaning near to Homer's *thymos*: the active conscious self, the living and breathing self. In this way, the *psychē* or the *eidōlon* becomes the principle of life, while in Homer (and later sometimes in Pindar) it seems to have been asleep when the person was alive and awake, and awake when the person was asleep or unconscious or dead. (Not that these rules of usage were ever quite consistently adhered to by any author.) Thus we read in Pindar (fragment 116 Bowra = 131 Sandys (Loeb)): 'The body of every man follows the call of mighty death; yet there is left alive a phantom or image (*eidōlon*) from his time of life, which alone stems from the gods. It sleeps while his limbs are active; but while he sleeps it often announces in dreams their [the gods'] decision of coming joy or sorrow.' We see that Homer's phantom *psychē*, which was a projection of all the terrors of extreme old age far beyond the grave, has lost some of its ghastly and ghostlike character, although there are some traces left of the Homeric usage.

25 Aristotle tells us that 'the poems known as Orphic say that the soul, borne by the winds, enters from the all into the animals when they breathe' (DK 1B11 = *De Anima* 410b28).

26 W. K. C. Guthrie, *A History of Greek Philosophy*, vol. I, Cambridge, 1962, p. 355.

27 G. Vlastos, 'Ethics and Physics in Democritus', in R. E. Allen and D. J. Furley (eds.), *Studies in Presocratic Philosophy*, vol. II, London, 1975, pp. 381–408.

28 Cp. Epicharmus, DK 23 B12: 'Only mind sees, only mind hears: all else is deaf and blind.'

29 Plato's *Republic* 530c–531c may be taken as evidence that the discovery was made by some Pythagorean. For the discovery and its ascription to Pythagoras himself see Guthrie, *A History of Greek Philosophy*, vol. I, pp. 221ff. See also Diogenes Laertius, *Vitae Philosophorum* VIII.12.

30 For the generalization of this problem see *C.&.R.*, Chapter 2, Section IV.

31 See also the brilliant article by Charles H. Kahn, 'Pythagorean Philosophy Before Plato', in A. P. Mourelatos (ed.), *The Presocratics*, New York, 1974, pp. 161–85.

32 See Plato, *Phaedo* 85e ff., especially 88c–d; Aristotle, *De Anima* 407b27 'many regard it as the most credible of all . . . theories'; and p. 21 of volume XII (*Select Fragments*) of the Oxford edition of *The Works of Aristotle* edited and

translated by Sir David Ross, 1952, where Themistius describes the theory as very popular.

33 I owe this question to Jeremy Shearmur, who also suggested that the relation might be like that of the Platonic ideas to matter.

34 See *O.S.*, Chapter 3, p. 26 and note 15.

35 Reading Guthrie, whose book (*A History of Greek Philosophy*, vol. III, Cambridge, 1969) contains the best presentation of Socrates known to me, has convinced me that Socrates' autobiographical remarks in Plato's *Phaedo*, 96a ff., are likely to be historical. I first accepted Guthrie's criticism (p. 423, n. 1) of my *O.S.* (vol. I, p. 308) without rereading what I had written. In preparing the present passage I looked up *O.S.* vol. I, again, and I found that I did not, on p. 308, argue against the historicity of the autobiographical passage (*Phaedo* 96a ff.), but against the historicity of the *Phaedo* in general, and of *Phaedo* 108d ff. in particular, with its somewhat authoritative and dogmatic exposition of the nature of the cosmos, especially of the Earth. This exposition still seems to me incompatible with the *Apology*.

36 C. H. Kahn, 'Sensation and Consciousness in Aristotle's Psychology', *Archiv für Geschichte der Philosophie*, 48, 1966, pp. 43–81. See also the remarks on W. F. R. Hardie's *Mind* article in Section II above.

37 Cp. *S.I.B.*, Part 1, Section 30, text to note 5.

38 See DK 68B45. Cp. also 68B187.

39 Concerning the incompatibility of certain parts of the *Phaedo* (especially *Phaedo* 108d ff.) with Plato's *Apology*, see note 35 above, and *O.S.*, vol. I, p. 308.

40 The historicity of this autobiographical passage is defended convincingly by Guthrie, *A History of Greek Philosophy*, vol. III, p. 421–3; see also note 35 above.

41 J. Beloff, *The Existence of Mind*, London, 1962, p. 141.

42 In modern times this second passage from Plato's *Phaedo* was repeatedly referred to by Leibniz in his various discussions of the mind–body problem. See further *S. I. B.*, Part 1, Section 50.

43 If one does not insist on this point – if, say, one says that the physical movements of our bodies can be in principle completely explained in World 1 terms alone, and that this explanation may merely be complemented by one in terms of meanings – then, it seems to me, one has unwittingly adopted a form of parallelism, in which human aims, purposes, and freedom become merely a subjective epiphenomenon.

44 The only exceptions were some of the Sophists, especially Protagoras. Subjective empiricism became important again with Berkeley, Hume, Mach, Avenarius, and with the early Wittgenstein and the logical positivists. I regard it as mistaken and I shall not devote much space to it. I regard as its characteristic doctrine the saying of Otto Neurath, 'Everything is surface: the world has no depth'; or the saying of Wittgenstein: '*The riddle* does not exist' (*Tractatus Logico-Philosophicus*, London, 1922, 6.5).

45 This method must be clearly distinguished from the theory of instrumentalism with which it was conflated by Duhem. (See *C. & R.* Chapter 3, p. 99, note 6, where references to Aristotelian passages discussing this method can be found, for example *De Caelo* 293a25.) The difference between this method and instrumentalism is that we put the truth of our tentative explanations to the test mainly because we are *interested* in their truth (like an essentialist: see below), though we do not think that we can *establish* their truth.

46 See my *O.S.*, vol. II, p. 16.

47 Newton, letter to Oldenburg, 2 June 1672. (Cp. Newton's *Opera*, ed. S. Horsley, vol. IV, London, 1779–85, pp. 314f.)

48 I. Newton, *Philosophiae Naturalis Principia Mathematica*, 3rd edn, London, 1726, Book III. Cp. also the letters to Richard Bentley, 17 January and 25 February 1692/3. See *C.&R.*, notes 20 and 21 to Chapter 3 (and text), and Newton's *Opticks*, London, 1730, query 31, where Newton mentions the possibility that attraction 'may be performed by impulse, or by some other means unknown to me'.

49 A further and complementary discussion of Newton's theory and its relation to essentialism will be found in *S. I. B.*, Section 51.

ESSAY 9

PLATO AND GEOMETRY

When writing on Plato in *The Open Society* (Chapter 6: 'Totalitarian Justice'), I came to comment on the Platonic theory of justice and Plato's distinction between 'arithmetical' equality and 'proportionate' (or 'geometrical') equality; and I appended to my note 9 of that chapter the results of a study of Plato and geometry, here reprinted in *Section 1*. I later added an addendum with the title 'Plato and Geometry', here reprinted as *Section 2*. After this follows *Section 3*, which contains Addendum II from *O.S.*, vol. I, entitled 'The Dating of the Theaetetus', written in 1961. The following *Sections 4 and 5* contain reprints of texts that were first published in this version in *Studies in Philosophy*, ed. J. N. Findlay, Oxford, 1966, as sections VII and VIII of my paper 'On the Sources of Knowledge and of Ignorance', which also appeared as the Introduction to *C. & R.*, but with fewer notes than here. *Section 6*, entitled 'The Cosmological Origins of Euclidean Geometry', is a discussion note on a paper by Professor Árpád Szabó, first published in *Problems in the Philosophy of Mathematics*, ed. I. Lakatos, vol. I, Amsterdam, 1967, pp. 18–20, and the final *Section 7* is a reprint of 'Plato, *Timaeus* 54e–55a', first published in *The Classical Review*, N.S. 20, 1970, pp. 4–5.

1 Plato and geometry (1950)

For Plato's views, in the *Laws*, on *political justice and equality*, see especially the passage on the two kinds of equality (*Laws* 757b–d) quoted below under (1). For the fact, mentioned in Plato's text, that not only virtue and breeding but also wealth should count in the distribution of honours and of spoils (and even size and good looks), see *Laws* 744c, quoted in note 20 (1) to Chapter 6 of *O.S.*, where other relevant passages are also discussed.

(1) In the *Laws*, 757b–d, Plato discusses '*two kinds of equality*':

> The one of these . . . is equality of measure, weight, or number [i.e. numerical or arithmetical equality]; but the truest and best equality . . . distributes more to the greater and less to the smaller, giving each his due measure, in *accordance with nature*.

. . . By granting the greater honour to those who are superior in virtue, and the lesser honour to those who are inferior in virtue and breeding, *it distributes to each what is proper, according to this principle of* [*rational*] *proportions*. And this is precisely what we shall call '*political justice*'. And whoever may found a state must make this the sole aim of his legislation . . . . : this justice alone which, as stated, is *natural equality*, and which is distributed, as the situation requires, to unequals.

This second of the two equalities which constitutes what Plato here calls 'political justice' (and what Aristotle calls 'distributive justice'), and which is described by Plato (and Aristotle) as '*proportionate equality*' – the truest, best, and most natural equality – was later called 'geometrical' (*Gorgias* 508a; see also 465b/c, and Plutarch, *Moralia* 719b f.), as opposed to the lower and democratic '*arithmetical*' equality. On this identification, the remarks under (2) may throw some light.

(2) According to tradition (see *Comm. in Arist. Graeca, pars* XV, Berlin, 1897, p. 117, 27, and *pars* XVIII, Berlin, 1900, p. 118, 18), an inscription over the door of Plato's Academy said: 'Nobody untrained in geometry may enter my house!' I suspect that the meaning of this is not merely an emphasis upon the importance of mathematical studies, but that it means: 'Arithmetic (i.e. more precisely, Pythagorean number theory) is not enough; you must know geometry!' And I shall attempt to sketch the reasons which make me believe that the latter phrase adequately sums up one of Plato's most important contributions to science. See also Section 2 below.

As is now generally believed, the earlier Pythagorean treatment of geometry adopted a method somewhat similar to the one nowadays called 'arithmetization'. Geometry was treated as part of the theory of integers (or 'natural' numbers, i.e. of numbers composed of monads or 'indivisible units'; cp. *Republic* 525e) and of their '*logoi*', i.e. their 'rational' proportions. For example, the Pythagorean rectangular triangles were those with sides in such rational proportions. (Examples are 3 : 4: 5; or 5 : 12: 13.) A general formula ascribed to Pythagoras is this: $2n + 1 : 2n(n + 1) : 2n(n + 1) + 1$. But this formula, derived from the '*gnōmōn*', is not general enough, as the example 8 : 15 : 17 shows. A *general formula*, from which the Pythagorean can be obtained by putting $m = n + 1$, is this: $m^2 - n^2 : 2mn : m^2 + n^2$ (where $m > n$). Since this formula is a close consequence of the so-called 'Theorem of Pythagoras' (if taken together with that kind of algebra which seems to have been known to the early Pythagoreans), and since this formula was, apparently, not only unknown to Pythagoras but even to Plato (who proposed, according to Proclus, another non-general formula), it seems that the 'Theorem of Pythagoras' was not known, in its general form, to either Pythagoras or even to Plato. (See for a less radical view on this matter T. Heath, *A History of Greek Mathematics*, Oxford, 1921, vol. I, pp. 80–2. The formula described by me as 'general' is essentially that of Euclid; it can be obtained from Heath's unneccessarily complicated formula on p. 82 by first obtaining the three sides of the triangle and by multiplying them by $2/mn$, and then by substituting in the result m and n and p and q.)

The discovery of the irrationality of the square root of two (alluded to by Plato in the *Greater Hippias* and in the *Meno*; cp. note 10 to Chapter 7 of *O.S.*; see also Aristotle, *Anal. Priora* 41a26f.) destroyed the Pythagorean programme of 'arithmetizing' geometry, and with it, it appears, the vitality of the Pythagorean Order itself. The tradition that this discovery was at first kept secret is, it seems, supported by the fact that Plato still calls the irrational at first *arrhētos*, i.e. the secret, the unmentionable mystery; cp. the *Greater Hippias* 303b/c; *Republic* 546c. (A later term is 'the non-commensurable'; cp. *Theaetetus* 147d, and *Laws* 820c. The term *alogos* seems to occur first in Democritus, who wrote two books *On Illogical Lines and Atoms* (or *and Full Bodies*) which are lost; Plato knew the term, as proved by his somewhat disrespectful allusion to Democritus' title in the *Republic* 534d, but never used it himself as a synonym for *arrhētos*. The first extant and indubitable use in this sense is in Aristotle's *Anal. Post.* 76b9. See also T. Heath, op.cit., vol. I, pp. 84f., 156f. and Section 2 below.)

It appears that the breakdown of the Pythagorean programme, i.e. of the arithmetical method of geometry, led to the development of the axiomatic method of Euclid, that is to say, of a new method which was on the one side designed to rescue, from the breakdown, what could be rescued (including the method of rational proof), and on the other side to accept the irreducibility of geometry to arithmetic. Assuming all this, it would seem highly probable that Plato's role in the transition from the older Pythagorean method to that of Euclid was an exceedingly important one – in fact, that Plato was *one of the first to develop a specifically geometrical method* aiming at rescuing what could be rescued from, and at cutting the losses of, the breakdown of Pythagoreanism. Much of this must be considered as a highly uncertain historical hypothesis, but some confirmation may be found in Aristotle, *Anal. Post.* 76b9 (mentioned above), especially if this passage is compared with the *Laws* 818c, 895e (even and odd), and 819e–820a, 820c (incommensurable). The passage reads: 'Arithmetic assumes the meaning of "odd" and "even", geometry that of "irrational".' (Or 'incommensurable'; cp. *Anal. Priora* 41a26f., 50a37. See also *Metaphysics* 983a20, 1061b1–3, where the problem of irrationality is treated as if it were the *proprium* of geometry, and 1089a, where, as in *Anal. Post.* 76b40, there is an allusion to the 'square foot' method of the *Theaetetus* 147d.) Plato's great interest in the problem of irrationality is shown especially in two of the passages mentioned above, the *Theaetetus* 147d–148a, and *Laws* 819d–822d, where Plato declares that he is ashamed of the Greeks for not being alive to the great problem of incommensurable magnitudes.

Now, I suggest that the 'Theory of the Primary Bodies' (in the *Timaeus* 53c–62c, and perhaps even down to 64a; see also *Republic* 528b–d) was part of Plato's answer to the challenge. It preserves, on the one hand, the atomistic character of Pythagoreanism – the indivisible units ('monads') which also play a role in the school of the atomists – and it introduces, on the other hand, the irrationalities (of the square roots of two and three) whose admission into the world had become unavoidable. It does so by taking two of the offending rectangular triangles – the one which is half of a square and incorporates the square root of two, and the one which is half of an equilateral triangle and incorporates the square root of three – as the units of which everything else is composed. Indeed, the doctrine that these two irrational triangles are the limits (*peras*; cp. *Meno* 75d–76a) or forms of all elementary physical bodies may be said to be one of the central physical doctrines of the *Timaeus*.

All this would suggest that the warning against those untrained in geometry (an allusion to it may perhaps be found in the *Timaeus* 54a) might have had the more pointed significance mentioned above, and that it may have been connected with the belief that geometry is something of higher importance than is arithmetic. (Cp. *Timaeus* 31c.) And this, in turn, would explain why Plato's 'proportionate equality', said by him to be something more aristocratic than the democratic arithmetical or numerical equality, was later identified with the 'geometrical equality', mentioned by Plato in the *Gorgias* 508a (cp. note 48 to Chapter 6 of *O.S.*), and why (for example by Plutarch, *loc. cit.*) arithmetic and geometry were associated with democracy and Spartan aristocracy respectively – in spite of the fact, then apparently forgotten, that the Pythagoreans had been as aristocratically minded as Plato himself; that their programme had stressed arithmetic; and that 'geometrical', in their language, is the name of a certain kind of numerical (i.e. arithmetical) proportion.

(3) In the *Timaeus*, Plato needs for the construction of the Primary Bodies an Elementary Square and an Elementary Equilateral Triangle. These two, in turn, are composed of two different kinds of *sub-elementary triangles* – the half-square which incorporates $\sqrt{2}$, and the half-equilateral which incorporates $\sqrt{3}$ respectively. The question why he chooses these two sub-elementary triangles, instead of the Square and the Equilateral itself, has been much discussed; and similarly a second question – see below under (4) – why he constructs his Elementary Squares out of four sub-elementary half-squares instead of two, and the Elementary Equilateral out of six sub-elementary half-equilaterals instead of two. (See Figures 6 and 7.)

Concerning the first of these two questions, it seems to have been generally overlooked that Plato, with his burning interest in the problem of irrationality, would not have introduced the two irrationalities $\sqrt{2}$ and $\sqrt{3}$ (which he explicitly mentions in 54b) *had he not been anxious to introduce precisely these irrationalities as irreducible elements into his world.* (Cornford,

254

Plato's Cosmology, London, 1937, pp. 214 and 231ff., gives a long discussion of both questions, but the common solution which he offers for both – his 'hypothesis', as he calls it on p. 234 – appears to me quite unacceptable; had Plato wanted to achieve some 'grading' like the one discussed by Cornford – note that there is no hint in Plato that anything smaller than what Cornford calls 'Grade B' exists – it would have been sufficient to divide into two the *sides* of the *Elementary Squares* and Equilaterals of what Cornford calls 'Grade B', building each of them up from four elementary figures *which do not contain any irrationalities*.) But if Plato was anxious to introduce these irrationalities into the world, as the sides of sub-elementary triangles of which everything else is composed, then he must have believed that he could, in this way, solve a problem; and this problem, I suggest, was that of 'the nature of (the commensurable and) the uncommensurable' (*Laws* 820c). This problem, clearly, was particularly hard to solve on the basis of a cosmology which made use of anything like atomistic ideas, since irrationals are not multiples of any unit able to measure rationals; but if the unit measures themselves contain sides in 'irrational ratios', then the great paradox might be solved; for then they can measure both, and the existence of irrationals was no longer incomprehensible or 'irrational'.

But Plato knew that there were more irrationalities than $\sqrt{2}$ and $\sqrt{3}$, for he mentions in the *Theaetetus* the discovery of an infinite sequence of irrational square roots (he also speaks, 148b, of 'similar considerations concerning solids', but this need not refer to cubic roots but could refer to the cubic diagonal, i.e. to $\sqrt{3}$); and he also mentions in the *Greater Hippias* (303b–c; cp. Heath op. cit., p. 304) the fact that by adding (or otherwise composing) irrationals, other irrational numbers may be obtained (but also rational numbers – probably an allusion to the fact that, for example, 2 minus $\sqrt{2}$ is irrational; for this number, plus $\sqrt{2}$, gives, of course, a rational number). In view of these circumstances it appears that, if Plato wanted to solve the problem of irrationality by way of introducing his elementary triangles, he must have thought that all irrationals (or at least their multiples) can be composed by adding up (*a*) units; (*b*) $\sqrt{2}$; (*c*) $\sqrt{3}$; and multiples of these. This, of course, would have been a mistake, but we have every reason to believe that no disproof existed at the time; and the proposition that there are only two kinds of atomic irrationalities – the diagonals of the squares and of cubes – and that all other irrationalities are commensurable relative to (*a*) the unit; (*b*) $\sqrt{2}$; and (*c*) $\sqrt{3}$ has a certain amount of plausibility in it if we consider the relative character of irrationalities. (I mean the fact that we may say with equal justification that the diagonal of a square with unit side is irrational or that the side of a square with a unit diagonal is irrational. We should also remember that Euclid, in Book X, def. 2, still calls all incommensurable square roots 'commensurable by their squares'.) Thus Plato may well have believed in this proposition, even though he could not possibly have been in the possession of a valid proof of his conjecture. (A disproof was apparently first given by Euclid.) Now, there is undoubtedly a reference to some unproved conjecture in the very passage in the *Timaeus* in which Plato refers to the reason for choosing his sub-elementary triangles, for he writes (*Timaeus* 53c/d):

> all triangles are derived from two, each having one right angle . . . of these triangles, one [the half-square] has on either side half of a right angle . . . and equal sides; the other [the scalene] . . . has unequal sides. These two we assume as the first principles . . . according to an account which combines likelihood [or likely conjecture] with necessity [proof]. Principles which are still further removed than these are known to heaven, and to such men as heaven favours.

And later, after explaining that there is an endless number of scalene triangles, of which 'the best' must be selected, and after explaining that he takes the half-equilateral as the best, Plato says (*Timaeus* 54a/b; Cornford had to emend the passage in order to fit it into his interpretation; cp. his note 3 to p. 214): 'The reason is too long a story; but if anybody puts this matter to the test, and proves that it has this property, then the prize is his, with all our good will.' Plato does not say clearly what 'this property' means; it must be a (provable or refutable) mathematical property which justifies that, having chosen the triangle incorporating $\sqrt{2}$, the choice of that incorporating $\sqrt{3}$ is 'the best'; and I think that, in view of the foregoing considerations, the property which he had in mind was the conjectured relative rationality of the other irrationals, i.e. relative to the unit, and the square roots of two and three.

(4) An additional reason for our interpretation, although one for which I do not find any further evidence in Plato's text, may perhaps emerge from the following consideration. It is a curious fact that $\sqrt{2} + \sqrt{3}$ very nearly approximates π. (Cp. E. Borel, *Space and Time*, London, 1926, reprinted 1960, p. 216; my attention was drawn to this fact, in a different context, by W. Marinelli.) The excess is less than 0.0047, i.e. less than 1½ pro mille of π, and a better approximation to π was hardly known at the time. A kind of explanation of this curious fact is that the arithmetical mean of the areas of the circumscribed hexagon and the inscribed octagon is a good approximation of the area of the circle. Now, it appears, on the one hand, that Bryson operated with the means of circumscribed and inscribed polygons (cp Heath, op. cit., 224), and we know, on the other hand (from the *Greater Hippias*), that Plato was interested in the adding of irrationals, so that he must have added $\sqrt{2} + \sqrt{3}$. There are thus two ways by which Plato may have found out the approximate equation $\sqrt{2}$

$+ \sqrt{3} \approx \pi$, and the second of these ways seems almost inescapable. It seems a plausible hypothesis that Plato knew of this equation, but was unable to prove whether or not it was a strict equality or only an approximation. [Figure 8 illustrates the argument of this paragraph.]

But if this is so, then we can perhaps answer the 'second question' mentioned above under (3), i.e. the question why Plato composed his elementary square of four sub-elementary triangles (half-squares) instead of two, and his elementary equilateral of six sub-elementary triangles (half-equilaterals) instead of two. If we look at Figures 6 and 7, then we see that this construction emphasizes the centre of the circumscribed and inscribed circles, and, in both cases, the radii of the circumscribed circle. (In the case of the equilateral, the radius of the inscribed circle appears also; but it seems that Plato had that of the circumscribed circle in mind, since he mentions it, in his description of the method of composing the equilateral, as the 'diagonal'; cp. the *Timaeus* 54d–e; cp. also 54b.)

If we now draw these two circumscribed circles, or more precisely, if we inscribe the elementary square and equilateral into a circle with the radius r, then we find that the sum of the sides of these two figures approximates $r\pi$; in other words, Plato's construction suggests one of the simplest approximate solutions of the squaring of the circle, as our three figures show. In view of all this, it may easily be the case that Plato's conjecture and his offer of 'a prize with all our good will', quoted above under (3), involved not only the general problem of the commensurability of the irrationalities, but also the special problem whether $\sqrt{2} + \sqrt{3}$ squares the unit circle.

I must again emphasize that no direct evidence is known to me to show that this was in Plato's mind; but if we consider the indirect evidence here marshalled, then the hypothesis does perhaps not seem too far-fetched. I do not think that it is more so than Cornford's hypothesis; and if true, it would give a better explanation of the relevant passages.

(5) If there is anything in our contention, developed in (2) above, that Plato's incription meant 'Arithmetic is not enough; you must know geometry!' and in our contention that this emphasis was connected with the discovery of the irrationality of the square roots of 2 and 3, then this might throw some light on the Theory of Ideas, and on Aristotle's much-debated reports. It would explain why, in view of this discovery, the Pythagorean view that things (forms, shapes) are numbers, and moral ideas ratios of numbers, had to disappear – perhaps to be replaced, as in the *Timaeus*, by the doctrine that the elementary forms, or limits (*peras*; cp. the passage from the *Meno* 75d–76a, referred to above), or shapes, or ideas of things, are triangles. But it would also explain why, one generation later, the Academy could return to the Pythagorean doctrine. Once the shock caused by the discovery of irrationality had worn off, mathematicians began to get used to the idea that *the irrationals must be numbers*, in

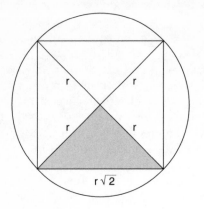

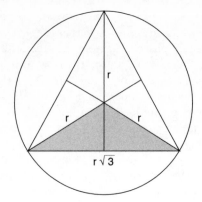

Figure 6 Plato's Elementary Square, composed of four sub-elementary isosceles rectangular triangles

Figure 7 Plato's Elementary Equilateral, composed of six sub-elementary scalene rectangular triangles

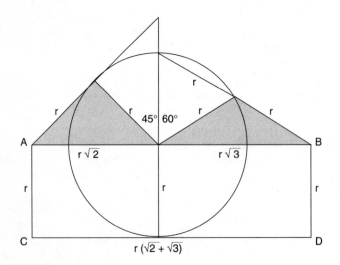

Figure 8 The rectangle ABCD has an area exceeding that of the circle by less than 1½ pro mille

spite of everything, since they stand in the elementary relations of greater or less to other (rational) numbers. This stage reached, the reasons against Pythagoreanism disappeared, although the theory that shapes are numbers or ratios of numbers meant, after the admission of irrationals, something different from what it had meant before (a point which possibly was not fully appreciated by the adherents of the new theory).

258

2   Plato and geometry (1957)

In the second edition of *O.S.*, I made a lengthy addition to note 9 to Chapter 6 (pp. 248–53). The historical hypothesis propounded in this note was later amplified in my paper 'The Nature of Philosophical Problems and their Roots in Science' (published as Chapter 2 in *C. & R*).

It may be restated as follows: (1) the discovery of the irrationality of the square root of two which led to the breakdown of the Pythagorean programme of reducing geometry and cosmology (and presumably all knowledge) to arithmetic, produced a crisis in Greek mathematics; (2) Euclid's *Elements* is not a textbook of geometry, but rather the final attempt of the Platonic School to resolve this crisis by reconstructing the whole of mathematics and cosmology *on a geometrical basis*, in order to deal with the problem of irrationality systematically rather than *ad hoc*, thus inverting the Pythagorean programme of arithmetization; (3) it was Plato who first conceived the programme later carried out by Euclid: it was Plato who first recognized the need for a reconstruction; who chose geometry as the new basis, and the geometrical method of proportion as the new method; who drew up the programme for a *geometrization of mathematics*, including arithmetic, astronomy, and cosmology; and who became the founder of the geometrical picture of the world, and thereby also the founder of modern science – of the science of Copernicus, Galileo, Kepler, and Newton.

I suggested that the famous inscription over the door of Plato's Academy (Section 1 (2) above) alluded to this programme of geometrization. (That it was intended to announce an *inversion of the Pythagorean programme* seems likely in view of Archytas, DK B1.)

In Section 1 (2) above I suggested 'that Plato was *one of the first to develop a specifically geometrical method* aiming at rescuing what could be rescued . . . from the breakdown of Pythagoreanism'; and I described this suggestion as 'a highly uncertain historical hypothesis'. I no longer think that the hypothesis is so very uncertain. On the contrary, I now feel that a rereading of Plato, Aristotle, Euclid, and Proclus, in the light of this hypothesis, would produce as much corroborating evidence as one could expect. In addition to the confirming evidence referred to in the paragraph quoted, I now wish to add that already the *Gorgias* (451a/b; c; 453e) takes the discussion of 'odd' and 'even' as characteristic of arithmetic, thereby clearly identifying arithmetic with Pythagorean number theory, while characterizing the geometer as the man who adopts the method of proportions (465b/c). Moreover, in the passage from the *Gorgias* (508a) Plato not only speaks of geometrical equality (cp. note 48 to Chapter 8 of *O.S.*) but also states implicitly the principle which he was later to develop fully in the *Timaeus*: that the cosmic order is a *geometrical order*. Incidentally, the *Gorgias* also proves that the word *'alogos'* was not associated in Plato's mind with irrational numbers, since 465a says that even a technique, or art, must not be *alogos*; which would hold *a fortiori* for a science such as geometry. I think we may simply translate *alogos* as 'alogical'. (Cp. also *Gorgias* 496a/b; and 522e.) The point is important for the interpretation of the title of Democritus' lost book, mentioned earlier in Section 1 (2) above.

My paper on 'The Nature of Philosophical Problems' (*C. & R.*, Sections IV–IX) contains some further suggestions concerning Plato's *geometrization of arithmetic* and of cosmology in general (his inversion of the Pythagorean programme), and his theory of forms.

Added in 1961

Since the above text was first published in 1957, in the third edition of *O.S.*, I have found, almost by accident, some interesting corroboration of the historical hypothesis formulated in Section 1 above, in the first paragraph under (2). It is a passage in Proclus' commentaries to the first book of Euclid's *Elements* (ed. Friedlein, Leipzig, 1873, Prologus ii, p. 71, 2–5) from which it becomes clear that there existed a tradition according to which Euclid's elements were a Platonic cosmology, a treatment of the problems of the *Timaeus*.

3   The dating of the *Theaetetus* (1961)

There is a hint in note 50, (6), to Chapter 8 of *O.S.* (p. 281), that 'the *Theaetetus* is perhaps (as against the usual assumption) earlier than the *Republic*'. This suggestion was made to me by the late Dr Robert Eisler in a conversation not long before his death in 1949. But since he did not tell me any more about his conjecture than that it was partly based on *Theaetetus* 174e f. – the crucial passage whose post-*Republican* dating did not seem to me to fit into my theory – I felt that there was not sufficient evidence for it, and that it was too *ad hoc* to justify me in publicly saddling Eisler with the responsibility for it.

However, I have since found quite a number of independent arguments in favour of an earlier dating of the *Theaetetus*, and I therefore wish now to acknowledge Eisler's original suggestion.

Since Eva Sachs (cp. *Socrates*, 5, 1917, pp. 531f.) established that the proem of the *Theaetetus*, as we know it, was written after 369, the conjecture of a Socratic core and an early dating involves another – that of an earlier lost edition, revised by Plato after Theaetetus' death. The latter conjecture was proposed independently by various scholars, even before the discovery of a papyrus (ed. by Diels, *Berliner Klassikertexte*, 2, 1905) that contains part of a *Commentary to the Theaetetus* and refers to two distinct editions. The following arguments seem to support both conjectures.

(1) Certain passages in Aristotle seem to allude to the *Theaetetus*: they fit

260

the text of the *Theaetetus* perfectly, and they claim, at the same time, that the ideas there expressed belong to Socrates rather than to Plato. The passages I have in mind are the ascription to Socrates of the invention of *induction* (*Metaphysics* 1078b17–30; cp. 987b1 and 1086b3), which, I think, is an allusion to Socrates' *maieutic* (developed at length in the *Theaetetus*), his method of helping the pupil to perceive the true essence of a thing through purging his mind of his false prejudices; and the further ascription to Socrates of the attitude so strongly expressed again and again in the *Theaetetus*: 'Socrates used to ask questions and not to answer them; for he used to confess that he did not know' (*Soph. El.* 183b7). (These passages are further discussed in Section 5 below, and in Essay 10, Sections IV–VII.

(2) The *Theaetetus* has a surprisingly inconclusive ending, even though it turns out that it was so planned and prepared almost from the beginning. (In fact, as an attempt to solve the problem of knowledge, which it ostensibly tries to do, this beautiful dialogue is a complete failure.) But endings of a similarly inconclusive nature are known to be characteristic of a number of early dialogues.

(3) 'Know thyself' is interpreted, as in the *Apology*, as 'Know how little you know.' In his final speech Socrates says:

> After this, Theaetetus . . . you will be less harsh and gentler to your associates, for you will have the wisdom not to think that you know what you do not know. So much my art [of *maieutic*] can accomplish; nor do I know any of the things that are known by others.

(4) That ours is a second edition, revised by Plato, seems likely, especially in view of the fact that the introduction to the dialogue (142a to the end of 143c), which might well have been added as a memorial to a great man, actually contradicts a passage which may have survived the revision of the earlier edition of this dialogue; I mean its very end, which, like a number of other early dialogues, alludes to Socrates' trial as imminent. The contradiction consists in the fact that Euclid, who appears as a character in the introduction and who narrates how the dialogue came to be written down, tells us (142c–d, 143a) that he went repeatedly to Athens (from Megara, presumably), using every time the opportunity of checking his notes with Socrates, and making '*corrections*' here and there. This is told in a way which makes it quite clear that the dialogue itself must have taken place *at least* several months before Socrates' trial and death; but this is inconsistent with the ending of the dialogue. (I have not seen any reference to this point, but I cannot imagine that it has not been discussed by some Platonist.) It may even be that the reference to '*corrections*', in 143a, and also the much-discussed description

of the 'new style' in 143b–c (see, for example, C. Ritter's *Platon*, vol. I, Munich, 1910, pp. 220f.), were introduced in order to explain some deviations of the revised edition from the original edition. (This would make it possible to place the *revised* edition even after the *Sophist*.)

4   On sources of knowledge and of ignorance

Plato plays a decisive part in the prehistory of Descartes' doctrine of the *veracitas dei* – the doctrine that our intellectual intuition does not deceive us because God is truthful and will not deceive us; or in other words, the doctrine that our intellect is a source of knowledge because God is a source of knowledge. This doctrine has a long history which can easily be traced back to least to Homer and Hesiod.

To us, the habit of referring to one's sources would seem natural in a scholar or a historian, and it is perhaps a little surprising to find that this habit stems from the poets; but it does. The Greek poets refer to the sources of their knowledge. These sources are divine. They are the Muses. 'The Greek bards', Gilbert Murray observes[1]

> always owe, not only what we should call their inspiration, but their actual knowledge of facts to the Muses. The Muses 'are present and know all things' . . . Hesiod . . . always explains that he is dependent on the Muses for his knowledge. Other sources of knowledge are indeed recognized. . . . But most often he consults the Muses. . . . so does Homer for such subjects as the Catalogue of the Greek army.

As this quotation shows, the poets were in the habit of claiming not only divine sources of inspiration, but also divine sources of knowledge – divine guarantors of the truth of their stories.

Precisely the same two claims were raised by the philosophers Heraclitus and Parmenides. Heraclitus, it seems, sees himself as a prophet who 'talks with raving mouth . . . possessed by the god' – by Zeus, the source of all wisdom.[2] And Parmenides, one could almost say, forms the missing link between Homer or Hesiod on the one side and Descartes on the other. His guiding star and inspiration is the goddess Dikē, described by Heraclitus[3] as the guardian of truth. Parmenides describes her as the guardian and keeper of the keys of truth, and as the source of all his knowledge.[4] But Parmenides and Descartes have more in common than the doctrine of divine veracity. For example, Parmenides is told by his divine guarantor of truth that in order to distinguish between truth and falsehood, he must rely upon the intellect alone, to the exclusion of the senses of sight, hearing, and taste.[5] And even the principle of his physical theory which he, like Descartes, founds upon his intellectualist theory of knowledge is the same as that adopted by Descartes: it is the impossibility of a void, the necessary fullness of the world.

In Plato's *Ion* a sharp distinction is made between divine inspiration – the divine frenzy of the poet – and the divine sources or origins of true knowledge. (The topic is further developed in the *Phaedrus*, especially from 259e on; and in 275b–c Plato even insists, as Harold Cherniss pointed out to me, on the distinction between questions of origin and of truth.) Plato grants that the poets are inspired, but he denies to them any divine authority for their alleged knowledge of facts. Nevertheless, the doctrine of the divine source of our knowledge plays a decisive part in Plato's famous theory of *anamnēsis* which in some measure grants to each man the possession of divine sources of knowledge. (The knowledge considered in this theory is knowledge of the *essence or nature* of a thing rather than of a particular historical fact.) According to Plato's *Meno* (81b–d) there is nothing which our immortal soul does not know, prior to our birth. For as all natures are kindred and akin, our soul must be akin to all natures. Accordingly it knows them all: it knows all things.[6] In being born we forget; but we may recover our memory and our knowledge, though only partially: only if we see the truth again shall we recognize it. All knowledge is therefore re-cognition – recalling or remembering the essence or true nature that we once knew.[7]

This theory implies that our soul is in a divine state of omniscience as long as it dwells, and participates, in a divine world of ideas or essences or natures, prior to being born. The birth of a man is his fall from grace; it is his fall from a natural or divine state of knowledge; and it is thus the origin and cause of his ignorance. (Here may be the seed of the idea that ignorance is sin or at least related to sin.)

It is clear that there is a close link between this theory of *anamnēsis* and the doctrine of the divine origin or source of our knowledge. At the same time, there is also a close link between the theory of *anamnēsis* and the doctrine of manifest truth: if, even in our depraved state of forgetfulness, we see the truth, we cannot but recognize it as the truth. So, as the result of *amamnēsis*, truth is restored to the status of that which is not forgotten and thus not concealed (*alēthēs*): it is that which is manifest.

Socrates demonstrates this in a beautiful passage of the *Meno* by helping an uneducated young slave to 'recall' the proof of a special case of the theorem of Pythagoras. Here indeed is an optimistic epistemology, and the root of Cartesianism. It seems that, in the *Meno*, Plato was conscious of the highly optimistic character of his theory; for he describes it as a doctrine which makes men eager to learn, to search, and to discover.

Yet disappointment must have come to Plato; for in the *Republic* (and also in the *Phaedrus*) we find the beginnings of a pessimistic epistemology. In the famous story of the prisoners in the cave (514ff.) he shows that the world of our experience is only a shadow, a reflection, of the real world.

And he shows that even if one of the prisoners should escape from the cave and face the real world, he would have nearly *insuperable* difficulties in seeing and understanding it – to say nothing of his difficulties in trying to make those understand who stayed behind. The difficulties in the way of an understanding of the real world are all but superhuman, and only the very few, if anybody at all, can attain to the divine state of understanding the real world – the divine state of true knowledge, of *epistēmē*.

This is a pessimistic theory with regard to almost all men, though not with regard to all. (For it teaches that truth may be attained by a few – the elect. With regard to these it is, one might say, more wildly optimistic than even the doctrine that truth is manifest.) The authoritarian and traditionalist consequences of this pessimistic theory are fully elaborated in the *Laws*.

Thus we find in Plato the first transition from an optimistic to a pessimistic epistemology. Each of these forms the basis of one of two diametrically opposed philosophies of the state and of society: on the one hand an anti-traditionalist, anti-authoritarian, revolutionary, and Utopian rationalism of the Cartesian kind, and on the other hand an authoritarian traditionalism.

This development may well be connected with the fact that the idea of an epistemological fall of man can be interpreted not only in the sense of the optimistic doctrine of *anamnēsis*, but also in a pessimistic sense.

In this latter interpretation, the fall of man condemns all mortals – or almost all – to ignorance. I think one can discern in the story of the cave (and perhaps also in the story of the fall of the city, when the Muses and their divine teaching are neglected[8]) an echo of an interesting older form of this idea. I have in mind Parmenides' doctrine that the opinions of mortals are delusions, and the result of a misguided choice – a misguided convention. (This may stem from Xenophanes' doctrine that all human knowledge is guesswork, and that his own theories are, at best, merely *similar to the truth*.[9]) The misguided convention is a linguistic one: it consists in giving *names* to what is non-existing. The idea of an epistemological fall of man can perhaps be found, as Karl Reinhardt suggested, in those words of the goddess that mark the transition from the way of truth to the way of delusive opinion.[10]

But you also shall learn how it was that delusive opinion,
Destined to pass for the truth, was forcing its way through all things.
Now of this world thus arranged to seem wholly like truth I shall tell you;
Then you will be nevermore overawed by the notions of mortals.

Thus though the fall affects all men, the truth may be revealed to the elect by an act of grace – even the truth about the unreal world of the delusions and opinions, the conventional notions and decisions, of mortal men: the unreal world of appearance that was destined to be accepted, and to be approved of, as real.[11]

The revelation received by Parmenides, and his conviction that a few may reach certainty about both the unchanging world of eternal reality and the unreal and changing world of verisimilitude and deception, were two of the main inspirations of Plato's philosophy. It was a theme to which he was for ever returning, oscillating betweeen hope, despair, and resignation.

5 Socrates' *maieutic* art of criticism versus Aristotle's induction (*epagōgē*)

Yet what interests us here is Plato's optimistic epistemology, the theory of *anamnēsis* in the *Meno*. It contains, I believe, not only the germs of Descartes' intellectualism, but also the germs of Aristotle's and especially of Bacon's theories of induction.

For Meno's slave is helped by Socrates' judicious questions to remember or recapture the forgotten knowledge which his soul possessed in its pre-natal state of omniscience. It is, I believe, this famous Socratic method, called in the *Theaetetus* the art of midwifery or *maieutic*, to which Aristotle alluded when he said that Socrates was the inventor of the method of induction.[12]

Aristotle, and also Bacon, I wish to suggest, meant by 'induction' not so much the inferring of universal laws from particular observed instances as a method by which we are guided to the point whence we can intuit, or perceive, the essence or the true nature of a thing.[13] But this, as we have seen, is precisely the aim of Socrates' *maieutic*: its aim is to help or lead us to *anamnēsis*; and *anamnēsis* is the power of seeing the true nature or essence of a thing, the nature or essence with which we were acquainted before birth, before our fall from grace. Thus the aims of the two, *maieutic* and induction, are the same. (Incidentally, Aristotle taught that the result of an induction – the intuition of the essence – was to be expressed by a definition of that essence.)

Now let us look more closely at the two procedures. The *maieutic* art of Socrates consists, essentially, in asking questions designed to destroy prejudices; false beliefs which are often traditional or fashionable beliefs; false answers, given in the spirit of ignorant cocksureness. Socrates himself does not pretend to know. His attitude is described by Aristotle in the words, 'Socrates raised questions but gave no answers; for he confessed that he did not know.'[14] Thus Socrates' *maieutic* is not an art that aims at teaching any belief, but one that aims at purging or cleansing[15] the soul of its false beliefs, its seeming knowledge, its prejudices. It achieves this by teaching us to doubt our own convictions.

Fundamentally the same procedure is part of Bacon's induction.

6 The cosmological origins of Euclidean geometry

(1) I should like first to say how much I too enjoyed Professor Szabó's wonderful paper. His thesis, that the axiomatic method of Euclidean geometry was borrowed from the methods of argument employed by the Eleatic philosophers, is an extremely interesting and original one. Of course, his thesis is highly conjectural, as must be any such thesis, in view of the scanty information that has come down to us about the origins of Greek science.

(2) Szabó, it seems to me, has only explained one fact of Euclidean geometry, how the *method* employed in it was invented. The question, to which he has offered a tentative answer is: 'How did Euclid come to adopt the *axiomatic method* in his geometry?' However, I wish to suggest that there is a second, perhaps more fundamental, question. It is this: 'What was the *problem* of Euclidean geometry?' Or to put it another way: why was it *geometry* that was developed so systematically by Euclid?

(3) These two questions are different, but, I believe, closely connected. I should like just to mention a historical conjecture of my own about this second problem.[16] It is this: Euclidean geometry is not a treatise on abstract, axiomatic mathematics, but rather a treatise on cosmology; that it was proposed to solve a problem which had arisen in cosmology, the problem posed by the discovery of irrationals. That geometry was the theory dealing with the irrationals (as opposed to arithmetic, which deals with 'the odd and the even') is repeatedly stated by Aristotle.[17]

The discovery of irrational numbers destroyed the Pythagorean programme of deriving cosmology (and geometry) from the arithmetic of natural numbers. Plato realized this fact, and sought to replace the arithmetical theory of the world by a geometrical theory of the world.[18] The famous inscription over the gates of his Academy meant exactly what it said: that arithmetic was not enough, and that geometry was the fundamental science. His *Timaeus* contains, as opposed to the previous arithmetical atomism, a *geometrical* atomic theory in which the fundamental particles were all constructed out of two triangles which had as sides the (irrational) square roots of two and three. Plato bequeathed his problem to his successors, and they solved it. Euclid's *Elements* fulfilled Plato's programme, since in it geometry is developed autonomously, that is, without the 'arithmetical' assumption of commensurability or rationality. Plato's largely cosmological problems were solved so successfuly by Euclid that they were forgotten: the *Elements* is regarded as the first textbook of pure deductive mathematics, instead of the cosmological treatise which I believe it to have been.

As to Professor Szabó's problem, why the *axiomatic method* was first employed by Euclid, I think that an analysis of the cosmological prehistory of Euclidean geometry may also help to solve this problem. For the methods of solving problems are frequently inherited with those problems. The Presocratics were trying to solve cosmological problems, and in so doing, they invented the critical method, and applied it to their speculations. Parmenides, who was one of the greatest of these cosmologists, used this method in developing what may perhaps have been the first deductive system. One may even call it the first deductive physical theory – or the last pre-physical theory before that of the atomists, whose theory originated with a refutation of Parmenides' theory (with the refutation, more especially, of Parmenides' conclusion that motion is impossible, since the world is full[19]).

None of this is inconsistent with the views of Szabó, who finds the origins of the deductive method in the Eleatic method of dialectic, or of critical debate. But the link with cosmology adds an extra dimension, in my view a necessary one, to his discussion. For it seems to me that the sharp distinction, on the basis of their different *methods*, between mathematics and the natural sciences would have been foreign to the Greeks. Indeed, it was the remarkable success of Euclid which brought about this distinction in the first place. For up to (and, in my opinion, including) Euclid, Greek mathematics and Greek cosmology were one or very nearly so. To understand fully the discovery of '*mathematical methods*', we have to remember the *cosmological problems* which they were trying to solve using these methods. Parmenides was a cosmologist; and it was in support of Parmenides' cosmology that Zeno developed his arguments which, as Professor Szabó stresses, inaugurated the specific Greek way of mathematical thought.

7 Plato, *Timaeus* 54e–55a

τρίγωνα δὲ ἰσόπλευρα συνιστάμενα τέτταρα κατὰ σύντρεις ἐπιπέδους γωνίας μίαν στερεαν γωνίαν ποιεῖ, τῆς ἀμβλυτάτης τῶν ἐπιπέδων γωνιῶν ἐφεξῆς γεγονυῖαν.

This sentence describes the oldest stereometric construction. Yet I have found no translation or commentary that does not misunderstand it.

The construction described is this. Take four equilateral triangles and arrange them so that any three adjacent plane angles complement each other to 180°; that is, to 'the most obtuse of the plane angles'. (For clarity, I am shading the triangle in the centre.)

Now bend up successively *two* of the non-shaded triangles so that they, together with the shaded triangle, make a solid angle. (Thus, in the order of the adjacent angles, the solid angle amounted to, or came up to, the

most obtuse of plane angles; and it was formed as a next step, or successively, after this most obtuse of the plane angles.) Then 'when four such
[solid] angles are produced, the first solid figure is constructed' (55a).

The presence of the diagram which Plato indicates somewhat sketchily,
assuming perhaps that it was well known, makes any elaborate verbal
description redundant.

I suggest the following translation:

Let four equilateral triangles be put together in such a way that any
three adjacent (σύντρεις) plane angles make one solid angle which is
formed successively after the most obtuse of the plane angles.

The sense remains about the same if we translate (constructing τῆς
ἀμβλυτάτης, as say, *gen. pretii*): ' . . . which in adjacent order was equal
to [or: came to] the most obtuse of the plane angles'.

The usual misunderstandings (e.g. in Archer-Hind, Bury, Cornford,
Taylor), which are grave, are due to (*a*) a failure to recognize the intended
geometrical construction, and (*b*) a translation of ἐφεξῆς as 'next in order
of *magnitude*'; which clearly makes no sense here.

In Euclid ἡ ἐφεξῆς γωνία means the adjacent angle. Although the first
of my two proposed versions seems to be the easier one, Euclid's terminology suggests, I think, that something like the second may deserve consideration. (Moreover, the construction of ἐφεξῆς with the genitive seems
unique, *at least* in Plato, and therefore perhaps not above suspicion; though
admittedly the genitive depending on γίγνομαι, while it occurs in
Aristophanes and Xenophon, would also be unique in Plato.)

I am grateful to Professor Charles Kahn for discussing the two suggested
versions with me (he feels that the second can hardly be right), and to
Professor W. K. C. Guthrie for permitting me to add to this note the
following comment from a letter of his:

> ἐφεξῆς certainly does mean 'adjacent' in Plato as well as 'succes-
> sively', as when at *Parmenides* 149a he says that for one thing to
> touch another it must be a separate thing but ἐφεξῆς. I think,
> however, (though I am a bit unsure of this – it is a difficult
> sentence) that the word order is in favour of taking ἐφεξῆς
> γεγονυῖαν closely together as 'formed successively.'

Notes

1 See Gilbert Murray, *The Rise of the Greek Epic*, 3rd edn, Oxford, 1924, p. 96.
2 See DK 22 B92 and 32; cp. also B93, 41, 64, and 50.
3 DK 22 B28 (see also B94 and cp. Orpheus DK 1 B14 and Plato's *Laws* 716a).
4 The '*goddess*' of Parmenides (DK B1, line 22) was identified by Sextus, *Adv.
Math.* VII, 113, with the goddess Dikē (of lines 14–17), in an otherwise
admittedly dubious interpretation. It seems to me that the text strongly
suggests this identification. The widely accepted view (cp. W. K. C. Guthrie,

A History of Greek Philosophy, vol. II, Cambridge, 1965, p. 10; L. Tarán, *Parmenides*, Princeton, 1965, p. 31) that Parmenides leaves his goddess 'unnamed' seems to me without foundation, though it has been supported by subtle arguments. Yet most of these arguments (especially Tarán's) make it incomprehensible why Dikē (and perhaps even Anankē in B8: 30) was not left 'nameless' also. My own positive arguments for identifying the 'goddess' with Dikē are two: (1) The whole balance of B1, down to line 23, and especially 11–22, suggests the identification, as the following details show: Dikē (though on the other view she would be no more than a turnkey) is introduced elaborately, in keeping with the whole passage; she is the main person acting from line 14 down to line 20 (*arērote*); also, the sentence does not seem to stop here – not indeed until the end of line 21, just before the 'goddess' comes in. Moreover, between line 20 and the end of line 21 no more is said than: 'Straight on the road through the gates did the maidens steady the horses.' This in no way implies that Parmenides' journey (elaborately described up to this point) continues any further; rather I find here a strong suggestion that, upon passing through the gates (where he must encounter Dikē), his journey ends. And how can we believe that the highest authority and main speaker of the poem enters not only unnamed, but without any introduction or any further ado – even without one epithet? And why should the maidens have to introduce Parmenides to Dikē (and 'appease' her) who, on the view here combated, is the inferior person, but not to the superior one? (2) If we believe (as I do) with Guthrie, op. cit., II, p. 32 (see also pp. 23f., and Tarán, op. cit., pp. 5 and 61f.) that there is ('cumulative') 'evidence that Parmenides, in his criticism of earlier thought, had Heraclitus especially in mind', then the role played by Dikē in the *logos* of Heraclitus (see the preceding note) would make it understandable why Parmenides in his *antilogia* cites her now as his authority for his own *logos*. (Incidentally, there seems to me no difficulty in assuming that in the important passage B8, line 14, Dikē is speaking about herself, but great difficulty in assuming that the 'goddess' speaks in these terms about her own turnkey or gate keeper.)

5 Compare also Heraclitus DK 22 B54, 123; 88 and 126 contain hints that *unobservable* changes may yield observable opposites.

6 For the relation between *kinship* and *knowledge* (cp. Russell's 'knowledge by acquaintance') see also *Phaedo* 79d; *Republic* 611d; and *Laws* 899d.

7 Cp. *Phaedo* 72e ff.; 75e; 76a–b. Like all great epistemological theories, the theory of *anamnēsis* (or of 'innate ideas') has influenced religion and literature. Bryan Magee has drawn my attention to Wordsworth's 'Ode: Intimations of Immortality from Recollections of Early Childhood'.

8 See *Republic* 546d.

9 Xenophanes' fragment here alluded to is DK B35:

These things are, we conjecture, like the truth.

For the idea of *truthlikeness* – of a doctrine that partly corresponds to the facts (and so may '*seem like the real*' or '*pass for the real*', as Parmenides has it here) – see *C. & R.*, especially pp. 236f., where *verisimilitude* is contrasted with *probability*, and Addendum 1 to Essay 1 above.

10 For the *naming* of what is non-existing (non-existing opposites) cp. Parmenides B9 with B8: 53: 'for they decided to give names'. Concerning the transition to the way of delusive opinion (*doxa*), see Karl Reinhardt, *Parmenides*, 2nd edn, Frankfurt-am-Main, 1959, p. 26; see also pp. 5–11 for the text of Parmenides,

DK B1: 31–2, which are the first two lines here quoted. My third line is Parmenides B8: 60, cp. Xenophanes B35. My fourth line is Parmenides B8: 61. (Added in 1979). The last word of B1: 31, *dokounta*, can be translated either by 'opinion' or by 'seeming' or 'appearance'. After some wavering, I stick to 'opinion' because it is the ideology that forces its way through all things. [Cp., however, p. 131 note 56, where *dokounta* is finally translated by 'appearance'. Ed.]

11 It is interesting to contrast this pessimistic view of the necessity of error (or of *almost* necessary error) with the optimism of Descartes, or of Spinoza, who, in his 76th letter, paragraph 5 (*Opera, Edito Tertia*, ed. J. van Vloten and J. P. N. Land, Amsterdam, 1914), scorns those 'who dream of an impure spirit inspiring us with false ideas which are similar to true ones (*veri similes*)'; see also *C. & R.* pp. 236f, and Addendum 1 to Essay 1.

12 *Metaphysics* 1078b17–33; see also 987b1.

13 Aristotle meant by 'induction' (*epagōgē*) at least two different things which he sometimes links together. One is a method by which we are 'led to intuit the general principle' (*An. Pr.* 67a22f., on *anamnēsis* in the *Meno*; *An. Post.* 71a7, 81a38ff., 100b4f.). The other (*Topics* 105a13, 156a4, 157a34; *An. Post.* 78a35, 81b5ff.) is a method of *adducing* (particular) *evidence* – *positive* evidence rather than *critical* evidence or counterexamples. The first method seems to me the older one, and the one which can be better connected with Socrates and his *maieutic* method of criticism and counterexamples. The second method seems to originate in the attempt to systematize induction logically or, as Aristotle (*An. Pr.* 68b15ff.) puts it, to construct a valid 'syllogism which springs out of induction'; this, to be valid, must of course be a syllogism of perfect or complete induction (complete enumeration of instances); and ordinary induction in the sense of the second method here mentioned is just a weakened (and invalid) form of this valid syllogism. (See also *O.S.*, note 33 to Chapter 11 and the Introduction to this volume.)

14 See Aristotle, *Sophist. El.* 183b7; cp. Plato's *Theaetetus* 150c–d, 157c, 161b.

15 Cp. the allusion to the rite called *amphidromia* – a purification ceremony after the birth of a child (which sometimes ended in the purge or exposure of the child) alluded to in *Theaetetus* 160e; see also *Phaedo* 67b, 69b/c.

16 The conjecture is stated more fully in 'The Nature of Philosophical Problems and their Roots in Science', Chapter 2 of *C. & R.*, Sections VIII–IX.

17 For references see *C. & R.*, p. 87, note 42.

18 All this is discussed at some length in Section 1 above.

19 *C. & R.*, pp. 79–83, and now especially in Essays 3–5 above.

ESSAY 10

CONCLUDING REMARKS ON SUPPORT AND COUNTERSUPPORT

How induction becomes counterinduction, and the *epagōgē* returns to the *elenchus*

Already before I wrote Addendum 18 to the 7th edition of *Logik der Forschung* (which I still consider fatal for the philosophy of induction), that is, in the summer of 1981, I had started work on a simplification and clarification of a new proof against probabilistic induction.

I should never have found this proof without receiving a letter written to me by David Miller, my friend and collaborator. I saw immediately the importance of this letter, and I gave a short account of its content in footnote 2 on page 326 of *Realism and the Aim of Science*. This footnote contained, however, something that neither of us immediately saw: it turned out to be the decisive impetus for the proof, which we eventually published in *Nature* in April 1983.[1] The present version contains a further simplification and improvement of the proof, together with some historical remarks about Aristotle and Socrates.

I

I begin with the definition of (probabilistic) support of *a* by *b*: *s*(*a*, *b*), the support of *a* by *b* in the sense of probability theory.

Definition: $s(a, b) = p(a, b) - p(a)$

The *support* of *a* by *b* is thus defined as the *increase in probability* of *a* in the light of the information *b* (owing to the occurrence of *b* after the comma). In

First published in Logik der Forschung, *8th edn, Tübingen, 1984, 19th addendum, pp. 445–52. {Translated from the German by the Editor with minor corrections and additions by the Author. In Section VIII, five short paragraphs have been carried over from Sir Karl's speech in honour of Sir John Eccles, 'Critical Remarks on the Knowledge of Lower and Higher Organisms', printed in* Experimental Brain Research, *Supplement 9, 1984, pp. 24f., Ed.}*

case $p(a, b)$, i.e. the probability of a, given b, is *greater* than $p(a)$, b *supports* (or sustains) the hypothesis a. If $p(a, b)$ is *smaller* than $p(a)$, then a is *undermined* by b. In this case $s(a, b) < 0$, and we speak of a negative support, or of a (positive) *countersupport*. In case $p(a, b) = p(a)$, then $s(a, b) = 0$, and we say that a is neither supported nor undermined by b: in this case a and b are (probabilistically) independent of each other.

II

Theoreticians of induction agree to interpret the positive *support* of a hypothesis h by an empirical test statement e as induction, and this interpretation can be defended by the following argument.

A *test statement* e for the hypothesis h is one that can be derived from h together with our background knowledge b (which, we assume, contains the initial conditions); that is, e follows from h in the presence of the background knowledge b. Accordingly we have

(1) $\qquad p(he, b) = p(h, b)$,

since in the presence of b, the statement he says no more than the statement h. From the multiplication theorem we may then conclude that

(2) $\qquad p(he, b) = p(h, eb)\, p(e, b) = p(h, b)$

and further, from a theorem of probability, $0 \leqslant p(e, b) \leqslant 1$, that

(3) $\qquad p(h, eb) \geqslant p(h, b)$.

We may, on the other hand, generalize our definition of $s(a, b)$ to three variables:

Definition: $\quad s(h, e, b) = p(h, eb) - p(h, b)$

(the support in the presence of b). If (1) is valid, then we find

(4) $\qquad s(h, e, b) \geqslant 0$.

That is to say, if e follows from h in the presence of b, then e supports hypothesis h in the presence of b, and $s(h, e, b)$ is always *non-negative*.

I shall now show that these in themselves valid derivations cannot be interpreted as an argument for induction. The argument is very simple (and analogous to the addition made in 1983 in Addendum 18; see *L.d.F.*, 8th edn, p. 442).

From (2) and the definition of support follow:

(5) $\qquad s(h, e, b) = p(h, b)/\, p(e, b) - p(h, b) = p(h, b)\,(1/p(e, b) - 1)$
(6) $\qquad s(h, e, b) = p(h, b)(1 - p(e, b))/p(e, b)$.

Now $(1 - p(e, b))/p(e, b) \geq 0$ obviously only depends on e; and whenever $p(e, b) < 1$, then $(1 - p(e, b))/ p(e, b) > 0$. This explains that when e follows from bb then the support is always positive. However, since this only depends on e, all those invalidating consequences follow which have been mentioned in the addition of 1983, mentioned above.

III

In the following I shall liberate myself from the assumption that e follows from bb (or any similar assumption) and show quite generally, for any statement h and for any statement e, that if there should be anything like inductive (non-deductive) support, then it must always be less than zero; that is: *all inductive support turns out to be countersupport.*

I am therefore going to work with $s(h, e)$ instead of with $s(h, e, b)$, since the derivations can be generalized without difficulty from two variables to three.

The following theorems are valid in general for any given statement h and for any given statement e:

Theorem 1. $s(h, e) = s(h \vee e, e) + s(h \leftarrow e, e)$.

Here $h \vee e$ is to be read 'h or e', a statement which is true if and only if at least one of its two components, h and e, is true; thus $h \vee e$ follows deductively from h as well as from e.

$h \leftarrow e$, to be read 'h if e', is true and only if h is true or e is false. ($h \leftarrow e$ is more usually written $e \rightarrow h$, 'if e then h'.) From e and $h \leftarrow e$ follows he. Therefore we have $p(h \leftarrow e, e) = p(he, e) = p(h, e)$. From this follows $s(h \vee e, e) = 1 - p(h \vee e) = p(\overline{he})$; $s(h \leftarrow e, e) = - Exc(h, e) = (1 - p(h, e)) (1 - p(h)) = ct(h, e) \, ct(h)$; see note 1. So we have

Theorem 2. $s(h \vee e, e) \geq 0 \geq s(h \leftarrow e, e)$.

Thus the first summand in Theorem 1 is always a positive support (or zero), while the second summand is either zero or negative – i.e. a negative support, a countersupport.

Theorem 3. $s(h \vee e, e) \geq 0$ is always positive, since $h \vee e$ follows from e, and so $p(h \vee e, e) = 1$. The explanation of the positivity of $s(h \vee e, e)$ is thus that the support of $h \vee e$ by e is a *purely deductive support*.

Theorem 4. The negative factor,

$$s(h \leftarrow e, e) = p(h \leftarrow e, e) - p(h \leftarrow e) = - Exc(h, e) \leq 0$$

(see note 1), is very interesting. The conditional statement $h \leftarrow e$ ('h if e', or 'h in case of e') is, if e is given as a premise, equivalent to the conjunction he. This is the reason why $p(h, e) = p(h \leftarrow e, e) = p(he, e) = p(h, e)$. Furthermore, $h \leftarrow e$ is the logically weakest (and therefore the absolutely most probable) statement, which is strong enough (in the presence of e) to have h as a consequence. Thus if e is given, then $h \leftarrow e$ is necessary and sufficient for h. Therefore $h \leftarrow e$ is precisely what, in addition to e, we need in order to get h: what is *not already deductively entailed* in e; precisely that statement by which e must be extended in order to give h. Any other statement x which can do that is stronger. And for any such statement x (which does not give too much but only $ex = he$) we have $x \leftarrow e = h \leftarrow e$, and from this

$$p(x \leftarrow e) = p(h \leftarrow e),$$

and further from this

$$s(x, e) = s(x \vee e, e) + s(h \leftarrow e, e),$$

as before. Nothing is therefore easier for any such x (in relation to e) than to distinguish between its purely deductive and its (in logic unambiguously determined) non-purely-deductive component:

$$x = (x \vee e)(x \leftarrow e).$$

Only the second component, $x \leftarrow e$, can be called 'inductive' or 'ampliative'. But its support by e is negative: it is a *countersupport*.

Theorem 5. If now, according to Theorems 1, 2, and 3, any support $s(h, e)$ can be described as the sum of a purely deductive support and a remaining negative support – that is, a countersupport – then we can say: the fact that some given support $s(h, e)$ is positive is explained by the support provided by e for its purely deductive component $h \vee e$; and the support from this component is bigger than the countersupport from the non-deductive component $h \leftarrow e$, that is, the countersupport $s(h \leftarrow e, e) = Exc(h,'e)$. If therefore the non-deductive factor is not zero, and if there exists something like an inductive component, then its contribution to the total support $s(h, e)$ is *always negative*. Since every non-deductive support is negative, then every inductive support (if it exists) is also generally a *countersupport*. Induction (to the extent it exists) is therefore *always counterinduction*.

IV

Here, I assert, ends the history of induction. It ends precisely at the place where, if we are to believe Aristotle, it began: with Socrates. For Aristotle called Socrates' method of *learning from examples* 'induction' (*epagōgē*). We may accept this. But the decisive examples in the Socratic argumentation were all *counterexamples*, and his way of inference distinguishes itself clearly from Aristotle's induction or *epagōgē*: the Socratic argumentation is the *elenchus*: the refutation, the countersupport, the undermining (of dogmas), in particular through the use of counterexamples.

V

I am most ready to admit that I have done Aristotle wrong many times. But I was, and I am still, provoked to protests by the development from the Presocratics and Socrates through Plato to Aristotle. For it is a development from critical rationalism to rationalistic dogma: to Aristotle's demonstrable science, to his idea that scientific knowledge (*epistēmē*) is secure and certainly true, since it is demonstrable knowledge.

Critical rationalism is the attitude of the Presocratics. They all emphasized (even Parmenides) that we mortals cannot really *know*, since we can have *no certain knowledge*. This critical rationalism reached its height in Socrates' method of refutation, the *elenchus*, which Parmenides was most probably the first to use.[2] This method was, of course, well known to Aristotle. For he characterizes Socrates' method (in *De Sophisticis Elenchis*) in the following way (perhaps without distinguishing Socrates' *elenchus* from his *maieutic*): 'Socrates', Aristotle writes, 'was in the habit of asking questions, but not of answering them; for he admitted that he did not know.'[3]

Yet it appears from the context[4] that Aristotle did not really believe Socrates when he again and again asserted that he did not know: Aristotle took these assertions as ironical gestures, as tricks, or perhaps as stock phrases by means of which Socrates tried to distinguish himself clearly from the Sophists; from the Sophists, who claimed to know and who asserted their possession of wisdom, but who really didn't know anything, and whose proofs as well as whose refutations were not really valid, but only served to make the better case appear the worse. Thus Aristotle may have truly believed that Socrates was wise, but that he only pretended not to know.

But Socrates, the searcher for truth, did not pretend; nor did the great searchers of truth before him. They knew that they did not know: and hardly that. Aristotle could not believe this. For he was the man of certain knowledge, of demonstrable knowledge (*epistēmē*).

VI

Aristotelian logic is the theory of demonstrable knowledge; and Dante was right when he called Aristotle 'the master of all who know'. He is the founder of the proof, the *apodeixis*: of the apodeictic syllogism. He is a scientist in the scientistic sense and the theoretician of scientific proof and the authoritarian claims of Science.

Yet Aristotle himself became the discoverer (or rather, the rediscoverer) of the impossibility of knowledge: of the problem of demonstrable knowledge and of the impossibility of its solution.

For if all knowledge, all science, has to be demonstrable, then this leads us (he discovered) to an infinite regress. This is because any proof consists of premises and conclusions, of initial statements and of concluding statements; and if the initial statements are yet to be proved, the concluding statements are also yet to be proved.

It is as simple as that.

VII

Nevertheless, Aristotle knew that he knew. Incapable of admitting to himself that there does not exist any knowledge in the sense of his idea of *epistēmē*; incapable of admitting that all knowledge is fallible knowledge, conjectural knowledge – even (as I often stress) the most convincing intuitive knowledge, and the knowledge of the natural sciences – Aristotle found a way out: *the theory of induction*, the leading onward, through examples, to the sight of the essence; and built into this, *the theory of definition*: the essential definition as the foundation of proof, as the principle (*archē*) from which the proof departs.

The general attitude that brought about this remarkable, though erroneous and fatal theory, and that immortalized the theory of induction until our own time, was *essentialism*, which Aristotle had taken over from Plato by weakening the Platonic doctrine of forms: the idea that in every thing (not outside it, as with Plato) there resides an essence, its *ousia* or essence or nature, which contains everything of importance to that thing – all that is worth knowing about that thing, and all that can be known about it. Although Aristotle took over this doctrine from Plato's doctrine of forms, he attributed it to Socrates.

For Aristotle the definition, or more precisely the definition of essence, became the 'first premise' (*archē*), the basic axiom of all proofs: it occupied an exceptional position, since it did not need to be (and could not be) proved deductively, i.e. syllogistically. (In those places where Aristotle appears to say the contrary, he thinks of induction as a kind of syllogism.)

It is the function of induction (*epagōgē*), the leading forward (of the pupil) through examples to the sight of the essence, to intuit the essence;

it is a kind of half-syllogistic proof, with the aim of securing the definition as true and correct. Yet many times Aristotle seems to be conscious of the fact that this induction is *not* a proof, not a demonstration. He says more often that *not all* scientific statements are demonstrable, and that the first principles cannot be demonstrable, since we are threatened by an infinite regress. But to my knowledge he does not say that, precisely for this reason, *no scientific statement* can be demonstrable. For the possibility of deriving an *undemonstrated* statement from another statement is no proof of it. It is especially clear that no scientific statement is demonstrable if, with Aristotle, one tries to identify certain and secure knowledge with syllo-gistically demonstrable knowledge. Aristotle's way out is in fact to con-sider induction as a kind of half-proof or perhaps as three-quarters of a proof.

It is clear that the invention of induction and the doctrine of essential definitions did not lead to the result hoped for: to a positive solution of the problem of certain and secure knowledge. And Aristotle attributed this invention, which he viewed with some uneasiness, to Socrates – to the man who did not use induction (*epagōgē*) by examples but refutation (the *elenchus*), which never tries to prove, but only to disprove; to the man, whom Aristotle did not really believe, who knew and said that he did not know.

But (as my friend Arne Petersen says) most people are terrified by Socrates' insight that we do not know. (Perhaps this was why they killed him.) And so they reach out for a theory of induction – a theory that presents what are in fact (as I think) our guesses, our conjectures, as the conclusions of inductive inferences, derived from observational (and there-fore they think secure) premises.

VIII

In our time they appeal to probability, and to the calculus of probability. Perhaps the explanation is the following.

In deduction we know the difference between a valid and an invalid inference. 'All swans are white, so if this bird is a swan it will be white' is valid while 'All swans are white, so if this is a herring it will be red' is invalid.

Induction is, of course, never valid; or rather, in those limiting cases in which it becomes valid (in which all cases have been observed) it turns into deduction. How, then, can we distinguish a 'good' inductive inference such as: 'All observed ravens are black, therefore all ravens are black' from a 'bad' inductive inference such as 'All observed ravens are black, therefore all herrings are red'?

The answer to this question is, presumably, this: an inductive inference must be highly probable. If the probability reaches 1, then the induction becomes a deduction. If it is near to 1, it is a good inductive argument. If it is less than $1/2$, it is a bad inductive argument, for this means that the negation of the conclusion is more probable than the conclusion.

Although this is only a first and a very rough approach to a probabilistic theory of induction, it indicates the need for such a theory. Since inductive inferences are not valid or secure, we must have some theory like probability theory to indicate better or worse, more nearly valid or more obviously invalid inferences.

We can write $p(x) = 1/6$ for 'The probability of x is $1/6$' and $p(x, y) = 1/3$ for 'The probability of x, given y, is $1/3$.' Here x may be the proposition 'The next throw with this die will be four' and y may be the information 'We regard only an even number as a throw.'

Now let a be 'The next throw will be two' and let b be 'We regard only an even prime number as a throw.' Since 2 is the only even prime, a follows deductively from b, and we have therefore $p(a, b) = 1$ for a case such that a is a deductive conclusion from the 'given' premise b. It has been hoped (at least since Daniel Bernoulli 1766) that for inductive inferences high probabilities could be reached, although of course short of 1.

But this is precisely not true, and as we have seen, it can be *proved* not to be true.

IX

All knowledge is conjectural knowledge. The different conjectures or hypotheses are our intuitive inventions (and therefore *a priori* – before experience, even though not *a priori* valid). They get weeded out through experience – through bitter experience – and so we become anxious to replace them by better conjectures: in that, and only in that, consists the contribution of experience to science.

All the rest – and so indeed all – is our own activity: our own search for testable consequences of our theories – for possible weak spots. We search for experimental conditions that allow us, if possible, to expose the errors of our theories. And even in our experiences, in our observations, in our sensations, we are active: active like the bats that are actively sending out their acoustic radar.

Notes

1 This proof in *Nature* (vol. 302, pp. 687f.) was based upon an algebraic derivation from the equation for the *Excess* (*Exc*(a, b); see *L.d.F.* p. 307), which I found in 1938 and some of whose advantages I had indicated on p. 396 of *C. & R.* There I introduced the definition:

Definition: $Exc(a, b) = p(a \leftarrow b) - p(a, b)$,

where '$a \leftarrow b$' can be read as 'a if b' and is the same as $b \rightarrow a$ ('if b then a').

The derivation shows that $Exc(a, b) = p(\bar{a}, b)\, p(\bar{b}) \geqslant 0$.

$$0 \leqslant p(\bar{a}, b)p(\bar{b}) = (1 - p(a, b))(1 - p(b)) = 1 - p(a, b) - p(b) + p(ab)$$
$$= 1 - (p(b) - p(ab)) - p(a, b) = 1 - p(\bar{a}b) - p(a, b)$$
$$= p(a \leftarrow b) - p(a, b) = Exc\,(a, b) \geqslant 0.$$

As $p(a, b) = p(a \leftarrow b, b)$ we then get:

$$p(a \leftarrow b, b) - p(a \leftarrow b) = -\, Exc\,(a, b) \leqslant 0.$$

$a \leftarrow b$ is therefore always undermined (countersupported) by b. (For a more detailed proof, see the *Philosophical Transactions of the Royal Society of London*, Series A (Mathematical and Physical Sciences), vol. 321, 1987, pp. 569–91.)

2 DK 28 B7: 5.
3 Aristotle, *De Sophisticis Elenchis* 33, 183b7. Still more freely: 'Socrates' routine was to pose questions and not to answer them.' It was, as a matter of fact, a question not about a habit but about a method.
4 Ibid. 'We have explained the reason' is likely to refer to 165a19–30.

APPENDIX
Popper's late fragments on Greek philosophy

ON PARMENIDES (II)

Fragment 0

Introduction

This paper continues and amplifies my first brief paper on Parmenides published in *The Classical Quarterly* in 1992; it was entitled 'How the Moon Might Shed Some of her Light upon the Two Ways of Parmenides' [Essay 3]. Here I shall refer to this earlier paper as Paper 1, and to the present one as Paper 2.

Paper 2 consists of the following sections:

1   More on Parmenides' Fragment B16.
    a   On the translation;
    b   On Aristotle's View;
    c   On Theophrastus' View;
    d   Where in the Poem does Fragment B16 belong?
2   More on the Relation Between the Way of Truth and the Unsurpassed Way of Conjecture through the World of Human Illusions.
3   Parmenides' Blind Sister: A Fairy Story.
4   The Proem.
5   Endnote.

The search for manuscripts on Xenophanes in Sir Karl's Nachlass *also brought out documents relating to Heraclitus, Parmenides, and Democritus, as well as some sketches for a paper on a geometrical proof in Aristotle's* Metaphysics. *As none of these turned out to be complete and final, they have been collected in this appendix as 'Popper's Late Fragments on Greek Philosophy'. Ed.*

APPENDIX

Fragment 1

1 More on Parmenides' fragment B16

Parmenides' fragment B16 is difficult to understand. It reads, in Theophrastus' version (with some well-known emendations), like this:

> What is at any one time in their much-erring sense organs' mixture
> That's what men use as a stop-gap for thought. For they take as equal:
> Reasoning powers of man – and his sense organs' nature or mixture.
> What in this mixture prevails, this is thinking in each man and all.

This, I hold, is a highly ironical attack on the same theory that Aristotle
mentions [in his *Metaphysics* 1009b21] and a few lines later ascribes to
Parmenides.

For B16 describes the theory thus. The changing content of our sense
organs, that is, the mixture of dark and light in our eyes, which constantly
changes, or of noise and noiselessness in our ears – in other words, our
sense organs' sensations – that is all that constitutes our consciousness; so
thought, thinking, reasoning is 'really' the same as the sequence in time of
our sensations. What prevails in our thinking – our thought – is the same
as what prevails at this moment in the senses.

This is the sensualistic empiricism which Parmenides hates and which
he scorns: he hardly argues against it except by ridiculing the doubleheads who hold such views [compare fragment B6: 5, translated here in
Section 1(d)]. In fragment B16, he attacks the same people [as in B6] by
wittily suggesting that their sensualistic theory of thought is true – for
those who hold it. They, indeed, are unthinking, thoughtless – unless we
mean (as they do) that, for each man and all, thinking = the change of our
sensations, and conclude that what prevails = what is at a moment the
stronger sensation.

(a) On the translation

I must admit that I have no longer any doubts about the interpretation of
B16 [outlined in several essays in this collection, especially Essays 3 and
4]. (So much so that I expect that everybody will say 'Of course, we always
have understood it that way!' And I even think that the 'limbs', and
perhaps even 'the much-bent limbs', will continue, 'for we always understood the Greek text'.)

My interpretation and translation fit both Aristotle and Theophrastus;
they fit Parmenides' intention and temper. As a valid criticism of the
eternal sensualist empiricism, it is of the utmost interest, for it shows,
among other things, that this empiricism must have existed, say shortly
before 500 BC, long before Protagoras and very long before Carnap.

Parmenides' irony and scorn are, of course, made unmistakable by the reference in the very first line to the πολυπλάγκτων μελέων, the much-erring sense organs. If this is misinterpreted ('much-bent limbs' is still the favourite mistranslation), then the irony is missed. Aristotle missed the irony because he misremembered πολυπλάγκτων and replaced it by πολυ-κάμπτων (a possible translation could be 'much-neglected'). So in his view there is no irony in fragment B16, and for Aristotle B16 gives a formulation of that sensualistic theory which Aristotle himself describes just a few lines before he quotes Parmenides.

(b) On Aristotle's view

Aristotle's quotation from Parmenides (B16) [appears in the] context of his *Metaphysics* 1009b12:

> And quite in general, it is because these thinkers suppose that [all] thought is sense impression, and that sense impression [in its turn] is a kind of physical change [in the sense organs], that they say that what appears to our senses will by [causal] necessity be true. For these are the reasons why . . . Empedocles and Democritus and almost all the rest are victims of opinions such as these. For Empedocles says that those who change their physical condition also change their thoughts.

Now come two quotations from Empedocles, and then Aristotle says:

> And Parmenides too elaborates the same view:
> What at each time in the much-humble organs of sense is their mixture,
> That is his thought as it comes to each man. For these two are the same thing:
> One is his thinking, and the other his sense organs' physical structure.
> What in this structure prevails is his thought, for each man and all.

In the sequence, Aristotle elaborates at length his presentation of the theory which he believes is held by Parmenides and many others. For example he writes (in 1010a1): 'But the reason why these thinkers hold such views is that . . . they suppose that reality is confined to sensible things.'

Now I say, first, that Aristotle's version of Parmenides B16, as here translated, fits perfectly into Aristotle's context: Aristotle thinks that Parmenides defends the under-valued senses, and that he supports the theory which he describes – a materialistic empiricism.

(The correctness of my translation of fragment B16 in Aristotle's version can hardly be questioned once Aristotle's *Parts of the Animals* is consulted, in which *melos* is exemplified as a sense organ like the eye.)

So everything here [seems] in perfect order.

However, secondly, when Theophrastus wrote on perception, he was at one place discussing Empedocles' problem: whether we perceive by associating with our momentary sense perception a *similar* one from the past or [a] contrasting one (that preceded it immediately). For reasons unknown, but probably because Aristotle had quoted Empedocles and Parmenides together, Theophrastus repeated the passage that Aristotle had quoted from Parmenides (that is, B16), correcting silently Aristotle's memory lapse. (He probably knew that Aristotle often quoted from memory and sometimes made mistakes.) Yet the passage did not really fit his context; and so he made a remark on Parmenides on death, which seemed to fit into the context, and which is quite interesting from another point of view.

(c) On Theophrastus' view

Thus we come to our second source of fragment B16, Theophrastus' *De Sensu* (DK 28A46), where he silently corrects his teacher's text. The new text, with *meleōn polyplanktōn* in the first line instead of Aristotle's *meleōn polykamptōn* (the only relevant difference), is therefore to be preferred. Theophrastus, like Aristotle, takes fragment B16 to represent Parmenides' own theory, and he undoubtedly does not attach much significance to Aristotle's slip of memory.

That, like Aristotle, he takes *melea*, to mean 'sense organs' and that he agrees with Aristotle's reading can be seen from the fact that (1) he is writing *de sensu*, and (2) his comment, immediately after quoting B16, is that 'he [Parmenides] regards perception and thought − *to aisthanesthai kai to phronein* − as the same'.

His other remarks are irrelevant to our problem of a clear translation of the meaning of fragment B16, and they actually seem to me wrong, with the exception of an interesting final remark from which we might be able to extract (it seems to me) one or even two literal quotations from Parmenides so far not recognized as such (although it may be difficult to say where the literal quotation ends):

τὸν νεκρὸν φωτὸς μὲν καὶ θερμοῦ καὶ φωνῆς οὐκ αἰσθάνεσθαι διὰ τὴν
ἔκλειψιν τοῦ πυρός,
ψυχροῦ δὲ καὶ σιωπῆς καὶ τῶν ἐναντίων αἰσθάνεσθαι.
καὶ ὅλως δὲ πᾶν τὸ ὂν ἔχειν τινὰ γνῶσιν.

Corpses cannot perceive light, heat, or sound: they are lacking all fire.
But they perceive the opposites, [darkness] and cold and silence.
Generally everything that exists carries a measure of thought.

(d) Where in the poem does fragment B16 belong?

Parmenides' fragment B6 describes the opinions of the mortals [as] chaotic, and their behaviour [as a] mirror [of] their opinions. So here is a place in what is assuredly a fragment of Part 1 of the poem (as opposed to Part 2, the illusions of the mortals) in which the goddess speaks of the false and dangerous opinions of the mortals (not of their best theories); and so fragment B16 might have followed here, with an introduction.

[In a letter addressed to me in August 1992] Professor Gadamer has raised an interesting and weighty objection to this proposal in referring to Parmenides' use of the word 'mixture'. It is, of course, true that 'mixture' plays an important role in Part 2 of the poem and that it may perhaps have been used as a technical term. But perhaps not; and on the other hand, πολυπλάγκτων and πολυκάμπτων are perhaps also technical terms, and used [by Parmenides] in the context of a theory of knowledge, as the roads are here Roads to Knowledge and the errors are wrong Ways.

[Let us consider fragment B6 more closely. In my translation it reads as follows:]

> Necessarily, what can be spoken or thought of, that must be.
> Being can be; but I ask you to ponder that non-being cannot.
> From this wrong road of inquiry, let me restrain you!
> Yet from a second one, too, on which ignorant mortals are stumbling,
> Fickle and double-headed: helplessly do they attempt to
> Govern the much-erring minds in their breasts. For along they are carried
> Stupefied men without hearing or sight, indiscriminate parties,
> Hordes which hold that To Be and Not To Be are all the same, and
> Not just the same: for this road will turn back with all those that are on it.

For this fragment, Burnet's interpretation seems to me an excellent guide! It will be seen that, from the fourth line on, the goddess turns from a characterization of a first wrong road by way of the mistaken idea that it represents (that Not Being can be) to a characterization of a second wrong road by way of the hopeless mortals who travel on it and by way of a scathing attack on the confusion of their opinions (that To Be and Not To Be are the same and not the same) – opinions that explain their hopelessly chaotic minds and actions.

Now it seems to me that fragment B16 might have been situated near this. It is, for example, conceivable that the goddess may have indicated that the totally confused mortals of fragment B6 are the same as those who think of their own thinking that (instead of trying to grasp logical connections) it is determined by what has just struck their senses or their sense organs.

Although at present I opt for placing fragment B16 in Part 1 of the poem, I wish to stress that the problem should be regarded as open.

Fragment 2

2 More on the relation between the Way of Truth and the unsurpassed Way of Conjecture through the world of human illusions

In Paper 1 [Essay 3] I treated the following problem.

Parmenides' great poem is intended, obviously, to describe a discovery which he wishes us to regard as a *divine revelation*; and he wishes to claim that it is a revelation received by himself, personally, from a divinity – a goddess.

I assume with Jaap Mansfeld that Parmenides has, indeed, had a personal experience of the intensity of an enlightenment, and that he tried to describe this great experience in words, especially in the proem, as a fast journey *from darkness to light* (B1: 9). This must have been an experience that solved a great problem for him.

My own problem in Paper 1 was: what could have been Parmenides' great problem that was solved for him by that divine revelation?

In the present Paper 2 I shall pursue a different problem: *What is Parmenides' view of the world?*

I shall at once proceed to a brief and somewhat dogmatic description and later to a critical defence of this description, based on the text.

I

Parmenides, like everybody else, owed much to the social environment in which he grew up. A valiant and original thinker, he owed much to the Milesians, especially to the great Anaximander, and to the refugees, Xenophanes and Pythagoras, who had brought with them many of the Milesian ideas and problems. Like his predecessors he was a cosmologist who studied the relationship between the Sun, the Moon, and the Earth, and who had made the most exciting and significant discoveries, both empirical and theoretical, that had been made since Anaximander.

Like his predecessors Parmenides looked upon the world in which we, mortal men, live and die, as a world of appearance – of *mere* appearances, as a world of mere human conjectures (*brotōn doxai*; B1: 30) which are uncertain; in contrast to the world of reality, the world of being, whose full truth was known only to the gods, who understood it and knew it with certainty – a truth as well-rounded (B1: 29) as even we may conjecture the Sun to be, and also the Moon, and the Earth.

Parmenides loved the world of appearance: he loved life with its birth, its sufferings, its unfaltering and eternal death; with its light, with its many colours, glowing colours that may subtly change into one another (B8: 41) and that may be subtly dimmed. He loved life, dominated (as he tells us) by its first-born god, Eros, the god of love; he loved its warmth, its poetry; he loved its adventures and misadventures, its hopes and its disappointments; its spiritual adventures, the rapid moves of thought, of discovery, the flash of spiritual enlightenment.

Yet Parmenides believed that, in truth and for the gods, all this, all the beauty and the excitement of our human world, our world of appearances, is but an illusion of the mortals. It is bound to pass away. In truth, and in reality, only cold death remains; and death remains for ever.

This is a tragic view of the world of the like of mortals, of the human condition. But it is not a view that is unheard of. It is almost always present in Greek poetry, in lyrical poetry and in tragedy, and often in epic poetry. But Parmenides attempts to give it an explanation.

His hypothesis is that the world of truth, of reality, is a material world; but that the world of appearance, the world of illusion – the world of beauty, life, and love – consists of man-made illusions. Parmenides explains it as something like a world of poetry, a world that results from language and human imaginative [dreams]; from the conventional giving of names *to* often non-real, non-existing no-things: to such non-material entities as light, love, music, poetry, works of art: to beautiful human illusions. They are not real, not truth – they are 'beguiling verses' (B8: 52), beautiful and comforting products of human imagination. But viewed from the point of view of divine knowledge, they are the results of an intellectual fall of man: it is the act of inventing – almost a lying invention – of a NO-THING, a NO-BEING, in addition to BEING (which is material).

This invented no-matter can only be an empty *name*, a name they gave by mere decision, by linguistic convention – to nothing: it was the name 'light':

> Two forms they made up their minds that they would give names to,
> But of these two, one was not permitted to have a name given,
> This is how they have gone astray.

The two names are 'light' and 'night'. And the man-invented illusion, the fall of man, is that the non-existing, the non-material, the beautiful light is thought of as existing.

But in this way, a whole world of illusion is created: the illusion that something exists that is non-existing, makes change possible and thereby movement. And so the world of experience becomes possible, and the world of uncertain human conjectures, of conjectural knowledge, of cosmology and cosmogony.

It is a world of extremes – light and night – but also of all inter-mediates which are explicable as the results of mixtures of various degrees; and so we may explain the changes of qualities such as 'changes of radiant colours', and the whole world of change and motion: the world of human opinion, of conjecture, of appearance is explained as the result of the intellectual fall of man. The world of appearances is explained as the world of human illusions.

These are the principles of Parmenides' explanation of the world as it appears to us: his cosmogony and cosmology. It is the consummation of the promise of the goddess (B1: 31–2):

> But you also shall learn how it came that illusive conjecture,
> Bound to be taken for real, was forcing its way through all things.

I have presented the 'Second Way' of the goddess, which I now prefer to call the Way of Illusion, by contrast to her first 'Way', which she calls the Way of Truth, the world of reality.

II

In the first part of her revelation, the Way of Truth, the goddess proves the properties of the world of reality, the world of real existence – the world of being, of matter, of things, of material objects. It is a world consisting of one full homogeneous sphere, a world in which there is no empty space and therefore no movement, no change, no time: a world of eternal all-presence. This is what the goddess calls the Way of Truth, in . . .

Fragment 2a

III   *The difficulty of Parmenides' argument*

Parmenides' central argument in its simplest form is:

1   *Being is.*
2   *Non-being cannot be being.*
    (For non-being = being is *absurd*; it cannot even be thought of.)
    Therefore
3   *Non-being cannot exist.*
    (The nothing cannot exist.)

This is all. Parmenides draws from it the conclusions:

4   *The void cannot exist.*
    (For Parmenides, being is what takes up space, *fills* space.)
5   *The world is full – a block.*
6   *Motion is impossible.*

This is a valid argument if it is assumed that

Being = impenetrable material (the full).

The argument can be refuted by assuming that

Both the full *and* the void are existing.

(It is not a problem that 'being' and 'existing' may be used as synonyms.)

In order to appreciate the argument better, we may consider a world in which *only the void* exists: an empty world, nothing but an empty space. According to Parmenides, such a world would be no-thing, just nothing. It would be non-existing. Who can say that Parmenides would be wrong? Who can say that such a world would have 'existence'?

On the other hand, it was the admission of the void – of nothing, non-being – that turned the Parmenidean theory into physics.

The Parmenidean argument is thus of outstanding importance in that supreme adventure of ideas which turned the almost unconscious tribal civilization of the East into the self-conscious (because cosmos-conscious) civilization of the West.

So far I have not even touched upon the problem of Parmenides' relation to language. My first thesis is that, basically, language problems play no role whatsoever in Parmenides' theory. Or in other words, my thesis is that Parmenides' argument, to be well understood, can be put in any objectivist language in which we can speak about the world and its inhabitants, whether ordinary Greek or Latin, English or French, or Italian, Spanish, or German.

Only after this has been made perfectly clear may we turn to the peculiarities of Parmenides' use of language – (1) his vocabulary; his theory of language, especially (2) his theory of legitimate name-giving, and (3) his logico-grammatical problems.

(1) *Vocabulary.* I find it especially striking that Parmenides' vocabulary is perfectly 'normal' except that he makes extensive use of words with the meaning 'way' or 'road'. They furnish his favourite metaphors. This is even more striking when in the largest and most important fragment, fragment 8 we find, in addition to 'ways' or 'roads', used metaphorically, that Parmenides' goddess, like one who fears to lose her way, introduces further the metaphorical use of 'signs' (B8: 2: σήματα) in the sense of road-signs or sign-posts that help us to find our way. These sign-posts are not, I believe, like our modern inscribed sign-posts, but they are all kinds of indicators that may help one to find one's way. This fact, together with

Parmenides' denial of all (sense) qualities except what later philosophers have called 'primary qualities' – the geometrical shape and spatial extension (size) of a body, its hardness, impenetrability, and weight, suggested to me that Parmenides' language was strangely similar to that of a child born blind.

For a blind child, the world – its environment – consists of ways leading to (touchable) unchangeable material locations that are indications or signs helping the child to identify its own location in a world that is essentially a structure of such unmoving material sign-posts.

(2) *Name-giving* plays the central part in Parmenides' 'philosophy of language'. Names (nouns) are the most important elements of the language, and they are given to certain things by an act of *convention* performed by human beings. This, again, is a theory towards which a blind child is tending because it finds that certain words, 'light' and 'darkness', 'red' and 'green', 'pointing' (in the literal sense) and 'looking', have (at first) no literal meaning, merely a metaphorical or a ritual use.

Like a ritual, which in fact is a *mere* convention, without practical significance, even though it may be connected with a pseudo-practical activity, the use of names that are unattached to touchable things leads to misunderstandings; and these misunderstandings may be grave – they may lead to illusions.

The worst of these, the illusion κατ' ἐξοχήν, is the illusion that there exists light, and not only darkness (= the normal state in which our movement is guided by touchable indicators of our position, by 'signs'). Talking of light (which does not exist) has led mankind to live in a world of illusions and often delusions, such as of colours, and even of changes of colours. . . . The world of illusions is often beautiful, and often threatening; especially if it leads to the disappearance and unreliability of important sign-posts, of some of the invariants on which we have to depend. . . .

It cannot be strongly enough emphasized that these peculiarities of language – I may call it 'the Blind Child Language' – are not referred to as an additional argument to that other argument given in *'Parmenides I'* [Essay 3] and here, briefly summarized, according to which *light is a no-thing* for Parmenides, since it is not material, not full.

For the atomists, up to and including Newton, light was a stream of weightless, or practically weightless, particles. I myself, when first struck by the 'Blind Child Language', stupidly did not connect it with my theory that Parmenides held light to be a *no-thing*. Yet after some time I realized, of course, that there was indeed a striking linkage between the 'Blind Child Language' and the 'light-is-nothing' theory that I had attributed to Parmenides. But I wish to stress, yet again, that my reasons for attributing this important theory to Parmenides are independent of my reasons for attributing to him the goddess's explicit proof that only matter can exist but not empty space or, of course, light (which should never have been named).

(3) Parmenides' strange *grammar* – conspicuous in the early stages of the goddess's proof – is well known. It consists of omitting from the phrase 'It is', in the sense of 'It exists', the subject 'It'. I believe that this is connected with the point (2) above, 'Parmenides' conventionalist theory of name-giving', in the following way. Parmenides is fascinated by his (or the goddess's) task of proving that *being can be*, but *not* not-being (or no-thing). But, so he feels, by using 'being' or even 'it' for a subject, he might be begging the question, and so invalidate his proof. He strongly believes that the no-thing is nothing and therefore cannot have anything attached to it – not even a name; not even a demonstrative or other pronoun, like 'this' or even 'it'. So *only things that exist ought to be referred to, and named*, since only they can be given a name. In other words, by using a noun, like 'being', or even a noun-replacing pronoun, like 'it', he would assume that *the thing exists* to which the noun or pronoun refers: for according to his conventionalist theory of name-giving, all name-giving that is logically legitimate makes precisely this assumption. (This is precisely what those mortal sinners overlooked who introduced the name 'light' without first making sure that there was such a thing – a thing that might legitimately be called 'light'.) He feared making a similar mistake by introducing 'it' or 'being' (or perhaps 'matter') without first establishing that there did, indeed, exist something to which the word in question was referring.

So I suggest that Parmenides' best-known grammatical peculiarity can be understood as a consequence of that theory which I have called his 'conventionalist theory of name-giving'. But while the latter theory may be explained as a part of the 'Blind Child Language', the omission of the subject in a few crucial places is, I should say, a result of a logical over-anxiousness not to commit the logical sin of begging the question.

Fragment 3

3 Parmenides' blind sister: a fairy story

In Paper 1 [Essay 3], I introduced (in the Endnote) the fairy-tale idea that Parmenides was brought up by (or with) a blind relative.

In elaborating this rather fantastic hypothesis, which is of no importance for my general argument about Parmenides' poem, I have been tempted to think that Parmenides was brought up by a sister, at least six or seven years older, who was blind and loved her brother, who greatly admired her: she was his guide and authority after the death of their mother.

He was taught to speak by her. She taught him poetry, and later he recited to her Homer and Hesiod. She was his ethical guide, and he owed much to her justice and discipline. She was for him a goddess and the source of wisdom. She taught him quite unconsciously that light is not fully real, but she might also have questioned the [very] existence of light *and* the void. When he received his revelation, she had died (perhaps from the same cause as their mother); he knew, however, how much of his revelation he owed to her – and to her judgement. He could therefore attribute his enlightenment to her. Perhaps he called her Δίκη (blind-folded); note that the goddess Δίκη was blindfolded at least in some representations.

Before his revelation, Parmenides was a knowing man, who had made discoveries. But he still lived in a world of illusions. Even his journey to the goddess was a journey to the light, the unreal.

What he and his sister had in common was the material world of touch, and the illusory world of poetry. From her he learnt that only touchables exist (materialism), that ways or roads are existing and among the most important realities. Also sign-posts exist and are most important: they tell you where you are. However, light, empty space, colours and change of colours, warmth, and movement are all non-existing.

Of course, this hypothesis of mine belongs to the illusory world of poetry. Still, it explains much that Parmenides says. (If, in addition, he was himself colourblind, it would explain even more.) And explanatory power is all one can ask of a hypothesis.

The following is a list of passages on which it may throw some light. Of these, B4 seems to me to get the most enlightenment; and it has *no* direct connection with the 'conventionalist attitude towards language' which led to the hypothesis. . . .

For a blind person, signs (*Anzeichen, Merkzeichen*, σήματα: B8: 55; B9: 1; B10: 2) are important; similarly ways, ὁδός: B1: 2, 5, 27; B8: 18; B6: 3; B2: 4; B8: 1; B7: 3; B8: 34; B8: 38; B19.

Real = firm (*fest*); dense = matter, body: πυκινὸν δέμας, B8: 59; compare Xenophanes, B14.

Then we have the emphasis on *going astray* (*in die Irre gehen*, πλάζω, πλαγκτός, πλανάω, as in πολύπλαγκτος! (B16). B9: 1 and B19 are obvious here. Even B3 appears a little different now, for somebody blind. B10: 2: the Sun here does not produce light: its effect is *burning*.

All this is apart from the stress on *names*, as in B19, B8: 53, and the other obvious 'conventionalistic' passages.

[The list of fragment numbers stems from a letter addressed to Professor J. Mansfeld, Utrecht, 3 January 1992. Ed.]

Fragment 4

4   The proem

(i)   The proem: one goddess or two goddesses?

The daughters of Helios drive Parmenides' chariot, pulled by divine mares, from night to light (B1: 1–20). They arrive at a marvellous locked door whose keys are held by the goddess Dikē. The divine maids persuade Dikē to unlock the door. Then we read (B1: 20–3):

> straight through the doorway,
> Wide enough just for a wagon, the maids lead the mares and the chariot.
> And the goddess received me graciously grasping my right hand,
> Speaking most kindly to me and addressing her verses as follows:

Then, after nine introductory verses, the goddess begins her revelation, Part 1, the Way of Truth, followed by Part 2, which I now call the Way of Conjecture and Illusion.

Fragment 4a

(ii)   A note on the proem: the rush to the goddess was an illusory tale

Assuming the truth of my hypothesis, how can we explain the proem? Does it not, indeed, contradict my hypothesis? For clearly the proem is Parmenides' journey to light and to the Goddess of Justice, who will reveal to him the truth. And this journey is described by him as a journey towards the light. Do we not, therefore, get the equation light = truth, rather than night = truth?

My hypothetical answer is this. The journey in the fast-moving carriage is, obviously, prior to the revelation that will teach Parmenides that movement is impossible and that light is not truth but an illusion. The blinding light of the revelation that taught Parmenides the awful truth did therefore really blind him; destroyed his eyesight (and his hearing, and even his tongue, his sense of taste[1] – but not his tactile sense!), all epistemic power. The very journey towards the blinding light of truth turned out to be an illusion – a pre-revelational illusion – like all our ambitious desires and loves. The blinding revelational experience that not only the phases of the Moon are unreal (but an illusion because they are due to the non-existing light), but also all that we know is merely through our senses (except the sensation of touching, of colliding with, some hard matter) did indeed reveal the truth – but at the cost of destroying the loved realities of life, which is change and movement towards light.

So the proem is compatible with the revelation of the Goddess of Justice. And the Goddess of Justice is *not* identical with the Goddess of Truth; rather it is the goddess who judges *the reliability of the witnesses* and with this, she also declares the just distribution between the two worlds, the world of objective truth and the world of our illusions. And considering what must have been the great content of Part 2, she was not unfair to this second world.

Fragment 5

5 Endnote

I am at the end of my story – the discovery of Parmenides' problem, and how it may have resulted from his discovery that the Moon is neither growing nor shrinking and that her phases are an illusion. I only wish briefly to add two short comments.

[The first is on Parmenides' idea about] primary and secondary qualities, which might show the influence of Xenophanes' 'honey versus figs' (and so his critique of anthropomorphism): object in physics – at any rate pre-Maxwellian physics – assumes media, especially air, as relevant to the senses of sight, hearing, and smell (perhaps taste, which is chemical), but touch is something different: it is direct mechanical action. So if it is asked why Parmenides trusts touch, there is an answer.

[The second remark is about Part 2 of the poem.] Part 2 is poetic – even tragic. What remains of Part 2, the Way of Human Conjecture, is a shambles. But we *know* that this very important part contained the natural philosophy of a great thinker and the greatest cosmologist in the tradition of Anaximander. We know from Plutarch and from the goddess (i.e. from Parmenides himself, B10) that it was an extensive and highly original work. And that Parmenides himself thought it not only unsurpassed, but not to be easily surpassed, [as he lets] the goddess make quite clear when she says of it (B8: 60–1):

τόν σοι ἐγὼ διάκοσμον ἐοικότα πάντα φατίζω,
ὡς οὐ μή ποτέ τίς σε βροτῶν γνώμη παρελάσσηι

Now of that world so arranged to seem wholly like truth I shall tell you,
Then at no time can you be led astray by the notion of mortals.

[This pronouncement as well as the remarks of Plutarch in B10 state] a tremendous programme, like [that of] Anaximander; and [then there is] the goddess herself, who thinks her own words beautiful and unsurpassed! Nevertheless, Parmenides has modestly to regard it as conjectural! (This was a tradition – perhaps inherited from Xenophanes.)

It is strange that the tradition, hinging on ἀπατηλὸν (B8: 52), which I translate 'beguiling', belittles the significance of Part 2 in spite of Plutarch's testimony, and so it must also belittle the significance of B8: 60, where the goddess herself testifies to both the beauty and the unsurpassable contents of Part 2.

Fragment 6

DEMOCRITUS AND MATERIALISM

By far the greatest of the founding fathers of atomism was Democritus. He inherited a materialist theory of the world which regarded the human soul as material. Thus in Democritus' atomist cosmology, the soul consisted, like all matter, of atoms – a peculiar kind of atoms, spherical and very small. Democritus also inherited the doctrine that the soul moves the body.

Thus in one sense, Democritus was a materialist monist: all that existed was atoms. Yet in another, quite as important sense he was a dualist: the movement or the activity of one kind of atoms, those constituting the soul, was more significant than the others: 'Men get happiness neither from their bodies nor from money, but from thinking straight, and thinking much' (B40). And in so far as there was an infinity of atoms in existence, Democritus was an extreme pluralist.

All later developments beyond materialism were a result of research into atoms and thus of the materialist research programme itself. (This is why I am speaking of the self-transcendence of materialism.) It has left the importance and the reality of matter and of material things – atoms, molecules, and structures of molecules – unscathed. One might even say that it led to a gain in reality, as will be explained here.

Atomism, or atomistic materialism, could until the discovery of the electron be described as the doctrine that all things consist of atoms, and that all change can be explained as due to the mixing and separating, the composition or dissociation, or more generally the motions and the push of atoms, that is, of unchanging and indivisible material corpuscles. This doctrine was highly speculative; this was recognized by the greatest of its founding fathers, Democritus. He realized, on the one side, that we needed sense experience to give us 'evidential support' or 'confirmation' (B8b: Κρατυντήρια) for the atomic theory; on the other hand, he realized that sense experience did not give us pure or true knowledge, but only 'dusky' or 'dark' knowledge (B11).

In the field of the theory of knowledge not only was he a sensualist, but he realized that there was a certain clash between his atomic hypothesis and sense experience. This he stated in the form of a conversation between the (conjecturing) intellect and the senses.

The intellect says: 'Colour – by custom; sweet – by custom; bitter – by custom. In truth [there is nothing but] atoms and the void.'

The senses reply: 'Wretched intellect! You get your evidence from us and then you try to overthrow us? Our overthrow is your downfall.'

The intellect can be interpreted (in the sense of Parmenides, B8: 53: *onomazein*; see also B6: 8: *nenomistai*) as saying here that, as only atoms and their movements in the void are real or true, 'sweet' and 'bitter', etc. are mere conventional names, or opinions, or perhaps illusions. (We may say that the intellect attacks the subjectivity of the senses.)

Fragment 7

ARISTOTLE'S MATHEMATICS MISUNDERSTOOD

Aristotle on the angle in a semi-circle (Metaphysics *1051a26f.*)

I

The central purpose of this paper is to clear up a misunderstanding that has affected, apparently since antiquity, the interpretation of the passage referred above which contains a beautiful proof, probably original to Aristotle, of the geometrical theorem that all angles in a semi-circle are right angles. There are two arguments that speak for Aristotle's originality: first, that Euclid's proofs (III.31) are different (indeed, they are not quite as elegant); secondly that if the proof had been well understood in the form in which I say that it was meant by Aristotle, it is difficult to believe that the misinterpretation could have arisen, or that it could have persisted.[2]

The extreme brevity of Aristotle's formulation of the mathematical proof is characteristic of him and shows the pride of a mathematician (or perhaps the pride of an amateur who wishes to impress the professional). In any case, I find it impressive; even exciting.

II

I have decided to adopt the following method of presentation. As an old teacher of elementary mathematics (now in my 92nd year of life and in my

74th year of (occasionally) still teaching a little elementary mathematics, I shall first explain carefully (in *Sections 1–2*) the interest of 'the theorem of the angle in the semi-circle', and next to it, Aristotle's beautiful proof, together with its two assumptions (in *Sections 3–4*). Then I shall discuss the text (in *Section 4*), and (in *Section 5*) propose a tiny emendation ($\dot{o}\rho\theta\hat{\eta}$ instead of $\dot{o}\rho\theta\acute{\eta}$) in 1051a28, which solves all problems.

Next I shall report on the interpretation of Sir David Ross (in his commentary), Sir Thomas Heath, and H. Tredennick (Loeb Classical Library). In my opinion these interpretations do an astonishing disservice to Aristotle, even that of the mathematician Heath: for a critical reader they all imply what Alexander hints:[3] that Aristotle promises to give a proof of the theorem in its universality, but fails to do so. I shall call this 'the traditional misinterpretation'; and I shall show that my proposed emendation fits the traditional misinterpretation as well as (or better than) it fits my own interpretation – that is, my proposed restitution of Aristotle's proof. That is to say, the proposed emendation would be almost neutral between these two interpretations and could be proposed from both points of view. On the other hand, my interpretation has the advantage of attributing to Aristotle a faultless and beautiful proof, rather than burdening him with an alleged proof that fails to fit his promise – and that is invalid!

My main work is thereby done, but two tasks shall be added (*Section 4*): an attempt to fit my interpretation with Aristotle's *Posterior Analytics* II.xi as well as with the purely speculative idea (*Section 5*) that Aristotle put up a trap for his students into which, however, the careful reader of the preliminaries would not fall – or so he hoped.

Fragment 8

ARISTOTLE'S MATHEMATICS MISUNDERSTOOD

(III *and parts of* IV *and* V)

Among the excellent scholars who have misunderstood, as I shall be suggesting, Aristotle's mathematics are Sir David Ross, Sir Thomas Heath, and Hugh Tredennick. I have not investigated German, French, and Dutch treatises on the subject, and it may well be that there are scholars who have anticipated some or all of my very simple arguments.

1 A remark on Euclid and his predecessors: proofs with and without assumptions

Everybody knows that Euclid is the main author of the axiomatic method in geometry: a most interesting and important method. It consists of making a few assumptions – if possible, intuitively simple and convincing ones – and then deducing from them, by purely logical means, the huge edifice of geometrical theorems.

It seems that many people think that there is no real alternative to the axiomatic method. One of those who thought so was Bertrand Russell. His instinct was against accepting it, but he gave in when his older brother told him that there was no alternative.

But Bertie's brother was misinformed, and he misinformed Russell: there are geometrical (and other) proofs that need no assumptions: absolute proofs. And among the predecessors of Euclid there are both geometricians who work from unproved assumptions or axioms, and geometricians who offer proofs – absolute proofs.

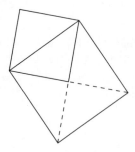

Figure 9

One example of these, known to every Greek scholar, is Plato's proof, in the *Meno*, of the theorem that the square over the diagonal of any given square has twice the area of that given square (see Figure 9).

Of this diagrammatic proof holds all that Aristotle says in *Metaphysics* 1051a26f. Thus it is an absolute, an intuitive proof, to be grasped and understood, without argument: you need hardly be acquainted with counting up to 4.

2   Some intuitive acquaintance with angles

In order easily to understand Aristotle's very interesting and beautiful proof (so badly misunderstood by experts) in his *Metaphysics*, it seems to me necessary to have some intuitive acquaintance with some very simple geometrical structures: angles, and triangles.

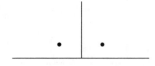

Figure 10

For Aristotle, one angle is the most interesting and important of all: the right angle (ὀρθή, . . .). Figure 10 is a drawing of two right angles R. We see that the right angle R is, essentially, one-half of a limiting case that I will call the 'stretched angle' S, which indeed is not an angle any longer but a straight line with a point P where there was once some ordinary angle such as a right angle, or, say, half of a right angle (see Figure 11).

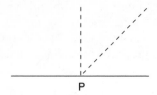

Figure 11

The three angles so far mentioned, R; S = 2R; R/2 (= 45°), are entirely different in appearance, in looks. An isosceles right-angular triangle ABC as in Figure 12 contains all three, as becomes clear if we consider it as half of a square standing on one corner.

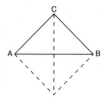

Figure 12

It is important to get acquainted with these angles and triangles as geometrical individuals in various positions, such as a square standing up like  and like

or a right-angular isosceles triangle standing up like 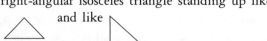 and like

or an equilateral triangle whether standing up like 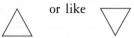 or like

The equilateral triangle is, of course, very important, and it is easily seen from Figure 13 that it has three equal angles which are each one-third of the stretched angle S (= 2R).

298

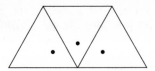

Figure 13

If we, in modern terms, count S = 2R as equal to 180°, then each of these three angles of the equilateral triangle has 60°. Also it is easily seen that Figure 14 is the upper half of a regular hexagon:

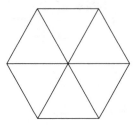

Figure 14

Each angle of a regular hexagon consists of two 60° angles and thus is of 120°.

In order to *understand* ancient geometry it is, I suggest, important to learn by acquaintance these angles of totally different shapes, which, however, can be similarly related by counting them as Plato's *Meno*-triangles. So we get some trivial and some not so trivial proofs. A very trivial proof is that of the theorem that a regular hexagon is divided by its three diagonals into six regular (equilateral) triangles. A not at all trivial but very simple proof is Aristotle's proof in the *Metaphysics*, that the angle in the half-circle is a right angle R.

We now approach one of the central problems of elementary geometry: the proposition that all triangles, whatever their specific shape, have the same sum of their internal angles.

While in the *Meno* theorem, only the size is generalized. . . .

3   Generalization of the proof of the sum of the three angles of a regular triangle

Two points determine a straight line through them. They also determine two circles each with the centre in one of the points and with their distance as radius.

Any triangle ABC can be shifted along the straight line through AB so that the point A after the shift assumes the position held by B before the shift, and the point C assumes the new position C', as shown in Figure 15.

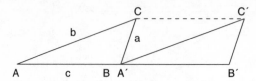

Figure 15

We say that the lines AC and BC' are 'parallel'; also the lines BC and B'C' and the lines BB' and CC'. Since ABC has been shifted into a new position BB'C', each point of the triangle BB'C' has been shifted by a distance equal to the distance AB. Therefore the dotted line CC' is equal to AB (and also to BB') . . .

4 Some characteristic angles

1. (Theorem) The sum S of the (inside) angles in any triangle is the same: it is the stretched angle of 180° and therefore equal to the sum of two right angles (S = 2R).
2. (Corollary) It is therefore, of course, also equal to the sum of the three equal angles (of 60° each) of any equilateral triangle.

As to Theorem (1) Aristotle asks: 'Why are two rights [which are equal to the stretched angle] equal to the [sum of the angles of a] triangle?'[4] And he replies: 'Because the angles about one point (above a straight line) are equal to [a stretched angle and so to] two rights. If the [dotted] line parallel to the side [A'–B'] were drawn already, the answer would be obvious.'

What I call the 'stretched angle' S, which is equal to 2R, is called by Aristotle two right (angles), *duo orthai* (or δύο ὀρθαί).

He thinks by this, of course, of the sum of ⌐ and ∟, that is ⊥ ; but also of $\frac{1}{2R}$, or $\frac{1}{2R}$, the result of that sum – my S; that qualitative figure half of which happens to be the figure ⌐, called R or ὀρθή: the right angle R.

When Aristotle thinks of my S, he usually speaks of 2Rs.

Let us now look at the text of the *Posterior Analytics* II.xi.

If, as shown above, the triangle ABC in Figure 16 is shifted to the right by the distance c, then the distance between C and C' must be c; therefore, as in the original case of the equilateral triangles,

Lemma: the 'middle triangle' is the same as the two other triangles, only with its point C″ down instead of up.

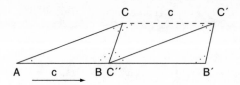

Figure 16

Theorem: The sum of the three angles in *any* triangle = S = 2R = 3 × 60°.

Employing the above lemma in Figure 17 it appears that BC'C is the same as ABC turned on its head, so that A is placed at point C', B at C and C at B; thereby it also becomes clear that α + β + γ = the straightened angle at B which is β + γ + α.

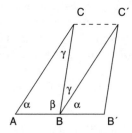

Figure 17

Fragment 9

5   *Aristotle's theorem, and a suggestion for an emendation to bring out his proof*

Why, then, is the angle in the half-circle a right angle, quite generally (καθόλου)?

In order to see that, one need only pay attention to the three equal straight lines in Figure 18: *two* that form the base, and the *third* which goes from the middle to the right angle. Then, as Aristotle says, 'if you know the previous theorem well, the answer will be obvious to you'.

What has to be shown is that, in the divided triangle,

α + β = R.

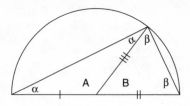

Figure 18

But as we have A + B = 2R, and, in the divided triangle, the two resulting triangles are both isosceles (since they are radii), then $\alpha = \frac{B}{2}$ and $\beta = \frac{A}{2}$.

But from A + B = 2R it follows that $\alpha\ (=\frac{B}{2}) + \beta(=\frac{A}{2}) = R(=\frac{A+B}{2})$.

This brilliant proof was, as I conjecture, cunningly formulated to perplex and to impress Aristotle's students. It certainly succeeded – perhaps beyond Aristotle's intentions – for it was misunderstood by some outstanding scholars such as Alexander in the third century and Sir David Ross, Hugh Tredennick, and Sir Thomas Heath in the twentieth century. Heath is the only author among the scholars mentioned who has seen that one cannot arrive at the general theorem, if one starts to consider the case of ⌂, but he does not give the solution.

Fragment 10

Geometrical arguments like those given above strongly suggest one emendation in *Metaphysics* 1051a27, namely replacing ὀρθή by ὀρθῇ (*dativus loci*); a kind of oversight that may have happened very early – perhaps in the very first of all manuscripts – and that may have led to all the misunderstandings. (It seems that all interpretations have taken ὀρθή to be adverbial – that is, 'by way of an angle that is right', 'perpendicular', or something similar.) Thus the point is here: if ὀρθῇ is taken to be a *dativus loci*, then Aristotle's proof is correct; if it is interpreted as adverbial, the proof is untenable.

Another, though less important, emendation concerns the same crucial passage, ἡ ἐκ μέσου ἐπισταθμεῖσα ὀρθή, where ἐπὶ στάθμην (meaning 'in a straight line [to]') could replace ἐπισταθμεῖσα, thereby allowing the translation 'from the middle to the right angle (in a straight line)', which fits well with the geometrical argument. (ἐπὶ στάθμην is found in Aristotle's *Part. Animal.* 657a 10: 'this is why nature has brought the nostrils together *in a straight line*'.)

Fragment 11

AN ARISTOTELIAN TANGLE OF HERACLITUS' AND XENOPHANES' THEORY OF THE SUN

Aristotle remarks (*Meteorologica* 355a13; compare DK 22B6) that if the Sun were a fire or a flame, then Heraclitus could not have said (as he did) that 'the Sun is new every day'; but rather 'the Sun is new at every moment'.

This remark of Aristotle is quite right, and Heraclitus himself would have said (I think) that this is what he meant – only that he preferred to put things in a way that can be misinterpreted by fools (whom he did not suffer gladly). But Aristotle's remark suggested to fools that, in saying that the Sun is new every day, Heraclitus wished to exclude that it is new unintermittently and that he even wished to exclude that it is a fire. But this suggestion to fools by Aristotle (as it turned out, it was widely accepted) is mistaken, for we have the report by Diogenes Laertius (DK 22A1) that the heavenly bodies are all flames held in bowls that are turned towards us with their hollow sides, and that the Sun is the brightest and hottest flame of them all. This is a refutation of the suggestion [attributed to Xenophanes that the Sun is new every day].

But is the attribution to Xenophanes of the doctrine that an entirely new Sun rises every day, rejected here, somehow confirmed by Heraclitus? For he said: 'The Sun is new every day.'

Not in my opinion. Heraclitus, as I reaffirmed long ago [*O.S.*, vol I, pp. 14f.], is the great discoverer of the fact that all things are processes – our children, who invisibly grow, all animals, all plants, but also the stones carried by a river, and the river itself with its banks, [whirlpools and falls] and, foremost, fire (and also the bronze or iron cauldron in which oil is burning), so that, indeed, 'all things are in flux' (as Plato put it). If that is his teaching, then, indeed, 'The Sun is new every day' would be only saying the same as 'The Sun is new every hour': it would say . . . Aristotle gets into a slight tangle.

There is nothing in that passage in the *Meteorologica* against Heraclitus believing that the Sun is fire and new all the time, like fire; on the contrary, a lot [is speaking] for it: obviously Aristotle had said so before. . . .

But cannot the theory of the many daily Suns of Xenophanes be supported by reference to the view of Heraclitus? For as we hear about him from Aristotle (*Meteor.* 355a13f.),

> for if it [the Sun] were fed in the same way as a flame – as these people say it is – then the Sun would not just be only, as

Heraclitus says, new on every day; rather it would be new all the time.

From this we obtain Heraclitus fragment B6:

The Sun is new every day.

Some scholars have derived from this that it was, indeed, the view of Heraclitus that there is a new *and different* Sun every day. But this is extremely improbable. If Heraclitus believed (B91) that

One cannot step twice into the same river,

then he most probably also believed as, indeed, Aristotle here suggests himself, that

The Sun is new incessantly.

Is it less clear to say 'every day' than to say 'every minute'? Is not every length of time chosen – day, hour, minute, second – equally arbitrary? (Besides, Heraclitus does not suffer fools gladly and might have chosen a period of time that may be misunderstood by fools precisely in the way they did.)

Some readers of the chapter from Aristotle's *Meteorologica* to which the passage which I quoted belongs did get the impression that Heraclitus is criticized by Aristotle for *not* saying (and perhaps not agreeing) that the Sun is new all the time (or continuously), and that Aristotle therefore seriously intends to imply that Heraclitus meant and stated that there is an entirely newly kindled Sun every day. (See, for example, Zeller–Nestle, *Die Philosophie der Griechen in ihrer geschichtliche Entwicklung*, Part I, 6th edn, Leipzig, 1919–20, pp. 859–60.)

I shall first argue that Aristotle does not suggest this, or had the slightest intention of conveying that this was Heraclitus' meaning. And I shall next argue that we have ample grounds in Heraclitus' fragments for saying that he did not mean that the Sun was newly kindled every day, as some scholars have understood fragment B6 to mean.

First to Aristotle.

Chapter II of Book II of the *Meteorologica* is devoted to a discussion of the hydrosphere – the sea; and this part is especially devoted to its saltiness, and to the rotation or circulation of water, its rise in the form of vapour into the upper region and its condensation by cold, and its falling to the ground in the form of rain.

As sometimes happens to him, Aristotle gets badly side-tracked from his theme, and begins to speak of the Sun: whether it is fed by moisture;

whether that is the cause of the solstice; and many more details. Then he happens upon a theory that he is going to object to: 'this theory of the Sun is based on the analogy between the Sun and a burning fire'. And he turns to combat this theory, and gets quite entangled. It is in this situation that he mentions Heraclitus' saying, together with its improvement (the Sun is new continuously); only to drop Heraclitus at once like a hot brick, and to proceed to an argument against the theory which he wished to combat.

Thus there simply is nothing whatever here except a momentary entanglement and the attempt to get some rhetorical relief by using something (Heraclitus was too timid in what he said) that looks like a joke he had used before for a similar purpose. Result: although we can, I suppose, use the quotation from Heraclitus, we cannot say that it is criticized – on the contrary, it looks as if Aristotle had used it before as a principle against a formulation of Heraclitus which he, Aristotle, could greatly improve.

And we can agree with Aristotle that it is an improved formulation of Heraclitus' meaning; in fact, of Heraclitus' theory that the Sun is fire (or flame), a process rather than a thing.

As far as Heraclitus' meaning is concerned, there is very little doubt that he meant that the Sun is fire ($\pi\hat{v}\rho$) or flame ($\phi\lambda\acute{o}\xi$); and also that Aristotle knew this (even though this last point is unimportant for our argument). For . . .

Notes

1 Some commentators suggest that 'even your tongue' in B7 refers not only to the sense of taste but to the power of speech. I think that this is a mistake: it is excluded by the context.
2 The theorem itself is credited to Thales, but without a proof.
3 Alexander of Aphrodisias, who taught philosophy in Athens around 200 AD, wrote commentaries on several of Aristotle's works. Ed.
4 *Metaphysics* IX. 4 and 5, and *Posterior Analytics* II.xi.

INDEX OF TRANSLATIONS

Presocratic fragments translated by Popper, occasionally inspired by others. The Diels-Kranz numbering (DK) has been used except where otherwise specified.

Page numbers in *italics* indicate the latest among different translations of a given fragment (thus 'DK28 B8: 60: *121*, 190, 264, *293*' signifies that two identical translations of B8: 60 on pages *121* and *293* are different from and *later than* those found on pages 190 and 264). The letter 'n' means 'note'.

This index has been prepared by Troels Eggers Hansen.

INDEX OF NAMES, AND
PASSAGES CITED AND
DISCUSSED

Page numbers in *italics* indicate quotations. The letter 'n' introduces references to note numbers. JM.

INDEX OF SUBJECTS

Page numbers in *italics* indicate the more important passages. The letter 't' in front of a page number indicates that the term is explained and discussed in the place referred to; 'n' stands for 'note'. Ed.

317